HITLER'S PERSONAL SECURITY

HITLER'S PERSONAL SECURITY

PETER HOFFMANN

The MIT Press
Cambridge, Massachusetts, and London, England

First MIT Press edition, 1979
Published in England by the Macmillan Press Ltd., 1979

Copyright © 1979 by
Peter Hoffmann

Printed and bound in the Unites States of America.

Library of Congress Cataloging in Publication Data

Hoffmann, Peter, 1930-
    Hitler's personal security.

    Includes index.
    1. Hitler, Adolf, 1889-1945 — Assassination.
2. Anti-Nazi movement.   I. Title.
    DD247. H5H654   1978   943.086'092'4   78-8932
    ISBN 0-262-08099-0

Contents

List of Illustrations

Foreword

The present investigation grew out of a study of *coup d'état* and assassination attempts made against Hitler by the German Resistance Movement from 1933 to 1945.[1] Witnesses to those events, survivors of the Resistance, and former members of Hitler's entourage, often categorically asserted that Hitler was much too well protected for any assassination attempt to succeed, or, on the contrary, that he was so poorly protected that almost anyone would have found it easy to kill him. It seemed worth while to try to find a documented, non-speculative explanation for this contradiction through an objective examination of the evidence.

The greater part of the files of Hitler's security agencies was destroyed in an air raid on 29 April 1944, and, at the end of the war, whatever had been accumulated again was destroyed by security authorities in central offices.[2] In the course of the last ten years, however, I discovered so much source material that had survived in more obscure places, often in the form of copies or drafts, or enclosures in correspondence, that a coherent description of measures taken for Hitler's personal security has become possible.

An earlier edition of this book appeared in German in 1975, although the English version was written before the German one. The interval proved beneficial in that a good deal of newly-discovered material and improved knowledge can be presented here.

I should like to thank the many archive and library officials whose assistance in my research was so valuable and indispensable, particularly the officials of the *Bundesarchiv* in Koblenz; of the *Bundesarchiv–Militärarchiv* in Freiburg i. Br.; of the *Politisches Archiv des Auswärtigen Amts* in Bonn; of the Legal Section of *Eidgenössisches Politisches Departement* in Berne; of the *Institut für Zeitgeschichte* in Munich; of *Württembergische Landesbibliothek* in Stuttgart; of the *Institut für Zeitungsforschung* in Dortmund; of McLennan Library at McGill University; the late Mr. Richard Bauer of the Berlin Document Centre; Messrs. Robert Wolfe, George Wagner, John Taylor and Don Cunliffe of the National Archives in Washington, D.C.; and Mrs. Agnes F. Peterson of the Hoover Institution in Stanford, California. I acknowledge gratefully the assistance and support of the McGill University Social Science Research Grants Sub-Committee and of the Canada Council which helped to make possible crucial aspects of my research. I sincerely thank the many witnesses of events described below who helped with information and documents, and whose names appear in the notes. I am most grateful to Mr. R. Raiber, M.D., in Wilmington, Delaware, who reviewed and criticised the manuscript, who offered numerous valuable suggestions and points of information, and who collaborated with me in surveying the remains of 'Wolfschanze' in order to help to produce a reasonably accurate map of this site of one of the best-known assassination attempts against Hitler. I owe thanks for particularly important items of information to Professor Charles Burdick, Mr. David Irving, Mr. Eugen Kreidler, Dr. Werner Maser, Mr. Philip Palmer, Mr. Karl R. Pawlas, Mr. Hellmuth Schöner, Professor Bradley F. Smith, Professor Lawrence D. Stokes and Mr. Fritz Tobias, and to Miss Eve Rosenhaft for her valuable contributions to the preparation of the manuscript.

P.H.

McGill University
Montreal, 1978

1. *The History of the German Resistance 1933–1945* by the same author (Macdonald and Jane's: London, 1977; and M.I.T. Press: Cambridge, Mass., 1977).

2. Party Chancellery correspondence concerning *Kriminalrat* F. Schmidt, Berlin Document Centre; statements by *Kriminaldirektor* (ret.) F. Schmidt and O. Günsche.

Abbreviations

BA	*Bundesarchiv* (Federal Archives), Koblenz
BA–MA	*Bundesarchiv–Militärarchiv* (Federal Archives–Military Archives), Freiburg i. Br.
BDC	Berlin Document Centre
FBB	*Führer-Begleit-Bataillon* (*Führer* Escort Battalion)
FHQ	*Führerhauptquartier* (*Führer* Headquarters)
Gestapo	*Geheime Staatspolizei* (Secret State/Political Police)
HQ	Headquarters
IfZ	*Institut für Zeitgeschichte*, Munich
KTB	*Kriegstagebuch* (War diary)
LSSAH	*Leibstandarte-SS 'Adolf Hitler'* (SS Bodyguard Regiment)
NA	National Archives, Washington, D.C.
NSDAP	*Nationalsozialistische Deutsche Arbeiter-Partei* (National-Socialist German Workers' Party)
OKH	*Oberkommando des Heeres* (High Command of the Army)
OKW	*Oberkommando der Wehrmacht* (High Command of the Armed Forces; Hitler's staff as Supreme Commander)
RSD	*Reichssicherheitsdienst* (*Reich* Security Service)
RSHA	*Reichssicherheitshauptamt* (*Reich* Security Head Office)
RuSHA	*Rasse- und Siedlungshauptamt* (Race and Settlement Head Office of the SS)
SA	*Sturmabteilung* (Stormtroopers, literally Storm Detachment; abbrev. 'St.A.' until ca. 1922)
SD	*Sicherheitsdienst* (Security Service)
SS	*Schutzstaffel* (literally Protection or Guard Detachment; originally *Saalschutz*—assembly-hall protection)
StA	*Staatsarchiv* (State Archives)
SSO	SS Officers' files in BDC
VfZ	*Vierteljahrshefte für Zeitgeschichte* (periodical)
Waffen-SS	Fully-militarised formations of the SS

1 Reasons and Objectives of the Investigation

Throughout his career as a political and military leader, Adolf Hitler got into situations in which his life was in acute danger. Throughout his career, he never tired of considering these dangers and what might be done to avoid them. At the same time he not only accepted danger as an inevitable part of his life, but he seemed to seek it. This, together with the fact that numerous unsuccessful attempts on his life were made, lends special importance to the question of how easy, or how difficult, it really was to assassinate Hitler. Was access to him easy or difficult for a would-be assassin? Was he protected adequately or inadequately? What was his own interest and involvement in measures designed for his protection? Which of the many assassination attempts failed as a result of security measures, and which failed for other reasons? An inquiry into these complex problems will provide insights into the thinking and psychology of the dictator, and contribute to an understanding of Hitler's catastrophic personality and its effects.

During all four years of the First World War, Hitler served at the Western Front, and he returned as a highly-decorated soldier, although he had only attained the rank of corporal.[1] During the years of his struggle for political power, 1919–33, there were countless occasions when he got into the midst of menacing, violent crowds and into assembly-hall fights. On one occasion, in 1922, he stormed up on to the speaker's platform and physically attacked the speaker, surrounded by an unfriendly crowd; he was sentenced to three months in jail for this. As late as 22 August 1939 he threatened to throw down the stairs personally anyone who proposed a compromise in order to prevent war. As a politician, he cannot be said to have shunned personal danger, whether he made speeches from a truck while unsympathetic crowds mobbed the vehicle, whether he risked being lynched in 'Red' Saxony, or whether he simply headed a political party advocating and practising brute force as a matter of principle and ideology. As a military leader in the Second World War, he often visited dangerous points at the fronts. Despite many examples of fearlessness, Hitler developed a preoccupation with assassins who might end his career abruptly before he could accomplish what he thought to be his mission. 'I might be murdered by a criminal, or by an idiot, at any time,' he said in his speech on 22 August 1939.[2] But he continued to take personal risks whenever it seemed necessary—and quite often when it did not.[3] In the end he allowed his own underground headquarters in the Berlin Chancellery to become part of the Front itself.

In the turbulent days after the fall of the Hohenzollern dynasty, political assassination was occasionally committed with official sanction. In the period from 1919 to 1922 alone, there were approximately 376 political assassinations in Germany. Rosa Luxemburg and Karl Liebknecht, leaders of the Communist *Spartakus-Bund* that had staged an armed revolt in January 1919, were murdered while in the custody of the Army, apparently on orders from commanding officers. Extremists of the political Left were special targets for political assassination, particularly after the bloody reign of the Soviet Government in Bavaria following the assassination of Kurt Eisner, the leader of the Bavarian extreme Left.[4] Its régime was suppressed even more bloodily by Freecorps troops led by General von Epp.

The Socialists and Communists were accused of having sabotaged the war effort with their peace agitation, and thus of being responsible for the defeat and its catastrophic aftermath. But politicians of the Centre and of the Right, conservative nationalists, were similarly singled out as targets for 'retribution' if they had favoured a negotiated peace publicly during the war, and if they had agreed that Germany must sign the Peace Treaty of Versailles and attempt to fulfil reparations demands to avoid enemy occupation. Matthias Erzberger, the Catholic Centre Party politician, had supported a peace resolution of the *Reichstag* in 1917; he had headed the German Armistice Commission in 1918; he had argued in the National Assembly in 1919 that Germany had no alternative to signing the Versailles Treaty and that her only hope was later revision; and he had taken the same position on the reparations issue. Several assassination attacks were his reward. An attempt by members of the Army failed in Weimar on the evening of the day on which the National Assembly and the Government decided to sign the Versailles Treaty to prevent the military occupation of Germany by Marshal Foch. Only a few days later, shots were fired at Erzberger's office in the Finance Ministry, and a hand grenade devastated a room thought to be his bedroom. In a third attack in Berlin-Moabit he was slightly wounded. Finally, in August 1921, he was murdered while hiking in the Black Forest, by members of an organisation set up for political assassinations and other acts of terror. This 'Organisation Consul' was composed of young veterans of the Freecorps led by Captain Ehrhardt, and they had been standing by to receive orders from some mysterious source.[5] Less than a year later, Foreign Minister Walther Rathenau was murdered on 24 June 1922 from a car that passed his own car as he was on his way to the Foreign Ministry. Rathenau had been Chairman of the Board of the giant electrical concern AEG; during the war he had organised German war production with superb efficiency; after the war he had favoured an effort to fulfil the unreasonable reparations demands in order to prove them unreasonable and thus get them modified. He was a supporter of the new Republic from conviction, and he was a Jew— two qualities that automatically made him a hated enemy to the extremists of the Right. Even the National Socialists became victims of political violence. By 1933 they mourned 228 members fallen for the Movement's cause—'comrades shot dead by Red Front and Reaction,' as the 'Horst-Wessel' Song called them.[6]

All politicians are in some degree of danger, especially in turbulent times when quasi-civil-war situations arise every few weeks or months. The man who often went by the cover name 'Wolf,' and who liked to hear himself called King of Munich in the early 1920s, was no exception. He was subject to the ordinary threats that prominent politicians are exposed to, and he attracted an amount of specific violence on the merits of the ideology he professed. He might have been the object of more assassination attempts if the Socialists and Communists had not held the belief that 'social,' impersonal forces rather than individuals were the essential agents of history. Individual assassination attempts were considered acts of anarchism.

From the very beginning of Hitler's political career, when he was an intelligence agent and counter-revolutionary propaganda agitator working out of a Munich Army garrison in 1919, through the period of the Bavarian Soviet Republic and of its suppression when many were suspected as collaborators and informers, Hitler's life was in danger. This did not change when, still working for Army Intelligence, Hitler came into contact with the party he soon joined. He left the Army in March 1920.[7] By 1921 Hitler had assumed full leadership in the Party, increasing his exposure, whilst the post-war situation in Germany continued to be marked by turmoil and violence.

Before considering in detail various security arrangements and their development, some theses will be stated:

1. Adolf Hitler attracted an above-average number of attempts on his life. All chancellors of Germany, from Bismarck to the present, were endangered by the designs of would-be assassins. But it is obviously pointless to compare chancellors by average numbers of assassination plots per year of tenure; too many factors are involved (inflation, enemy occupation of parts of the territory, revolutionary and civil-war situations, the presence of deranged persons, the phenomenon of 'follow-up crimes,' the accidental combination of assassin and opportunity, and so on). There is no method of counting assassination attempts that remained unknown, so that comparative lists mean little. A great number of known attempts may suggest good security measures that led to their discovery, or, equally, bad security measures that failed to discourage would-be assassins. The conclusion from few attempts to good

security could be equally erroneous. There can be no doubt, however, as will be shown below, that security precautions mounted for Hitler's safety exceeded all that had ever been done for any of his predecessors. Compared to the extent and intensity of precautions, the number of assassination attempts against Hitler was extraordinarily high.

2. Through the years, security precautions were constantly intensified, especially after surprising gaps had been discovered, or attempts on Hitler's life had been made or prematurely revealed. But intensification was not necessarily synonymous with greater effectiveness. Indeed, almost every increase in security contained its own negation.

3. There is no evidence to suggest either unusual or inefficient efforts to protect Hitler against accidents.

4. Hitler himself took considerable interest in details of the protection of his own life, but he often took risks not justifiable from a security standpoint.

5. Hitler himself often defeated the efforts to guarantee his personal security.

6. Many security efforts were self-defeating, either due to inadequacy of personnel, to over-organisation and over-bureaucratisation, or to regulations and methods too complex to be implemented and supervised.

7. Upon analysis of security precautions, both those theoretically possible and those actually taken, it becomes clear that there were limits beyond which security could not be provided, and beyond which risks had to be accepted. The limits were defined by the need of the protected Leader to continue to lead effectively, and by certain facts of human nature. They include the Leader's need for contact with those whom he is leading, for information and its corroboration from diverse sources; they include the impossibility of making any inhabited environment absolutely free of potential threats caused by human beings; and they include the human weaknesses of guards, varying intensity of effort, corruptibility, routine, lack of imagination, and fatalism.

2 Before 1933

Adolf Hitler the Party Leader required protection almost from the start of his career, not only as a public political figure, but as the leader of one of the most aggressive, violent and vindictive political organisations in Germany. There were in the 1920s many paramilitary, clandestine and illegal organisations in Germany. There were citizens' militias and Freecorps formed to suppress rebellions in Berlin, Hamburg, Bremen, or on the Ruhr, or to repulse Polish troops trying to occupy Silesia before the plebiscite under the auspices of the League of Nations had given an indication of the wishes of the population; there were paramilitary organisations employed by various political parties in demonstrations, rallies, assemblies and street battles; and there were underground organisations formed to counteract the work and influence of the Allied Control Commission, to prevent cooperation between the Commission and German individuals and authorities, and to murder those who were considered to have become traitors to the German nation. In such conditions, the National Socialists managed to surpass other groups in notoriety for violence. They advocated 'brute force' against 'enemies,' and they practised it.

As early as September 1920 they would bodily throw out of assembly halls any people advocating points of view differing from what the National-Socialist speaker had just said. In November 1921 Hitler spoke in Munich's 'Hofbräuhaus' to a crowd containing a large proportion of antagonistic labourers from the Majority-Socialist Party (MSP), from circles connected with their newspaper *Münchner Post*, from the Independent Socialists (USP), and from the Communist Party. There had been some talk and some warnings that the rally might be disrupted by these participants. Hitler was the main speaker, the topic was 'Who Are the Murderers?' An assassination attack had been made against Erhard Auer, a Majority Socialist and prominent *Landtag* deputy, on 25 October, and it was generally thought that Hitler would discuss it. The Nazis had in the room only some fifty of their SA (Storm Detachment) and *Ordnungsmänner*, and there were about three hundred or more antagonistic people present. At many tables, beer steins were being collected for the expected or planned battle.[1] The police later also found brass knuckledusters, ends of brass pipe, rods, a flick-knife, and other items of comparable usefulness. When the battle occurred, touched off by a remark from someone in the audience, approximately 150 steins were smashed, also numerous chairs and several tables, and a number of shots were fired in the direction of the speaker's rostrum, and *from* there as well (Hitler himself carried a pistol on public occasions, throughout his political career). There were many injuries, none of them serious. The police arrived, but before they had sufficient strength to close the rally, the Nazi SA had restored order and had frightened or pushed out most of the three hundred disrupters. Hitler continued his speech for about twenty minutes before the police finally closed the hall.

There were other battles, notably street battles with left-wing organisations in Munich in the summer of 1922, during demonstrations against a Law for the Protection of the Republic. This law was the response of the democratic parties to the assassination of Foreign Minister Rathenau by a clandestine revenge organisation affiliated with the 'patriotic' organisations of the Right. Hitler's own ideas on this matter are characteristic. It made no sense for a few courageous idealists to punish a few minor traitors while most of the big shots were left unharmed, and the idealists themselves were thrown in jail and wiped out in turn. The sensible thing to do was for a German people's court 'to sentence and execute several tens of thousands of the organising criminals of the November treason and everything that goes with it. This would also teach the little traitors an everlasting, necessary lesson.'

In October 1922 Hitler and hundreds of SA participated in a 'German Day' held in Coburg by *völkisch* organisations. They had invited Hitler to come 'with a few others,' but it was useless for Hitler to take part in such an event unless he could demonstrate the strength and invincibility of his Movement. A special train was scheduled to transport the SA troops. In Coburg the Nazis were told they must not unfurl their flags nor let the music play nor march in formation as they made their way to the centre of the city. They ignored these instructions and, when a street battle did not immediately develop, the Nazis provoked one by repeating their march after they had bullied the police into passivity. The SA soon dominated the streets. There were further incidents during the night, and Social Democrats and Communists tried to organise new counter-demonstrations for the next day, but only a few hundred of their people turned up, while the SA once again dominated and terrorised the city. When, in the evening, the railway workers refused to operate the special train back to Munich for the returning SA, Hitler threatened to take along hostages from the ranks of the Social Democrats and trade-union leaders and to have the train operated by his SA. The railway workers gave in.[2]

As Hitler himself pointed out, the significance of this victory could hardly be overestimated. It had proved that not only the Left could organise and deploy 'masses' in the streets and in assembly halls, but that the Right could do it just as well. The Right claimed to represent the people truly, by representing what was national, patriotic, *völkisch*; now the Right could 'prove' it by numbers and by brute strength. The legal government had no authority, neither police or military forces were sent in to restore order.

Many of these battles must be seen as events in a civil war in which certain armed organisations sought to dislodge or defend, respectively, the government of the Republic. The *Reichswehr*, in its various parts, played a most ambiguous role in this context. Hitler exploited his own and his Party's close association with the *Reichswehr* throughout his career. In fact, and notwithstanding sociological analyses of the NSDAP and its later sources of support, the early growth of the Party was sponsored directly by the Bavarian *Reichswehr* command, and it was aided by the participation of former or active *Reichswehr* officers.[3] It was Captain (General Staff) Karl Mayr who ordered Hitler to investigate the German Workers' Party (DAP) in the autumn of 1919 when Hitler still worked in Army Intelligence. Captain Mayr was in charge of section Ib/P (intelligence) in the Bavarian *Reichswehr* Group Command in Munich. But Ernst Röhm represents the Army influence in the early history of the NSDAP most strikingly. Coming from a family of royal officials in Munich, he took a full course in classics in secondary school and in 1906 he joined No. 10 Infantry Regiment ('Regiment, The King') of the Royal Bavarian Army. He served with distinction as a Front Line officer and in General Staff positions throughout the war, making a name for himself as a fearless leader and superb organiser.[4] After the Armistice of 1918, Röhm served under Colonel (later General) Ritter von Epp in a Freecorps that eventually (24 July 1919) formed the nucleus of the new Bavarian *Reichswehr* contingent as the 21st Rifle Brigade. He was in charge at various times of personnel administration, of the supply section, and of organisational work for unofficial military and paramilitary outfits. His work included provision and storage of weapons, ammunition and equipment, and concealment of these supplies from unsympathetic Allied inspection. Röhm had many contacts with politicians of the Right and Left, and early in 1920, probably in January, he joined the DAP, still before it was renamed NSDAP, not long after Hitler, when the Party had less than 150 members (Röhm's membership number was 623, but the numbers began at 501, for 'optical reasons'). From the day he joined, he 'rarely missed a meeting, and each time he was able to bring the Party a friend, mainly from the *Reichswehr*. Thus we fellow-fighters from the *Reichswehr* contributed many building blocks to the rise of the young movement.'[5] In the 1923 Beer Hall *putsch*, Röhm occupied and held for close on twenty-four hours, against hostile *Reichswehr* forces, the District Command building in support of Hitler's *coup d'état* attempt; Heinrich Himmler, a member of the paramilitary

Reichskriegsflagge whose Bavarian section was led by Röhm, was there, too, as standard bearer.[6]

In later years Röhm became leader of the SA. Strictly speaking, the SA was not a personal security force of the NSDAP leader. The first organised such group, called *Ordnertruppe* (stewards troop), came into being early in 1920 at the beginning of the Party's large-scale public activities.[7] The *Ordnertruppe* became the mother of the *Schutzstaffel* (SS), which had been known originally as *Saalschutz* (assembly-hall protection). This *Saalschutz*, often appearing as an integral part of the SA, was led by Emil Maurice, a hero of political brawls and Hitler's bodyguard and chauffeur. Maurice was a watchmaker by trade; he had served with the anti-aircraft artillery in the First World War, and with Freecorps 'Oberland' from 1919 to 1921. From 1919 he was member No. 594 of the DAP and NSDAP, respectively; after the refounding of the NSDAP in 1925 his number was 39. In 1926 he became member No. 2 in the SS. He was with Hitler in Coburg in 1922, and in the march on the 'Feldherrnhalle' on 9 November 1923. Julius Schreck (Party No. 53 after it was refounded, SS No. 5) became Maurice's successor, for a short time. The group included men like Ulrich Graf (former cheap-meat butcher), Christian Weber (a former horse-trader and one-time beer-hall bouncer), Max Amann (Hitler's former sergeant), and Rudolf Hess (assistant to Professor Karl Haushofer, who was an authority on Geopolitics and a First World War general). Some of the others were soldiers whom Hitler knew from the war; all were young, brawny toughs, and convinced that terror must be broken by terror. Hitler himself had developed an appreciation of the force of strong-arm arguments during his years in Vienna before the war (1909–12), when labourers had thrown him off a construction site where he had tried to harangue them.[8]

In the summer of 1920 the *Saalschutz* began to take shape, and by spring of 1921 it was organised into sub-groups called hundreds. They were officially known at this time as *Turn- und Sportabteilung der NSDAP* (Athletics and Sports Detachment of the NSDAP).[9] Despite their organisational connections, however, the *Saalschutz* and the SA served different purposes. The date Hitler himself regarded as the birthday of his *Sturmabteilungen* (SA) is 3 August 1921, immediately after he had threatened to withdraw from the Party, and had blackmailed its executive committee on 29 July into giving him full powers. At the same time Captain Ehrhardt functioned as midwife by commanding several of his own Freecorps officers to assume organisational duties in the NSDAP's SA.[10] Other political parties formed similar paramilitary formations at the same time; the Social-Democrats had their 'SA.'[11] Hitler entered into an alliance with Freecorps leader Ehrhardt, and it was no mere coincidence that the 'alliance' was formed when the *Einwohnerwehren* (irregular militia forces) were being dissolved after 28 July 1921 in fulfilment of a Versailles Treaty stipulation. In his memoirs, Röhm managed to refer apocryphally to a complicated event fraught with political and military implications: 'My particular interest was directed to the SA of the NSDAP for which, upon Hitler's request, Captain Ehrhardt had made available officers of his Brigade as organisers.'[12] Schulz and Tillessen, the murderers of Erzberger, members of 'Organisation Consul,' also came, as well as Naval Lieutenant von Killinger. At times, in 1921, the shock troops for meetings of the NSDAP came from the regular *Reichswehr's* Mortar Company 19. Naval Lieutenant Hans Ulrich Klintzsch was sent by Ehrhardt to be the first commander of the new SA. Those assigned from Brigade Ehrhardt continued to regard themselves as members of the Freecorps, subject to Ehrhardt's orders, and 'militarily' responsible to him, while they were 'at Hitler's disposal for his political tasks.' Some appeared to be there more to gather intelligence than to assist the NSDAP. While Klintzsch and another officer, Wegelin, served in the SA, they were paid by Ehrhardt's Freecorps. In May 1923 they returned to it, but others remained in the SA.[13] In short, the SA was organised primarily as a *Wehrverband* (a military organisation), only a small number of SA men served as bodyguards and in 'stewards troops' (*Ordnertruppe*). At times the SA received military training from *Reichswehr* units, and the SA's disguise as a mere propaganda organisation of a political party was convenient to men like Röhm and Ehrhardt at the time.

The Party Leader's 'stewards troop' played a special role and formed the nucleus of a new organisation. In his book *Mein Kampf* Hitler used both terms, *Ordnertruppe* and SA to refer to this special guard. It received its baptism of fire in the famous beer-hall battle in Munich's 'Hofbräuhaus' on 4 November 1921. Rudolf Hess and Emil Maurice were there, and both were seriously injured in the battle, but the group were so fanatical, brutal and successful that they managed to drive the opposition out, after guns had been used on both sides in the final stages of the battle. Official NSDAP accounts claim that no more of the Party's meetings were disrupted until 9 November 1923. But there were other baptisms of fire, such as the one on Munich's Königsplatz during a rally to protest against the Law for the Protection of the Republic, when the SA successfully battled the Reds for the 'right of the street,' and when some 800 SA terrorised the city of Coburg, long a left-wing stronghold, in October 1922.[14]

The small SA detachment at the 'Hofbräuhaus' had undergone a ritual of instruction by Hitler before the meeting: he told the group they would have to prove their loyalty today; they must not leave the room before the end unless they were carried out dead; he himself would stay inside until the end and he did not believe that any of them would desert him; but if he saw a coward he would personally tear off his swastika armband and badge (their only uniform then). Through the years of his leadership, Hitler reserved and exercised his privilege of personally instructing and swearing in his bodyguards. The ceremony was later embroidered by the use of a 'blood standard' on to which some of the dead of 9 November 1923 had fallen and had spilled their blood. After 1933 the annual swearing-in ceremonies for bodyguards were held at the 'Feldherrnhalle.'[15]

By the winter of 1922/23 Hitler's practice of having himself accompanied by a special armed bodyguard was well established. They were usually Amann, Graf, Hess, Klintzsch, Maurice, and Christian Weber. But some changes were indicated when the SA more and more slipped from Hitler's control during the Ruhr Struggle of 1923, and when the Party Leader could no longer be sure of the loyalty of such men as Klintzsch. SA strength had increased from about one thousand at the end of 1922 to more than two thousand. The SA was now far more a *Wehrverband* (militia organisation) controlled by men like Lieutenant-Colonel Kriebel (leader of *Vaterländische Kampfverbände*—patriotic combat leagues) and Röhm, than the political propaganda troop that Hitler wanted. The changes that occurred in the spring of 1923 in the SA also involved Hitler's personal security force.[16]

In March 1923 Captain Göring, formerly Richthofen's successor as commander of the 'Flying Circus' of fighter planes in World War I, was given command of the entire SA. An elite guard unit was set up as a *Stabswache* (staff guard). They were the successors of the old *Ordnertruppe*; its members wore black hats with skull and cross bones, and black-rimmed swastika armbands. In May the *Stabswache* numbered twenty men; they were incorporated as *Stosstrupp Hitler* (Hitler Assault Squad, sometimes translated Hitler Shock Troop) organised by Lieutenant (ret.) Joseph Berchtold and by Hitler's later driver Julius Schreck. They met regularly in Munich's 'Torbräu' at the Isar Gate.[17] The seeds were sown for a more fiercely and unquestioningly loyal élite organisation, which, by 1931, was large enough to provide Hitler's bodyguard, and a secret police within the Party and SA as well. In short, *Ordnertruppe*, *Stabswache* and *Stosstrupp Hitler* were early forms of the SS. The new *Stosstrupp Hitler* numbered about one hundred men initially. At a reunion on 9 November 1933, sixty persons signed their names, led by Hitler, Lieutenant (ret.) Brückner and Julius Schaub, and including Maurice, Dr. Weber, Christian Weber, Kriebel, Ulrich Graf, Berchtold, Walter Buch and Hans Kallenbach. A few of the reunionists were veteran *Ordnungsmänner* from 1920 (Ludwig Schmied, Hans Haug, Maurice, Chr. Weber, Wilhelm Briemann jun.). Dr. Weber and Kriebel, leaders of paramilitary organisations before and during the 1923 coup, were there as prominent participants of the Beer Hall *putsch*. In 1935 the reunion group (some forty-eight, this time, including Maurice) met again.[18]

On 8 November 1923 *Stosstrupp Hitler* had occupied the 'Bürgerbräu-keller' and established Hitler's short-lived control of the *putsch* situation. Hitler entered the hall with part of this armed Assault Squad including Hanfstaengl, Rosenberg, Amann and 'three men, his constant companions,' Ulrich Graf, Emil Maurice and Rudolf Hess.[19] Graf carried a machine pistol. Other Squad members installed machine-guns at the entrances. While Hitler was in a side room with Dr. von Kahr (head of the Bavarian Government), General von Lossow (Commander Bavarian *Reichswehr*) and Colonel Seisser (Munich Police Chief), 'talking them into' joining a revolutionary government, Graf was there with his machine pistol, and Hitler himself was also armed. On 9 November the Assault Squad formed one of the three columns marching side by side towards 'Feldherrnhalle'—from left to right—*Stosstrupp Hitler* led by Hitler himself; SA Regiment Munich led by Lieutenant (ret.) Brückner (later Hitler's Chief Adjutant); and *Oberland* led by Dr. Weber. Hitler's bodyguard, usually referred to as his 'personal escort,' or 'personal entourage,' was integrated in the *Stosstrupp*; Ulrich Graf was always at Hitler's side.

The marchers apparently hoped, by a mere show of strength, to sweep a fearful government off its feet, and to bring the population on to their side—in Bavaria at least, and perhaps in the *Reich*. The events of November 1918 seemed to be a precedent. Although there is some question concerning the 'peaceful intentions' of marchers intending to overthrow a government and marching through the city with loaded rifles, as many did, the march was obviously not designed to develop into a battle with regular troops: the standards obstructed the view of the marchers; the leaders were in front of the main force, preceded only by standard-bearers and a line of skirmishers with drawn pistols, and so could all be cut down in the first volley, robbing the marchers of direction and command. This was in fact what happened. The marchers never deployed to return fire in any organised manner, but most of them simply dispersed.[20] Ludendorff refused to take shelter when shots rang out. 'Clad in the invincible armour of his arrogance,' as one historian put it, but also in the knowledge of the immense respect he commanded among Germans, especially veterans of the war, Ludendorff walked on through the firing line of the provincial police unharmed, to be arrested a few minutes later. Hitler, on the other hand, was definitely being fired at. Scheubner-Richter, who was walking next to him, was killed instantly, apparently pulling Hitler down with him; Graf threw himself in front of Hitler as the leader was going down, stopping a handful of bullets that could have killed Hitler, and that inflicted serious injuries upon his bodyguard.[21]

After the *putsch*, the *Stosstrupp* was outlawed, along with the SA, and the NSDAP itself. Hitler was tried and sentenced to five years in prison,

MUNICH CITY MAP 1937

1. Munich City Centre 1937

achieving national status (or notoriety) through the trial. After his release on 20 December 1924, he was still convinced of his World-Historic Mission, and that without him the entire Movement would disintegrate—as it had begun to do already. The Movement was not, in Hitler's opinion, a collective, impersonal, socio-political force, but entirely dependent on its *Führer* who personified it. Clearly, nothing would be more important than the preservation of so unique a life. As Hitler put it later: 'I told myself then that I needed a bodyguard, even a very restricted one, but made up of men who would be enlisted without restriction, even to march against their own brothers.'[22] The contradictions remained: the Leader had to take risks to be effective. Still, security was now gradually increased.

On 27 February 1925 the NSDAP was founded anew. A day before, Hitler had decreed that the SA was to be re-founded. Its remnants had been led by Röhm, while Hitler had been in Landsberg, and now Röhm was still in command. But soon fundamental differences about the nature and function of the SA developed between Hitler and Röhm, which led to Röhm's (and Brückner's) resignation, effective 1 May 1925. For more than a year there was no central leadership of the SA, only a loose chain of responsibility, from the *Gauleiter* (regional Party leaders) who controlled the regional SA, to Hitler, the Party Chairman.

From about July 1926 Captain (ret.) Franz Pfeffer von Salomon, former Freecorps commander and now a *Gauleiter* in Westphalia, was mentioned as the next SA commander. He assumed command formally as OSAF (*Oberster SA-Führer*, Supreme SA Leader) on 1 November 1926.[23] Pfeffer was given 'political guidelines,' but full powers in organisational and disciplinary matters, and in implementing the directives of the political leadership of the Party. Membership in the Party was made a pre-condition for membership in the SA (this rule was not enforced in every case, and not even generally after January 1933); military terms (*Kompanie*, *Zug*) were replaced by such terms as *Schar*, *Trupp*, *Sturm*, *Standarte* (squad, troop, storm, standard); unit size was adjusted to local conditions. In small Party cells the SA was an informal affair; in communities with larger Party memberships the SA was clearly organised and recognisable as a distinct part of the Movement. Total SA strength is estimated for 1927 at over 10,000, two years later at over 30,000, and by 1930 at some 60,000.[24] But there was a tendency to prefer former Army officers for positions of SA leaders, and little or nothing was done to train an indigenous SA leadership.[25] Pfeffer apparently failed to understand the political combat Hitler had in mind—marching, propaganda, psychological impact, grass-roots canvassing and campaigning, selling Party newspapers, putting up posters—and he prepared the SA instead for hand-to-hand combat. But his concept of the SA as the core of a future mass army, as eventually taking over the *Reichswehr*

from within, was not accepted by Hitler, who wanted to avoid antagonis-
ing the *Reichswehr*.

In July and August 1930, after *Reichstag* elections had been called for
September, friction between Pfeffer and Hitler became acute when
Hitler rejected Pfeffer's demand that some SA leaders be given *Reichstag*
seats. Pfeffer resigned on 12 August. At the same time, difficulties
between *Gauleiter* and SA leaders such as Captain (ret.) Stennes, who
was *OSAF Stellvertreter Ost* (Deputy Supreme SA Leader East), and
financial difficulties in the SA, the misery of many SA rank-and-file who
were unemployed and starving, and resentment at the life style of Hitler
and his lieutenants, led to a list of grievances submitted to Stennes by
unit leaders. They demanded that a fixed proportion of Party income
be earmarked for the SA; and that the SA be removed completely from
the political organisation and from the authority of the *Gauleiter*. In
August 1930 the SA in the eastern districts and in Berlin went on strike,
led by Stennes, thus in effect paralysing the Party's election campaign
in Berlin.[26] Stennes' men invaded Goebbels' Berlin Party offices on the
night of the 29 August. The SS guards there were under Stennes' command and he had announced they would be relieved by SA guards, but
the SS had locked the doors and barricaded themselves in the Party
offices. The SA then broke down the doors, and the SS were manhandled
and beaten by the SA. On the same day Pfeffer left his post as Supreme
SA Leader.

Hitler, who was in Munich, was alerted by Goebbels and rushed to
Berlin. He confronted first the troopers and then the rebellious leaders.
All were extremely hostile, and one SA leader is said to have grabbed
and shaken Hitler by the necktie, to the great horror of Hess who could
not prevent it. Hitler accepted significant parts of the Eastern SA's
demands, and he announced that he was taking over the position of
OSAF, now styling himself *Partei- und Oberster SA-Führer* (Party and
Supreme SA Leader), effective on 2 September 1930.[27] This also meant
that Hitler personally was in command of the SS, which was still a part
of the SA (until 1934). In future the next in command of the SA after
Hitler was the Chief of Staff of the SA. This was to be Röhm's position,
who was then an instructor with the Bolivian Army, in the rank of a Lieutenant-Colonel, and whom Hitler cabled at once, asking him to return.
For the interval Pfeffer's Chief of Staff Otto Wagener attended to affairs,
and on 5 January 1931 Röhm took his duties. Stennes remained in
his post, so as to prevent the Eastern SA from defecting *en masse*, but
it was clear that the conflict was not over, and that Hitler's position as
Party Leader and even his personal security remained threatened.

About the time the NSDAP as a whole was re-founded, in February
1925, Hitler's bodyguard, the *Stabswache* (Staff Guard) was revived,
numbering eight men including Maurice and Erhard Heiden, now led

by Julius Schreck (after Schreck's death in 1936, Himmler called him 'Adolf Hitler's first SS man'). Soon it was renamed *Schutzstaffel* (Protection Squad), or SS. On 9 November 1925 it received this name officially. Schreck, who succeeded Maurice as Hitler's driver, was in charge for a short while of the fledgling SS, numbering about one hundred by the end of December 1925. He was voted out of the top position by his colleagues for his naivety. From 15 April 1926 until March 1927 Joseph Berchtold led the SS and resided in its Central Office at 50 Schellingstrasse in Munich.[28] He was confirmed SS *Reich* Leader in November 1926 by Pfeffer. In an order dated 4 November 1926 the OSAF (Supreme SA Leader) Pfeffer declared the SS an independent organisation beside the SA but under the command of the OSAF.[29] Schreck had sent out a circular on 21 September 1925 requesting all Party cells to form SS quads. Their size was determined by Pfeffer in November 1926 as 'one leader and ten men,' but he forbade the formation of SS squads in places where the SA was not yet strongly represented. Soon Berchtold became dissatisfied with the humble position of the SS and resigned, to be succeeded from March 1927 to December 1928 by Erhard Heiden.

The SS men were frequently made to act like errand boys of the SA, selling newspapers and subscriptions, soliciting new Party members from door to door, pasting posters on walls, etc. At the same time they felt and acted like an élite. They had stricter entrance requirements than the SA, and stricter discipline. They attended all the discussion meetings of the Party members; they never spoke there, nor were they allowed to smoke during the meetings or leave the room before they were over. This sort of behaviour, the requisite toughness and brutality for their 'special tasks,' and the black hats bearing skull-and-crossbones insignia, could hardly fail to make the SS seem sinister and awe-inspiring despite their small number (still only about 280 men in 1929).[30]

On 6 January 1929 Heinrich Himmler, who had been deputy SS *Reich* Leader since 1927, was made *Reichsführer SS* (SS *Reich* Leader). His career in the Movement had begun when he was standard-bearer in Röhm's paramilitary *Reichskriegsflagge* (*Reich* War Banner) organisation at the Munich War Ministry on 9 November 1923. After the *putsch*, from July 1924, Himmler had served as general assistant, propagandist and secretary to a Landshut pharmacist and SA leader, Lieutenant (res.) Gregor Strasser, who led one of the fragments of the *völkisch* movement while the Party was outlawed, and who became *Gauleiter* for Lower Bavaria in 1925. Himmler's rise began when he became Strasser's deputy as *Reich* Propaganda Leader of the Party in September 1926. Now he could reside permanently in Munich since Strasser moved the Lower Bavarian Party office to Munich. Five years later, as *Reich* Leader of the SS, Himmler was once again a subordinate of Röhm. But his close association with the two most prominent competitors of Hitler for power in the Party, who were murdered in 1934, did not thwart Himmler's career in the Nazi hierarchy.[31] Coming from a Bavarian middle-class family, as the son of a father who was once the tutor of Prince Heinrich of Wittelsbach, it was natural for Himmler to become an Army officer.[32] The war's end stopped his career, he took a diploma course in agriculture, but through the Freecorps, paramilitary and *völkisch* organisations he found a new outlet for his peculiarly pedantic fanaticism.

Soon after Hitler had assumed the SA leadership, and with it that of the SS, Himmler began to stress the separate development of the new élite. He declared it responsible 'first of all for police duty within the Party' on 7 November 1930, and he decreed that no SA leader could give orders to any member of the SS, or vice versa. Nine days after Röhm had assumed his post as SA Chief of Staff, on 14 January 1931, the *Reich* Leader of the SS, Himmler, was nevertheless declared subordinate to Röhm.

The SS grew in strength as well as in influence. In January 1929 there were only 280 SS men, but by December there were 1,000, by December 1930, 2,727, and 10,000 by October 1931.[33] There were, of course, ample reasons for tightening security precautions within the Party and around the person of its Leader. New crises arose, and as the SS grew larger it needed to be kept under surveillance itself, and at the same time the Party and its leaders needed better security.[34] Röhm issued SA Orders No. 3 and No. 4 on 25 February 1931 to set up a *Sicherheitsdienst* (SD, security service) for the protection of the leaders of the Party, and to turn over to the *Reichsführer SS* command over this new security service as well as giving him responsibility for the 'protection of the Hitler rallies in the entire *Reich* territory.' Gradually the SD acquired considerable independence within the SS; its personal-protection functions became more indirect through a concentration on intelligence work and general secret-police duties in the SS and in the Party.

Despite the precautions initiated on 25 February 1931, the second Stennes revolt of 1 April 1931 was an even more serious affair than the first, although the new intelligence network enabled Hitler to make early efforts to head it off.

When Röhm had returned from Bolivia, Stennes had warned him of Hitler's faithlessness, and of the incompetence and lack of principles of the entire Party leadership group.[35] Röhm had evaded a direct reply and had begun to carve up Stennes' command area, while increasing the strength of the SS there. Suddenly, on 1 April 1931, Stennes learned from the morning paper that he had been given a desk job at the Brown House in Munich, as Chief of Organisation. Within hours, telegrams from the East German SA leaders poured into the Brown House demanding Stennes' reinstatement, and Stennes refused to obey Hitler's order. Stennes' challenge was a dangerous threat in view of the great number

of followers personally devoted to him; in 1929 he had already controlled 15,000. Once again they occupied the Berlin Party offices, over-
powering the SS guards, and they also occupied the printing shop of
Goebbels' paper *Der Angriff*. Hitler was forced to call in the Berlin police
to turn out the occupants. He confirmed his order to Stennes, Stennes
again refused to obey, and was in due course expelled from the Party
and from the SA, and his followers were also threatened with expulsion.
After a few weeks the rebels ran out of money, and most of them stopped
supporting Stennes. Some left the SA and NSDAP, however, and followed Stennes into a new National Socialist Combat Movement. Stennes
joined up his organisation with Otto Strasser's Combatant Union of
Revolutionary National Socialists, founded labour service camps for
those of his men who were unemployed, and looked around for allies.
But neither the Freecorps veterans, nor the Centre Party, nor the League
of National-German Jews wanted any part of Stennes. In September
1931 he and Otto Strasser separated.

In March 1933, a few weeks after Hitler had been appointed *Reich*
Chancellor, SS men took Stennes into 'protective custody.' Frau Stennes
got in touch with Göring, who protected his former fellow-cadet against
an SS assassination squad, and highly-placed friends—including the
Papal Nuncio, the Archbishop of Cologne, and Stennes' father (who
knew Ludendorff)—interceded on his behalf. It was finally Göring, then
Ministerpresident of Prussia, and his Chief of the Prussian Secret State
Police, Diels, who got Stennes out of Germany to the Netherlands,
whence the refugee travelled to England and on to China. He joined
the staff of Generalissimo Chiang Kai-shek and worked with the Chinese
dictator's bodyguard and security service, also commanding his Headquarters Air Transport Detachment.[36]

Hitler liked to attribute his eventual victory over Stennes to the SS.
He probably knew better, but he had clearly seen his need for more and
more personal protection against disappointed followers as well as bona-
fide enemies. He wrote to the commander of the Berlin SS, a city refuse
disposal engineer, Daluege: 'SS man, your honour is loyalty.'[37] But this
was not enough. In April 1931 Reinhard Heydrich was expelled from
the Navy for moral turpitude. On 14 June 1931 he developed his ideas on
a counter-intelligence service within the SS to Himmler, who liked them
and put Heydrich in charge of what was at first called Ic Service on
29 July 1931.[38]

Whilst the new intelligence-gathering service contributed to greater
overall security, there were ample reasons for vigilance in protecting the
life of the *Führer* more immediately. Hitler frequently got into dangerous
situations, as during the Kapp *putsch* in 1920, when he had flown to Berlin
to try to participate. *En route* his plane had to land in Jüterbog, and
it was promptly surrounded by a menacing mob of 'Communists.' As

Hitler carried two passes, one for the 'Whites' and one for the 'Reds,'
he had only to show the appropriate one to get petrol for the rest of
the journey (he was nevertheless late for this *putsch*).[39] He had another
close shave in Red Thuringia in 1923; and once in Leipzig people were
taking shots at his car. On 15 March 1932 shots were fired at a train
in which Hitler, Goebbels and Frick rode from Munich to Weimar; on
30 July 1932 an assassination attempt was made against Hitler in Nuremberg; in June 1932 he had barely escaped an ambush on a road near
Stralsund. In Freiburg i. Br. rocks were thrown at his car, and one of
them grazed his head; he jumped out swinging his whip, and the startled
attackers ran away. During the election campaigns of 1932 (two presidential campaigns and two parliamentary elections, not counting provincial and municipal elections) Hitler had taken to flying from city to
city in a gruelling schedule of speaking engagements, addressing crowds
in three or four cities on the same day, and often standing up in his open
Mercedes car as he rode through teeming and hostile mobs. Sepp Dietrich, now the leader of Hitler's immediate SS bodyguard (which will
be described in detail below), would usually arrive a few hours earlier
at the next airfield, with a few SS officers, to make preparations for
Hitler's arrival and to check security arrangements against disruptions
by individuals or organised opponents.[40] Hitler himself was accompanied
by old followers and bodyguards such as Schaub, Brückner, Otto Dietrich, Hanfstaengl, Schreck, Kempka, Gesche, Gildisch and others.

On 5 July 1930 Hitler bought a house for the Party central offices
in Munich, only a few blocks from the centre of the city and from 'Feldherrnhalle,' at 45 Brienner Strasse, between Karolinenplatz and Königsplatz: a building known as the 'Barlow-Palais,' built in 1828, and for
some years the residence of the Italian Legation to the Royal Bavarian
Court. It cost one and a half million Reichsmarks, which the Party raised
through a special compulsory contribution from its members.[41] A good
deal of criticism was heard, such as why a workers' party needed a palace,
but Hitler christened the building the '*Braunes Haus*' (The Brown House)
and managed to subdue the critics. The Party moved in early in January
1931.

Security regulations existed here at least since September 1931. On
25 January 1932 Hitler as OSAF, through his Chief of Staff Röhm, issued
detailed new regulations for the security services in and around the
Brown House.[42] They stressed 'defence against Marxist-Communist
attacks, and the prevention of police encroachments.' *Reichsführer SS*
Himmler was put in charge of security in and around the Brown House
and attached buildings. The security service was composed of both SS
and SA men, in three groups of twenty each, plus three in reserve for
each group. A shift on duty was composed of fourteen men and three
leaders. They were subdivided into three shifts in turn which were on

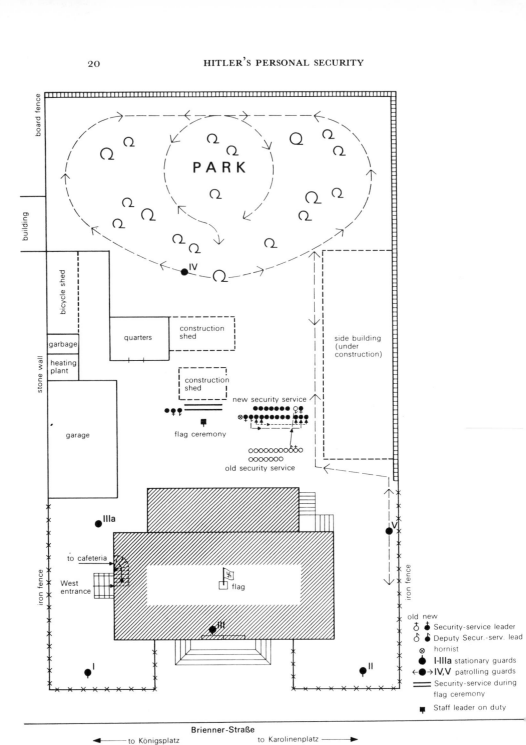

Security-service sketch of 'Braunes Haus' Munich 1932

2. Guard pattern, Brown House, Munich, 1932

guard duty two hours at a time. SS and SA were not mixed, but teams of each organisation served tours of duty on three consecutive days in turn. Criteria of qualification for guard duty included length of membership in the SA or SS, and 'need,' unemployed men being preferred. Initial appointments were made from two lists prepared by the Leader SA Sub-group, Munich—Upper Bavaria, Wilhelm Helfer, and by the commander of No. 1 SS Battalion Munich, Sepp Dietrich. Changes could be made only after application to the *Reichsführer SS*, and it was expressly forbidden to draw security men from SA or SS groups outside Munich without written permission from either Röhm or Himmler.

The diagram illustrates the elaborate procedures. From eight to ten security men were always inside the building, in a guard room, ready to be called out to assist those on post. At least six men constantly guarded the building entrance and a park area behind the house. At night, two men patrolled the park. Every one of the guards had to keep an eye out for conspicuous bystanders or persons apparently observing the building, even if such persons were doing so inconspicuously. They were instructed to prevent and if necessary break up any gatherings of people, including Party members, SA or SS members, even on the public pavement outside the fence. The image of the Party required that its headquarters have an orderly, respectable look about it; the Stennes revolt was still fresh in everyone's memory; and the 'enemies' of the Left might sneak up in disguise. For the same reasons, the cafeteria entrances had to be observed closely so that unauthorised persons could not enter. NSDAP membership cards had to be shown to enter the cafeteria; those wishing to enter the Brown House itself needed a special pass. Office employees had passes admitting them during office hours only, higher-ranking officials and employees working beyond regular hours carried red passes, members of the Supreme SA Leadership Staff and of the SS *Reich* Leadership Staff carried yellow passes. Neighbouring buildings had to be watched for suspicious activities, and the deputy guard leader was required to patrol the streets around the entire area between 8 p.m. and 6 a.m. All guards had to wear uniform (SA or SS), without 'watch-chains, handkerchiefs, etc. being visible,' and without any 'objects that could be considered weapons.' The Party armies were constantly under the threat of being outlawed.[43] But the guards around the Brown House did carry gas pistols which could temporarily disable.

These security precautions could be completely useless if an assassination plot against one of the leaders was hatched inside the Brown House, as in March 1932 when the Supreme Party Judge, Major (ret.) Walter Buch, Martin Bormann's father-in-law, wanted to have Röhm assassinated.[44] A murder squad was formed and given precise instructions on 14 March 1932 to kill Röhm and several members of his immediate staff, among them Karl Leonhardt Count Du Moulin-Eckart who resided in room No. 50, Brown House, and who was the SA's Chief Intelligence Officer. It was not Brown House security, but pangs of conscience, that saved the SA leaders, and gave them another lease on life until the 'Night of the Long Knives' in 1934. The would-be assassin was standing in front of the Brown House one day, when, on a sudden impulse, he went inside, told Du Moulin-Eckart everything he knew and helped him to unveil the plot and its background. Meanwhile Buch suspected that all was not going well and tried to have the assassin assassinated; three shots were fired at the man, but missed. Finally even Himmler, in charge of all Party security, became aware of the goings-on. The result of all the knowledge that was around by now, and that found its way into the press, was anti-climactic. Himmler had a talk with Buch which 'settled the matter.' Röhm, on the other hand, already suspicious (since the beginning of the attacks upon him for his homosexual practices he had surrounded himself with a special *Stabswache* or bodyguard), went to Magdeburg to see his old friend Mayr who had joined the Social-Democrats and was one of their *Reichsbanner* organisation leaders. Röhm tried to get incriminating material on an SA leader whom he (wrongly) suspected as the man behind the plot. Two of the victims-to-be, however, Count Du Moulin-Eckart and Count Spreti, dragged a go-between for the would-be assassin and Buch into court in October 1932, and the go-between was convicted of instigation to murder and sentenced to six months in jail.[45] Strangely, Buch's career does not seem to have suffered in the least through this outrageous affair.

The guards were really helpless, too, in the face of police 'encroachments' mentioned in their instructions. The Brown House was occupied by Green Police (provincial police) on 13 April 1932 after the SA had been outlawed, and it was not vacated until next day. On 4 July 1932, after a new prohibition of uniforms had been declared, the Munich Police Directorate demanded that the uniformed guards be withdrawn, agreed to allow them at the side entrances, but then sent over a criminal-police squad who tried to lure the guards out so that they could be arrested on public ground, and they succeeded with one of them. In the afternoon a large detachment of Green Police with carbines and machine-guns appeared, occupied the neighbouring buildings, and invaded the Brown House over the fences. The house remained occupied until noon next day; all the guards were arrested, along with all employees who were found wearing uniforms, and taken to Police Headquarters.[46] They were later released.

3 Head of Government

When Adolf Hitler became *Reich* Chancellor on 30 January 1933, he acquired new means of protecting his person, but also a new set of threats and dangers. Soon Hitler went about improving the protective measures that had been, so far, routinely available to chancellors.

After the assassination of Foreign Minister Rathenau on 24 June 1922, new directives for the protection of the Chancellery were prepared in August 1922, though they were not finally issued until September 1923. A group of eleven officers of the IA (Political) Section of the Berlin Criminal Police were charged with responsibility for security in the Chancellery; four of them had to be on duty there at all times. The group was immediately subordinated to the Minister of the Interior and the Chief of the Chancellery. The officers had to patrol the garden and the streets around the Chancellery, and the building itself. One of them had to accompany the Chancellor whenever he left the Chancellery. When the Chancellor rode in a car, his escort had to sit next to the driver and observe all oncoming or passing cars and passers-by, he had to decide when the car should be stopped or accelerated, and he was warned that premature intervention was as embarrassing as belated action in a moment of real danger could be fatal.[1] There was, of course, no lack of real dangers. The new Chancellor of 1933 became heir to a long tradition of assassination plots.

Chancellor Brüning on 9 April 1931 had received a small cardboard roll containing an explosive device made of matchsticks and five grammes of gunpowder. It was detected in time and it did no harm. Only a short while earlier, Dr. Goebbels had received a device of the same type. The police believed a Communist was responsible in both cases.[2] In another incident, on 15 November 1932, while Papen was Chancellor, a woman clutching a dagger was apprehended in the Chancellery after she had gained access unnoticed through a side-entrance.[3]

The majority of early threats against Hitler's life were of the same sort, but he attracted a considerably greater number of them than his predecessors. Hitler knew this well, and he was justified in worrying about attacks by Communists, Jews and Catholics who were being systematically persecuted and mistreated. Several of the attempts of 1933 were the work of Communists; there followed several by Jews; in 1938 a Catholic theology student made several assassination attempts; and the perpetrator of the beer-hall explosion of 1939 had once been a member of the *Roter Frontkämpferbund* (a Communist ex-servicemen's organisation).[4] In 1933 there were at least ten attempts that the police considered serious; and at least four in 1934.

A telegram addressed to Hitler on 9 February 1933 by a school-teacher said: 'Just learned that poison for your Excellency was sent to the Chancellor's Palace.'[5] Also in February, the Bavarian Legation in Berlin corresponded with the Bavarian Government and with the *Reich* Ministry of Justice about threats against Hitler's life voiced by a former Communist and Nazi (in this order), Ludwig Assner, who wrote from Palaiseau (Seine-et-Oise) under the date of 18 February, and who promised he would not rest until he had shot down Hitler, unless President von Hindenburg had dismissed the Chancellor by the 10th of March. He knew Hitler, he said; he knew the man was mad, and that he had no constructive goals and no character; he would only turn Germany into rubble and ashes, and plunge her into nameless misery. In another letter addressed to the German Embassy in Paris, Assner claimed he had allies in Germany who would act if he were prevented. Assner's assertions appear better founded after his prophecies were fulfilled, of course; at the time he wrote, and in view of his demand for a large sum of money in exchange for which he was willing to desist, the seriousness of his intentions was doubted. Still, the police took precautions and notified border points.

In February and March 1933 the air was buzzing with threats and dangers.[6] Some of these were fabrications by Himmler, who feared he might miss the boat in the general power-grab after Hitler's appointment as Chancellor. Himmler was still in Munich and without a major government post. But enough of the threats were real.

Hitler had a vivid idea of them, as he told the Prussian *Gestapo* Chief, Diels, in 1933: 'One day a completely harmless man will establish himself in an attic flat along Wilhelmstrasse. He will be taken for a retired schoolmaster. A solid citizen, with horn-rimmed spectacles, poorly shaven, bearded. He will not allow anyone into his modest room. Here he will install a gun, quietly and without undue haste, and with uncanny patience he will aim it at the *Reich* Chancellery balcony hour after hour, day after day. And then'—so Hitler continued with wide-eyed fixed gaze—'then, one day, he will fire!' Diels' recollection is not infallible; the *Reich* Chancellery did not have a balcony until 1935. But Hitler's suggestions as to what his bodyguards should look for were certainly useful.

At the beginning of his career as Chancellor the dangers were numerous, of bewildering variety, and difficult to pin down. In the early months of 1933 the police were tipped off about assassination plots at least once a week. They would learn that some anonymous person planned to hand Hitler a bunch of flowers and through the flowers squirt poison into his face. Another plan was to have a doctored fountain-pen explode in Hitler's hand. Then a crystal-ball gazer reported that a tunnel had been dug under the Potsdam Garrison Church where Hitler and his Cabinet were to meet President Hindenburg and many high-ranking officials and military officers for a ceremony. During the ceremony a large sack full of dynamite was to blow the *Reich* Government to kingdom come. The police did find tunnelling in progress under the Church: cables were being installed so that the proceedings could be broadcast simultaneously. Another report had it that Hitler's plane was to be shot down from another aircraft, during a flight to East Prussia. A former Freecorps fighter and convert to Communism, probably Captain Beppo Römer, had managed to gain admission to the *Reich* Chancellery regularly for many days before being discovered by an SS guard—whereupon he did not return. On the day of the scheduled opening meeting of the Prussian State Council presided over by Göring, his *Gestapo* Chief, Diels, suddenly had a telephone call from an excited police detective who said there was a time-bomb ready to go off at any moment in the coal cellar of the Prussian Ministry building, so that the entire State Council would be blown to bits; as a precaution, he had arrested all the construction workers around the building because inquiries had revealed that Communists were among them. There was in fact a strange object on the threshold of the cellar; it looked like a small torpedo, and no one wanted to touch it. Explosives and bomb experts were aroused everywhere by telephone, and the arrested workers shook with fear of going up with the building. But eventually it developed that the dangerous object had been a container of packing cord back in the days when Bismarck was in charge of the Ministry.

On 27 February the *Reichstag* building was destroyed by arson, and immediately 'the Communists' were blamed, especially when the arsonist, a Dutchman named Marinus van der Lubbe, turned out to have been, in fact, a member of a Communist organisation. The next day an Emergency Decree suspended all civil and personal liberties guaranteed by the Weimar Constitution and threatened the death penalty for attempts to commit political crimes such as assassination.[7] All this could only increase tensions in the last few days before the important *Reichstag* elections of 5 March. Many Social-Democrats and Communists were frustrated by the lack of direction and initiative shown by their leaders, and some believed that assassination of Hitler was a necessity for which they must sacrifice their lives. One of these plotters, a ship's carpenter named Kurt Lutter, was arrested on 3 March and accused of having planned and prepared with other Communists to kill Hitler with explosives at an election rally in Königsberg on 4 March.[8]

Throughout the 1930s there were reports of conspiracies and plans to assassinate the *Führer*. Some reports contained detailed, feasible plans, such as for an assassin to gain entrance to the Chancellery in the guise of a workman, or for an attack with a high-powered rifle with telescopic sight and silencer. Hitler was informed of many of these plots, and they worried him, but time and again he was driven to take great risks, as if under compulsion like a self-destructive gambler. There were at least seven assassination plans that came to the attention of the authorities in 1934 and 1935, when some reaction could be expected from the group around Otto Strasser after his brother Gregor had been murdered, along with Röhm and other SA leaders.[9] The SA crisis itself, of course, was a source of danger for Hitler.

The conflict between SA and *Reichswehr* had been long smouldering. Hitler's programme, vague as it was in other respects, had always included a drastic increase of the armed forces. The *Reichswehr* leadership wanted good soldiers, and there were many in the SA. But it was impossible to absorb some 500,000 SA in 1933 into a 100,000-man *Reichswehr* (even if it was, in reality, somewhat larger than the strength stipulated by the Versailles Treaty).[10] Röhm believed the SA ought to be the basis for a new national army; the *Reichswehr* leadership was opposed to this idea. Both the danger of a *Reichswehr putsch*, and Röhm's noisy declarations of his ambitions, forced Hitler to make a clear and painful decision.

How much there was to any plans of the SA to stage a *coup d'état* in June or July 1934, and perhaps to assassinate Hitler, is still a matter of dispute. In his speech in the *Reichstag* on 13 July 1934, after the massacre, Hitler claimed that Röhm had planned to have him assassinated by *SA-Standartenführer* Julius Uhl. As the SA was sent on a four-week furlough for all of July, there must be doubts at least about the timing of any alleged *coup*. In any case Hitler decided to take preventive action.[11]

Beginning on 30 June and ending about 2 July 1934, at least eighty-three, probably close on 200, 'enemies' were arrested and summarily shot in all parts of Germany.[12] The victims were picked up individually by SS and supporting police details, at home or *en route* to a conference Hitler had ordered Röhm to call for 30 June at Bad Wiessee where Röhm was on holiday. Hitler personally led the expedition to arrest Röhm and his associates in the 'Pension Hanselbauer' at Bad Wiessee, south of Munich, since only his personality and his uncanny control of people were likely to neutralise the danger of resistance by Röhm and his followers—resistance that might have led to a catastrophic conflagration.

The scene at the 'Pension Hanselbauer' about 6.30 a.m. on 30 June was ugly and wild, by all accounts.[13] Carrying his whip and his pistol, and followed by Brückner, Schreck, Goebbels, Röhm's successor Lutze, and others including some criminal-police officers from Munich, all with guns in their hands, Hitler went from bedroom to bedroom, beginning with Röhm's, awakening the revellers, and declaring them traitors and under arrest. Within little more than an hour, a few SS men and criminal-police officers packed them off, in two buses rented by Schreck in Bad Wiessee, to Stadelheim prison just outside Munich, to be shot. The few SA guards at the 'Pension Hanselbauer' had been overpowered and locked up in the cellar.

As Hitler and his entourage, including *Stosstrupp Hitler* veterans and SS bodyguards, were about to drive off back to Munich, Röhm's own *SA-Stabswache* arrived. They did not quite know what to do, as their leader, *SA-Standartenführer* Julius Uhl, was under arrest in the cellar of the 'Pension Hanselbauer.' But they were at first reluctant to leave, and assumed an increasingly threatening attitude towards Hitler as they began to understand the situation. The *Führer* did some fast and fierce talking, and he got them to climb back into their lorry and drive off towards Munich. Outside Bad Wiessee they had second thoughts and stopped again, setting up their machine-guns on both sides of the road. Hitler and his people felt uneasy enough to take the southern, longer route out of Bad Wiessee and to return to Munich via Rottach and Tegernsee.[14]

The shootings of the arrested began on the same day—at the SS barracks in Berlin-Lichterfelde, in some cases in the victims' homes, and in Stadelheim prison. Röhm was shot in his cell on 1 July by Theodor Eicke and Michael Lippert, the Dachau Concentration Camp commandants. Amann and Hess had competed for the honour of shooting Röhm personally, but the Dachau Camp guards, subsequently *SS-Totenkopfverbände* (SS Death's Head Formations), got the nod. As Eicke put it in a letter to Himmler in 1936: 'On 30 June 1934 we were given an important task.'[15]

Himmler's SS served Hitler well in carrying out the arrests everywhere in Germany, in protecting the *Führer's* life during his dangerous trips, and during his confrontation with his enemies. The SS was rewarded by being made a Party organisation independent of the SA on 20 July 1934. Within two years, Himmler and the SS controlled all German police forces.[16]

The elimination of competitors removed dangers but also created new ones. Disgruntled Nazis were now added to Communists, Social-Democrats and Jews as potential originators of plots against Hitler's life.[17] A vast conspiracy was believed centred in Paris and Prague, and Otto Strasser's Black Front was found to be behind a plan to blow up Nazi Party buildings in Nuremberg, to murder Julius Streicher or perhaps Hitler himself in December 1936. A Jewish student, Helmut Hirsch, was arrested, tried and put to death after he had confessed to having been sent by Otto Strasser to carry out the plan. Again, in 1937 and 1938, a group of German *émigrés*, Black Front sympathisers and Jews plotted in Czechoslovakia to kill Hitler. Other plots were hatched in Switzerland

and in Great Britain, while the German opposition within were beginning to produce plans and attempts of their own to do away with the dictator.

A Jewish student of medicine in Berne, Switzerland, named Felix Frankfurter, had hoped to assassinate Hitler, and instead murdered the *Führer's* deputy in Switzerland, Wilhelm Gustloff, in Davos in 1936. The background of this assassination was interwoven with the complicated policy of Germany toward the Jews living within her borders, and toward Palestine. SS authorities were furthering the emigration of German Jews, and they had intimate contacts with the Jewish intelligence service Hagana. Thus they learned from one of its leading members, Feivel Polkes, that he had been informed of David Frankfurter's attack, and in the hope of obtaining more information about 'the numerous threats against the *Führer's* life and assassination plans (*Alliance israélite universelle*, Paris),' the contacts were pursued. *SS-Hauptscharführer* Eichmann of *RSHA Abteilung* II, 112 arrived in Haifa on 2 October 1937 to meet Polkes in order to gain more information and to further arrangements for the emigration of German Jews; on 10 and 11 November 1937 he saw Polkes in Cairo since Polkes could not meet Eichmann in Haifa during the Arab riots. Polkes seemed to confirm suspicions about involvement of the *Alliance israélite universelle* in the Gustloff assassination.

The *Gestapo* (Secret State Police) further learned of plans originating in Italy with connections to Switzerland and Britain in April 1938. In the same year, Alexander Foote, an Englishman working as a spy for the Soviet Union, investigated the chances of assassinating Hitler and found them favourable. He had had no difficulty in getting quite close to the *Führer* in his favourite Munich restaurant, the 'Osteria Bavaria', and he was able to report that there would be no difficulty in planting explosives. But he did not receive instructions to act. Some other attempts will be dealt with below, after some basic security arrangements have been described.

4 *Reich* Security Service

During the Weimar Republic, police authority was almost entirely in the hands of provincial governments. Prussia represented more than half of German territory, population, industrial and economic resources, and it had the largest police force. Bavaria, like Prussia, had historical precedent for a large and relatively autonomous police force. There had been only a small measure of central police authority during the Weimar years. Before 1933, security details for chancellors came from Department IA in the Berlin Presidium of Police. Within Department IA, a political-police section called *Centrale Staatspolizei* (Central State Police) developed. It cooperated with the corresponding police organisations in the other German provinces and served *de facto* though not *de iure* as a central German police bureau.[1]

Only Prussia and Bavaria had political police forces of importance. Besides Department IA of the Berlin Presidium of Police, itself ultimately under the authority of the Prussian Ministry of the Interior, there was in the Prussian Ministry of the Interior a Prussian Political Police. In April 1933 Göring as Prussian Minister of the Interior created the *Preussisches Geheimes Staatspolizeiamt* (*Gestapa*, Secret State Police Bureau) with offices located at 8 Prinz-Albrecht-Strasse where Department IA had already been moved a few days earlier. Rudolf Diels, who had headed Department IA, now became Göring's deputy as Chief of *Gestapa*. The *Gestapa* remained under the jurisdiction of the Prussian Ministry of the Interior until 30 November 1933 when it was by law made a separate branch of the Prussian internal administration. Now it was responsible directly to the Prussian Ministerpresident rather than to the Prussian Minister of the Interior.[2] Although they were the same person, they might not always be, and Göring preferred simple methods of control to having to attend to a great mass of administrative detail. He remained Chief of the *Geheime Staatspolizei* (*Gestapo*) for a time, but day-to-day administration was turned over to the Deputy Chief and Inspector-General of the *Gestapo* and Chief of *Gestapa* (20 April 1934); the Prussian Ministry of the Interior was consolidated with the *Reich* Ministry of the Interior under Dr. Frick; and the administration of the Prussian Political Police became part of the domain of the *Gestapo*.

On the day of Hitler's appointment as Chancellor, Göring was already well established in Berlin as Speaker of the *Reichstag*, and soon as virtual dictator of Prussia, the largest and most important of all the provinces.

Himmler was still in Munich, far from the centre of power. But Himmler had something that Göring lacked: the presence and authority of an organisation he controlled, the SS, throughout all of Germany. In 1930 Göring had considered assuming leadership of the SA once more, and he had discussed this with Stennes, but when Stennes had explained to him the work that was involved Göring had dropped the idea, and now he was without a *Reich*-wide power base. The *Gestapo* did not penetrate the SS, but the SS penetrated the *Gestapo*. Step by step Himmler moved himself toward Berlin. On 9 March 1933 he was made President of Police in Munich; on 16 March he was put in charge of the entire Bavarian Political Police, as Political Assistant Secretary in the Bavarian Ministry of the Interior. In the course of 1933/34 Himmler managed to become chief of all the provincial political-police forces, with the exception of Prussia and Schaumburg-Lippe.

In Prussia Göring's power and control seemed impregnable. He controlled the entire government as Ministerpresident, the Ministry of the Interior, and the police forces (although his Prussian Police Chief, Daluege, was an SS officer). In the first weeks after Hitler's appointment as Chancellor, Göring had (illegally) enlisted the SA in Prussia as an auxiliary police and sent them to round up, beat up and throw into concentration camps 'enemies of the state'. But he soon found that he was unable to control the activities of the SA, and by then there had been appointed so many municipal and rural police chiefs who were SA officers that control of the Prussian Police began to slip from Göring's hands. Irregular SA concentration camps, some fifty in Berlin alone, were an element of anarchy that neither Göring nor Hitler could tolerate in the interests of orderly government and of their own power. The one-time chief of Department IA and now Göring's Prussian *Gestapo* Chief, Rudolf Diels, began raiding the illegal SA torture chambers, with Göring's half-hearted approval; but the competition, Himmler's and Heydrich's SS and SD, were gradually infiltrating Prussia.

In the autumn of 1933 Himmler had asked Hitler's permission to move the SS and SD head offices to Berlin, but Hitler had only allowed the establishment of branch offices there. The *Reich* Minister of the Interior, Dr. Frick, and even more so the high-ranking civil servants immediately under him, wanted control of all German police forces, as part of a centralist *Reich* reform. Neither Frick nor Himmler could quite extend their control over the strongest provincial chieftain, Göring, for the time being, but in March and April 1934, with the conflict between *Reichswehr* and SA about to erupt, all three found it wise to compromise. Göring retained the position of Ministerpresident in Prussia, and the Prussian Ministry of Finance also remained independent; but all other Prussian ministries and agencies passed under the appropriate *Reich* ministries' competence. An interim solution was found for the Prussian *Gestapo*: Göring remained as its Chief, but Himmler became Deputy *Gestapo* Chief and Inspector-General on 20 April 1934, succeeding Diels, and Heydrich became Himmler's deputy and Chief of the Prussian *Gestapa* Bureau. Arthur Nebe, also an SS officer already in the Prussian hierarchy, became Chief of the Prussian *Landeskriminalamt* (Provincial Criminal Police Bureau).

The SS now controlled the most important sections of the police forces in all German provinces. Himmler was Göring's deputy only in theory. Most of the orders were given and most of the administrative work was done by the ambitious, hard-working puritan, not by the jovial morphine addict, Göring, whose bursts of independent and outrageous activity too often alternated with spells of passivity. Himmler reached a peak in his career on 17 June 1936 when Hitler decreed that the Party office of SS *Reich* Leader be institutionally combined with that of Chief of German Police. Other peaks were to follow as the SS became a new quasi-revolutionary army through numerical increases, through the foundation of the *Waffen-SS* (military SS), and when Himmler became *Reich* Minister of the Interior in 1943, and (nominally) Commander-in-Chief of the Home Army on 20 July 1944.

'At the time of the national rising in Bavaria' in March 1933, as Himmler put it in a letter on 31 March 1934, a *Führerschutzkommando* (*Führer* Protection Group), sometimes called *Kommando z.b.V.* (Special Task Group), was formed for the new Chancellor by Himmler's authority and orders. 'With the assumption of command [by Himmler] over the political police forces in the provinces of Württemberg, Baden, etc., the activities of this *Kommando* were extended to the provinces. With the assumption of command by the *Reichsführer-SS* over the Prussian *Gestapo*, the activities of the *Führerschutzkommando* were also extended to Prussia.'[3] Thus the beginning of the reorganisation of the Chancellor's personal security may be dated March 1933, and its completion for April 1934. The personnel files of the *Führerschutzkommando* Commander, Police Captain Johann Rattenhuber, show that he was in command from 15 March 1933. But as late as 28 December 1933 Rattenhuber's letterheads described him as Adjutant to the Commander of Political Police in Munich (Himmler); in November 1934 his letterhead read '*Geheime Staatspolizei—Führerschutzkommando.*' Only in 1935 did Rattenhuber's *Führerschutzkommando* become a separate *Reich* agency; it was now called *Reichssicherheitsdienst.*

In his letter of 31 March 1934 Himmler further stressed that, as the *Führer* Protection Group had to guarantee the *Führer's* 'unconditional safety' in the Chancellery and wherever else he happened to be, they must be 'tried and trusted National Socialists, and furthermore excellent criminal-police officers of unconditional reliability, utmost conscientiousness in fulfilment of duties, good manners and physical dexterity.' But the commanding officer, as well as many of his subordinates, was first of all a professional police officer. Rattenhuber was born in 1897, graduated from a higher secondary school, and studied for two terms at a business college, joined the Army and served in Front Line positions from 1916, receiving a second lieutenant's commission in October 1918. He served in a Freecorps until 31 March 1920, then joined the Bavarian *Landespolizei* (provincial police) in Bayreuth, was promoted to lieutenant in 1925, and to captain in June 1933. His appointment was not based on any early Party merits. He did not even become an NSDAP member until 1 May 1933 (membership No. 3,212,449). His appointment as Commander of the *Führerschutzkommando*, 'with the title of *SS-Standarten-führer*,' is dated 15 March 1933. His deputy, Peter Högl, was a Party member only from 1 April 1933 (No. 3,289,992); he had preferred the *Bayerische Volkspartei* to the NSDAP before Hitler's appointment as Chancellor. In a political character reference written by the Party Office in Munich on 22 January 1937, it was stated that Högl 'had not come forward as a vicious enemy of the NSDAP. In as much as he has only profited from the National Socialist State, it may be assumed that by now he has adopted the idea of National Socialism. He is considered an honest comrade so that no more political reservations should exist against his promotion.' A number of other members of the *Führerschutzkommando*, however, were NSDAP members and supporters from earlier dates.

In its earliest days, the *Führerschutzkommando*, which was composed mostly of Bavarian criminal-police officers, could operate only in Bavaria, where Himmler's authority was undisputed. In the *Reich* Chancellery, the criminal-police officers of the Berlin Police IA Department were forced into the background by Hitler's personal *SS-Begleit-Kommando* (SS Escort). Hitler refused to allow any bodyguards other than his SS Escort to accompany him in the early months of his rule, but Himmler's criminal-police *Führerschutzkommando* tried to follow him around surreptitiously. One day in the spring of 1933, in Munich, Hitler noticed another car following his own and that of his SS Escort, and he instructed his driver, Kempka, to increase the speed of his supercharged Mercedes so that the strange car could no longer keep up. It developed that the strange car contained Himmler's policemen. Hitler, however, retained a strong aversion to policemen of any kind, apparently derived from his experiences in the Years of Struggle. It was not until the spring of 1934 that he finally accepted the professional criminal-police guards, so that they were enabled to operate in the entire *Reich* territory.

The strength of the new *Führerschutzkommando* was set at first at nine criminal-police officers plus two who were assigned to Himmler personally, and their commander; in 1935, the number was set at seventeen criminal-police officers and one commanding officer. Salaries, board, room, travel and equipment costs were to be defrayed temporarily by the individual provinces from which the officers had come. Hotel costs in Berlin, where the Group's headquarters was to be located in future, were much higher than the budget allowed, however. Therefore, *SA-Gruppenführer* Brückner, Hitler's Chief Personal Adjutant, rented apartments for the Group at 40 Kanonierstrasse (now Glinkastrasse). (Brückner was Chief Adjutant up to October 1940, when he was dismissed after he had had a row with Hitler's Chief Steward Kannenberg; Brückner's successor was Julius Schaub.[4]) Captain Hans Baur, Hitler's pilot, and Baur's two radio operators were also quartered there. The head office was at 8 Prinz-Albrecht-Strasse from where it was moved to 64 Kochstrasse in 1938, and to 5 Hermann-Göring-Strasse in 1940. When the apartments proved too small, a house was acquired for the Group in 1940 at 4–6 Kronenstrasse.

Costs, in addition to salaries for the officers in 1934, came to 80,068 Reichsmarks and included remodelling the apartments, salaries for a cook and two charwomen, rent, two Mercedes cars, and maintenance. The money came from the budget line for 'measures for the protection of people and state' for 1934, and *Reich* Minister of the Interior Dr. Frick had the amount transferred to the purser's office of the Prussian *Gestapo*.

At the end of 1934 the *Reich* Minister of the Interior asked the *Reich* Minister of Finance, the State Secretary and Chief of the Chancellery, and Brückner to join him in a conference on 18 December 1934, to discuss the administrative and financial affairs of the *Führerschutzkommando*. But Brückner could not come and a new date was set for 12 January 1935; this time the *Reich* Minister of Finance, Count Schwerin von Krosigk, the State Secretary and Chief of the Chancellery, Dr. Lammers, the Chief Adjutant to the *Führer* and Chancellor, Brückner, and the *Reichsführer SS*, Himmler, 'also as Inspector of the Prussian *Gestapo*,' were invited; but now the conference had to be postponed because Himmler could not come.

Eventually, the conference was held on 13 February 1935. Participants were: State Secretary in the *Reich* and Prussian Ministry of the Interior Pfundtner; Counsellor Erbe and Counsellor Dr. Gisevius of the *Reich* and Prussian Ministry of the Interior; Brückner; the Commander of the *Führerschutzkommando*, Police Captain and *SS-Obersturmbannführer* Rattenhuber; Counsellor Wienstein of the *Reich* Chancellery; Counsellor Schmidt-Schwarzenberg of the *Reich* Ministry of Finance.

All details of guarding Hitler and the Chancellery were reviewed by Counsellor Wienstein: the details included four criminal-police officers salaried by the Presidium of Police in Berlin; four gendarmes paid by the *Reich* Ministry of the Interior; thirty-one men from the *SS-Leibstandarte 'Adolf Hitler'* (SS Bodyguard Regiment) whose salaries were paid by the *Reich* Ministry of the Interior; fifteen *Führerschutzkommando* officers from the criminal-police forces of the various provinces and paid by them. Pfundtner argued that obviously the work of the *Führer's* Protection Group was a *Reich* matter and should therefore be paid for by the *Reich*, the only question was under what Government agency the Group was to operate. This was not merely a problem of finding an appropriate line in the *Reich* budget, but also one of authority, so that it could not fail to cause political manœuvring. There seemed to be three possibilities: attaching the *Führerschutzkommando* to the *Reich* Ministry of the Interior; or to the Chancellery; or to the *Gestapo*. The *Reich* Ministry of the Interior was willing to assume budgetary responsibility; the actual immediate authority of the *Führer's* Chief Adjutant seemed to favour attachment to the Chancellery; mainly technical reasons could be offered for subordinating the Group to the *Gestapo*. This was still only a Prussian agency, but closely connected with other German police forces through the person of the *Reichsführer SS* whose organisation, the SS, was a branch of the NSDAP, and thus more and more an integral part of the State.

Captain Rattenhuber then described the current composition of the *Führerschutzkommando*. There were five branch bureaux for security service with the *Führer*, with *Reich* Ministers Göring, Hess and Goebbels, and with Himmler. Two additional branch bureaux provided security for other *Reich* Ministers on travel, and for visiting foreign statesmen. An eighth bureau investigated reports of assassination plans, and a head office had primarily administrative functions. The crews of Hitler's plane and accompanying plane were included in the *Führerschutzkommando*: one major, one captain, four criminal-police inspectors. The Group's total thus came to seventy-six persons, not counting purely clerical personnel. Of these, a total of sixteen (not counting the air crew) were engaged exclusively in protecting the Chancellor.

Counsellor Gisevius presented the view of Ministerial Director Daluege, who was the Chief of Department III (Police) in the *Reich* and Prussian Ministry of the Interior, arguing for attaching the security bureaux to the Prussian *Gestapo*. This could have added to Frick's powers who, as *Reich* Minister of the Interior, hoped to establish control over all German police forces. Gisevius said the bureaux were too small for following up widely ramified assassination plans, and that they also lacked the necessary specialised training. The desired level of security could be achieved only if information available at the *Gestapo* and at the *Landeskriminalamt* (Provincial Criminal Police Bureau) was exploited in the closest cooperation with the security groups. If these became a separate agency, the danger of insufficient cooperation would be increased.

Captain Rattenhuber opposed Dr. Gisevius' argument, saying that the *Gestapo* had its own tasks and interests and had not always cooperated with the security groups. Counsellor Wienstein (Permanent Deputy to the State Secretary in the Chancellery, Dr. Lammers) added that attachment to the Chancellery would create an unmanageable burden without an increase in personnel.

Schmidt-Schwarzenberg then spoke for the *Reich* Ministry of Finance and supported Gisevius' creation of *Führerschutzkommando* positions in the *Reich* budget would make the individuals holding the positions less interchangeable, and deprive them of promotion opportunities; all police forces would soon be consolidated as one *Reich* organisation in any case, and therefore it would be best to leave unchanged for a while longer the current arrangement whereby the security officers were paid from provincial funds.

Brückner then said there was no reason to wait for the police forces becoming one unified *Reich* organisation; on the contrary, making the *Führerschutzkommando* a *Reich* authority would be a logical step in this direction. Gisevius and Schmidt-Schwarzenberg were opposed. But Pfundtner supported Brückner by favouring budgeting at least of the command positions of the *Führerschutzkommando* separately in the *Reich* budget. Total costs were estimated at 709,000 Reichsmarks.

Another conference was held on the same topic two days later, this time in the *Reich* Chancellery; participants were Captain Rattenhuber, his Paymaster Trenkl, Schmidt-Schwarzenberg, Dr. Gisevius, Counsellors Dr. Killy and Steinmeyer of the Chancellery.[5] It was agreed that organisational issues could not be settled before areas of competence and authority had been clearly defined. It was agreed that the *Führerschutzkommando* be organised as effective on 1 April 1935, the start of the new budget year. Rattenhuber promised to submit a list of all officers and their current positions in time for another conference a week hence. But he did not keep this promise, and inquiries by Steinmeyer on 13 March showed that Rattenhuber was not in Berlin and not expected to come back before the return of the *Führer*, who was in Bavaria until 15 March.

When Hitler had returned, Rattenhuber, on Saturday, 16 March 1935, demanded a conference on the same day in the Chancellery and insisted that the *Führerschutzkommando* be subordinated to Himmler and annexed to the Chancellery; Brückner demanded it, said Rattenhuber and his Paymaster Trenkl who had come with him that Saturday afternoon. Steinmeyer and Wienstein of the Chancellery, however, were in favour of annexing the *Führerschutzkommando* to the *Reich* Ministry of the Interior, and on the following Monday Lammers noted that Himmler had assured him there was no objection to this.

Finally, after further negotiations with Rattenhuber, it was all settled in a conference between the *Reich* Ministers of Finance and of the Interior, Count Schwerin von Krosigk and Dr. Frick, on 29 March 1935, and in a cabinet meeting on the same day. The *Führerschutzkommando* budget and the operating costs for the *Reichssicherheitsdienst* (*Reich* Security Service)—this seems to be the first time the more comprehensive term was used officially—were to be listed together in the budget of the *Reich* Ministry of the Interior. The estimate was still some RM 700,000; at the end of May the *Reichssicherheitsdienst* settled for RM 500,000. By 1937, however, its budget reached RM 1,062, 800.

Neither had Himmler succeeded in bringing under his control all German police forces as yet, nor had Frick got control of the *Führerschutzkommando*. The tug-of-war for control of Hitler's personal bodyguard continued.

In October 1935 Himmler seemed to have won. He got Hitler to make him Chief of the entire *Reichssicherheitsdienst* (RSD, *Reich* Security Service) as Hitler's and other prominent government members' protection groups were called officially since 1 August 1935. But Rattenhuber was still the Commander and took most of his orders, especially for day-to-day operation, from Hitler directly or through one of his aides (Brückner, Bormann, Schaub): Himmler was not given more than administrative authority, in practice, but he was now better able to integrate the RSD into the Party and SS system.

Incidentally, the question of naming the RSD caused some confusion in November 1935; Himmler asked Hitler to have the *Reichssicherheitsdienst* (*Reich* Security Service) renamed *Reichssicherungsdienst* (*Reich* Securing Service) to distinguish it from the *Reichssicherheitsdienst* in the Saar Province where this term was used for the *Staatspolizei* (State Police).[6] Hitler did not wish for the change, however, and he replied through Lammers on the day after Himmler had written that the Saar Province would simply have to change the name of its *Staatspolizei* because the term *Reichssicherheitsdienst* had already been written into the *Reich* budget. Frick did a little research of his own and came up with the information that the *Staatspolizei* Bureau Saarbrücken was never called *Reichssicherheitsdienst*. Himmler explained lamely that the term *Reichssicherheitsdienst* had been *considered* for the *Staatspolizei* Bureau Saarbrücken shortly before the return of the province to Germany in 1935, and asked Frick to regard the matter as closed.

At the time of Himmler's appointment as Chief of the *Reichssicherheitsdienst*, Lammers also wrote him (22 October 1935) that the *Reichssicherheitsdienst* (RSD), budgeted within the *Reich* Ministry of the Interior, 'will be subordinated to you. You are given full command authority over the members of the *Reichssicherheitsdienst*, and in this capacity you will be subordinated immediately to the *Führer* and Chancellor. Your command authority also results in your being solely responsible for the *Reichssicherheitsdienst*.' Himmler was further authorised to dispose of the funds allocated to the RSD within the laws and he was charged with responsibility to the *Reich* Court of Audit for every expenditure. But: 'The *Führer* and Chancellor has reserved for himself the appointment of the members of the *Reichssicherheitsdienst*.' Proposals for appointments were to be submitted through Lammers, with a copy to the *Reich* Minister of the Interior.[7] This procedure was followed by Himmler when he submitted a list of fourteen appointments for approval on 30 October 1935. The number of proposed appointments grew to forty-five before Hitler signed the letters of appointment. But before they were sent to the appointees, Lammers submitted the entire list to Deputy of the *Führer* and *Reich* Minister Rudolf Hess for approval, asking if there were any reservations against any of the appointments. As Wienstein put it in a marginal note: since the *Führer* was making all the appointments personally, his deputy had to be heard in all cases. Himmler was informed by Lammers that Hitler had signed the appointments, but that Lammers could not yet send them over to Himmler. According to the Decree of the *Führer* and Chancellor of 24 September 1935 regarding participation of the Deputy of the *Führer* in appointments of government officials, the approval of the Deputy was required for all appointments made by the *Führer* and Chancellor personally. Himmler must have been long used to such setbacks and disappointments. This letter showed him that the struggle for control was still on, and it is an illustration of Hitler's system of dividing authorities so that he always retained final and decisive control. Even after Himmler had become *Chef der Deutschen Polizei im Reichsministerium des Innern* (Chief of German Police in the *Reich* Ministry of the Interior) in June 1936, his control over the RSD was not increased. Hess, incidentally, raised no objections, and the letters of appointment were sent to Himmler on 13 November 1935.

The immediate RSD commanders were Rattenhuber and his deputies, Detective Inspector of Criminal Police Högl and Police Inspector Kiesel.[8] All took orders directly from Hitler, Hess, Bormann, or Brückner. Himmler tried many times, even via his position as Chief of German Police, to gain full control of Hitler's RSD bodyguards; but Martin Bormann got a good deal further towards this goal.

Bormann had begun his rise in the hierarchy of the NSDAP in 1933 as Chief of Staff (*Stabsleiter*) to Hess. By August 1938 he was officially declared a member of 'the permanent entourage of the *Führer*.' He managed to expand his influence constantly through the years, until he controlled the entire NSDAP organisation and was able to interfere in the operations of most government and even military agencies. On 12 May 1941, two days after Rudolf Hess's spectacular flight to Britain, Hitler decreed that the former Office of the Deputy of the *Führer* was henceforth to be known as Party Chancellery, and that it was under the immediate authority of the *Führer* himself. Bormann had already been, in effect if not in name, Secretary of the *Führer*, and he headed the Chancellery of the Leader of the NSDAP. On 29 May 1941 Hitler further decreed that the *Leiter der Partei-Kanzlei* (Head of the Party Chancellery), Martin

Bormann, had the authority of a *Reich* Minister, and that wherever the term Deputy of the *Führer* was used in laws, ordinances, decrees and orders, the term *Leiter der Partei-Kanzlei* was to take its place. On 8 May 1943 Hitler once more clarified Bormann's position, apparently upon Bormann's request and because there had been difficulties: Bormann was not only Head of the Party Chancellery but was also entrusted by the *Führer* with many 'special assignments' outside the range of competence of the Head of the Party Chancellery, and Bormann was then acting as Secretary to the *Führer*, carrying out '*Führer* Orders' which had the force of laws.[9]

In the RSD, professional excellence and loyalty were intended to be enhanced by elaborate swearing-in ceremonies in the presence of the *Führer* himself. The tradition of such ceremonies went back as far as the famous beer-hall battle of 4 November 1921.[10] All newly appointed RSD officers were sworn in on 9 November; the place was always Munich's 'Feldherrnhalle,' and Himmler administered the oath in the presence of Hitler.

Every government official and all military men had to take a regular oath of office; after President von Hindenburg's death, it was given the following form, required by law from 20 August 1934: 'I swear: I shall be faithful and obedient to the *Führer* of the German *Reich* and People, Adolf Hitler; I shall observe the laws and fulfil my official duties conscientiously, so help me God.' Counsellor Wienstein in the *Reich* Chancellery insisted that members of the RSD had to take this oath if they were to become government officials with all implied rights and privileges. The slightly different wording of the oath taken at the 'Feldherrnhalle' would not do, he said, it was not the one prescribed by law. Consequently, the official oath was administered to the RSD in 1936 and on subsequent occasions when new officials were appointed.

The personal oath of loyalty sworn at the 'Feldherrnhalle' by the RSD (and by all SS men) was stronger: 'I swear to you, Adolf Hitler, as *Führer* and Chancellor of the German *Reich*, loyalty and bravery. I vow to you and to my superiors designated by you obedience to the death. So help me God.' Neither in this nor in the official oath was there any mention of the nation or the constitution; in the second one, even the laws were eliminated. Personal loyalty was put above the law, and the circumstances in which the oath was administered as well as the use of the familiar form (second person singular) made it more personal and more personally binding. The relative importance of the two oaths was stressed by the long delay before the original forty-five RSD men finally took the official oath. Thirty-seven RSD men, including the commander Rattenhuber and his deputy Högl, as well as Hitler's personal pilot Hans Baur, had not taken it by April 1936.

Throughout the twelve years of Nazi rule there were instances when

Hitler insisted on his direct control of organisations he considered to be of vital importance; the RSD was one. In January 1942 Lammers contemplated alleviating the burden of Hitler's many official duties, seeing that the *Führer's* health was deteriorating rapidly. But Hitler firmly insisted on signing every RSD man's appointment document in his own hand in every case. Again, in 1944, it was emphasised that, while the *Reichsführer SS* was 'Chief' of the RSD and Rattenhuber was his deputy as commander, 'the *Führer* had reserved for himself personally the command of the RSD.' The RSD had become a separate *Reich* agency not subordinated institutionally to any other *Reich* authority (Ministry of the Interior, Chancellery, *Reichssicherheitshauptamt* (RSHA, *Reich* Security Head Office), but only to the *Führer* himself.

The various RSD detachments were assigned as follows: Bureau 1 was always with the *Führer* and also in charge of local security at his Obersalzberg retreat; the Munich and Berchtesgaden *Ortsdienststellen* (local bureaux), 8 and 9 (formerly 7b), and *Ortsdienststelle* Berchtesgaden (organised in 1936) were also earmarked primarily for the security of the *Führer*. Other detachments were assigned to Göring (No. 2), Ribbentrop (No. 3), Himmler (No. 4), Goebbels (No. 5), Frick (No. 6), Minister of Food Darré (No. 7). This was the final order of the detachments in 1944, after a number of changes had occurred. In 1937, Bureau 3 had been Hess's detachment; there were three more bureaux in 1937 than in 1935. Bureau 8, described in 1935 as a combined head office and investigation service was merely the Munich detachment in 1937. There were some seventeen bureaux by 1944. No. 7 was no longer (as in 1937) assigned to *Reich* Minister Darré but to Minister Frank in Prague; No. 10 to *Reich* Minister Seyss-Inquart in the Hague; No. 11 to *Reich* Commissar Terboven in Oslo; No. 12 to Grandadmiral Dönitz; No. 13 to *Reich* Commissar Dr. Best in Copenhagen; No. 14 to *SS-Obergruppenführer* Kaltenbrunner, the Chief of RSHA; one each without a number to Dr. Ley and to *Gauleiter* Koch; a *Sicherheits-Kontrolldienst Reichskanzlei* (Security Control Service in the *Reich* Chancellery) had been added, also without number, in December 1939.[11]

The routine tasks of RSD detachments included providing personal security for the functionaries to whom they were assigned; investigation of assassination plans (independently, despite some necessary cooperation with the *Gestapo*); constant surveillance of places (headquarters, buildings, hotels, etc., where protected persons were likely to stay), for example, in Berlin the 'Krolloper,' in Munich the 'Osteria Bavaria,' in Vienna the Hotel 'Imperial,' etc.; periodical complete checks of such buildings with the assistance of craftsmen and experts in the detection of explosives, listening devices, etc; personnel checks on those employed at the various sites; checks on neighbouring sites; thorough checks of meeting halls, arenas, etc., before appearances of the *Führer* or other dignitaries; constant surveillance of such places until after the event, including all buildings and persons within a certain radius; security along access roads, on airfields and at railway stations.[12] Bureau 9 was charged in 1937 with responsibility for surveillance of all foreigners and strangers in the area, in cooperation with authorities in Berchtesgaden and Bad Reichenhall.

In 1935 there were forty-five RSD officers (not counting crews of Hitler's planes), some twenty of whom were detailed for Hitler's security, the rest being administratively employed, manning various investigative and screening positions in the branch offices, and guarding a number of other government officials. By 1936 there were fifty-six positions in the RSD, and in the draft budget for 1937 the total came to 100. By 1939 there were some 200 RSD men, and about 400 by the end of the war.[13]

The majority of the original RSD men came from Bavaria, most of them from a Bavarian municipal or provincial police force; only about 10% of the RSD came from parts of Germany outside of Bavaria. Those who were not Bavarians were Thuringians (two) or Prussians.[14]

Former members of the RSD are inclined to say that only professional qualifications were criteria for RSD appointments. While it is true that SS ranks were given to every member regardless of whether he wished for one or not, and while it is also true that background, training and professional qualifications were looked at closely in considering candidates, there were other equally important criteria: political orthodoxy and loyalty were required.

Most of the RSD men were NSDAP members, with a sprinkling of them *Alte Kämpfer* (Old Fighters) who had joined the Party before 1933, some of them participants in the March to the 'Feldherrnhalle' in which sixteen Nazis were killed by Bavarian provincial police. A list of sixteen *Führerschutzkommando* officers drawn up by Rattenhuber on 30 November 1934 gave no NSDAP membership information for six of the names, and listed two as NSDAP members who had joined the Party in 1931, one who had joined in 1932, and seven who had joined after 30 January 1933.[15] Close to half of those active in the RSD in 1939 did not become Party members until 1 May 1937, when Himmler saw to it that all RSD members were given NSDAP memberships; but almost all held SS ranks before 1934, and Party membership was taken for granted and nearly automatic for SS members.[16] SS membership implied NSDAP membership, as the SS was a branch organisation of the NSDAP.

In May of 1934 Göring, as Prussian Ministerpresident and Chief of the Prussian *Gestapo*, declared that for the protection of Hitler only those were suitable who were 'tried and trusted National Socialists.' Immediately after the Röhm massacre, most of the RSD officers received promotions 'occasioned by the Röhm Affair,' as Himmler put it, and effective from 1 July 1934. 'Unconditional reliability' and loyalty were rewarded.

By the autumn of 1936 these principles were written into a law that allowed and encouraged promotions, at shorter intervals than regularly provided, for 'proven National-Socialist candidates for higher government service who also meet the qualifications' for the positions for which they were being considered. The preference shown to NSDAP and SS members for government service also applied to the RSD. Persons not eligible for NSDAP and SS membership were not considered eligible for RSD service. All RSD men had to show proof of their 'German-blood descent.' 'Jewish descent' was not considered 'German-blood descent' by the Nazis. In 1933 the *Reichstag* rubber-stamped the 'law for the restoration of the professional civil service corps' which forced most Jewish civil servants into retirement. The Nuremberg Laws of September 1935 stated (among other things) that Jews could not be civil servants.[16]

On duty the RSD wore—before the war—black SS uniforms, or civilian clothes, depending on whether their duties required an 'official,' visible appearance, or an inconspicuous one such as on a visit to the opera or to a restaurant, or on under-cover duties. The uniforms facilitated the RSD's work at Hitler's official residences where his bodyguards sometimes had to deal with loud and troublesome followers of the *Führer*, or with police officers outside Berlin where the RSD men were not personally known. Rattenhuber's overall authority over local police forces in connection with Hitler's personal security had been established early. On 12 December 1934 Heydrich, as deputy of *Der Politische Polizeikommandeur* (Himmler), had written from Berlin to all regional political-police chiefs: all police officials who are locally detailed for Hitler's protection will be placed under Rattenhuber's command for the duration of Hitler's visit; the political-police forces must make available as many officers as Rattenhuber will request, for as long as he will specify.[17]

At the beginning of the war the RSD were given field-grey SS uniforms with the insignia appropriate to their military police ranks.[18] They were integrated into the war machine, whose master from 1 September 1939 usually referred to his residence as *Führerhauptquartier*.

The RSD personnel assigned to Hitler were declared by the *Oberkommando der Wehrmacht* (OKW, Armed Forces Supreme Command) to be *Wehrmacht* officials for the duration of the war. Detachments guarding other ministers were not included in this regulation. Hitler's RSD was put under the authority of the Chief of OKW (Keitel) administratively, with the Commander of RSD (Rattenhuber) the immediate subordinate of the Chief of OKW in this respect; militarily, the higher authority was also the Chief of OKW. This did not change Hitler's and Himmler's operational and administrative authority, nor did it curtail the exercise of this authority through Bormann, Brückner and others. The rights and

3. *RSD detail in Prague, 16 March 1939 (from left): Johann Driesle, Otto Feuerlein, Johann Rattenhuber, Karl Zenger*

4. *Peter Högl, Julius Schaub, and Heinrich Himmler (from left) at 'Wolfschanze,' 25 July 1944*

privileges of the RSD were expanded to give them the greatest possible freedom of movement and authority within the military framework in which they had to fulfil their functions during the war when Hitler spent most of his time in military headquarters. The RSD men were given the status of secret military police officers. Soon they were called, accordingly, *Reichssicherheitsdienst Gruppe Geheime Feldpolizei z.b.V.* (*Reich* Security Service Secret Military Police Group for Special Assignment).[19] They were given appropriate identification papers and secret badges. The RSD men had the right to request assistance from the military police or any other *Wehrmacht* soldier or officer in urgent cases, and to arrest *Wehrmacht* members if they surprised them *in flagrante delicto* at whatever the RSD thought a soldier ought not to be doing. In cases of suspected espionage they could have the suspect arrested in consultation with the local military commander. If necessary, the RSD were allowed to wear the uniforms of any branch of the armed forces as a disguise. Uniforms had the effect of plain clothes in a military environment. They could pass all military check-points by merely showing their pass or badge. In military installations and areas, they had to use only those passes and papers that identified them as serving with the Secret Military Police Group for Special Assignment. They were empowered to enter any military building, use any military communication facility, and to demand to ride in any military vehicle. They could demand food and lodging when needed in connection with their duties. In a civilian environment and *vis-à-vis* civilians, however, the secret-police badge was to be used as proof of authority.

5 Hitler's SS Escort

Hitler's personal *SS-Begleit-Kommando* (SS Escort) had its origins in the earliest history of the NSDAP. Significant dates in its development are 4 November 1921, for the baptism of fire of the bodyguard in Munich's 'Hofbräuhaus'; March 1923, for the organisation of the *Stabswache* (Staff Guard) by Göring; May 1923, for the formation of *Stosstrupp Hitler* (Hitler Assault Squad) by Berchtold and for the incorporation of the *Stabswache* in *Stosstrupp Hitler*.[1] From this the *Schutzstaffel* (SS) was formed in 1925, from which Hitler took his personal bodyguard before and after 1933, although after his appointment as Chancellor the regular police bodyguards were available to him. In the spring of 1933, when the strength of the SS had grown to 50,000, the *SS-Leibstandarte*, or SS Bodyguard Regiment, was organised as Hitler's own 'palace guard' from which his SS Escort details were taken.

The commander of the Bodyguard Regiment, Sepp Dietrich, born in 1892 in Hawangen (Bavaria), had joined the Army as a volunteer in 1911, served in the field during the war, and was discharged as a *Vizewachtmeister* (vice-sergeant). He served in 'Oberland' Freecorps from 1920 to 1926, and in the Bavarian *Landespolizei* (provincial police) from 1920 to 1923. On 9 November 1923 he marched to Munich's 'Feldherrnhalle' with *Sturm-Bataillon* 'Oberland'. Participation in Hitler's *putsch* put an end to Dietrich's police career. He joined the SS in 1928 and rose through the ranks to *SS-Gruppenführer* (equivalent to major-general) by 1931, and he was a *Reichstag* deputy from 1930. In the 1932 election campaigns he commanded the SS guards accompanying Hitler, with overall authority over SS details providing security for the *Führer*, and usually preceded him to places of public appearances in order to organise and inspect security arrangements. After 30 January 1933 Dietrich played an important role in the build-up of the SS as a military formation, and in the war he distinguished himself as a Front Line commander of SS troops in Russia and in France.[1a]

On 17 March 1933 Sepp Dietrich was ordered by Hitler to form a new *Stabswache* out of the existing SS units. This new *Stabswache* was composed at first of several *SS-Sonderkommandos*, such as *SS-Sonderkommando z.b.V. Berlin*, *SS-Sonderkommando München*, and such units as *Adolf Hitler Standarte* and *Kommando Zossen*. The Berlin *Stabswache*, billeted initially in Alexanderkaserne near Friedrichstrasse Station, numbered 120 men. Wherever Hitler went, the most reliable SS men, organised as *Sonderkom-*

mandos, were to be available to him locally for his protection. Within a few months, however, the *Sonderkommandos* were either combined in the larger *SS-Leibstandarte*, or allowed to develop locally and regionally into separate units which had only secondary importance when Hitler was in their area.

The new *Stabswache* had duties around Hitler and his residences: cordoning-off at public appearances, guard duties in and around the *Reich* Chancellery and the private residences, guard duties at central NSDAP offices including Himmler's, Göring's, Heydrich's, Dr. Ley's and Darré's, and at the *Gestapo's* central offices, also at Tempelhof airfield where government planes usually departed and arrived.[2] The unit was kept available for general security tasks, and it was used in the Röhm massacre. During the war, parts of the élite troops were always used in the heaviest fighting, as a spearhead and as a model fighting unit. But they were almost never used to guard Hitler's military headquarters during the war. The defence of these against any intruders or surprise attacks (such as airborne assaults) was the duty of the *Führer-Begleit-Bataillon* (*Führer* Escort Battalion) which was recruited from Army and Air Force units (Infantry Regiment 'Grossdeutschland' and Regiment 'General Göring'). Only Hitler's personal SS Escort was on duty within the military headquarters—as everywhere else where Hitler happened to be.[3]

At the 1933 NSDAP Rally in Nuremberg (30 August to 3 September) the *Stabswache* (or remaining *Sonderkommandos*) which had in the meantime reached regimental strength was renamed officially as *Leibstandarte* '*Adolf Hitler*' (sometimes also referred to as *Adolf Hitler Standarte*), or Bodyguard Regiment 'Adolf Hitler'. On 4 November 1933 it was decreed that all future orders and directives issued by Himmler to the *Leibstandarte* were no longer to be sent to the *Reich* Chancellery where Sepp Dietrich resided and had his office, but to the *Leibstandarte* barracks at 'Berlin-Lichterfelde, Kadettenanstalt'—an indication of the permanence of the new organisation. On 9 November 1933 the entire *Leibstandarte*, numbering 1,000 officers and enlisted men, swore the oath of personal obedience and loyalty to Hitler at the 'Feldherrnhalle', in the same words as had the RSD when they had become SS members. After November 1933 the name usually employed for the organisation (*SS-Verfügungstruppe*, or SS Special Duty Troop) became *Leibstandarte-SS 'Adolf Hitler*' (LSSAH).[4] The LSSAH, as a part of the SS, was ultimately commanded by Himmler, under Hitler's authority. But in reality Dietrich took his orders from the *Führer* directly, rather than through Himmler. The LSSAH was never fully integrated into the SS, and Himmler only managed to establish a certain technical and administrative authority over it, never full command authority. Hitler would not dream of allowing one man to control all of his Black Guards, and when Himmler now and then had to insist that certain procedures be followed in the LSSAH, he was forced to 'ask' Dietrich, since he had no power to command him.[5]

The example of the LSSAH also shows that the amalgamation of Party and State which Hitler had decreed in a law of 1 December 1933 did not always proceed smoothly. When the LSSAH had theoretically become a state agency by this law, a *Reich* budget line had to be found for Hitler's private bodyguard regiment.[6] A few months before, on 22 September 1933, the Prussian Minister of the Interior, Göring, had sent to the President of Police in Berlin, Levetzow, to the Prussian Chamber of Audit and to the *Reich* Chancellery new salary regulations for the '*Leibstandarte* of the *Reich* Chancellor and the *Stabswache* of the Ministerpresident,' to become effective on 1 October 1933. The strength of the *Leibstandarte* was given as 1,000, that of Göring's *Stabswache* as 253.[7] On 22 December 1933 Secretary of State Grauert in the Prussian Ministry of the Interior declared officially that the *Leibstandarte* was being used exclusively for the protection of *Reich* agencies and was not subordinated to any Prussian agency; only temporarily, until a more satisfactory solution could be found, the *Leibstandarte* was to be budgeted within the budget of *Landespolizeigruppe Wecke z.b.V.* (Provincial Police Group Wecke for Special Assignment).[8] This organisation had been formed on 8 March 1933 for the special disposition of Göring and it was used as his personal guard until the RSD took over this assignment in 1935. At least until January 1935 it was billeted in the former Königin-Elisabeth-Gardegrenadier-Kaserne at 5 Königin-Elisabeth-Strasse in Berlin-Charlottenburg, and in the Lichterfelde Cadet barracks where Hitler's *Leibstandarte* was also housed. Police Major Walther Wecke, incidentally, long a Nazi supporter in the Berlin police force and organiser of secret dossiers on 'unreliable' police officers since March 1932, was working out of the Prussian Ministry of the Interior, purging 1,457 'unreliable' officers from the Prussian Police.

Grauert called the present arrangement 'hardly satisfactory' and requested budgeting for the *Leibstandarte* under some *Reich* ministry. Therefore Dr. Lammers, as State Secretary of the *Reich* Chancellery, asked *Reich* Minister of Finance Schwerin von Krosigk to budget the security force in the *Reich* Ministry of the Interior.[9] Then a bureaucrat in the *Reich* Ministry of Finance suggested budgeting in the Chancellery budget, to which a Chancellery official objected vigorously in February 1934, saying that the Chancellery budget could not be kept secret, and the fact that 1,000 men of a paramilitary force were organised and budgeted very much like *Reichswehr* units could lead to 'conclusions undesirable from a foreign policy point of view;' the restrictions imposed by the Treaty of Versailles were still in force. Furthermore, the official continued, an officially-decreed salary structure for the LSSAH might lead to claims for equal pay as well as for pay by the *Reich* for all the rest of the SA and SS. There were by now more than three million in the SA, and the SA was then the greatest menace to all established authority, including Hitler's own. The official requested a decision by the Chancellor. On 8 February 1934 Counsellor Wienstein informed Counsellor Woothke in the *Reich* Ministry of Finance of the Chancellor's decision: the LSSAH's budget was to be carried in that of the Ministry of the Interior, as a lump sum, without itemisation. The reasons for this, said Wienstein, could not be committed to writing, but he would be glad to inform Woothke orally.[10]

It was not merely through budgetary and other administrative means that the amalgamation of Party and State was being advanced. In particular, the SS was meant to be much more than a military force at the disposal of the *Führer*: it was meant to be spread throughout Germany and through all phases of national life as a ubiquitous network. As Police General Daluege put it in a long memorandum in December 1938: 'It had been the one wish of the *Führer* through the amalgamation of police and SS, to have new men and officers come from the SS leadership schools and from active SS formations whenever possible.' Unfortunately, this hope had not quite been fulfilled: 'Of 800 SS men who left the LSSAH on 1 October 1937 after their four-year term of service, only 13 enlisted for service with the police.' Daluege attributed this deplorable state of affairs to poor wages and hard working conditions in the police forces. Nevertheless, the goal remained, as Himmler stated it in a circular of 1 July 1941: 'the building of a unitary State Security Corps of the National Socialist *Reich*, and the fusion of the members of the German Police with the SS.' To this end, policemen were encouraged to join the SS. And in 1944: 'Members of the police who fulfil the requirements of the SS will become members of the SS. As SS members they will wear on duty the uniform of the SS or SS insignia on their police uniforms. The leadership corps and all replacements of the men will in future be taken from the ranks of the SS. Thus the police will be permeated by the SS.'[11]

Conditions for membership in the SS included 'Aryan' ancestry from 1800 at least, from 1750 for officer ranks. In 1940 an enlisted SS man was dismissed on grounds that no one could be tolerated in the SS who had a Jewish ancestor after the Thirty Years' War.[12] A clean political past was also required, as well as physical fitness, a certain minimum height (1.80 metres in 1934, 1.78 metres in 1936), and 'Nordic' appearance.

Party membership of LSSAH men, on the other hand, was not as strictly insisted upon as one might expect. On 6 March 1934 the *Leibstandarte* reported to the *Reichsführer SS* an actual strength of 986 as at 1 March 1934; of these, 45 were not members in the NSDAP, and 136 of the 941 members were 'without membership number.' In 1937 some

1,400 LSSAH men were inducted into the NSDAP *en bloc*, apparently without being scrutinised individually before being granted NSDAP membership. According to official statistics published in 1937, 11% of all SS were not Party members nor had they applied for membership by 1 July 1937. The non-membership percentage was 27% for the *SS-Verfügungstruppe*, which included the LSSAH. It was higher only among the *SS-Totenkopfverbände* (SS Death's Head Formations), at 29%. Two of Hitler's later SS adjutants, Richard Schulze (who also used the double name of Schulze-Kossens) and Max Wünsche, did not become NSDAP members until 1 May 1937 and 1 March 1938, respectively.[13]

The history of the *SS-Begleit-Kommando 'Der Führer'*, Hitler's personal SS Escort, as a formal organisation, begins at least a year before that of the *Leibstandarte*. Sepp Dietrich and Hitler's driver, Julius Schreck, could not, in the increasingly busy and turbulent months before Hitler's rise to power, personally look after all necessary security measures, let alone lead the guard details. On 29 February 1932, the *SS-Begleit-Kommando* was formed under a leader who had only guard and security duties. Twelve SS members were chosen from various units and presented to Hitler at Berlin's 'Kaiserhof' hotel by Sepp Dietrich and by their various unit commanders, in the presence of Himmler (Hitler had made the 'Kaiserhof' his Berlin headquarters from 3 February 1931).[14] Eight of the candidates were selected: Franz Schädle, Bruno Gesche, Erich Kempka, August Körber, Adolf Dirr, Kurt Gildisch, Willy Herzberger, and the first commander of the detail, Bodo Gelzenleuchter. During the months of prohibition of uniforms, the *SS-Begleit-Kommando* wore motorcycle overalls and blue caps without insignia. Their weapons were sjamboks, and later, when permits could be obtained, they carried pistols. After 30 January 1933 they almost always wore SS uniforms. Those who had joined the SS before that date wore chevrons on their right sleeves. SS men who had transferred directly from the police to the SS after 30 January 1933 were given chevrons with a star, so that most of the RSD officers were hardly distinguishable from their colleagues in the SS Escort.[15]

The new *SS-Begleit-Kommando* did not include any of the 'permanent companions' of the *Führer*, most of whom had long since risen to higher positions in the Party hierarchy.[16] Josef Berchtold was editor of the periodical *Der SA-Mann* and later occupied a leading position in the editorial staff of the *Völkischer Beobachter*; Rudolf Hess was Deputy of the *Führer* and a *Reich* Minister; Alfred Rosenberg was, among other things, Chief of the Foreign-Policy Office of the NSDAP, and of the *Reich* Bureau for the Fostering of German Publications; Max Amann was *Reichsleiter* of the NSDAP for Press Affairs, and headed the NSDAP's publishing house, Eher Verlag (*Zentralverlag der NSDAP*); Dr. Ernst (Putzi) Hanfstaengl headed the Foreign-Press Office in the *Führer's* Deputy's Staff;

3. The *Führer* has decided that in this one and only exceptional case Maurice as well as his brothers could remain in the SS, because Maurice had been his very first companion, and because his brothers and the entire family Maurice had served the Movement with rare bravery and loyalty in the first and most difficult months and years.

4. I decree that Maurice must not be entered in the SS Clan Book, and that none of the descendants of the Maurice family may be admitted into the SS.

5. The Chief of the Race and Settlement Head Office receives a copy of this Minute with the request of most strictly confidential treatment; only the Chief of the Clan Office is to be informed.

6. For myself and for all my successors as *Reichsführer SS* I state that only Adolf Hitler himself had and has the right also for the SS to decree an exception with regard to blood. No *Reichsführer SS* has or will have for all future time the right to allow exceptions from the requirements of the SS regarding blood.

7. I oblige all my successors to maintain most strictly the position laid down in point 6.

The Reichsführer SS

[signed] H. Himmler

1. Two copies to the Chief of the Race and Settlement Head Office
   (a) one closed and sealed for Maurice's marriage file
   (b) one for the information of the Chief of the Race and Settlement Head Office and for the Chief of the Clan Office.

2. One Minute for Maurice's personnel file, also closed and sealed, after confidential information to

[signed]	seen Heissmeyer	(a)	Chief of SS Head Office
[signed]	seen Heydrich	(b)	Chief of SS Security Head Office
[signed]	seen Wolff	(c)	Chief Adjutant
[signed]	seen Schmitt	(d)	Chief of Personnel

[signed] H. Himmler

Maurice remained banned from the inner circle around Hitler, but he enjoyed his *Führer's* protection to the very end of the Nazi era. No disciplinary action was taken against him when he knocked down an old man in September 1935 who had unwittingly blocked the road for Maurice's car with his bicycle; for Christmas of the same year, Himmler sent Maurice a present regarded as an honour in the SS (an SS candle-holder). Maurice was promoted on 30 January 1939 to *SS-Oberführer*; he operated a watch store; he was a member of the *Reichstag*; he was vice-president of regional chambers of commerce and trade; from

January 1940 to October 1942 he served in the *Luftwaffe* as an officer. After the war, he got off relatively easily, considering the atmosphere of revenge then prevalent; a de-Nazification court sentenced him to four years hard labour.

Some of those engaged in the protection of their *Führer* were really security risks, and could hardly be regarded as reliable in any but the ideological sense. This was true even of the leaders of the *SS-Begleit-Kommando*.

Bodo Gelzenleuchter, the first commander, soon left the organisation and accepted a lucrative position connected with horse-racing. His successor was Willy Herzberger, an *SS-Sturmhauptführer*, who was in turn succeeded from 11 April 1933 to 15 June 1934 by *SS-Sturmführer* Kurt Gildisch. Gildisch had been trained as a schoolteacher but had not been able to find a position; he had joined the Prussian Police; in the autumn of 1930 he had been suspended for National-Socialist activities, and had been fired from the Berlin Police on 10 March 1931. He had joined the SA on 1 April 1931, and transferred into the SS on 29 September 1931. In June 1934 Gildisch was removed from the *SS-Begleit-Kommando* because of his drinking habits, as Sepp Dietrich recalled in 1953. Despite his satisfactory performance as the murderer of Dr. Klausener on 30 June 1934, Gildisch continued to have difficulties with his drinking and resulting behaviour, so that he was expelled from the NSDAP and from the SS in 1936. At the start of the war he was allowed to join the military SS (*Waffen-SS*) and distinguished himself through bravery. In 1953 he was sentenced to 15 years in gaol for the murder of Dr. Klausener.[18]

SS-Obersturmführer Bruno Gesche followed Gildisch as commander of the *SS-Begleit-Kommando;* his deputies were *SS-Untersturmführer* Franz Schädle and *SS-Untersturmführer* Walter Dirr.[19] Gesche was born in Berlin in 1905, the son of a former technical maintenance sergeant and office helper; in questionnaires Gesche gave his occupation as 'labourer' and 'bank employee,' variously. He liked soldiering, and he had ambitions, but an officer's career in the selective and numerically restricted armed forces was not open to an elementary-schoolboy, even though he had taken some additional courses in a business school. He joined the SA and NSDAP as early as 1922 (Party membership No. 8,592), and in one *curriculum vitae* he said he had lost a job with a bank in 1923 because of his political activities. In October 1928 he transferred from the SA to the SS where he became member No. 1,093.[20]

Gesche had a reputation for unusual daring, bravery and effectiveness with his fists, but he had quarrels with higher-ranking SS leaders to whose conception of an ideal SS officer and *Führer* bodyguard he did not conform. When he criticised publicly the security precautions during Hitler's speech in Selb on 14 October 1932, SS Group Command South in Munich demanded Gesche's reduction in rank and his removal from the *SS-Begleit-Kommando* on the grounds that he was undermining the image of the SS and particularly of the SS Escort as an exceptionally conscientious and disciplined organisation. But Gesche was merely reprimanded in front of the assembled SS Escort.[21]

Jealousy on Himmler's part may have played a role in these events. Himmler tried repeatedly to gain control of the SS Escort, unsuccessfully. In 1935 he caused it to be administratively incorporated in the *Reichssicherheitsdienst* (RSD) and suspended salary payments to SS Escort members from the LSSAH, which was their parent unit. Gesche immediately went to see Sepp Dietrich, who caused Himmler to reverse his decision.[22] When Himmler wanted to discipline members of the *SS-Begleit-Kommando*, he also tended to sustain set-backs, particularly in Gesche's case.

Gesche appears to have been so well liked and so respected for his early merits in the Years of Struggle that neither friction with higher-ranking SS leaders nor occasional over-indulgence impaired his standing seriously. On 26 September 1938 he had to promise the *Reichsführer SS* in writing to abstain from the use of spirits for three years. After a few months Himmler lifted the prohibition, although he had decreed under 21 December 1937 that SS men guilty of abuse of alcohol must promise to abstain for twelve years or resign from the SS. Touble surfaced again in April 1942, and a new three-year prohibition was imposed by Himmler when Gesche was accused of behaviour that had 'given rise to criticism' after he had threatened a fellow SS man with his pistol. He was sent to a basic-training camp, and then transferred to the Caucasus Front. (Only later, after the fall of Stalingrad in January 1943, when apparently forced statements by German prisoners-of-war in Russian hands became known, an order was issued to prevent the transfer to the Eastern Front of anyone who had served in the *Führer's* Headquarters; but it was not strictly obeyed.) Gesche was wounded, and by 28 December 1942 he was back at Hitler's Headquarters, again in command of the *SS-Begleit-Kommando*, although his behaviour had clearly shown that he was a security risk.[23]

Gesche's position was somewhat weakened. On 22 December 1942 Hitler transferred some of the SS Escort commander's authority to his SS Adjutant, *SS-Hauptsturmführer* Richard Schulze(-Kossens), ordering him to assume disciplinary and administrative powers, to issue guidelines for training and deployment of the SS Escort, and to appoint and dismiss its members (though not without Hitler's approval in every case). Schulze's deputies were to be *SS-Hauptsturmführer* Darges and Pfeiffer. Conflicts resulted occasionally, as when Gesche ordered the transfer of a member of Hitler's SS Escort without consulting Schulze, and Schulze repealed the order.

Somehow Gesche got through the years 1943 and 1944. But in

December 1944 his career as commanding officer of the SS Escort came
to an end, almost at the same time as the war and the régime came to
an end—or else Gesche might have been rehabilitated once more. On
20 December 1944 Himmler wrote him: '1. You have again threatened
a comrade with a pistol while intoxicated and fired shots senselessly. 2.
I became aware in 1938, as well as through reports in recent years and
months that you are a drunkard without any self control. 3. Since I have
no use for drunkards in the SS leaders' corps, I reduce you in rank to
SS-Unterscharführer. Only as an act of clemency and in consideration of
your long SS membership, I allow you to remain a member. 4. I shall
give you the opportunity to serve in the Dirlewanger Brigade and perhaps wipe out the shame you have brought on yourself and the entire
SS, by proving yourself before the enemy. 5. I expect you to refrain from
the consumption of alcohol for the rest of your life, without any exception. If your will power has been so destroyed by alcohol that you are
not capable of making such a decision, I expect you to submit your request to be released from the SS.' Gesche did not learn the contents of
this order until 11 January 1945.[24]

One hardly knows which to think more grotesque—the fact that
Himmler had been unable for so long to remove from command of the
SS-Begleit-Kommando a man with such negative qualifications for guarding the *Führer's* life, or Himmler's order that Gesche practise abstinence
for the rest of his life, when the end of the war and the end of the SS
were merely a matter of weeks away, and when Gesche was virtually
sentenced to death by the transfer to Dirlewanger's penal unit. At any
rate, *SS-Gruppenführer* Hermann Fegelein (Hitler's later brother-in-law,
through Fegelein's marriage to Eva Braun's sister) interceded for Gesche,
with *SS-Gruppenführer* M. von Herff, the Chief of SS Personnel Main
Office, who adopted the argument that Gesche, as a former member
of the *Führer's* HQ, must not serve on the Eastern Front, therefore not
with Dirlewanger. Gesche distinguished himself in combat with 16 SS
Division '*Reichsführer SS*' in Italy, Hungary and Slovenia, and he survived
the war.[25] Schädle commanded the *SS-Begleit-Kommando* during the
remaining weeks of the war, 'under directives from *SS-Sturmbannführer*
Günsche, to whom the *Führer* transferred authority over the Escort.'

At first, in 1932, the *SS-Begleit-Kommando* numbered only eight. By
1937 it had grown to seventeen, and by June 1941 to thirty-five. On
15 January 1943, the total strength of the SS Escort was thirty-one SS
officers and 112 men, of whom thirty-three were engaged in escort duties,
taking turns in groups of eleven. The rest were valets, orderlies, drivers,
couriers, and guards for residences not in use at the time.[26]

SS-Ordonnanzoffiziere (special missions staff officers) and SS Adjutants
(*Persönliche Adjutanten* from the SS, aides-de-camp) also acted as bodyguards.[27] During the war, one or two of them were always present at

military situation conferences with Hitler, although they had no legitimate military function there; they were required, however, to read the transcripts of conference protocols for completeness and accuracy. On the other hand, Himmler's liaison officer in Hitler's HQ, *SS-Obergruppenführer* Karl Wolff, was not allowed to be present during situation conferences and was forced, upon Himmler's orders, to try and collect information from the SS aides on what went on at the conferences; his successor, *SS-Gruppenführer* Fegelein, was allowed to be present at the conferences only in the last months of the war.

At first Hitler's aides were associates from the Years of Struggle in the 1920s. Thus *SA-Obergruppenführer* Wilhelm Brückner was titled by 1934 *Persönlicher Adjutant des Führers* and subsequently *Chefadjutant des Führers* until 18 October 1940, having served Hitler as an aide for many years before 1933. *SS-Gruppenführer* Julius Schaub, who had also been in Hitler's entourage constantly since the mid-1920s, and a *Persönlicher Adjutant* through October 1940, succeeded Brückner as Chief Adjutant and retained this position to the end of the war. (Hitler's Chief *Wehrmacht* Adjutant, Lieutenant-General Schmundt, in the course of the war assumed many of the SS aides' administrative functions, and he became more widely known as *Chefadjutant* than any of the SS aides.) Schaub did not stay with Hitler in the *Reich* Chancellery Bunker until the very end; he moved to the Obersalzberg area with other members of Hitler's personal staff a few days before the end.

Other *Persönliche Adjutanten* who, besides attending to day-to-day administrative and organisational affairs of Hitler's life, were in part responsible for his security, included: *SS-Sturmbannführer* Paul Wernicke; *SS-Obersturmführer* Ludwig Bahls who died in 1939 having joined Hitler's staff in 1938; *SS-Hauptsturmführer* Max Wünsche (to December 1940); *SS-Obersturmführer* Hansgeorg Schulze (-Kossens) was an *SS-Ordonnanzoffizier* from October 1939 to August 1941, until he was transferred to the Russian Front where he was killed in action. From 3 October 1941 his brother Richard, an *SS-Sturmbannführer*, served with Hitler as *SS-Ordonnanzoffizier*, with several intervals for tours of Front Line duty, and from 27 October 1942 to mid-December 1944 as SS Adjutant (*Persönlicher Adjutant des Führers*). He had been Ribbentrop's *Persönlicher Adjutant* from April 1939 to January 1941. *SS-Hauptsturmführer* Hans Friedrich Georg Pfeiffer was an *SS-Ordonnanzoffizier* in Hitler's entourage from 23 October 1939 to 31 July 1942, as successor to Bahls, and subsequently an SS Adjutant; he was killed in action in June 1944. *SS-Obersturmbannführer* Fritz Darges had been M. Bormann's adjutant from 1 July 1936 to 31 October 1939 before he joined Hitler's staff as an SS aide on 21 October 1940. He was *Persönlicher Adjutant des Führers* from 1 March 1943 to 18 July 1944 (although for purposes of his personnel files his transfer did not become effective until August 1944). Darges made himself *persona non grata* in the *Führer's* HQ in a number of ways, until his somewhat precipitate departure on 18 July 1944.[28] *SS-Sturmbannführer* Otto Günsche (then an *SS-Hauptsturmführer*) succeeded Darges. Günsche served in the *SS-Begleit-Kommando* from 1 May 1936, then as an *SS-Sturmmann*, he was an *SS-Ordonnanzoffizier* with Hitler 1940–41, with tours of training and Front Line duty following; he became a *Persönlicher Adjutant* to the *Führer* in January 1943, serving alone for two months when Darges was recovering from wounds and Schulze(-Kossens) and Pfeiffer were ill. From August 1943 Günsche was doing Front Line duty again in Russia, and in March 1944 he was back in the *Führer's* HQ while Schulze(-Kossens) was at Bad Tölz SS leadership school and Pfeiffer wanted Front Line duty. Now Günsche shared the work with Darges, until 18 July 1944; he was alone again until the beginning of August when Schulze(-Kossens) returned, and again after mid-December 1944. Günsche stayed on in Hitler's immediate entourage until the *Führer's* suicide in the *Reich* Chancellery Bunker on 30 April 1945.

Hitler's valets were also members of the *SS-Begleit-Kommando*, and they played important roles in his personal protection. Karl Krause was Hitler's First Valet from 18 July 1934. He had come from the Navy.[29] On 16 September 1939 he was dismissed by Hitler after he had lied to him once too often, having tried to convince Hitler that a certain mineral water was the brand Hitler customarily used—while in fact Krause had forgotten to bring it along. Krause was back in 1940, but only for a short time. Otto Meyer, another valet, had to go when Hitler found out that Meyer let his relatives use the *Führer's* box in a certain theatre. Heinz Linge had joined the SS as a bricklayer's apprentice in 1932, at the age of nineteen, becoming SS member No. 35,795 and NSDAP member No. 1,260,419. He made the SS his career and joined Sepp Dietrich's new *Stabswache* on 17 March 1933, became a member of the LSSAH, and later of the *SS-Begleit-Kommando*. By 1935 he had become one of the principal valets in Hitler's personal service, and was eventually given the title of *Chef des persönlichen Dienstes beim Führer* (Chief, Personal *Führer* Service), about 1939. Wilhelm Schneider, another valet, was transferred to the Front during the war when Linge found that Schneider's weakness for poker games interfered with his duties. Hans Junge, killed later on the Russian Front, was in the SS Escort from 1 July 1936, and moved into one of the vacated valet positions, until July 1943. At least one of the valets was always at Hitler's side or following him, carrying whatever was needed, overcoats, pills, sandwiches, binoculars. They had to keep Hitler's clothes ready, take newspapers and messages to his bedroom, accept flowers during public appearances, and they had to be ready to shoot down any would-be attacker or to throw themselves in front of the *Führer* to protect him. Linge stayed with Hitler until the very end, helping to burn his body on 30 April 1945.

All the *SS-Begleit-Kommando* men were, in the early years of their service at least, young and strong, good-looking, physically trained and fit, but they were without higher education, and really without serious occupation and discipline. Their lives were often hard, as when they were forced to travel in open cars in any kind of weather, sometimes for twenty-four hours or more without rest, having to stay vigilant at the same time. But often they had far too much idle time; they moved on a social level not their own, and the temptations were many. Considering these handicaps, and considering that such colourful characters as Gesche were responsible for Hitler's safety, it is surprising that the many breakdowns of security remained without serious consequences. It is less surprising that the RSD officers looked upon their amateur colleagues with a considerable amount of condescension. M. Bormann's complaint was well founded, though belated, when he wrote to Himmler on 17 November 1944: 'For years, conditions in our *Begleit-Kommando* have caused me concern; the *Begleit-Kommando* lacks strict leadership, the men only do a little guard duty, and its scheduling is handled just as laxly as all other *Begleit-Kommando* matters. The officers of the *Begleit-Kommando* feel equal to regular troop officers, though they can neither master the duties of these troop officers nor do they want to accept them. The lax leadership seemed tolerable when the *Begleit-Kommando* was small. The group benefited from years of experience of all the members on the *Führer's* many trips. Since this travel activity has ended and in face of the constant expansion of the *Begleit-Kommando*, its leadership ought to be particularly tight. The less tightly an agency is led, the larger it automatically grows: everyone pushes off on to others as many of his duties as he can.'[30] The dangerous result of the swelling of the *Begleit-Kommando's* ranks was, Bormann continued, that the older members achieved higher and higher ranks which were in sharp contrast with their low-level duties. They could in fact no longer be used as orderlies, runners, and telephone-operators, but they actually demanded runners and orderlies for themselves in sufficient numbers. 'If automatic promotions of *Begleit-Kommando* members continue, we shall have totally intolerable conditions. I have pointed this out repeatedly to *Oberstgruppenführer* Dietrich.' Himmler replied on 25 November that he shared Bormann's concern and added: 'These men, many of whom were promoted to higher ranks by the *Führer* himself, are today in no way so physically fit and young that they represent the protection for the *Führer* that they were originally supposed to provide.' But Bormann knew well, Himmler wrote, that the *Führer* had most strictly prohibited Himmler and Dietrich from transferring any of the older men in the *Begleit-Kommando*. 'The *Führer* once said to *SS-Oberstgruppenführer* Dietrich: as long as he lived he would not let go a single one of these men.'

6 Hitler's Escort Detachment and Other Security Groups

In addition to RSD and SS Escort, a number of other security organisations were in operation for Hitler's protection. For trips and public functions, between five and eleven members of each of the RSD and *SS-Begleit-Kommando* were combined to form the *Führer-Begleit-Kommando* (*Führer* Escort Detachment). The lines between police guard and SS became nearly indistinguishable to outside observers when the *Führer-Begleit-Kommando* operated as a unit.[1] The lines of command were unified only in the person of Hitler himself. But RSD and *SS-Begleit-Kommando* still moved in separate groups, even in separate cars, when they were combined as the *Führer-Begleit-Kommando*, and each had a keen consciousness of being different, of having special and different duties.

Among security forces of less immediate attachment to Hitler, there were the LSSAH as a whole, the regular police, the *Gestapo*, the SA and the regular Army. Whenever there was construction taking place in one of Hitler's residences there were workmen's control posts, such as in the Obersalzberg area where construction never quite ceased until the very end of the war. The New Chancellery, too, was such a vast object that the many regular guard organisations—RSD, SS, *Wehrmacht*, Police—still did not seem sufficient to make certain that unwelcome manipulations could not occur. This was felt most keenly after Georg Elser's near-successful assassination attempt of 8 November 1939. Loyal henchmen of the Party were in charge of security in the Munich beer-hall, but Elser had found it easy to spend some thirty nights in the building, working on the installation of his explosive device. Later on, even the tapwater running through pipes everyone else was connected to was regularly analysed if it was also used in Hitler's household.[2]

There had been since 1935 an internal *Sicherheitsdienst* (Security Service) in the *Reich* Chancellery for doorman and surveillance service. Shortly after Elser's attack in 1939, a new *Sicherheits-Kontrolldienst* (Security Control Service) was set up in the New Chancellery and adjoining buildings.[3] It was expressly charged with supervising the existing *Sicherheitsdienst* in the New Chancellery as well as the similar organisations yet to be created for the adjoining buildings. It began operations by 12 December 1939, and its responsibilities included patrolling the Chancellery, the Presidential Chancellery, the Private Chancellery of the *Führer*, and the Supreme SA Leadership Office. It was intended 'to provide unified security service for the entire *Reich* Chancellery complex,' and 'to make impossible in future such acts of sabotage as that of 8 November 1939.' Therefore the patrols should be experienced craftsmen who could intelligently keep under surveillance any construction and repair work in the buildings. In addition, the new *Sicherheits-Kontrolldienst* was to supervise and control 'all persons in the *Reich* Chancellery area' including the existing security services. This may not have been entirely realistic, but it was understandable in the hysteria following the Elser attempt.

The new *Sicherheits-Kontrolldienst*, also referred to as *Kontrollmänner* (Control Men), was to consist primarily of experts in certain trades and crafts, but it was actually recruited to a considerable extent from retired police officers. Its initial strength was forty-five, to be increased to fifty in 1940. The men were all armed with Walther PPK 7.65 pistols and flashlights, and they wore special uniforms. Rattenhuber, Commander of the RSD, was put in charge of the new *Sicherheits-Kontrolldienst*.

The flying personnel for Hitler's aeroplanes were not integrated into an existing security force such as RSD or SS Escort (at first there was not yet an Air Force). Instead they were given commissions as police officers, so that in fact still another independent group directly responsible to the *Führer* was created.[4] Rattenhuber did not command it immediately, and Himmler had as much or as little authority over it as over the RSD and the operations of the *SS-Begleit-Kommando*.

Finally, there was the *Führer-Begleit-Bataillon* (*Führer* Escort Battalion). It came from what eventually developed into *Panzer Division 'Grossdeutschland,'* and its job was to guard Hitler's military headquarters and to accompany him on trips to Front Line command posts. It was first organised as *Kommando 'Führerreise'* in June 1938, and it accompanied Hitler on his trips to the Sudetenland in October 1938 and to Prague in March 1939. After 23 August 1939 the outfit was known as *Frontgruppe der FHQu. Truppen*, and as *Führer-Begleit-Bataillon* after November 1939.[5] Its home address was the barracks of Regiment 'General Göring' in Döberitz, outside Berlin (later in Berlin-Reinickendorf West, Spandauer Weg 42). Like the later, war-time *Führer-Begleit-Bataillon*, so its prototypes were commanded until January 1940 by Erwin Rommel, then a Colonel. Its functions will be described in connection with headquarters security. More on the functions of the other escort and security forces will be related in dealing with Hitler's residences, and with outings.

There was rivalry and friction among the numerous security services, and sometimes they got in each other's way, potentially reducing rather than increasing security. Much of this rivalry was based on differences in background and training, as between regular Army and SS guards, or between SS guards and RSD who came from criminal-police forces. The SS were trained above all as soldiers and as unquestioning, unreflective palace guards always ready to overwhelm any intruder ruthlessly, to shield their master with their bodies, perhaps to throw themselves on to a tossed grenade to protect the *Führer*. The RSD, on the other hand, were trained as professional criminal-police officers and were accustomed to using a methodical, scientific approach to security. They had to investigate points to be visited beforehand, they sought intelligence from local *Gestapo* offices, they gathered information on assassination rumours throughout Germany, they had to be able to prevent the planting of bombs, to discern the lone assassin in a crowd if possible. Their work was much more demanding intellectually, and the same physical endurance was expected of them as of the *SS-Begleit-Kommando*, particularly when travelling day and night, rain or shine.

7 Transport

Cars

When Hitler left his residence, private or official, he almost never walked or used public transport, except to take a walk for health or relaxation. As early as 1923 he owned a car, a red Benz, in which he drove to the 1923 Beer Hall *putsch*; he employed a chauffeur who doubled as bodyguard.[1] After 1933, he rarely rode in his car without having it followed by a car-load of SS Escort men, plus a car-load of RSD after 1934. Hitler usually sat next to the driver (except on ceremonial occasions) with one of his valets, usually Krause or Linge, sitting behind him. They were armed, and during the war they carried machine pistols. Of course, they had to be sure and quick in reacting to any dangerous situations. As the commanding officer of Hitler's *SS-Begleit-Kommando* was slightly cross-eyed, Hitler once joked (as Linge recalls): 'Linge, I am glad that Gesche does not sit behind me; he might shoot me in the back.'[2] For security reasons, Hitler insisted that insignia, flags and other paraphernalia be kept at a minimum, except on official and publicised occasions. He always believed that the way to achieve the greatest degree of security was to be inconspicuous and well protected at the same time. As he put it during lunch at his Headquarters on 3 May 1942: 'As far as possible, whenever I go anywhere by car I go off unexpectedly and without warning the police. I have also given Rattenhuber, the Commander of my personal Security Squad, and Kempka, my chauffeur, the strictest orders to maintain absolute secrecy about my comings and goings, and have further impressed on them that these orders must still be obeyed even when the highest officials in the land make enquiries. As soon as the police get to hear that I am going somewhere, they abandon all normal procedure and adopt emergency measures, which, to say the least of it, are most alarming to normal people, and yet they never seem to realise that it is just these emergency antics which are conspicuous and draw attention where no attention is desired. I had a splendid example of this sort of thing when, at the time of the *Anschluss*, I went to Vienna and Pressburg. The police raised the alarm along the whole route both from Vienna to Nicolsburg and on to Pressburg—an action which was all the more dangerous because they simply did not have the necessary forces at their disposal to guard the roads. Apart from this, the *Gestapo* plainclothes men dressed themselves in such an astonishing collection of clothes—rough woollen mackintosh coats, ostler's capes and so forth—

that I, and indeed any moron, could recognise them for what they were at a glance. When I gave orders that we were to follow a route other than the one agreed upon and were to stop, like any other citizen, at the traffic lights in the villages, I was able to continue my journey un-noticed and unmolested.'[3]

If he could help it, Hitler never used any other cars than his own Mer-cedes-Benzes. As early as 1934, it was stated that he did 'not tolerate a car manufactured by another company in his escort and entourage.' Only when his own cars were not available he might occasionally use a Horch or some other large car.[4] On Obersalzberg, around his 'Berghof' retreat, Hitler frequently had himself chauffeured back from a walk to the 'Mooslahnerkopf' tea-house in a Volkswagen, partly to avoid being recognised. During the war it was nothing to Hitler to have a set of his cars (one for him and at least two for his escorts) driven hundreds of miles to a point to which he took a plane, such as from 'Wehrwolf' HQ in the Ukraine, or from Slominsk to Smolensk or to Saporoshe, just to use the cars for a distance of two or three miles at some military head-quarters, even though the generals there could have supplied him with enough good cars.

The red Benz Hitler rode to the Beer Hall on 8 November 1923 was his fourth car.[5] Before it, Hitler had owned two Selve cars. The red Benz was confiscated by the Bavarian Police after the *putsch*, and repossessed by the NSDAP in 1933; in the meantime it was used 'by the Bavarian Police in combating the National Socialist Movement.' After his release from Landsberg prison, Hitler struck a defiant pose holding on to a Benz outside the city gates. Numerous Benz and Mercedes-Benz cars were pur-chased for the use of Adolf Hitler and his immediate entourage through the years. The order ledgers of the Daimler-Benz Corporation between 1929 and 1942 list some forty-four cars ordered for the *Reich* Chancellery, for the RSD, or for 'Administration Obersalzberg c/o *Reich* Leader Mar-tin Bormann.' These cars were all of the largest, strongest type produced by Daimler-Benz. The majority of them were folding-top tourers which Hitler preferred; only four large saloon cars are listed as delivered for the *Führer's* use after 1933 in the order ledger; Kempka knows of only one, and even this was hardly ever used.

Probably the earliest armoured cars for Hitler's use were three proto-types called Type 540KW24, delivered to the *Führer's* Adjutants' office as touring cars in 1935. The armour consisted of a 4-mm steel body, 25-mm windshields and windows, and bullet-proof tyres (20-chamber tyres). This vehicle had an eight-cylinder, 5.4-litre, 177-hp supercharged engine and it could travel at 106 mph. Kempka, however, does not recall ever having driven Hitler in one of these cars.

Touring cars of Type 520G4W31 and 131 were manufactured from 1934 until 1939, and delivered up until 1940. They were built with three

1 400 PS engine
2 20-cell tyres
3 40-millimetre bullet-proof windows
4 Hitler's seat, raised 13 millimetres
5 Hitler's footrest, raised 13 millimetres
6 Aluminium parts to reduce weight
7 Spare wheels, used to protect engine
8 Electromagnetic circuit blocking the doors
9 Manganese-treated armoured plating
10 300-litre gasoline tank
11 Nickel-silver radiator
12 Hitler's standard
13 Overall 18-millimetre armour plating

Mercedes-Benz 770KW150II

Mercedes-Benz 770G4W31

Mercedes-Benz Grosser Mercedes W150, 7.7 litres

6. *Three automobiles Hitler used*

axles and could be used for cross-country travel as well as for parades and other occasions when speed was not required. They had 5-litre (W31) and 5.252-litre (W131) eight-cylinder engines delivering 98 hp (W31) and 113 hp (W131) respectively. But according to Kempka, Hitler used only the large 7.7-litre cars which could go up to 75 mph. These cars were used preferably on public or semi-public occasions, and on visits to theatres of war. They had 30-mm windshields, the roll-up windows on both sides of the front seats were 20 mm thick, and the rear side-windows were 30 mm thick. The back of the rear seats was reinforced with 8-mm steel plate and came up as high as the tops of the passengers' heads. With 8-mm steel doors and an equally reinforced enclosure for the driver's leg room and floor plates, this car was moderately bullet-proof against the hand-guns and rifles then in use. The bullet-proof tyres were taken off, however, because they caused heavy vibration. Ordinary tyres with extremely low air pressure had to be used for the sake of Hitler's oversensitive stomach. Since his cars were only canvas-top tourers, however, protected (moderately) only at their sides, shots and grenades could be dropped in from above, and Hitler liked standing up in his car, thus raising head and chest well above the light armour—although he declared later that it was foolish (for others) to do this, after Heydrich was assassinated in Prague in May 1942: 'Since it is the opportunity which makes not only the thief but also the assassin, such heroic gestures as driving in an open, unarmoured vehicle or walking about the streets of Prague unguarded are just damned stupidity, which serves the country not one whit.'[6] His bodyguards were forced to keep close to him and, on triumphal occasions such as a ride into Danzig in September 1939, to try to catch or deflect the many bouquets that people tossed from balconies and windows, and to make certain none of them hit the *Führer*. They had to watch for unusual missiles, and in an emergency they were to signal Kempka to accelerate and speed out of range.

Hitler's chauffeur, Erich Kempka, who had succeeded Julius Schreck upon the latter's death on 16 May 1936, and had been named *Chef des Kraftfahrwesens beim Führer und Reichskanzler* (Chief of the *Führer's* and *Reich* Chancellor's Fleet of Cars), reports that the *Führer* refused to have a fully-armoured car until 1939, and that he consented to using one only after Elser's attack; but the records of the Daimler-Benz Company show that orders for a more heavily-armoured car for Hitler's use were placed beginning at least on 22 July 1938, and that a fully-armoured saloon car had been delivered, on 15 April 1939, in time for Hitler's fiftieth birthday, and apparently on Kempka's initiative.[7] It was a large saloon known as Type 770KW150II; it was delivered to the Presidential Chancellery of the *Führer* and *Reich* Chancellor. This new version of the 'large Mercedes' 7.7-litre, built from 1930 on, had a 394-hp eight-cylinder

7.665-litre supercharged engine; it reached speeds of up to 112 mph. It was fully armoured all around with 18-mm steel plate, the windscreen and windows were made of 40-mm bullet-proof glass. The spare tyres, mounted in the front wings at the sides of the hood, just in front of the running boards, were covered with steel armour-plate as additional shields. The car used ten gallons of petrol and a quart of oil for every 66 miles, and it weighed 10,528 lb empty. Hitler used the armoured limousine only a few times. Photographs of public appearances usually show him in a touring car. A number of variations and prototypes such as a 6-litre, V-12, 167-hp engine tourer, were in Hitler's fleet of cars. But the types described earlier were the ones mostly used.

Martin Bormann had a hand in all orders for Hitler's cars. He informed the Daimler-Benz Company on 4 June 1936 by registered mail that *SS-Sturmbannführer* Kempka had been put in charge of Hitler's fleet of cars after the death of *SS-Brigadeführer* Julius Schreck, that all bills and correspondence were to go through Kempka to Bormann, and that orders were void unless they came from Bormann in writing. In February 1937 Bormann found it necessary to remind one of Hitler's SS aides, *SS-Hauptsturmführer* Wernicke in Berlin, that this regulation had been approved by Brückner last June.[8]

Hitler's fleet of cars grew, of course. In 1935, maintenance costs were budgeted for four RSD cars (RM 6,000 for tyres, RM 20,000 for petrol, and RM 4,000 for repairs). In 1936 there were eight passenger cars available for RSD security and escort duties with the *Führer—Führerkolonne* (*Führer* Convoy)—and with a number of *Reich* Ministers. Garages were located in a house specially built for the chief chauffeur and the head valet in Saarlandstrasse. But only in 1935 Rattenhuber had had to plead for a car for the RSD by describing the grotesque difficulties they encountered in accompanying the *Führer*. On visits to the opera for instance, in Hamburg, Bayreuth or Berlin, an advance detail was sent to the site to check it against possible dangers and threats, and to set up the scene for a smooth arrival. But in order to go there the detail had to request a car from the *Gestapo*, who sometimes could not provide one, so that the RSD had to catch a taxi. There had been times when part of Hitler's escort were forced to travel by taxi, and even by tram or bus when a taxi could not be found quickly, as in a downpour.[9] Such difficulties arose particularly when a planned visit to a theatre was not announced to the escort until the last minute—in the interests of secrecy, which was thus simultaneously defeated. Hitler often made decisions on the spur of the moment—or he tossed a coin if he could not make up his mind whether to go, say, to Weimar or to Bayreuth.

Rattenhuber's plea for more cars was successful. In the 1937 RSD budget, three new cars were provided for: a 5.4-litre supercharged Mercedes for Darré's detail, and two 7.7-litre supercharged Mercedes for the

Führer's escorts. The reason given for the purchase of the latter two was that the escort cars stationed in Berlin and Munich were too slow to keep up with the *Führer's* car on the highway. Each of the two Mercedes cost RM 27,500.[10]

Serving the *Führer* was hard on both cars and drivers. It was so demanding that Rattenhuber stated flatly that RSD men would ordinarily have to retire no later than at the age of fifty. The drivers always had to risk their lives to protect the *Führer*. They had to be ready to ram an oncoming car that threatened to get in the way of the *Führer's* car, or to swing out suddenly into the left-hand lane to prevent other cars from passing (in Germany, of course, one drives on the *right*). It was dangerous for a column of cars to be passed in traffic, it could not be tolerated that strange cars got between Hitler's car and the escort cars, and it was always possible to shoot the *Führer* in his open tourer from a passing car, like Rathenau, or to force it off the road at a prepared ambush point. Hitler himself talked about the dangers of motor car journeys, especially about possible attacks from suspicious cars following his car. But he had seen to it that they could not harm him: his driver would simply turn on a strong searchlight installed at the rear and blind the pursuer—a lesson Hitler said he had learned from the Rathenau plot. In July 1934 the Berlin Police received a complaint about such a searchlight which illuminated 50 metres of road behind a car while it was moving forward—instead of the 10 metres permitted by law if the car were in reverse gear. Investigation revealed that 'all automobiles of the *Reich* Chancellery were equipped with such searchlights for special reasons.'[11]

With all this, accidents were often difficult to avoid, and escort cars frequently got into scrapes with other cars. Many a passer-by, usually a woman, was so surprised by Hitler's unexpected appearance that she stood motionless in the middle of the street, unable to move. Once in a while, such a woman was run down by a car of the *Führer-Begleit-Kommando* because the driver could not stop or swerve in time. Often the crowds got so thick, too, that the escort men had to stand on the running boards of Hitler's car, or run alongside to make room, and to prevent the fanatically enthusiastic masses from storming the *Führer's* car, or from being run over.

Trains

The Head of Government had at his disposal, upon sufficient advance notification, railway trains composed of a specified kind and combination of Pullman cars. Special trains had to be scheduled so that they fitted in between trains in the regular, published, timetables. The *Reichsbahn* (*Reich* Railways) had kept available appropriate coaches for the Emperor, for visiting Heads of State or other dignitaries, and for the

Heads of State and Government in the Republic. Private persons and organisations might rent Special trains on occasion. Hitler made use of Specials for himself and for his entourage after his appointment as Chancellor.

In 1937, 1938 and 1939 new coaches were built for a permanent Special train for Hitler that was not to be available to others. For the greatest possible security, all coaches were constructed entirely (except the windows) of welded steel. Most of them weighed well over sixty tons. By January 1939 there existed two versions of *Führersonderzug* (*Führer* Special): one for peace-time travel, and one for a State of War. Peacetime *Führer* Specials were usually composed as follows, in order: locomotive, baggage and power-engine car, *Führer's* Pullman (No. 10206), conference car, escort car, dining car, two sleeping cars for guests and entourage, Pullman coach, personnel car, press chief's car, baggage and power-engine car.[12] A State of War was envisaged by the *Reichsbahn* authorities at least as early as January 1939, and they decided that the *Führer* Special should then be named *Führerhauptquartier* (*Führer's* Headquarters); but it came to be code-named 'Amerika.' It was completed and put into service in August 1939. Surviving *Reichsbahn* documents indicate this sequence of cars: locomotive (later two), armoured anti-aircraft car with 2-cm guns and a 26-man crew, baggage and power-engine car, *Führer's* Pullman (No. 10206, in which his Chief *Wehrmacht* Adjutant, his Chief Personal Adjutant and a valet were also quartered), conference car with communications centre including several teletype machines, escort car for 22 *SS-Begleit-Kommando* and RSD men (but only 7 + 7 and 2 commanding officers accompanied Hitler in 1941), dining car, two sleeping cars for entourage and guests (Schaub was given the compartment originally assigned to Ribbentrop's liaison man because Schaub 'does not wish to sleep over the axle'), bath car, dining car, two cars for personnel (secretaries, cooks, aides, signal corps men), press chief's car with communication centre including a 700-watt short-wave transmitter, baggage and power-engine car, anti-aircraft car.[13] The sequence was changed slightly during the war. The *Führer's* Pullman, the dining car and the sleeping cars could be connected with the postal telephone network during stops. When the Special was not used it was parked at Tempelhof repair depot in Berlin.

Secrecy of advance arrangements was a major security precaution, and considerable efforts were made to ensure it, upon Hitler's insistence. Brückner had wanted to know from Transport Ministry officials if it would be possible to inform their railway people as late as one or two hours in advance if the *Führer* Special was required. The Minister, himself a veteran railwayman, replied personally that the strictest secrecy of arrangements was ensured where Transport Ministry and railway officials were concerned, and that if there had been any breaches of secrecy, they had not been caused by them. But if the *Reich* Railway were to use the greatest possible care in preparing Special train runs, a certain minimum of time was essential.[14] It was impossible to ensure the necessary intensive guarding of all stretches of track, the personnel could not be guaranteed to be on post, barriers at crossings might not be closed early enough, if the Ministry had only an hour or two to wire and telephone all these hundreds of people. Many hours were often required just to work out a schedule because it had to be fitted into an existing tight timetable which sometimes had to be changed accordingly.

7. *Hitler's Special Train 'Amerika' at Mönichkirchen, April 1941*

Even the availability of locomotives, railway personnel and railway police could be a problem at short notice. If the Special were to depart from a Berlin station other than Anhalter Station, up to two hours were needed merely to shunt the train to its departure station, and advance notice on the evening before was required for early morning departures (4 and 5 a.m. from Berlin, 3.53 and 4.50 a.m. from Munich). It was therefore highly advisable (if breakdowns, confusion and delays were to be avoided) to inform the railway authorities as early as possible of an intended journey—even if it was not yet definitely decided upon. It was better to order the Special and to cancel it again than to order it on short notice.

Brückner replied that short-notice runs were required only on the Berlin–Munich and Munich–Berlin route, and that the Adjutant's office was making every effort to inform the Ministry travel office as soon as the *Führer* had given the order—only 'this is not always possible with as much advance notice as desired.'[15] Brückner only hinted at a chief difficulty: the *Führer* used to give his travel orders only a very short time in advance, because he believed, as he liked to say, that living irregularly and appearing unexpectedly was one of the best methods of preventing assassinations. Brückner thought that two hours' advance notice should be sufficient for runs to and from Munich since a number of permanent schedules (ghost runs) were established for this route. Safety must not suffer, said Brückner, and the *Führer's* security must be guaranteed at all times. However: 'With regard to security in general, I believe it is best guaranteed if a journey is unannounced.' This applied especially to railway security: 'for security is not guaranteed if railway policeman Schulze or Meier and thereby their entire families know that the *Führersonderzug* will roll into a certain station at a certain time.' Therefore the Adjutants' office had already arranged with an official in the Ministry to have the railway police practise their security operations twice a week, irregularly, for runs permanently fitted into the railway timetable, so that not even the railway police knew whether they were actually protecting the *Führer* Special and the *Führer*, or only a ghost run.

The *Reichsbahn* had had its own Regulations for Trips of Certain Persons (Regulation 470) for some time. The version that applied through the Second World War was valid from 1 September 1937, and re-issued on 1 June 1941.[16] The Regulations defined conditions of special-train runs for Certain Persons, and code-words for the railway police, for provision of additional railway personnel and guards along the route, for guards travelling aboard the train, and for any other preparations as for scheduled and unforeseen stops. Regularly scheduled trains were normally not to overtake Specials: freight trains or maintenance trains were not to meet or run parallel with Specials; if there was a time conflict between a Special and a regular train, as when one of them was late, the Special had to be given the right-of-way. Reserve locomotives had to be kept on hand, particularly where tracks were slippery or headwinds strong, or where delays had to be made up. Trains following behind a Special could not be allowed to proceed from a given station until at least five minutes after the next station ahead had reported the Special's passage.

As the most important security regulation for trips of Hitler and of those ranking closely behind him (code-word *Sondersicherung*—Special security), the entire projected route of the Special, as from Berlin to Munich, or from Berlin to one of the war-time headquarters, was travelled, no more than ten to fifteen minutes in advance of the Special, by the chiefs of the various railway subdistricts (*Betriebsamt*). The officials, taking turns at district boundaries, rode on a locomotive to which a baggage car or a few passenger coaches might be added on occasion. The advance locomotive had to be treated by all railway personnel as a Special train so that any dangers threatening the *Führersonderzug* or other Special would be attracted by the advance locomotive.

The system had a weakness of course. Theoretically, an attacker with inside information and knowledge of the system could set up, hours or days in advance, an explosive charge under the tracks for manual ignition via electric cable; he might hide himself in a forest near the tracks, at the end of his cable, and ignite the charge just as Hitler's Pullman passed over it, having allowed the advance locomotive to pass by unharmed. But the entire route of the Special was patrolled in short, one-man sections; an attacker thus needed the support of at least one or two of the permanent railway guards. If Hitler was to be killed, the explosive charge had to be powerful enough to blow to bits the entire coach and those preceding or following it (depending on the order of cars), since Hitler might not happen to be in his Pullman at the time of the explosion; it would not do to cause the train to be derailed. Obviously it would be difficult, to say the least, to install such a vastly powerful explosive charge and to conceal it against premature detection. Only a very reckless attacker who was relatively indifferent to his chances of success would be willing to accept the odds; too small a charge might not kill Hitler, a very large one might be discovered. An attacker also needed up-to-date inside information not only from the railway environment but from Hitler's immediate entourage. This was extremely hard to obtain, even for an insider. Such information was also unreliable due to Hitler's tendency to decide on travel plans and on the mode of transport literally at the last minute whenever possible (more on this will be said under 'Travel'). If a trip were announced, and if the date and mode of transport were fixed in advance, there were so many more guards and patrols than for 'unofficial' trips, and there would be so many onlookers, that the chances of success for any attack grew extremely small.

Hitler's and Göring's Special trains were accompanied by railway-police detachments during the trip, who were placed under Rattenhuber's command. Railway technicians travelling aboard the train had to look after any defects *en route*, and they had orders to examine thoroughly all carriages of the train from the security point of view as soon as the train had reached its destination. All aspects of Special-train runs, such as points and times of departure and destination, route, stops, had to be kept strictly secret. Uninvolved *Reichsbahn* officials and family members of those involved were strictly not to be told anything about Special-train runs. The number of those who had to be informed had to be kept to the minimum, and the information given to individuals was not to exceed the minimum necessary for their various functions. All written information relating to schedules and other aspects of a Special-train run had to be returned to higher railway offices upon completion of the trip; there they were counted to ensure the return of every copy, and then destroyed. At stops, and departure and destination stations, platforms on both sides of the trains had to be clear of any luggage, parcels, boxes, mail-bags, etc. Underpasses in stations and *en route*, stairways and similar danger points had to be guarded and kept free of any loiterers. Additional regulations for publicised trips provided for the cordoning-off of stations, crossings and the like by police, SA and SS units (in the manner to be described in the chapters dealing with Hitler's public appearances). If Hitler or Göring or any others entitled to *Sondersicherung* left the train, or boarded it, the railway police were responsible for security between the train and the station gates; regular police, SA and SS were responsible between gates and automobile. The dignitaries were also accompanied by their respective bodyguards, of course. All security measures in the vicinity of Hitler's person were always under Rattenhuber's overall authority, direction and command.

During the war years, all Special trains—Hitler's, Göring's, Keitel's, the *Wehrmacht* Leadership Staff's, Ribbentrop's, Himmler's—were given code-names. Hitler's *Führersonderzug* was known as 'Amerika' until 31 January 1943; then it was re-named 'Brandenburg.' Most code-names for Special trains were changed as from 1 February 1943. Göring's Special was initially known as 'Asien' 1 and 2, later as 'Pommern' 1 and 2; Keitel's Special was known as 'Afrika,' but from 1 February 1943 as 'Braunschweig,' Ribbentrop's was 'Westfalen' (unchanged), Himmler's 'Heinrich,' later 'Steiermark' (temporarily in 1944 as 'Transport 44') the *Wehrmacht* Leadership Staff's two specials were called 'Atlas,' later 'Franken I' and 'Franken II.'[17] For all of these, timetable slots were arranged, with times during which the various Specials could be contacted by telephone or wire in predetermined stations *en route*. In such stations the communications centres of the trains could be connected by a few cables and plugs within minutes to the telephone and teletype network desired (Army, Navy, Air Force, SS, Post Office, Railway—each had their own). When the trains were in motion, communication was carried on by radio. During the war, when the Specials ran outside German *Reich* territory, as in France and Poland, the extent of security operations was increased vastly, and the *Führersonderzug* did not run at night.

Hitler had little contact with the population on his train trips, but in the first two years of the war, as in the 1930s, he still showed himself at his window during stops. Such appearances were usually unplanned and dangerous. The enthusiastic public might run up to the *Führer's* train *en masse*, crossing tracks and platforms, and breaking through thin security cordons. Then someone might have hurled a hand-grenade through the open window; or Hitler might have his arm wrenched off when he reached down to shake a hand. Once the *Führersonderzug* is said to have stopped, by chance, alongside a trainload of Jews destined for an extermination camp, and the eyes of murderer and victims met. But Hitler wanted to see neither 'these things' (as they are called by former members of his entourage), nor the destruction caused by Allied bombing, and he usually kept his curtains drawn during trips in the later years of the war. When he returned by train from his Western Headquarters 'Amt 500' (near 'Adlerhorst') to Berlin in January 1945, he was surprised and depressed by the extent of destruction in the city.[18]

In the last days of the war, shortly before 8 May 1945, Hitler's Special was parked in Bruck, near Zell am See, in Austria. It was used by some members of Hitler's personal staff who had gone south to prepare a new headquarters for him in 'Alpine Redoubt,' and by General Winter and his staff (*Wehrmachtführungsstab Süd*) who boarded the train at Hofgastein. Hence they travelled through the tunnel to Mallnitz. When Germany capitulated to the Allies, Hitler's Pullman (No. 10206) was blown up and destroyed here.[19] The rest of the train travelled to Saalfelden and remained there until the end of May; then it went on to Pullach near Munich, where it was taken over by the American Army. Most of the carriages were used by American and British military authorities, and returned to German authorities in 1950, 1951 and 1953. One of the carriages was still used in the Federal Chancellor's Special train in the 1960s.

Aeroplanes

In the political campaigns of 1932 Adolf Hitler made the most extensive use of flying that any German politician had ever made, speaking in as many as five cities in one evening. In 1932 he hired Lufthansa Captain Hans Baur (a NSDAP member from 1921), and a plane from Lufthansa, saying that Chancellor Brüning (against whom he was running) had the advantage of using the radio, and there was no better way of competing with him than by trying to be in as many different places as possible in as short a time as possible. In campaigns of two to three weeks each, Hitler arranged to speak in some sixty-five cities per campaign.[20]

After his appointment as Chancellor, Hitler made Captain Baur his permanent personal pilot and got him to organise the government flying group. Hitler always insisted, with perhaps one exception, that only Baur should fly him.[21]

On his first two series of campaign flights in March and July 1932, Hitler used a Rohrbach Ro VIII Roland aeroplane ('Immelmann I'). The Junkers Ju 52, one of the most reliable aeroplanes ever built, was

a. Junkers Ju 52, on a Front visit in Poland, 10 September 1939; Heinz Linge on far right

b. Focke-Wulf FW 200 Condor V 3, 'Immelmann III,' 1937

c. Focke-Wulf FW 200 Condor C-4/U-1, 1942

8. Hitler's Aeroplanes

d. Focke-Wulf FW 200 Condor C-4/U-1, 1942

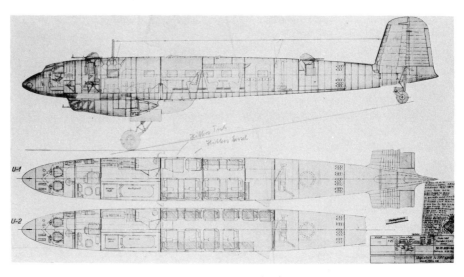

e. Focke-Wulf FW 200 Condor C-4/U-1 (top) with Hitler's seat and steel floorplate, and C-4/U-2 (bottom) for entourage, 1942

8. *Hitler's Aeroplanes*

f. Hitler's seat with parachute

put into service by Lufthansa in 1932, and in November of that year Hitler used it on his campaign flights. At landing points, SA or SS men guarded the aircraft while Hitler gave his speech in the city. The Ju 52 was also used in 1933 and in the years following. Hitler's personal plane was named 'Immelmann II' and carried the registration number D-2600 which was not changed until the war, so that airfield personnel always knew that Hitler's aeroplane was arriving when permission to land was requested for 'D-2600,' and would extend the appropriate preferential treatment.[22] Baur remembers, however, that on 30 June 1934 Hitler did not use this but another aircraft of the group; that Röhm had asked the Munich airport manager to let him know as soon as Hitler had landed; and that the manager at first had not been aware of who was in the plane, that he was told immediately after it had landed not to mention Hitler's arrival to anyone, and that consequently Röhm had not been warned. Kempka, on the other hand, remembers having radioed for Hitler's cars during the flight, so that there could have been some advance warning after all. Hitler's meeting with Röhm and other SA leaders had been arranged for this day, but not for the early hour.

Three Ju 52 were available to Hitler by 1937; Hess and Göring had one each at their disposal, and by 1937 Himmler also had one, so that the government squad consisted of six Ju 52. In 1937 the first two four-engined Focke-Wolf 200 Condor were built; the third one became Hitler's plane 'Immelmann III.'[23] This plane was much faster than the Ju 52 (which Hitler continued to use on many occasions), and it was noted for its non-stop Atlantic crossings. In 1942 a new improved version of the Focke-Wulf FW 200 Condor was put into service for Hitler.

The 1942 Condor had four machine-guns and stronger engines of 986 hp each, such as those used by the *Luftwaffe* for naval reconnaissance. It could remain in flight for fifteen hours. Under Hitler's seat there was a trap door; in case of danger, he could open it by pulling a red lever, and, with a parachute, jump through it to safety (see Illustration 8e).[24] In the autumn of 1944 this escape system was improved in a new aircraft, the Junkers Ju 290 A-6, by an additional ejector mechanism. The Ju 290 was a flying-fortress capable of flying 6,000 kilometres non-stop, and it was armed with ten large-calibre machine-guns (1.5 and 2 cm). Three of these planes were modified for Hitler. His seat was enclosed by 12-mm steel armour-plates; the window panes were made of 50-mm thick bullet-proof glass; floor and ceiling had additional armour-plates where Hitler sat. In case of danger, he only had to pull his red lever, and an escape door would be opened hydraulically, whereupon the *Führer* would slide out, on his seat, and drop to the ground by a parachute—in the seat. Tests with dummies were successful.[25] By the end of the war, Baur commanded thirteen Condor of the improved type, as well as several Ju 290. He was lord over a total of some forty aeroplanes, including Ju 52, some Heinkel He 111, and some smaller machines such as Fieseler Storch and Siebel aeroplanes. A Fieseler Storch was kept on hand to fly Hitler out of Berlin in April 1945, in case Hitler had decided not to die there.[26]

The aeroplanes of the government group were constantly under guard, and those used by Hitler were guarded by RSD and SS (LSSAH) details.[27] It had taken some efforts and manœuvring of the SS guards before they were satisfied, after 30 January 1933, that all those guarding or handling Hitler's planes were politically 'reliable.' Two officers of the Tempelhof airfield air police were removed in March 1933, upon urgent demands of the SS guards, because the police officers' anti-National-Socialist or Marxist attitudes (respectively) were a threat to security. SS Security Service of SS Flying Squad East demanded full authority for guarding Hitler and his aeroplanes at the airfield, including political surveillance of maintenance personnel, and power to arrest any 'suspects approaching the aeroplanes.' Servicing, repairs and loading (luggage) at any airport were soon only carried out in the presence of the flight engineer or another crew member, and in the presence of the guards. Objects not specifically authorised were not allowed on the plane; there was a general prohibition against parcels, mail and unauthorised luggage.

Before every one of Hitler's plane trips a test flight of ten to fifteen minutes at certain altitudes was mandatory. No passengers were allowed on the plane during these test flights. They served general safety requirements, but they would also reveal explosive devices linked with a barometer and set to go off at a certain altitude; therefore it was necessary to reach cruising altitude during the test flight. This was useless if an explosive device on the plane depended on a timer, and if the would-be assassin was familiar with the routine and with Hitler's plans. But if the departure time was kept strictly secret, as required, and if the luggage regulations were enforced, only an insider in Hitler's most intimate circle had a good chance of success in an assassination attempt. Later in the war, in 1944, when rumours of assassination plots became rather frequent, security was tested at irregular intervals by sham acts of sabotage against Hitler's plane. One of them was not discovered by those guarding and checking the plane.

Secrecy and unpredictability were as important for the security of Hitler's flights as for other modes of travel, and he often emphasised this. It was easier to ensure in air travel than in travel by railway or road where hundreds and hundreds of people had to be informed well in advance. Hitler therefore insisted that all 'his people'—valets, security personnel, chauffeur, pilot, physicians—must be close at hand at all times. He wanted to be able to summon them at a moment's notice. Baur often had to bring along his planes empty (two or three, so that the entire entourage could be transported) when Hitler travelled by train, as through France to the Spanish border to see General Franco at Hendaye in 1940—just in case Hitler suddenly decided to fly part of the way. In many cases, as on the trip to Hendaye, an automobile convoy of the *Führer-Begleit-Bataillon* also travelled on a parallel route in order to be available at a moment's notice.[28] This allowed Hitler to keep travel plans and methods unpredictable, and also to rush back to Berlin or to a Headquarters in a crisis.

An incident in September 1933 illustrates, however, what Hitler and his aides were up against in trying to enforce strict secrecy. Hitler wanted to visit the village of Öschelbronn, near Pforzheim, that had burned down completely, but the *Gauleiter* of Baden, Robert Wagner, had been informed by the *Gestapo* that Hitler planned to fly to Karlsruhe in strict secrecy—whereupon Wagner had seen fit to call out hundreds of SA to the airfield, and many more ordinary spectators were also attracted. Hitler was extremely angry. At the airfield in Berlin (Tempelhof), the commandant had beseeched and implored Baur to let him know where the flight was bound for; he was under strict orders from the Air Ministry to inform them of every one of Hitler's flights, including the destination, so that air safety procedures could be activated. Baur had refused to reveal anything and left it up to Hitler, and Hitler had said that if his pilot told him he did not need special safety procedures then he did not need them. After the customary ten-minute trial flight without him, Hitler boarded the plane and Bauer took off northward, towards

Hamburg, just to mislead anyone who tried to guess where the flight was bound for; later he turned and headed south-west towards Karlsruhe. And then, in Karlsruhe, the great throngs were waiting, and they had also gathered along the road to Öschelbronn, causing a delay through which Hitler missed another appointment. He had intended to take part in the funeral of ten SA men who had been killed in an automobile accident; the funeral was to be held in Bochum. Instead of going back to Karlsruhe airfield to continue the trip, he had himself driven to Böblingen airfield near Stuttgart and ordered Baur to bring the plane there, but it was too late to get to Bochum in time, and thunderstorms added to the delay.[29]

On a similar occasion, when again the police had leaked Hitler's travel plans, he did not even land at the port of destination, Nuremberg, when he saw the crowds, but ordered Baur to land at Fürth where some cars were hired on the spot to take the *Führer's* party to the funeral he had wanted to attend in Nuremberg and back again.

Once, in March 1936, on a trip from Munich via Stuttgart to Wiesbaden, Hitler stayed overnight in Stuttgart. Huge crowds gathered in front of his hotel, and Hitler's aides let it be known that he planned to fly on from Böblingen airfield, near Stuttgart. Baur was ordered to stay there until evening and not to land in Wiesbaden before 6 p.m.; Hitler would take his car and evade the crowds. But some clever mayor along the route had telephoned the Frankfurt radio station, which now broadcast reports on Hitler's progress so that people in the next towns along the route were always alerted in advance. Hitler's cars could only move at a snail's pace, in some villages the farmers put their wagons across the road to help persuade Hitler to stay a while, and the police and guards had to walk along to prevent children from getting run over.[30]

Hitler's frequent use of aeroplanes illustrates strikingly the contradictions and limitations of his quest for personal security. In order to avoid informing hundreds or thousands of railway employees, he preferred the risks of flying—thunderstorms, the constant danger of running out of petrol before finding a landing place, a burning wheel that could cause the plane to explode in flight or in take-off or landing. Fog might force an emergency landing, and emergency landings are never safe; if the ground was soft from rain, the wheels could get stuck, causing the plane to stand on its nose and crash. In June 1942 Hitler flew from Rastenburg to Micheli near Wiborg in Finland to visit Fieldmarshal Mannerheim; upon landing, a wheel started burning because of a faulty brake and the plane narrowly escaped catching fire. If the Rastenburg runway had been longer and the wheel had started to burn there, and had been folded into place under the wing, near the fuel tanks, the plane carrying Hitler would very likely have crashed.[31] In foggy weather Baur often had to fly at such low altitudes that the danger of crashing into a hill was acute, especially if he lost his bearings due to radio signals from the ground being misleading. Hanfstaengl, then Hitler's foreign-press secretary, remembered having seen Hitler in scarcely-concealed fear of death when Baur once got lost over the Baltic Sea—one of the very few occasions that Hanfstaengl could recall when Hitler had shown physical fear.[32] In cases of mechanical failures in the air, the dangers were greater than on the ground, or even on water. But there were dangers everywhere. Derailment or car crash had high degrees of probability; ships could sink or burn, yet Hitler took a number of short boat trips, as in April 1934 on the battleship *Deutschland* to Norwegian waters, or between Wilhelmshaven and Heligoland in 1939, sharing the *Robert Ley* with about a thousand holiday-makers.[33] It is true that opportunities for assassination attacks were fewer in flying. Advance information could be limited to a handful of persons. If Baur appeared at the airfield half an hour before take-off, people got a clue, but he often flew other members of the Government and foreign dignitaries. He might have been instructed to be seen at the airfield in order to mislead any observers. Rattenhuber's and Gesche's men could be presumed to be loyal and reliable, and in any case they did not get much advance warning themselves. Yet the risks apart from plots were so extraordinary in air travel that one must assume as part of the motivation for its preference a trait in Hitler's character frequently manifested: his tendency to gamble and to take risks when he did not have to. He took his risks consciously, in air travel as well as in other types of travel; he insisted that high-ranking persons (e.g. fieldmarshals) who accompanied him, as on a flight to the Front, should not share his plane with him, so that in case of a crash no more higher leaders would be killed than was inevitable.[34] But he managed to pretend complete unconcern when he realised he had narrowly escaped death, as he did on numerous occasions, including the burning-wheel incident, and once on a flight to Army Group South in 1943— an incident which will be related in another context.

8 Public Appearances

In his first year in power Hitler often liked to have tea at the 'Kaiserhof' hotel near the *Reich* Chancellery, and to listen to the Hungarian band that played there. A corner table was reserved regularly for Hitler. But within a few days of the start of these visits the place was filled to capacity at the hours when Hitler liked to come, and it became apparent that it was always the same elderly ladies who sat at the tables next to Hitler's. His pilot Hans Baur recalls that Hitler made a remark to the effect that he really preferred younger ladies; Rattenhuber was instructed to investigate. It was discovered that the elderly ladies paid the waiters to reserve seats for them and to tell them when the *Führer* was expected so that they could come and watch him have his tea. Hitler began to avoid the 'Kaiserhof,' but not public cafés and restaurants altogether. He continued to frequent such favourite haunts from the Years of Struggle as Munich's 'Café Heck,' or the 'Osteria Bavaria,' well into the war. A diary apparently kept by Bormann contains notes for the years 1937 to 1941 indicating that Hitler always participated in the Party Founding Day celebrations in Munich's 'Hofbräuhaus' on 24 February, and on some of these occasions the chronicler recorded 'afterwards "Café Heck" as usual,' or 'afterwards "Osteria" and "Café Heck".'[1] Obviously, the staff in these places had ways of making other guests behave so that the *Führer* felt reasonably at ease. RSD officers also had to search basements and other rooms in such buildings, *SS-Begleit-Kommando* men took over the tables next to Hitler's, and, during the war, SS men were posted as guards in front to see to it that onlookers could not get in.

In Bad Godesberg Hitler preferred to stay at 'Rheinhotel Dreesen' from the mid-1920s when he had been treated very well there by the proprietor, Fritz Dreesen, although Hitler had been politically unimportant after his release from Landsberg prison. Once, after January 1933, he found the hotel completely empty. He had got used to big crowds gathering at all the hotels where he stayed, and to the ovations. Upon inquiry, he learned that one of his bodyguards had arrived with the advance party and had ordered some 1,200 people out of the garden restaurant, for security reasons. Hitler was angry and demanded the instantaneous return of the public. Eventually they were re-assembled and the garden restaurant filled up again, with Hitler sitting at his table among all the other guests, taking his tea.[2]

At rallies and parades, and at the Nuremberg Party rally each year, the regional *Gauleiter* was in charge of the arrangements. This applied to events 'beyond the framework of the Party' as well.[2a] Security was often inadequate, as when Party officials responsible for the organisation of the event broke the rules against photographing. Hitler's Naval Aide, Rear-Admiral von Puttkamer, once became so concerned that he mentioned these conditions to Rattenhuber. But the security chief said that nothing could be done about them, except to keep Nuremberg under the closest possible observation.

In cases of announced appearances, it was necessary to cordon off the streets through which Hitler was to pass, considering that even 'secret' journeys often turned into triumphal processions as people spread the news by telephone from one town to the next. If cordoning-off was necessary, Hitler did not want police in uniform at the rally site or near it, nor along the route he travelled to or from it. It was all right to use uniformed police for telephone or runner services, and to use the minimum force necessary for maintaining order at rendezvous points and approach routes for rally participants. Never were uniformed police to be used to form cordons and lanes for Hitler to walk through. If political authorities who organised the rally requested police assistance, it was to be granted, but only in the form of offered advice, and without the implication that police officers assumed any responsibility. The public were to have as much freedom of movement as possible, but the path of marchers and other rally participants had to be clear. Officers of the political police forces of the provinces were to be employed in accordance with the wishes of RSD commander Rattenhuber, who acted as their commanding officer.

On 'secret,' not publicly-announced occasions, visible security efforts would attract crowds and make even more of an effort necessary. Therefore such visits had to be *strictly* secret, and the best way to ensure this was for Hitler not to tell anyone his plans until minutes before he wished to carry them out, as he well recognised. Breakdowns of secrecy, however, were not uncommon. On 23 May 1939 the *Führer* wished to visit the Berlin 'Wintergarten' variety theatre opposite Friedrichstrasse Station in the Hotel 'Central.' In order to avoid attracting attention and the usual resultant congestion and discomfort, Hitler wanted to come only (as he usually did) after the auditorium lights had been switched off. When Rattenhuber arrived there at 7.45 p.m., ahead of the *Führer*, there were already several people standing about awaiting Hitler's arrival, as Rattenhuber gathered from their conversation; he found that 'Wintergarten' employees had told them Hitler was coming but that they must not tell anyone else. After the 'Wintergarten' visit Hitler had planned to stop at a beer-hall called 'Franz Nagel,' and he was expected here, too, although the visit was to be 'spontaneous.' Two waiters were standing in front of the place, and they told Rattenhuber they had been informed by 'Wintergarten' staff. Hitler changed his mind and did not go to the theatre at all. Later, during the same evening, Rattenhuber escorted Hitler to the 'Kasino der Deutschen Künstler' (Club of German Artists), and again found a small crowd there, including a policeman who said he had been sent by Herr Benno von Arent, *Reichsbühnenbildner* (*Reich* Stage Designer) and leader of *Kameradschaft der Deutschen Künstler*, much esteemed by Hitler.[2b]

More such incidents will be related in the Chapters on Travel and Residences below: at this point, security measures on the occasions of Hitler's public appearances, and their success, will have to be examined.

On 9 March 1936 Hess, as the *Führer's* Deputy, decreed an extension of central authority for security measures at the *Führer's* public appearances.[3] An older directive of 23 September 1934 said: 'The *Führer* has ordered that the local *Gauleiter* as representative of the Movement shall have overall responsibility for rallies and mass marches in which the *Führer* participates. This applies also to occasions that transcend the framework of the Party.' This fundamental directive was reaffirmed now, on 9 March 1936, and it remained in force until Elser's assassination attempt of 8 November 1939. But in 1936 Hess had added: 'On such occasions the *Reichsführer-SS* or a higher SS leader designated by him is alone responsible for all cordoning-off and security measures.' This took security authority out of the hands of the *Gauleiter* and put it back into the hands of Himmler, of the RSHA, and to all intents and purposes into the hands of the RSD, where it had been placed, in effect, as early as 1934. It was not always easy to heed Hess's further injunction that the *Gauleiter* and SS leaders settle any differences of opinion in cooperative discussions, but this generally seems to have been achieved, and police, SA, Party functionaries and SS coordinated the necessary measures. This was facilitated by Himmler's appointment as Chief of all German Police on 17 June 1936. But the directive was not applied to the annual 'Bürgerbräukeller' event in November.

Detailed Cordoning-off Instructions told the SS units employed what to do.[4] If there was to be a ship christening, a ground-breaking, a Party rally, a road-opening in the presence of the *Führer*, or a visit to a disaster area, the regional *SS-Oberabschnittsführer* (SS Higher Section Leader) had to get in touch immediately with the appropriate *Gauleiter* and determine the nature of the occasion, the length of the *Führer's* visit, the extent of the event, etc. A security staff was formed for preparation of security measures, and a detailed cordoning-off plan set up in cooperation with police and Party organisations. Before the plan was finally set, the entire terrain on which crowds, organisations and the *Führer* were to appear, including approach and departure routes and railway and airport areas, had to be inspected and surveyed, regardless of whether Hitler was expected to arrive by car, train or plane, in case his plan 'as often

happens, is changed at the last moment (plane instead of train, etc.).'
'Unforeseen' approach and departure routes had to be looked at, reserves
had to be set aside to cordon off unplanned routes on short notice. During
the inspection, danger points had to be noted, such as viaducts, narrow
lanes, stretches of road where the view was obstructed, building corners,
parks, bushes, patches of trees and forest. If it seemed advisable, danger
points had to be put under surveillance twenty-four hours in advance
of the event. After the inspection, and after the desired intervals between
cordoning-off personnel had been determined, the size of the force was
calculated.

Even in the planning stage, the mood of the population had to be
gauged and taken into consideration. 'All measures must be taken in
such a way that their usefulness and necessity are clear to the reasonable
public. They are to be applied helpfully and without useless hardships
where it is a case of enthusiastic people who want to see the *Führer*.
Pedantry only has negative effects. On the other hand, the measures must
be taken quietly, firmly and without any wavering when generosity is
no longer possible. If there is any resistance to security arrangements,
they must be enforced without hesitation, if necessary with all appropriate ruthlessness and with the assistance of police forces.' The 'surveillance
of foreigners subject to suspicion, or of other unreliable elements' was a
matter of course and must be initiated by police authorities.

Normally the cordoning-off plan was secret. It had to contain the following information: precise description of area, with sketches; approach
and departure routes; position of security staff and command centre,
with names of commander and deputy; boundaries of cordoning-off sections with names of leaders responsible for the section (sections must not
begin or end at crossroads); strength and name of units deployed in sections; police district headquarters where arrested persons could be taken;
rendezvous and assembly points; first-aid points; parking areas; information on admission of certain persons into cordoned-off areas (press,
photographers) and on their passes; units for particular points such as
railway stations, airports, grandstands, parking areas, specific buildings;
telephone and radio cables had to be designated clearly; preparations
had to be made for communication through runners or telephone
cables independent of public lines, etc.; guards and observers of SS and
police in plain clothes had to be assigned to trees, monuments, balconies,
window-sills, etc., which must be kept free of spectators and under constant surveillance; special observation posts had to be set up to keep an
eye on building entrances, windows, balconies and roofs of buildings,
either by observing them from a distance or by occupying them.
Reserves had to be stationed at appropriate points so that an unruly
mob could be dealt with quickly. 'In order to ensure constant information of occurrences which might disturb the events, the cordoning-off,

or the regulation of traffic, the public should be observed by SS men in civilian clothes (with guns). These observers and SS civilian patrols (which cannot and shall not replace members of the *Sicherheitsdienst, Gestapo* or criminal police) ... are to report on all important observations to the SS leader who gave them their assignment. These reports are to be made inconspicuously so that outsiders cannot tell that the civilian is actually an SS member.'

Usually there were two cordons set up, an inner one and an outer one. The outer one closed off an area in which all traffic with vehicles was prohibited or at least very much limited, and in which pedestrians were subject to restrictions and surveillance. The inner ring sealed off the place of the coming event, e.g. market-place, town hall or theatre. The areas cordoned off were to be cleared in zones, moving from inside outwards. The cordoning-off orders must be passed down all the way to non-commissioned leaders in writing, and they had to state precisely what was to be cleared and sealed off: streets, squares, bridges, viaducts, pavements, open-air stairways, buildings. The sealed-off area was to be kept as small as possible so that the available security forces would be sufficient; but safety valves had to be prepared in case the public broke through a cordon. If this happened, the cordon might have to give way, but had to be prepared to force people—by forming funnels or wedges— into side streets. On large open places such as airfields the cordons had to be particularly tight because there were no lines of buildings reinforcing them and stopping the masses; here it might be necessary to have available a reserve troop on horseback, and to use stricter methods than in a city. In any case, cordoning had to begin early enough to ensure that, in the restricted areas, no masses had already congregated who would have to be forced out.

Lanes formed by schoolchildren, sports club members, factory workers, etc., could not be substituted for an SS cordon. They might be permitted, but an SS cordon had to be in front of them. Even if the Army formed the lane, 'SS in modest numbers had to be assigned for intervention if necessary.' The SS cordon always had to be so close that SS men could grip each other's hands if necessary; in some cases the intervals between the men had to be so small that one could get a grip of the belt-lock of both his left-hand and right-hand neighbour—or at least of his left-hand neighbour, if one hand was to remain free for the use of a weapon. If the public stood several ranks deep, additional SS men, besides the ones in front, had to be placed behind the public. Those forming the actual cordon holding back the public were to alternate in facing the public and the area where things were happening (Plates 9a–d). Depending on the requirements of the situation, every second, third or fourth man had to stand facing the spectators. Those facing them had to keep them under observation 'in order to intervene at danger points,

Cordoning-off a street and security measures for the *Führer's* car

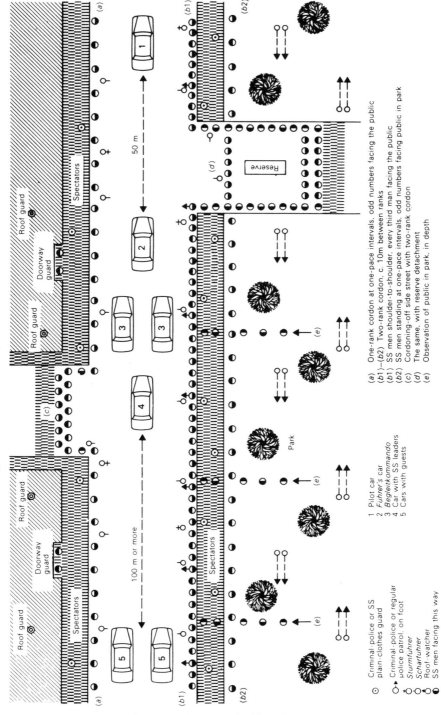

Roof guard
Doorway guard
Spectators

1 Pilot car
2 *Führer's* car
3 *Begleitkommando*
4 Car with SS leaders
5 Cars with guests

⊙ Criminal-police or SS plain-clothes guard
♂ Criminal-police or regular police patrol, on foot
Sturmführer
Scharführer
Roof-watcher
SS men facing this way

(*a*) One-rank cordon at one-pace intervals, odd numbers facing the public
(*b1*)–(*b2*) Two-rank cordon. c. 10m between ranks
(*b1*) SS men shoulder-to-shoulder, every third man facing the public
(*b2*) SS men standing at one-pace intervals, odd numbers facing public in park
(*c*) Cordoning-off side street with two-rank cordon
(*d*) The same, with reserve detachment
(*e*) Observation of public in park, in depth

9. Cordoning-off patterns for SS cordons, 1937

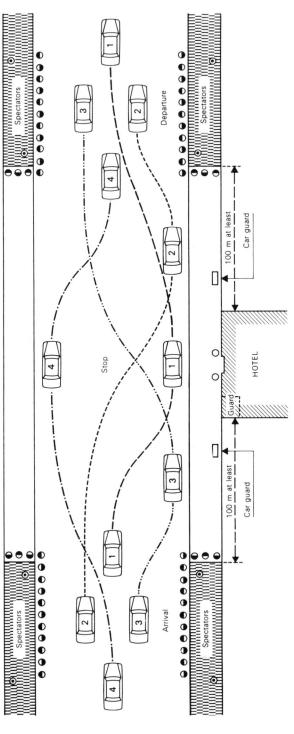

Security for the *Führer* when travelling by car, showing Arrival, Stop, and Departure

Spectators
Departure
Spectators

Stop

100 m at least
Car guard

Guard

HOTEL

100 m at least
Car guard

Spectators
Arrival
Spectators

1 *Führer's* car
2 and 3 *Führer-Begleit-Kommando*
4 SS leaders

○ ○ Double sentry
◉ Plain-clothes guard (criminal-police or SS)
● SS men facing this way

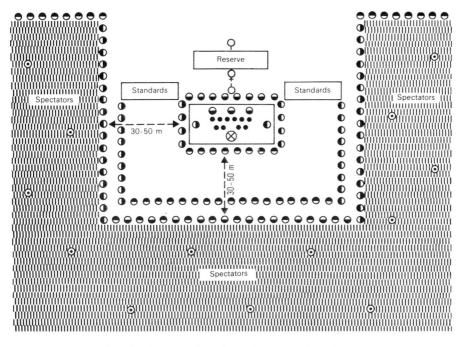

Security for a grandstand or other open-air position

⊗   *Führer*   ♂̄   Commander of *SS*

●   *Führer's suite*   ♂   Deputy commander of *SS*

◉   Plain-clothes guard   ◑   Cordon men facing this way

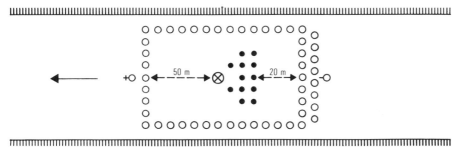

Security for the *Führer* on foot

⊗ *Führer*   ● *Führer's suite*   ♂̄ Commander of SS   O SS men   ♂ Deputy-Commander of SS

to prevent crimes (pickpocketing, endangering of security, assassination).' The same purpose was served by the instruction to place 'children and old persons' in front whenever possible. SS men were told they must not be distracted by the arrival of the *Führer*, or by other events.

Where the *Führer* was passing through in his car convoy, every seventh or eighth man in the cordon had to observe the roofs opposite his side of the street, and every 50 to 100 metres guards had to be posted on those roofs. Two SS posts were stationed in each building entrance, behind the spectators, and every 50 to 100 metres a plain-clothes SS man was posted for observation of the public from behind. If the spectators were standing on a pavement along a park or other open area, rather than along a solid housefront, another SS cordon with intervals of three to four metres had to be stationed along the park behind the spectators; every hundred metres a barrier of at least three SS men had to extend some ten metres into the park, at right angles to the path. Reserves for use in cases where the cordons were broken through had to be stationed inside the inner ring so that they could be deployed without delay. Reserves designed to prevent outside disturbances had to be stationed outside the cordons.

The forces to be used were first of all those of the *SS-Verfügungstruppe*, primarily of the *Leibstandarte-SS 'Adolf Hitler'* (LSSAH). Only if these forces were insufficient, could other units, especially SA formations, also NSKK or *Reichsarbeitsdienst* (RAD, *Reich* Labour Service), be employed, under the command of their various unit leaders (SS leaders were not to command other units immediately, only through their respective leaders).

No one was allowed to pass through cordons except security officers, organisation officials, physicians, injured and sick persons. Press reporters and photographers had to be sent to designated points where they might pass through the cordons; if it seemed indicated, their passes had to be examined. 'Unknown persons without valid passes must under no circumstances be allowed to pass the barriers.' Those breaking through, presumably out of enthusiasm, were to be admonished and to be led back behind the cordon, provided they were not subject to suspicion. 'Those subject to suspicion are to be arrested, to be searched for weapons, and to be taken to the nearest police station or collection point for arrested persons.' SS men thus had immediate police authority; the local police was made an executive arm of the SS: 'The SS cordon man is the superior official of the leaders of all other organisations. Therefore he must see that he gets his way. In many cases he will experience difficulties from higher-ranking leaders (passing through the cordon); he will then have to act with particular firmness, though politely.' Weapons were not to be used without orders except in cases of self-defence, or in order to deal with a criminal caught in the act. It was strictly forbidden to eat, drink, smoke, read, talk to the public, or to salute anyone (including the *Führer* himself) so as not to diminish vigilance. Only SS leaders from *Untersturmführer* up were to salute, and only if they were standing in front of the cordon line.

Hotels, town halls, tents and other buildings used by the protected persons during events had to be guarded twenty-four hours in advance of the event. New arrivals in hotels had to be scrutinised very closely. Guest rooms and other public rooms and garages had to be 'thoroughly searched for signs of intended crimes or acts of sabotage.... The service personnel of hotels and assembly rooms used in the event must be given inconspicuous reliability checks.' Not later than an hour before the building opened it had to be cordoned off by SS, all adjoining streets had to be cleared entirely, no one was allowed within 50 metres of the building, and all except a few easily supervised entrances had to be closed and sealed off. At passage points in the cordon, SS members in the local police (local residents) were to be stationed for surveillance, so that strangers passing themselves off as, say the city treasurer, could not get through unless authorised. From the building entrance to the actual assembly room, SS had to form a shoulder-to-shoulder lane. Emergency exits had to be prepared, especially from the speaker's rostrum. Lighting, public-address systems and telephone equipment had to be guarded by experts and by SS signal troops. Before the start of the event 'the entire building is to be searched by clever SS members (police officers), with the assistance of the building supervisor, from roof to cellar;' double guards were to be placed at attic and basement entrances, as well as at all entrances and exits of the building. 'In the building, especially in the assembly room, observers in plain clothes must be posted. The balconies must be specially observed. Any persons subject to suspicion, particularly persons with packages, must be stopped at once and taken to the security leader.'

If structures or areas in the open air were used in an event, these and their environment were to be guarded 'for days in advance by plain-clothes police officers;' this had to be arranged with the appropriate police authorities. No later than on the morning of the event, a new and thorough search had to be made of the grandstand or other locality, and, from now on, a close watch had to be kept until after the end of the event. All structures or areas in the open air must be secured by double cordon-lines, with 2 metres distance between the two cordons. Every second man in the cordon nearest to the spectators had to face these. The distance between the speaker or protected person and the public must be as large as possible, 'at least thirty metres, to limit throwing and hitting accuracy.' Observer posts, 'some in plain clothes, with binoculars where appropriate,' were to be stationed at elevated points, and among the public. 'Any person giving rise to suspicion must be seized at once and turned over to police.' Reserves were to be stationed immediately behind the speaker's rostrum or grandstand.

From the moment of the *Führer's* arrival at the airfield, railway station, or outskirts of the town, the commander of the *Reichssicherheitsdienst* (RSD) detail or of the combined *Führer-Begleit-Kommando* had command authority over all further police measures; all steps taken so far had to be reported to him; all of his directives had to be followed in the vicinity of the *Führer*, by all those on cordoning-off duty. Times set for car trips, drives, processions were to 'be kept secret as long as possible,' equally the routes if they had not been cordoned off officially, and alternate routes had to be designated and prepared so that changes were possible without any advance notice. Usually three minutes before Hitler would pass through, a car of the SS or police and two motorcyclists were to drive along the cordoned route with a yellow flag as the signal for the beginning of a period of utmost vigilance and alertness, strictest maintenance of the cordons, and detour of all other vehicles. In some cities it might be useful to let a pilot car precede the *Führer's*, but in most cities Kempka knew the routes. Any pilot cars had to drive 50 metres ahead of the *Führer's* car, which was in turn followed at the shortest possible interval by the two cars of RSD and *SS-Begleit-Kommando* (the combined *Führer-Begleit-Kommando*), then by a car-load of SS officers, and behind them at 100 or (preferably) more metres distance the cars with other guests and the rest of the entourage. If this made the procession too long, the guest cars might have to be detoured to their destination through side streets. When Hitler's car stopped in front of the hotel, assembly hall, city hall, etc., the two *Führer-Begleit-Kommando* cars stopped immediately in front and behind the *Führer's* car on the same side of the street, and the SS leaders' car in the same position as the *Führer's* car, on the opposite side of the street. In departure, the original order was restored. If the *Führer* was to walk a distance, say, from hotel to market-place, he was surrounded by a square cordon of SS men walking with him, 50 metres in front, 20 metres behind, and on the sides with as much distance as feasible, depending on the width of the streets. This system was used only when Hitler was to walk along a route that was not officially cordoned off, otherwise he was merely accompanied in loose order by his adjutants, bodyguards and guests or hosts if any. His valet and bodyguard Heinz Linge recalls that Hitler frequently went ahead and opened his own path through the crowds on unexpected occasions.

In case of 'unusual occurrences,' the directives said, the worst thing was lack of decision. The assassination of King Alexander of Yugoslavia and of the French Foreign Minister Louis Barthou on 9 October 1934 was a case in which this had led to panic and confusion. Therefore: 'At the first sign of an assassination attack, the SS leaders nearest the place of the attack must immediately take over and cause the cordons on both sides to swing into positions at right angles to their original positions so that 25 metres in front and behind the car with the attacked person the route is sealed completely from house to house; the car with the intended victim must leave the danger area as fast as possible. No car, no persons except police, judicial authorities, and physicians, are to be allowed in or out of the sealed-off area.' At the same time, the nearest side streets had to be opened and cleared by appropriate moves of the cordons, so that the *Führer* or other target might depart quickly, 'for in the festival street more assassination attempts have to be expected (assassination of Austrian Heir to the Throne in Sarajevo).' So much was to be learned from the assassination of King Alexander and Barthou that a film of the assassination was made available to regular, criminal and municipal police forces in order for them to arrange showings of it for all personnel used in cordoning-off duties during state visits. The directives, however, made no mention of the possibility of attacks from upper-storey windows, balconies and roofs, or of an explosive attack prepared underground (as in the assassination of the Spanish Ministerpresident, Blanco, in December 1973 in Madrid); they only seemed to reckon with attacks made out of doors and at ground level. This is clear from instructions on what to do to make certain the background of the crime could be cleared up: 'If the public get a hold of the assassin or suspects and try to lynch them, the SS must wrest them from the masses, take their weapons from them (suicide!), and hold them in the nearest house until the police arrive. The interrogation of the guilty person is of great importance for the uncovering of widespread conspiracies. It must not be prevented by the death of those involved.' This, too, was a lesson learned from the assassination in Marseilles.

The measures sketched above were used throughout the 1930s and part of the 1940s. Some of them had been applied at the Olympic Games of 1936. The *Gestapo* mounted comprehensive efforts to smash any remaining Social-Democrat and Communist underground organisations in 1935 and 1936. In Berlin alone, 2,197 persons belonging to left-wing circles were arrested during fourteen months in 1935 and 1936; in all of Germany, 11,687 persons were arrested in 1936 for Socialist activity.[5] Equally, every effort was made to ensure the utmost in security during the Olympic Games, by keeping under surveillance all suspicious characters who crossed the borders into Germany.

The Winter Games were held in Garmisch-Partenkirchen from 6 to 16 February. The LSSAH was employed in almost every phase of security operations when Hitler participated. SS uniforms were to be seen everywhere. Rattenhuber and Sepp Dietrich shared the direction of security operations.[6] RSD officials gave the directives, and the Bavarian Political Police office in Garmisch-Partenkirchen was charged with carrying out local security precautions, such as observation of hotels, buildings and crowds during Hitler's arrival and departure. Cordoning-off operations were in the hands of Sepp Dietrich with 200 men and five officers. The men were put up in the local schoolhouse, and a directive pointed out that there were twenty-four inns they might visit, but the 'Traube' ('Grape') was not recommended as its proprietor had the reputation of being a 'non-National-Socialist.'

On opening day, 6 February, Hitler arrived on his *Führer* Special at 10.22 a.m. at Kainzenbad, a few minutes from Garmisch-Partenkirchen station, coming from Munich. At the station he was greeted by *Reich* Minister of the Interior Frick, *Reich* War Minister Colonel-General von Blomberg, Minister of State Adolf Wagner, *Reich* Sports Leader von Tschammer und Osten, and by the Presidium of the Organising Committee of the Fourth Olympic Winter Games. Hitler then walked past a *Wehrmacht* guard of honour, and proceeded on foot to the Olympic ski stadium. It was forbidden for photographers to follow the *Führer*, but the security directives gave them places at the station. SS men formed a lane through which Hitler walked, while an RSD detail set up guards for the Special train as soon as it had been moved to a railway siding in Garmisch-Partenkirchen. On the day before, officers of the Bavarian Political Police had searched the main building of the Olympic ski stadium and had guarded it during the twenty-four hours before Hitler's arrival. They were instructed to observe the public along the path to the stadium, and particularly on the stands near the *Führer's* seat. All territory around the stands from which the *Führer's* seat could be seen had to be patrolled constantly by secret-police officers on skis. At Kainzenbad station, plain-clothes railway police had to provide security.

Similar security measures were in effect for Hitler's other visits to the Games, such as on 13 February, and during the Summer Games in Berlin from 1 to 16 August, when Hitler visited the Games almost daily. It is worth noting that he always took the same route. This did not matter much in the Winter Games, for he attended only a few times. But in the summer his aides pointed out to him that he might give an assassin an easy chance by taking the same route at the same time every day. Hitler refused to allow any changes. The RSD tried to make his way as safe as possible by holding all landlords along the route responsible for keeping out of their houses all untrustworthy strangers.

At autumn manœuvres of Second Group Command in the Schlüchtern area in September 1936, LSSAH and *Wehrmacht* soldiers shared security service during Hitler's motor trips into the manœuvre area. No. 26 anti-tank unit was to give support only if necessary. *SS-Gruppenführer* Sepp Dietrich was in charge of 300 *Leibstandarte* men; a major (Major Stollbrok) commanded the Army unit. Both received their orders from Hitler's Chief *Wehrmacht* Adjutant, Lieutenant-Colonel Hossbach. Two hundred and fifty-two SS men were on duty. But the LSSAH men were alone responsible for external security at the compound where Hitler and his entourage were quartered—on the Army's grounds.[7] The implications of the Supreme Commander of the *Wehrmacht* bringing his own private non-*Wehrmacht* guards to protect himself while inspecting the *Wehrmacht* are obvious.

On a similar occasion on 19 and 20 August 1938, when Hitler reviewed troops in Military District II (Stettin), he did bring his personal bodyguard, who followed him in two cars from the railway station to the manœuvre fields and everywhere else, but no SS troops as at Schlüchtern in 1936.[8] Along the approach route, civilian employees of the troop command were placed to greet the *Führer*, and they were supported by members of the *Deutsche Arbeitsfront* (DAF, German Labour Front), by pupils from the local schools, and by other local residents. Cordoning-off duties were performed by Army soldiers outside and inside the training camp and manœuvre grounds. Hitler observed artillery target practice, held conferences with commanding officers, and attended a dinner with officers of the Military District. At twenty-minute intervals, the officers sitting at his table retired to make room for another shift that sat and talked with the *Führer*, according to a schedule worked out by the District Command staff—while the *Führer-Begleit-Kommando* ate in the kitchen. The Bormann brothers (Martin and Albert), *Gauleiter* Schwede-Coburg and *SS-Sturmbannführer* Dr. Brandt (but no bodyguard members) were scheduled to sit at Hitler's table. On his way back to his *Führersonderzug*, where he spent the night, Hitler drove through a 'torch-lit lane.' Only moderate cordoning-off was arranged for the following day.

A major annual occasion for a public appearance was the day on which Hitler had been appointed Chancellor, 30 January 1933, now generally referred to as the Day of the Seizure of Power, and also known as Day of National Resurgence.

The day's festivities usually included (in the years 1933–39): at 10 a.m. a review of the LSSAH on the Wilhelmsplatz; at 1 p.m. a *Reichstag* meeting in the Kroll Opera building (the *Reichstag* meeting hall, ever since its own building had been burned in February 1933) where the *Führer* addressed the deputies as usual; at 5 p.m. the Cabinet had one of its rare meetings in the Chancellery; at 8 p.m. Hitler enjoyed a torch-light procession of NSDAP members from the Greater Berlin area, and he was joined by eighty-four foreign diplomats who were invited to view the procession from within the Chancellery.[9]

Two thousand SS men were detailed to cordon off the parade areas in the morning, Wilhelmstrasse was sealed off from Vossstrasse to Unter den Linden, and forty-five *Gestapo* officers were ordered to keep Wilhelmsplatz and Wilhelmstrasse under close surveillance. RSD patrols observed the outside of the Chancellery, and RSD officers had to check the guest list at Hotel 'Kaiserhof' nearby, twice, in the afternoon on 29 January and at 8 a.m. on 30 January. All security measures directly connected with the parade had to begin an hour in advance, and were to end only after Hitler had returned to his apartments. During the *Reichstag* session, 4,000 SS men cordoned off the surrounding area under the command of Sepp Dietrich himself; only half of the men could be drawn from the LSSAH; the rest came from other SS units stationed in Eastern Germany. The entire approach area from Vossstrasse to the Kroll Opera was sealed off so that Hitler would have a clear route for his cars to come

10.   Incident during 'election' campaign, 31 March 1938

and go. *Gestapo* secured sections of Hitler's route from *Reich* Chancellery to Kroll Opera as follows: from Vossstrasse to the corner of Unter den Linden, 50 officers; from Unter den Linden to the Brandenburg Gate, 50 officers; from the Brandenburg Gate to the Victory Column (then at Königsplatz, in front of the *Reichstag* building), 40 officers; from the Victory Column to the Kroll Opera, 50 officers. Safety measures were very much needed at the Kroll Opera, as Hitler remarked at lunch in May 1942: 'the five-metre-wide lane leading to the Kroll Opera in Berlin, for example, is one of the potentially most dangerous bits of road I know.' The Kroll Opera building was searched on 29 January at 5 p.m. and patrolled throughout the night; a second search was scheduled for 9 a.m. on 30 January, and a third one for 11 a.m., from which time onward the building was kept under constant surveillance until after the meeting. Police officers were stationed at all entrances, hallways, near the Government chairs and around the speaker's rostrum, and behind the stage curtain, all over the stage area and backstage rooms, in the attic above the Government chairs, at all gallery entrances, in the press box and auditorium areas, etc. An advance party of eight RSD officers led by Högl had to check out the path Hitler was going to walk from his car to the speaker's rostrum, and to station themselves along it. Rattenhuber himself was present and in charge during the *Reichstag* meeting. But SS guards were not, on this or on subsequent occasions, as conspic-

11.   Hitler in Stuttgart, on Königstrasse with Führer *Escort, during 'election' campaign,*
1 April 1938

uously in evidence as on 13 July 1934, when four SS bodyguards in steel helmets stood behind the *Führer* while he made his speech 'justifying' the murder of Röhm, Röhm's friends, and other 'enemies.'

RSD officers were reminded to prohibit all unauthorised photography; those authorised had identification cards and an armband. Photography with flash-bulbs was prohibited even for authorised photographers. It was also prohibited to photograph from the other side of the men cordoning off the crowds, and it was forbidden in the strongest possible terms to hand to Hitler any flowers, letters, packages and the like, or to throw any objects whatsoever in his direction.

Every time Adolf Hitler visited anywhere publicly in the 1930s, in 'election campaigns,' as in March and April 1938, there were great crowds, and neither were they completely controlled, nor were the houses along Hitler's route searched consistently. Moreover, some children, women and sometimes men always managed to run up to Hitler's car and hand him flowers or a letter, or request his autograph.

Flower-tossing, in particular, was a threat to security that the authorities had to address themselves to frequently. General flower-tossing would make it extraordinarily easy for a would-be assassin to toss a bomb disguised as a bouquet, and to get away without being recognised. Orders against flower-throwing were issued repeatedly, but the practice could never be completely suppressed, at least before the war. A decree of 18 June 1935 of the *Reich* and Prussian Ministry of the Interior forbade flower-throwing in the presence of the *Führer*, clearly without effect, for in September 1936 Himmler wrote to subordinate police authorities that despite warnings, people were still throwing flowers and bouquets into automobiles carrying 'leading personalities of Party and State,' and that it definitely had to stop.

An order by Hess repeated the prohibition in August 1938, and on 30 November 1938 Daluege wrote to all *Reichsstatthalter* and other appropriate officials in the *Länder* that, as orders not to throw any flowers into Hitler's car had been frequently disregarded, all leaders of the Party and of its organisations were now instructed to take away before Hitler's passage all flowers that any onlookers might have in their hands, and that shortly before Hitler did come through a motorised patrol must check once again and collect whatever flowers could be seen. But the bad habit had not been stamped out even in 1939. Children and young girls were still tolerated when they handed bunches of flowers to the *Führer*, though his hands barely touched them before a bodyguard grabbed them from behind. Of course, if some foul deed was committed concurrently with the handing over of flowers, the intervention of the bodyguard could come too late.[10]

On 1 April 1938 Hitler visited Stuttgart while on a wide-ranging speaking tour, during the 'election campaign' for a new *Reichstag*. Security was minimal. The City Hall was searched by officers of the criminal police and of Heydrich's *SS-Sicherheitsdienst* (SD). Plain-clothes officers were charged with hotel surveillance in Stuttgart and the surrounding suburbs. Streets on which Hitler rode into town were guarded and kept under surveillance. Nevertheless, Hitler's car was very nearly mobbed when he rode down the Königstrasse. Flower-tossing was taboo, but tolerated by the security forces. On one occasion, a child trying to run up to Hitler's car with flowers was first caught and held back by a security man, then carried and lifted up to Hitler's car after all and allowed to hand over her gift.[11] It was not very likely that an assassin would use a child for his purpose. Besides, the use of violence of any kind in restraining crowds in the immediate vicinity of Hitler was bound to create a bad impression and had to be avoided.

A year later, Hitler's fiftieth birthday was a big event in Berlin.[12] The day before was also used for congratulations, in order to accommodate innumerable throngs of well-wishers. On 19 April 1939 newly-promoted SS officer candidates were presented to their *Führer*; the NSDAP leadership corps, headed by *Führer* Deputy Rudolf Hess, congratulated Hitler at 7 p.m.; they were followed by surviving members of the old *Stosstrupp Hitler* and by others who had participated in the 1923 March to 'Feldherrnhalle.' At 9 p.m. Hitler and fifty car-loads of invited guests rode down the East–West Axis to Adolf-Hitler-Platz and back again to open this monumental new multi-lane avenue officially. The 'population' stood on both sides, having been marched there under SA or SS escorts in closed columns (not an unusual method of providing the desired crowds of enthusiasts). A population of 513,000 was required to foregather by 6 p.m. at specified rendezvous points, 80,000 here, 30,000 there, and so on, and to take their places in formation by 8.30 p.m., all along the route Hitler would travel. The public were not permitted to leave before 9.30 p.m. The route from the Chancellery to the 'Siegessäule' (Victory Column), where Professor Albert Speer, now Hitler's favourite and foremost architect, officially reported to Hitler the completion of the monumental avenue, was cordoned off by SS, SA, and NSKK from 7 p.m. At 10.35 p.m., after Hitler's return from his ceremonial ride down the East–West Axis, 5,900 members of NSDAP organisations and delegations held a torchlight procession past the Chancellery which the *Führer* viewed from the balcony in the presence of the heads of the *Wehrmacht* and the SS, of Goebbels, Bormann and his personal bodyguards. SS men formed a tight lane through which the procession moved along the Wilhemstrasse, as Hitler always preferred to have SS perform cordoning-off duties in the immediate vicinity of his reviewing points on such occasions. After a 'Lights Out' ceremony, at Wilhelmsplatz, the evening ended with a choir presentation by members of the LSSAH at 11 p.m. in the *Reich* Chancellery courtyard.

The events of the birthday itself also began with musical efforts on the part of the LSSAH: at 8 a.m. the regimental music serenaded Hitler in the Chancellery garden. There followed a parade of the LSSAH and other SS units, viewed by Hitler from the *Reich* Chancellery in Wilhelmstrasse, at 9 a.m. At 9.20 the Apostolic Nuncio offered his congratulations, followed by the Governor of Bohemia and Moravia, Baron Neurath, and the former President of Czechoslovakia, Hachá, and by Slovak Ministerpresident Tiso. Then it was the Cabinet's turn to offer congratulations, and there followed representatives of the *Wehrmacht* leadership headed by Fieldmarshal Göring; after the Mayor of Berlin and some other delegations, *Gauleiter* Forster of Danzig handed Hitler a document making him an honorary citizen of Danzig. At 11 a.m. the Great Parade on the East–West Axis was reviewed by Hitler, and in the afternoon diplomats were received.

There were obvious opportunities for attacks amidst all this traffic in the Chancellery, and in all the coming and going. Hitler himself once described, about a year earlier, how an assassin could operate: 'Imagine that, while we are gathered here, a lorry passes through the Wilhelmstrasse. Right in front of the *Reich* Chancellery it has a flat tyre or other breakdown. The driver leaves to get help, and meanwhile the lorry, loaded with dynamite, blows up and buries us under the ruins of the Chancellery.'[13] This was precisely the opportunity that offered itself to the drivers of the commanders-in-chief of the Army, Navy and Air Force, or of some of the other dignitaries who were driven into the courtyard.

En route to the Great Parade at 11 a.m. there were the obvious security gaps that Hitler was well aware of. He travelled with five aides and bodyguards (including the driver) in an open touring car, followed by cars carrying more *Führer-Begleit-Kommando* men and the heads of the *Wehrmacht*. SS, SA, police and NSKK cordoned off the approach route. As Hitler said in May 1942 regarding such public appearances, it would be 'easy for some fanatic armed with a telescopic-sighted rifle to take a shot at me from some corner or other; any likely hole or corner, therefore, must be kept under careful observation.'[14] But there were limits to such observation. Despite considerable efforts, it was impossible to keep every building completely under surveillance along the route from the Wilhelmstrasse, Behrenstrasse, Charlottenstrasse, Französische Strasse, Werderstrasse, Schleusenbrücke, An der Stechbahn, Schlossfreiheit, and where Hitler reviewed the troops. Hitler rejected the search and occupation of every house, really a necessity if security was to be as thorough as possible, as too great an imposition on the populace. In the parade area, only LSSAH cordoned off the streets and pavements (security section VII, Berlinerstrasse from Charlottenburg Bridge to Knie) and behind the SS lines regular police had to look after the crowds. Hours before the parade, security forces had to take up their positions, some as early as 6 a.m. There were two reviewing stands opposite one another on Berlinerstrasse in front of the *Technische Hochschule* (Institute of Technology), between Knie and Charlottenburg Bridge.

Hitler had his place on the north side of the street, flanked by generals and admirals with their aides, by Ribbentrop, Göring, Brauchitsch, Raeder, Keitel behind him, and of course the inevitable black uniforms of some ten *Führer-Begleit-Kommando* officers immediately behind these dignitaries. On the opposite side, the reviewing stand was reserved for invited guests, including the diplomatic corps and the *Reich* Government. The police were instructed to make certain that the guests presented an orderly picture, and that aisles and stairways were kept open. But east and west of the reviewing stand opposite Hitler's stand, the picture was less than orderly. There were people standing on first and second-floor window-sills, on home-made scaffolding, and on a jungle of long and short ladders leaning against houses and trees.[15] Hitler was right: it could have been easy for someone with a telescopic-sighted rifle to shoot him from over there, although a conspicuously large number of those standing on window-sills and ladders and roofs were SS and policemen. Nevertheless, Hitler never knew how close he came to being shot at during one of those parades.

Colonel Mason-MacFarlane, the British Military Attaché in Berlin, lived at No. 1 Sophienstrasse, with a view to where Hitler usually reviewed the big parades in Berlin. He had long been convinced that Hitler's policies were leading to war. The German dictator, he maintained, would never stop blackmailing and raping countries right and left until the Powers put a stop to it.[16] After the occupation of Prague, even the ambassador, Sir Nevile Henderson, who had long thought that Hitler could be trusted, came round to the view that appeasement was not working. But Mason-MacFarlane was always a few steps ahead of the Ambassador, as the Chargé d'Affaires in the Embassy, Sir George Ogilvie-Forbes wrote to Mr. Strang on 29 March 1939: 'The Military Attaché here is in a very warlike mood and is anxious that we should declare war on Germany within the next three weeks! It was suggested to him privately that he should first express his views in writing.' This he did, and he advised strongly that war against Germany be brought about *now*, on two fronts at once, as this would guarantee victory—but no one could say how much longer conditions would be so favourable. It was generally assumed, of course, that the French Army was capable of offensive action, but that time was not on the side of the Western Powers as the German Army was improving its strength and performance with every month that passed.

Mason-MacFarlane's written suggestion was not adopted by the Foreign Office, and so he made another one, orally: 'In London . . . I had strongly urged that Hitler should be assassinated. My residence in Berlin was barely 100 yards from the saluting base of all the big *Fuehrer* reviews. All that was necessary was a good shot and a high-velocity rifle with telescopic sight and silencer. It could have been fired through my open bathroom window from a spot on the landing some 30 feet back from the window.' The din of music, marching and cheering would have drowned out the sound of the rifle shot so that it could not have been traced—even though the house was within the police cordon. This idea, too, was rejected in London.

It might have been difficult for an assassin in the crowd or from a building nearby to act, or for someone to get a good place in a house from which to shoot. But what if one of the many machine-gunners passing

12a.   Hitler in Berlin, on Unter den Linden, followed by Führer Escort, guests and entourage, 1 May 1939

12b.   Hitler in Berlin, on Unter den Linden, with Führer Escort, passing Soviet Embassy, 1 May 1939 (in the car, from left: Goebbels, Linge, Ley, Hitler, Kempka)

in review had suddenly turned his weapon on Hitler's stand and opened fire?

Ample opportunities also existed at the annual Party rallies in Nuremberg. A sharpshooter in one of the houses along the route through Nuremberg could have picked Hitler off in his open car. Although his bodyguards who followed him in several cars studied the crowds along the streets very intently and looked up at the upper-storey windows, they could not have protected him against a well-aimed shot from an attic window, nor perhaps against a bomb thrown from a window. Hitler himself once singled out the Nuremberg Party Rally as the event where he was exposed to the greatest degree of danger.

Every 8th and 9th of November throughout the 1930s, Hitler and his old fellow fighters of the 1923 *putsch* gathered for a commemoration and social evening in Munich's 'Bürgerbräu' Beer Hall at Rosenheimerplatz where Hitler had fired a shot at the ceiling to start a national revolution. Regularly occurring occasions were ideal for would-be assassins. Consequently such occasions required particularly thorough security measures.

On 8 November 1935 the coffins of the sixteen who were shot at the 'Feldherrnhalle' in 1923 were taken there again for a commemorative observance late in the night; earlier, at 7 p.m., the *Alte Kämpfer* (Old Fighters) had met and Hitler had addressed them; then the procession with the coffins had passed through Siegestor on its way to 'Feldherrnhalle' where they lay in state until the next day. During the night the new SS members were sworn in in Hitler's presence. On 9 November the historic March was repeated with as many of the original participants as possible, starting from the 'Bürgerbräu' Beer Hall at Rosenheimerplatz, across the Ludwigsbrücke, through Isartor and Tal, turning into Weinstrasse at Marienplatz, then into Perusastrasse, and finally passing through Residenzstrasse to 'Feldherrnhalle.' After some ceremonies, including the firing of sixteen shots, the coffins were taken to Königsplatz where they were finally laid to rest in two temples at the east side of the square. In later years, sixteen wreaths were laid at 'Feldherrnhalle' on the night before 9 November, and then taken along by the marchers on the next day to Königsplatz.

The Munich *Gauleiter's* office declared in 1936: 'The ceremonies of 8/9 November 1935, during which those who had fallen in 1923 have taken up Eternal Watch at Königlicher Platz, have created the basis for the "National Socialist Procession". Therefore, this year's ceremonies as well as those of all future years must be arranged exactly as in 1935.'[17] Thus anyone who bought one of the programmes sold in the street knew exactly what would take place, that year, next year and the year after that: the meeting at the 'Bürgerbräu' in the evening of 8 November, the swearing in of new SS men at 'Feldherrnhalle' during the night, the March to 'Feldherrnhalle' on 9 November, and its exact route and order: Julius Streicher, the Nuremberg *Gauleiter* and notorious Jew-baiter, marched in front of the Blood Standard which was followed by two ranks of the 'leadership group,' marching twelve or more abreast where the streets were wide enough. They included such redoubtable *Alte Kämpfer* and allies as Lieutenant-Colonel Kriebel, Max Amann, Alfred Rosenberg, Hermann Göring, Dr. Weber, Rudolf Hess, Heinrich Himmler, Hans Frank, Wilhelm Frick and others. Behind them there followed the *Alte Kämpfer* decorated with the Blood Order medal (for having participated in the original March), then those without it, then the *Reich* leaders of various sections and organisations of the NSDAP, *Gauleiter*, leaders with general rank in the SA, SS and NSKK, then newly-inducted Hitler Youth, then several companies of SA, NSKK, RAD and SS. The procession began at 12.10 p.m. and reached 'Feldherrnhalle' at 12.50 p.m. All along the route, pylons were placed on which oil was burning in basins; each pylon bore the name of one of the sixteen fallen comrades, and every time Hitler passed one, a caller sang out the name. This was accompanied by continuous drum rolls alternating with the 'Horst-Wessel' Song in slow march tempo. The entire length of the marching route was cordoned off by SA on both sides—SA not SS, uniforms dominated the scene. At 'Feldherrnhalle,' when the wreaths were placed, sixteen shots were fired in the air, there was more music, and then the procession went on to Königsplatz, preceded from 'Feldherrnhalle' onward by two companies of *Leibstandarte-SS 'Adolf Hitler.'* When all the thousands of uniformed marchers had taken their positions on Königsplatz, the scene of an early battle of the SA with political rivals, a shot was fired, the music ('Deutschland' Song from 'Feldherrnhalle' onwards) ceased, Hitler stepped forward and strode to a point between the two temples, then a second shot rang out, the flags were lowered, and the *Leibstandarte* band played Hanfstaengl's Funeral March. Then the sixteen names were called out again, and at each name the 12,000 Hitler Youth, boys and girls, and all the other formations, shouted 'Here!' After this, Hitler placed wreaths in the temples, Hess declared the Hitler Youth inducted into the Party, the SS watch marched up to the temples and took up positions, and finally, to the strains of the 'Horst-Wessel' Song, Hitler got into his car and rode off through the centre of the square. In 1936, all of this cost approximately 1,239,740 Reichsmarks, including oil for 276 pylons at 20 Reichsmarks a fill, 5,000 torches at 0.30 Reichsmarks apiece, and 40,000 Reichsmarks for unforeseen expenses.

In 1938, in the third year after the establishment of the official Nazi procession, a Swiss theology student, Maurice Bavaud, on vacation from a seminary in north western France, had come to Germany to assassinate the *Führer*. Hitler may have referred to Bavaud and his friends in his

remark about 'those fanatics who have been goaded to action by das-
tardly priests.'[18] Bavaud went to visit relatives in Baden-Baden, posing
as an ardent admirer of the *Führer*. His relatives included Leopold Gut-
terer, a high-ranking official in Goebbels' Propaganda Ministry, in
charge—of all things—of preparation of public and semi-public events
in which Hitler participated, such as the events of 8 and 9 November.
After a few days Bavaud left Baden-Baden and took a trip to Basle and
bought a pistol with ammunition, and then went to Berlin.

After scouting around in Berlin and Berchtesgaden for several days
for an opportunity to get near Hitler, pretending he was a newspaper
correspondent and an ardent admirer of the *Führer*, Bavaud met a Major
Deckert in a Berchtesgaden café. Major Deckert was most helpful when
he learned of Bavaud's heart's desire—to see the *Führer* in person. A personal interview was out of the question, Deckert said; the *Führer* was
so busy that he could not even see Dr. Lammers, Chief of the *Reich* Chancellery, who had been waiting for an interview for days. In any case,
the *Führer* was away from the 'Berghof' quite often during this time. He
took trips to Bratislava, Vienna and Nicolsburg in late October, and
to Munich and Nuremberg in the first days of November. But during
the commemorative observances in Munich on 8 and 9 November the
Führer would most likely be present; during the March, one might see
him at fairly close range from a certain café. It is of more than mild
interest from a security point of view that Major Deckert was Lammers'
security aide from at least 1936, currently working in the Berchtesgaden
branch of the *Reich* Chancellery while Hitler and Lammers were spending more time there than in Berlin.

Bavaud followed Deckert's advice, took a train to Munich, and went
about establishing himself at a point near the marchers from which he
might shoot Hitler with a pistol. He tried to obtain a ticket to one of
the reviewing stands, but everywhere, at the City Hall, at the Foreign
Press Office, at the 'Feldherrnhalle' Guard he was told that there were
no more tickets available. Finally, on 3 or 4 November, posing as a Swiss
journalist, he managed to get a complimentary ticket at the Office for
9 November. The ticket was for a seat on the Holy Ghost Church reviewing stand, a very useful spot for Bavaud's purpose, at the western end
of the street named Tal, just before the place where the March entered
Marienplatz through a narrow archway. Later it was discovered that
Bavaud was the only foreigner who had obtained such a ticket, and that
he was never asked for identification, not even when he came to take
his seat on 9 November. Bavaud obtained his ticket in violation of M.
Bormann's edict of 15 July 1938 that complimentary tickets for events
in which the *Führer* participated 'must be issued under the strictest controls and only to specially invited guests.' This breach of regulations is
the more remarkable in view of the shots fired by Herszel Grynszpan

at Legation Counsellor Ernst vom Rath in Paris on 7 November (Rath died soon afterwards). There were other reasons for tight security, such as the recent rape of Czechoslovakia; but security was, in fact, poor.

Bavaud first went off and bought some more ammunition for his pistol, and rented a boat at Ammer Lake near Herrsching, not far from Munich, where he practised shooting at small paper boats he launched from his boat; he also shot at targets fixed on trees in a forest near Pasing. Back in Munich, he bought a programme for the forthcoming ceremonies, determined the exact route of the March, and walked down its entire length to find the best spot. He finally settled on the reviewing stand to which he already held a ticket.

On the morning of 9 November he took up his seat so early that he managed to get into the first row. The loaded pistol was in his overcoat pocket. If he could not get a clear and close enough range from his position, he planned to leave his seat and run up to Hitler and shoot him as he was passing the reviewing stand. It turned out, however, as the leadership group approached, that the distance for an accurate pistol shot was too great, and the range was clear only for the few short moments when Streicher and the three men with the Blood Standard had come so close that they no longer covered Hitler in the centre of the first rank of the leadership group; at this point, Hitler was still rather far off for a pistol shot. Besides, as Bavaud told it later (an explanation that Hitler accepted), the SA men solidly lining the kerb in front of him unexpectedly obstructed his view with their arms raised for the Hitler salute as the *Führer's* group approached. When the distance between Hitler and Bavaud was shortest, it was impossible to shoot in any case because those marching on Hitler's left were in the way. This situation was worsened by the necessity for the marchers to form narrower ranks of no more than six or seven abreast so that they could pass through the archway after the Holy Ghost Church, and by the presence of three security men marching on each side of the leadership group and looking into the crowds very intently. One might have more easily dropped a grenade among the marchers from an upper-storey window at Marienplatz, or fired at them from such a vantage point; several assassins throwing bombs from the pavement might also have succeeded. But a man wedged in among the crowd in the first row of a reviewing stand, immediately behind the solid line of SA, had to expect to have his pistol knocked out of his hand before he could even begin to take aim. Even for a good shot the chances would have been poor. Bavaud, of course, was not a master marksman. The idea of running up to Hitler now proved equally impractical. Bavaud gave up this attempt when he saw how crowded the situation was. But he still hoped to kill Hitler.

He then used a 'letter', actually an empty envelope he claimed contained a letter of introduction to Hitler from the National-Radical

French Deputy, Pierre Taittinger, to try to obtain a personal interview. On 10 November he took a train to Berchtesgaden again, learned there that Hitler was not in the area, and returned to Munich. On 12 November he went to the Brown House, but was advised to try getting in touch with *Reich* Chancellery offices. Hitler had meanwhile returned to Berchtesgaden, and Bavaud followed him again. After some more futile efforts, however, he ran out of funds and got on a train headed for the French border. He was arrested in Augsburg, having been discovered without a valid ticket. The gun was found on him, and gradually the *Gestapo* got his story from him. He was tried by the People's Court in December 1939, sentenced to death, and beheaded in 1941 (after Swiss efforts to save his life had collapsed).

In 1939 there were many reasons for Hitler not to participate in a March: in war it was not wise to expose an essential leadership group to a situation that might be exploited by enemy agents or by someone trying to avenge the occupation of his homeland; and there were good reasons for Hitler wanting to be in Berlin on 9 November, such as decisions about the planned Western Offensive. Maurice Bavaud's assassination attempt, of which Hitler was well aware, may have contributed to the decision.[19] At any rate, there was no March in 1939. Hitler merely planned to drive to 'Feldherrnhalle' and to Königsplatz on 9 November to lay wreaths.

Hitler certainly had no idea that on the eve of Maurice Bavaud's attempt to shoot him, another would-be assassin reconnoitred the opportunities for an attack at the 'Bürgerbräu' Beer Hall. On the following day, this man watched the same March during which Bavaud wanted to make his attack, but found the situation unfavourable. He was Georg Elser, an unusually able Swabian cabinet-maker with Communist sympathies, who believed that the workers had been deceived by Hitler, and that the dictator's policy had led to war and must be halted.

After the Beer Hall gathering of 8 November 1938 was over, Elser visited the place and found that anyone could come and go freely when it was open for business. He decided to prepare a bomb that could be installed in the pillar in front of which the podium was set up from which Hitler always delivered his address.[20] The collapse of this pillar alone would bring down parts of the ceiling and the gallery on to the Party élite gathered below; the force of the explosion would do the rest. In the months following, Elser systematically stole explosives at a firm in Heidenheim where he worked, and then some more from a quarry near Königsbronn. If stealing explosives had been easy, buying a box of rifle ammunition was even easier; Elser simply walked into a rod-and-gun shop and made the purchase, no questions were asked. During Easter week in 1939 he paid a visit to the Beer Hall to take the measurements of the pillar and to draw a sketch of the hollow he had to prepare for his bomb. He experimented with mechanisms to detonate an explosive charge without a fuse, and he learned to pre-time it exactly. In August he moved to Munich and started on a series of thirty to thirty-five nights during which he managed to hide in the Beer Hall after closing time. In the first three nights he sawed out part of the wood-panelling that covered the column, just above the floor level of the gallery, and made it into a door that could be removed and reinstalled quickly. Many nights followed in which bricks and cement were removed little by little. Elser always gathered up all the debris in a sack attached to the growing hollow and carried it out of the building during the busy noon hour of the day following a night's work. He even lined the finished hollow with steel plate and cork to protect the timing mechanism of the bomb against nails that might be driven into the woodwork when decorations were put up in the banquet hall below, and also to try to prevent the discovery of the hollow space in case security men tapped on the pillar in search of suspicious things. He was a good judge of clock movements as he had been buying them for years to build his own beautifully handmade cases for them, and he obtained the best he could find, known as Westminster movements. He would not rely on only one of them; he installed two in the pillar. He set the two movements to release, by means of two independent mechanisms, three striker pins that would simultaneously hit three detonator caps setting off three booster charges which finally ignited the mass of the explosive. In the night of 1 to 2 November Elser installed his bomb—without the clocks—and the explosive in the pillar. On 3 and 4 November he intended to install the clock mechanisms; but one night he found a door closed that he had expected to use, and on the next night he found the space in the pillar too small for the boxes with the clocks. He had to take them back again to make alterations. On 5 November, a Sunday, he came again, with the modified boxes, used the main entrance and bought a ticket for a dance that was in progress, went up to the gallery, and watched the proceedings until people started to leave. He went into hiding until everything was quiet, then worked for about six hours to install and set the clocks. With some pride he recounted during his interrogation, after the attack and his arrest, that he had solved the problem of setting the time for the explosion three days in advance with a margin of error of no more than fifteen minutes. The clocks were set for 9.20 p.m., three days later. He left Munich on the morning of 6 November for Stuttgart, but returned to Munich on 7 November to double-check his work in the Beer Hall, spending one last night there in hiding, again undetected by anyone. There had never been anyone to try and keep track of people who went in.

One marvels at the ease with which Elser was able to work. The explanation is bizarre from a security point of view. In November 1936 there had been a dispute between Christian Weber and the Munich President of Police Freiherr von Eberstein as to who was responsible for the *Führer's* security in the Beer Hall. Hitler had decided: 'Here in this gathering, I am protected by my Old Fighters led by Christian Weber; police responsibility ends at the entrances.' This was confirmed specifically for the 1939 gathering in the programme prepared by the Munich *Gauleiter's* office: 'Overall responsibility for the event in the "Bürgerbräukeller," for receiving the *Führer* and the guests of honour, for control of participants, for security inside, and for seating arrangements: *SS-Brigadeführer* Weber.' Outside the building SS uniforms were much in evidence where pavements and approach routes were cordoned off, but inside, systematic security measures of any kind were lacking. The building was not searched in the days before 8 November, as the Kroll Opera in Berlin had been before the festivities of 30 January at least from 1937 on, nor was it patrolled the night before.

Beginning in August, Elser managed to spend over thirty nights in the Beer Hall. He usually came about 8 p.m. and ordered a meal, then wandered up to the gallery towards 10 p.m., and waited in hiding until the place was closed and all had become quiet. Then he would work until 2 or 3 a.m., take a nap until opening time in the morning, and casually wander out through the back door, across the brewery yards behind the building. He was seen sometimes, but never stopped or questioned. Elser was a small man, looking inconspicuous; the building with its two entrances was used by many people as if it were an alley between two parallel streets. Elser was caught after closing time at least once, but the manager let him go. Elser had made friends with some of the Beer Hall employees, and perhaps with the manager. Once in a while, someone unlocked a door during the night, listened or wandered about for a few moments, then locked the door again and went away. Elser never tried to see who the person was, but assumed it was someone giving the room a superficial check. Only on the day of the gathering, on 8 November, a criminal-police officer came in to look the room over. He was an *Alter Kämpfer*, Party member from 1920, and *Stosstrupp Hitler* veteran, Josef Gerum by name, who had been with the Munich *Gestapo* until summer 1939, when he had volunteered for army service. On 8 November he happened to be in Munich on furlough. Security was thus still in the hands of the Party rather than the RSD, the local police, or the LSSAH. Gerum was merely told to take over 'security in the "Bürgerbräukeller" during the Hitler speech.' As SS officers, both Weber and Gerum had to be aware of the various security directives issued during the last six years. One cannot therefore avoid the conclusion that the Munich authorities were grossly negligent in their handling of security at the 'Bürgerbräukeller.' In a speech in June 1942, *Gestapo* Chief *SS-Gruppenführer* Heinrich Müller complained of difficulties encountered on earlier occasions when the Party had insisted on the exclusive right to organise security and refused to let in any police officials; after the 1939 assassination attempt, he added, this had been changed fundamentally.

Elser's ultimate failure to kill Hitler has given rise to speculation about a plot behind the plot, a publicity stunt, even an SS plot to kill the *Führer*. Hitler himself contributed to the chorus of those who declared it impossible that Elser had acted alone when Himmler reported just that. Hitler remarked that he was certain the British Secret Service were behind the attempt. This seemed a plausible version to some people after the kidnapping by *Gestapo* agents of two British spies, Major R. H. Stevens and Captain S. Payne Best, on the Dutch border near Venlo on 9 November. But Elser always claimed he acted alone, and all the known facts show that he could and most likely did. On the other hand, it is inconceivable that Hitler would endanger his life and stake it on the functioning of some clockwork mechanism set by someone else, merely to bring off a publicity stunt. The stories about plots are understandable, however. A number of people wished to do away with Hitler; there were radicals in the Resistance, and the Army leadership firmly believed that a German attack in the West would lead to Germany's defeat. It was, after all, the Chief of the General Staff himself, General Halder, who had developed the habit of going to interviews with Hitler with a loaded pistol in his pocket, and with the intention of shooting him.[21] Evidence to connect such Resistance circles with Elser, however, has never surfaced.

The course of events in the 'Bürgerbräukeller' was something like this: by 6 p.m. on 8 November the Beer Hall was jammed to capacity; the Party leaders and 3,000 *Alte Kämpfer* were awaiting their *Führer*. Sepp Dietrich was there with Kriebel, Rosenberg, Bouhler, Amann, Himmler, Hans Frank, Goebbels, Dr. Weber, Streicher and Ribbentrop. Hardly any SS uniforms were noticeable, even Julius Schaub was wearing a Party uniform. Then, shortly after 8 p.m., the band struck up the Badenweiler March, the Blood Standard was carried in, the *Führer* came, and exuberant cheers arose among the three thousand. Hitler shook some hands, went to the rostrum, made his speech, concluded his remarks and walked out at 9.07 p.m. Hardly had the *Alte Kämpfer* settled back down with their beers when Elser's bomb went off mightily at 9.20 p.m., as it had been set to do, causing chaos and destruction throughout the Beer Hall. It killed six *Alte Kämpfer* and a waitress outright, and another *Alter Kämpfer* died afterwards in hospital; over sixty persons were injured, sixteen seriously.[22]

At the time of the explosion, Hitler was on his way to the railway station. He had spoken briefly compared to previous occasions, and he had begun somewhat earlier than usual, at 8.10 p.m., five minutes earlier

13a. Hitler speaking at 'Bürgerbräukeller,' Munich, 8 November 1939; behind him Jakob Grimminger, Bearer of the Blood Standard of 1923; behind the swastika flag, the pillar with Georg Elser's time-bomb ticking in it

13b. 'Bürgerbräukeller,' Munich, after explosion of Elser's time-bomb; the rostrum was in the centre

than the schedule provided for 1939. 'Important government affairs' were the official explanation for his early departure, and for his failure to take part in the March and other events on 9 November.

Hitler wanted to be back in Berlin by the morning of 9 November. As this was a time when fog frequently shut down the airfields, Baur could not guarantee a flight for the morning of 9 November; Hitler therefore decided to go back to Berlin in his *Führersonderzug* which was scheduled to leave at 9.31 p.m.[23] Ten minutes were not sufficient time to get from the Beer Hall to the station by car unless the streets were cleared entirely; he had to leave at least fifteen to twenty minutes before departure time.

Until a day before the actual event, Hitler had not planned to come at all. Instead of his usual speech, Hess was to have given a radio address. Only on 7 November, perhaps as late as 8 November, Hitler decided to go to Munich after all.[24] He flew to Munich on 8 November. A March was not planned for this year, perhaps for security reasons. But no one had reckoned with an assassin who worked for a whole year, completely alone, without ever telling anyone what he was up to, as patiently and as skilfully as Elser. That is why he almost succeeded. It is also clear why he failed. Hitler's behaviour in the days before 8 November and on 8 November was, at least in part, security-motivated. The very asset that helped to bring Elser so near to success, his isolation and silence, also prevented him from learning anything about changes in Hitler's plans. Even if he had known of them he could hardly have gone back into the Beer Hall to reset the clocks.

Elser was arrested as he tried to cross into Switzerland on the evening of 8 November. Two customs officers were listening to Hitler's speech over the radio when they noticed the suspiciously-behaving person near the border fence, and they went out and arrested him. There was so much disbelief about Elser's story, however, that the *Gestapo* ordered him to build his bomb once again. He did so in a very short time, and the contraption was used for instructional purposes in the RSHA (SS Central Security Office). Elser was kept in Dachau Concentration Camp, on Hitler's orders, possibly for a later trial at which the machinations of the British Secret Service were to be exposed, possibly because of his admirable abilities, perhaps merely because no decision to do otherwise could be obtained from Hitler. He was finally killed by order of Heinrich Müller, who had obtained a ruling from Hitler through Himmler, in April 1945.[25]

Elser's assassination attempt made a general overhaul of security precautions inevitable. It was completed by the beginning of March 1940. The new regulations were sent from the office of the *Chef der Sicherheitspolizei und des SD* (Chief of Security Police and Security Service), signed by Heydrich, the Chief of SD, to Section Chiefs of the RSHA, to the

Chief of Regular Police, to the Higher SS and Police Leaders, to the Inspectors of Security Police and SD, to the Criminal Police Directorates, to Martin Bormann, to Brückner and to Rattenhuber.[26]

This sixty-page directive on 'security measures for the protection of leading persons of State and Party' set up a protection service section headed by *SS-Sturmbannführer* Franz Schulz in the RSHA.

Beyond the tightening-up of security that was the main purpose of the new directives, they contributed to closer coordination of the work of the RSD, and that of the RSHA and its agencies in general, and of the *Gestapo* in particular. Rattenhuber had resisted such coordination in 1935, when his organisation was founded in the form in which it operated from then on, though the *Gestapo* continued to try to adhere to the principle of close cooperation and exchange of all relevant information.

But the Elser incident had shown that a much more far-flung organisation was necessary if there was to be any hope of preventing such attacks in the future.

Now Heydrich declared the supreme task within the overall activities of the RSHA to be 'all measures for the prevention of assassination attempts against leading personalities of the *Reich* and of foreign states when they are on German soil.' Combating all enemies of the State was the general purpose of the RSHA, the letter stated, and *Reich* and foreign statesmen had to be protected; but: 'Here the protection of the *Führer* precedes *every* other task.' And: 'In every case the basic assumption must be that any assassination plan, no matter how well organised, will founder on the meticulously and minutely prepared security measures.' For this purpose a special protection agency was being set up within the Security Police (comprising criminal police and *Gestapo*) and the SD of the SS, which in turn were centrally controlled and directed from RSHA. This was the new hierarchical structure: 1. A sub-section for protection service was created in *Amt IV (Gestapo)* of RSHA as *Ref. IV A 5a*. The sub-section was headed by *SS-Sturmbannführer* and Criminal Police Director Franz Schulz. His office was declared the central coordinating agency for all security-police measures of protection for Hitler and other statesmen, and the central collection-point for all information on assassination plans. 2. In all regional *Gestapo* head offices an office for protection matters was installed, and also in some district *Gestapo* offices, subordinated to the regional *Gestapo* head offices.

The security service bureaux in the regional and local *Gestapo* offices in a specified list of cities where Hitler frequently appeared at public events were charged, in addition to investigating reports of planned attacks and putting on certain security measures as required, with the *constant* surveillance of the sites of Hitler's public or semi-public appearances. On the list, among other places, were Berlin as the seat of the Government; Munich as the capital of the Movement where Hitler had an apartment and where the Beer Hall *putsch* was commemorated each year; Nuremberg as the city of the *Reich* Party Rallies; Weimar as the city of the first national Party Convention (1926) and of the National Theatre. The office chiefs of the protection-service sub-sections at these places were to do nothing but organise the protection of the *Führer*; they were not to be given any other work, nor could they be transferred to another branch office or given other assignments within their own regional or local office without permission from Heydrich. Where Hitler appeared rarely and irregularly, however, protection-service chiefs could be allowed to combine with their position that of head of the intelligence section within their *Gestapo* office. In all cases, the security office chiefs' immediate superior was the head of their *Gestapo* office. The protection-service office chief also had to take orders from the Higher SS and Police Leader and Inspector of Security Police and SD, who could overrule the regional and local *Gestapo* officials in security matters. Himmler and Heydrich could order exceptional measures, for example if security operations extended over more than one region. They could then set up a security staff which carried overall responsibility while implementation in detail was still in the hands of regional or local authorities. For events in which Hitler, Göring or the *Führer's* Deputy participated, overall direction belonged to the Higher SS and Police Leader in every case. For Berlin, Heydrich reserved overall direction for himself, and also for events outside Berlin if he planned to be present and expressly assumed overall direction.

The *Gestapo* were given more authority in security matters than they had had before, Party functionaries had little say now, and the entire security network was more closely integrated and centrally controlled than before. But Heydrich's authority, or that of the RSHA, never extended over the *Führer's* personal bodyguards, the RSD and the *SS-Begleit-Kommando*. On the contrary, Heydrich stated in his covering letter that: 'The RSD (*SS-Standartenführer* Rattenhuber, Chief) is the proper authority and responsible for the immediate and personal protection of the *Führer* and of those persons who are given a bodyguard. This authority is unalterable on *all* drives, trips, mass rallies, etc. Furthermore, the RSD is the proper authority and responsible for security measures in the *Reich* Chancellery, in the *Führer's* private residence, and on the Obersalzberg. For all other security measures in the wider environs of these persons, including routes of approach and departure, the *Gestapo* is the proper authority and responsible. The wishes of the RSD in actual cases are to be accommodated, as I require generally that all regional and district State Police offices cooperate with the RSD intensively and without friction. The Chief of RSD has the right to issue directives for carrying out security measures in the immediate environs of the *Führer*. He also bears personal responsibility for this.'

The sixty pages of specific security directives contain little that was radically new. Most of the instructions were a restatement and re-emphasis of long-standing requirements. But they do represent an attempt at putting order into precautionary measures whose necessity had become so painfully apparent through the Beer Hall blast—whether the British Secret Service had pulled the strings behind the scenes or not; and they gave more precision and clarity to older directives such as the ones written into the SS cordoning-off instructions referred to above.

Security precautions were categorised into three main groups. Firstly, a differentiation was made between periodically recurring public events, public events not periodically scheduled, and state visits. The directives had no bearing on security at Hitler's residences or headquarters, nor on his immediate protection during trips except in the narrower vicinity of the site of a public event. Secondly, the directives differentiated between stages of security precautions. General advance precautions had to be in effect the whole year round; specific advance precautions were related to the prospective site of the event, and they were to begin at least three months in advance of the event. In the last stage of prepara-tions, all precautions were reviewed, and security measures for the dura-tion of the event were started; finally, post-event security went into effect. Thirdly, the directives differentiated between three rings of security around the site of the event: a general security zone of the wider environment of the site; a narrower security radius of 1 to 500 metres, depending on local conditions (larger, for instance, in cases of buildings farther away than 500 metres but with a clear field of vision to the site), which included the localities of the event as well as paths of approach and departure for the persons specially protected; and the inner security zone immediately around the site. Fourthly, the forces providing security were structured into a staff led by the regional or local *Gestapo* chief to deal with overall security not under Rattenhuber's immediate control; a command staff if the localities to be protected were very sprawling, or if there were several places at a distance from each other at which parts of the event took place successively; command posts; and task forces with section commando squads (for specific parts of the approach and departure routes), special-task commando squads (for security in rooms, at danger points, overpasses and underpasses, for searches and occupa-tion of houses, identity and admission card checks, precautionary investi-gations and occupation of hotels, disreputable buildings, hiding places, restaurants and cafés, construction sites, subway entrances, sewage in-stallations, etc.) and reserve commando squads. Security staffs had to be formed for officially-announced, large mass events, and they had to be subordinated either to the *SS-Reich* Leader immediately (for the largest events), or to one of three offices: the *SS-Hauptamt* (SS Head

Office), the Head Office of Regular Police, or the RSHA (*Reich* Security Head Office). Staffs were enjoined to have available all appropriate map material, telephone numbers and names for all security men operating in their sections, and to maintain liaison with others at all levels, from regional staffs down to men on the line who had to know the colleagues positioned next to them, by sight at least. While the protected event was in progress, men on the line had to maintain sight-contact. These security forces, as opposed to SS or SA formations who might be used to cordon off areas, would normally be wearing civilian clothes, unless this made them more conspicuous in their environment than uniforms. Tags or pins by which they might have recognised each other were taboo. The directive stressed that security had to be inconspicuous to be effective, and that any mass deployment of security forces should be avoided if possible; it was unnecessary if advance measures were carried out thoroughly. Security men were told not to make themselves conspicuous by standing straighter than anyone else, by interfering in insignificant incidents, by being overly officious, or by trying to do the job of the uniformed regular police. On the other hand, inconspicuousness must not be overdone. If special-task squads had to rendezvous, this should not be done so inconspicuously that group leaders could not find the men of their groups.

Provision had to be made in case telephone communication broke down or was unavailable. This was most likely to occur in cases of 'disturbance,' precisely the moment when good communications were needed most. Sufficient numbers of couriers with cars and motorcycles had to be kept in readiness against such a contingency. This in turn required that overall security staff and command staffs be located outside the security zones and away from areas where masses of people were expected to gather. Specialists, technicians, chemists, explosives experts, etc., were to be assigned to special-task squads as needed. Fully-motorised reserve commando squads were at the disposal of the command staffs. Numbers of required forces must be calculated not merely according to numbers of participants and crowds but according to danger points that had to be covered. Only the very best men were to be used, even in seemingly not very dangerous places. All or most of the men had to carry pistols.

All measures had to be completely and thoroughly reviewed for every individual event, whether recurring or non-recurring. In every single case it had to be determined whether they could be carried out, and whether they appeared useful, appropriate and sufficient. The maxim was: 'Every precaution that becomes habitual routine loses its value.' Routine measures applied unthinkingly simply because they had been used before might well prove inadequate. Therefore none of the precautions must be set up before a thorough investigation was made of the localities involved. Many of these instructions seem self-evident. But it was also clear that guidance and orders were necessary where performance had failed to reach the mark, and where officials found it unsafe to act without orders. So they were told to issue clear and complete instructions for every individual event; to begin precautions early so that hasty measures would not endanger the operation; to avoid conspicuousness and fatigue by not mounting security operations too early.

For each event, detailed written secret orders had to be prepared under the direction of regional or local security officers at least forty-eight hours in advance, and copies had to go to RSHA, to the Higher SS and Police Leader, to the Inspector of Security Police and SD, to the Inspector of Regular Police, to the regional or local SD Section, and to the RSD.

General advance measures included intelligence gathering aimed at all 'circles of enemies' inside and outside Germany, to be intensified when the date for an event approached. All reports of planned sabotage, violence or attacks against the protected persons had to be transmitted at once to the RSHA and to the local or regional *Gestapo* office concerned, and all reports, even seemingly insignificant and unimportant ones, even ludicrous ones, had to be followed up thoroughly. An 'A-file' had to be kept constantly up-to-date on all 'enemies of the State' living in the wider or immediate vicinity of places that must be protected. Security forces were to use the files kept in criminal-police offices on the mentally ill who were at large, on professional criminals, on a-social elements and on all foreigners. Another file had to contain details on *all* persons who lived or worked within 500 metres of the site of regularly-recurring events, who had storage areas there or garages or offices, or who made deliveries there. All of these had to be subjected to security checks of 'the most thorough' kind based on political, criminal and moral criteria. At least once every year, all these investigations must be repeated. Every new arrival within the security radius, every departure, must be recorded. Persons judged 'unreliable' must be removed from within the security radius under appropriate pretexts, and, if this was not feasible in individual cases for serious reasons, they must be marked for preventive action during the security operation. Preventive arrests of suspicious characters, whether resident or transient, were authorised; further instructions had to be requested in such cases from RSHA Section IV (*Gestapo*) in Berlin. At least three months in advance of regularly-recurring events, checks on foreigners and all other persons entering or leaving Germany had to be intensified at all border points, airports, seaports, garages, boarding houses and tenement houses, disreputable hotels, restaurants, bars, notorious hideouts of criminals, railways, highways, and especially in the vicinity of protected sites. All persons crossing the border had to be recorded and subjected to thorough checks under pretext of customs and currency regulations. Those under any suspicion had to be announced to *Gestapo* offices at their place of destination so that they might be kept under surveillance. Up-to-date files of persons suspected of planning sabotage or other violence could be obtained from the RSHA when needed. Suspicious newspaper advertisements also had to be looked into.

Other preparatory steps included: compilation of files of politically and generally reliable specialists such as physicians, engineers, chemists, building specialists, explosives and gas experts, food experts, locksmiths, masons, plumbers, chimneysweeps, watchmakers, divers, scaffold builders; procurement of up-to-date maps showing sensitive areas to a scale of 1 : 25,000 including precise ground-plans of all appropriate buildings with recent modifications, with sewage systems and other sanitary installations. These materials and files had to be locally available at all times, they were not to be gathered only in the last weeks before a coming event. Danger points, such as corners, high buildings offering good shooting range, factory areas with hiding places, had to be marked in advance in the maps in red or bold black ink. House owners were required to provide to the *Gestapo* all relevant information on changes in buildings, fences, walls, gates, etc., in the sensitive neighbourhoods. When changes were made at a site of an event, such as the Berlin Sports Palace, or the Munich 'Bürgerbräu' Beer Hall, the architect had to get in touch with the *Gestapo*, and the workmen were investigated as to their political reliability.

Locally deployed security forces had to be able to enter any house within the security radius at any time to investigate. They had to have in their possession a collection of keys to buildings, basements and attics, garages and storage areas, and to the object of the security measures, such as the 'Bürgerbräu' Beer Hall. Buildings within the security radius, as well as basements, empty rooms, and garages, had to be kept locked and under observation, either by owners, inhabitants, factory security personnel, or police officers. Owners and building superintendents were held responsible for any untoward activities during security operations, such as unauthorised strangers entering buildings and sites. They had to make sure that nothing could be thrown from balconies, that only authorised persons gained admittance, and that no objects usable as missiles, or other dangerous things, were hidden by decorations and flags.

Sites of recurring events had to be subjected to controls at least once per month on an average, but at irregular intervals, and with the assistance of appropriate experts able to detect unauthorised changes and signs of attempts to install hidden explosive devices. Frequent spot checks had to be made of traffic in and out of the radius, new arrivals were to be put under constant surveillance for a time after their first appearance, criminal records (if any) of persons present within the radius had to be updated every year, suspicious foreign or domestic trips by these people had to be looked into, persons in the A-file had to be observed, tabs had to be kept on weapons and ammunition purchases, on thefts of weapons and explosives, and permanent contacts with informers within the radius (local policemen, Party members, nightwatchmen, deliverymen, etc.) had to be established. In short: 'All activity within the security radius must be kept up with, investigated and checked by constant, inconspicuous but energetic and appropriate surveillance. Nothing must be allowed to occur within the security radius that will not at the same time, at the latest, become known to the respective security office.'

A complete (secret) review of all advance security measures was required in the period beginning four weeks before an event, and ending one week before it. Preferably, the site of the coming event was to be kept closed to the public during this 'renewed examination of the site in every regard with a thoroughness that could not be surpassed.' It extended to 'basements, attics, side- and secondary rooms of all sorts, sewage systems, sanitary installations, floors, walls, pillars, ceilings, furniture and decorations, platforms and stands or other temporary structures, cables, transformer stations, underpasses, overpasses, lampposts, monuments, advertisement pillars, sandboxes, garages, telephone booths, mailboxes, scaffolding, above-ground electric power lines, grandstands, pylons, flagpoles, etc., etc., and all applicable achievements of science and technology are to be employed, such as listening, sensing, and screening devices, spotlights, etc. Furthermore, explosives experts must be called in to indicate on the basis of their experience those spots especially suited for assassination attempts with explosives.'

Needless to say, even tighter surveillance was ordered for the last few days and hours before the event. No one could now be allowed into the security radius or the site without a pass issued or approved by the *Gestapo*, and all passes had to be collected again after the event. Rooms and buildings that could not be locked up securely had to be watched constantly until after the event. Deliveries and packages arriving within the security radius during the last weeks must be examined by *Gestapo* officials. Any preparatory work still required in the last days, such as the setting up of stands, was subject to uninterrupted supervision by them. 'In particular, hollow places that will be closed in the course of such work must be very thoroughly examined before they are closed, and must be watched constantly afterwards.'

From the time of the final review until the event was over, hotels and boarding houses earmarked during preparatory measures had to be kept 'inconspicuously occupied if they appeared particularly suspicious or if they had windows facing the site of the event.' All automobile traffic in the security zone and around the site was to be closely and constantly observed by regular police. If another event took place at the protected site between the time of the general review and the specially-protected event, for example a dance in the 'Bürgerbräu' Beer Hall, a new general review had to be mounted to make sure nothing had changed; it was expressly prohibited to combine two reviews, or to have the main security check of the site only a short time before the sensitive event. Any prophylactic arrests had to be made in this final stage, though arrests were restricted to the absolutely necessary minimum from a security point of view; if it was not possible to remove a suspected person entirely from society this side of gaol walls and concentration-camp fences, it was usually better in cases of recurring events not to arrest him, lest he go into hiding before the next time and the more effectively conceal from the authorities his dark intentions—if any. *Gestapo* forces were required to take part in admission controls, too, on the maxim that the most superb security precautions are worthless if they are not coupled with the most meticulous admission checks. No persons in 'preventive custody' in the vicinity (in police custody, judicial custody or in a concentration camp) might be released now, except by special permission of RSHA. Any convicts, mentally disturbed persons or alcoholics who were released shortly before the critical time had to be put under surveillance.

The directives concluded with general remarks. The longer in advance a date for an event was known to the public—which of course applied to all regularly recurring ones, but also to a number of others that were announced in advance—the more intensive security measures had to be. On the other hand, when events or the participation of the prominent persons were intentionally scheduled only at a very late time, security preparations had to be limited to what was absolutely necessary so that the purpose of the late announcement was not defeated: 'This more or less unexpected participation of leading personalities in events constituted the most effective protection.' Still, no feasible precautions must be neglected. The history of crimes showed 'that assassins take into account every circumstance and every accidental occurrence. Thus it must not surprise anyone that such elements plan assassination attempts even for events at which prominent persons may be expected to appear only at the last minute.'

After the event, security must not be relaxed, either, especially in places of regularly-recurring events: 'It has been found repeatedly that carefully-planning assassins have used the time after an event when the public were allowed free "inspection" of the site to search out the possibilities.' Elser had done this in 1938. Finally, the reader of the directives was cautioned not merely to read them and put them aside, but to refer to them constantly and to make them the basis of uninterrupted training and practice. 'It is precisely that which seems trivial in these directives which is usually considered so trivial that it is overlooked or forgotten.'

On 30 May 1942 Hitler spoke at Berlin's Sports Palace before 10,000 officer candidates, their instructors, and invited guests, as he had done only weeks earlier on 14 February. On both occasions he came in his Special from 'Wolfschanze' HQ in East Prussia, and returned after the speech. An assassination attack had been made, as recently as 27 May, upon *SS-Obergruppenführer* Reinhard Heydrich, Chief of Security Police and Deputy Protector for Bohemia and Moravia, on his way to work. He had been riding in an open car, and a bomb thrown under his car had injured him fatally; he died on 4 June. The assassin had at first tried to shoot Heydrich, and the victim and his chauffeur were drawing their guns to shoot down the assailant, but an associate then hurled the bomb. The attack on Heydrich was referred to in the specific security directives for Hitler's unannounced semi-public appearance on 30 May 1942, stressing the need for tight security. The attack on Heydrich and an act of sabotage committed against an exhibition called 'The Soviet Paradise' showed, said the directives, that the terrorist instructions of the Soviet and British intelligence services were being heeded; 'obviously the terrorists aimed to kill the *Führer* because he was the guarantor of German victory.'[27]

Secrecy was fundamental: 'The event and the security measures are strictly secret.' It was arranged with *Wehrmacht* authorities to prohibit the use of public telephones in the Sports Palace by members of the audience, and to make certain that no one left the building before the event was over. Sentries were posted at all telephone booths during the day of the speech.

Considering, however, that the event was secret and that crowds were thus not likely to gather, security precautions were truly massive. On the whole, Heydrich's 1940 regulations were applied. But many measures designed for public events made known in advance were now applied to an event that could hardly be known to the population at large, at least as far as Hitler's own participation was concerned. These security measures were apt to arouse curiosity and attention, thus making necessary more extensive measures which were, however, not taken, so that those actually taken rendered *themselves* ineffective, or partially ineffective.

Some 450 criminal police, *Gestapo* and regular policemen were deployed to provide security, and to watch every possible source of danger, every garden and park, construction site, storage area, subway and elevated railway installations, gateways, underpasses, hollow spaces of any kind, air shafts, temporary structures such as scaffolding, houses with balconies and all houses from which one had a far-ranging view over the approach and departure routes, mailboxes, vending machines, hydrants, fire-extinguishers 'in the immediate danger area.' In the street, during the period of deployment of security forces, spectators had to be observed from behind, and at the same time the streets, pavements and house-fronts on the opposite side had to be watched. All security men had to be in 'eye-contact' with at least two of their comrades, but they were forbidden to stand together. Tossing of flowers and of any other objects had to be prevented. No one was allowed to climb upon scaffolding, monuments, masts, trees, fences, traffic signs, vehicles, or other things elevating him above ground-level. It had to be seen to most strictly that shortly before or during the passage of 'the persons to be protected' no suitcases, packages, bags or other containers were deposited anywhere along the route or inside the Sports Palace. If any such objects turned up, they must be carefully examined, and removed from the security zone; whoever had brought them must be arrested or searched for immediately. All vehicles parked along the route had to be checked as to whether they contained any suspicious persons or objects. 'Jews and other elements open to suspicion' were to be ordered out of the security area, and if need be they had to be taken into custody for the duration of the security measures.

If all this was done, it could not fail to arouse curiosity and attention amongst the population. The effort at secrecy became questionable if policemen, in plain clothes or in uniform, examined all cars parked along the route, opened hoods and luggage compartments, searched houses; and if they started arresting people and ordering them out of the area. Other activities connected with the event, too, could attract attention: officially authorised photographers were expected to be there; certain cafés and restaurants had to be occupied by police officials 'especially on the upper storeys,' and patrons of the cafés and restaurants had to be observed inconspicuously; empty buildings (apparently also a euphemism for ruins) were to be patrolled thoroughly and 'kept free of any persons on the street side while the *Führer* is passing by;' the balcony of 'Café Telchow' which had a good view to Potsdamerstrasse and Potsdamerplatz was occupied by two policemen; sand boxes along the streets (for use in air raids, against incendiary bombs) were put under surveillance, likewise piles of construction materials; a policeman was posted at the public toilet at Bülow- and Potsdamerstrasse; sewers and cable tunnels had to be checked for explosives, and afterwards a detail of nine *Gestapo* officers guarded the sewers and tunnels all along the route; at Potsdam Bridge all vessels nearby were checked out.

No effort was spared in the Sports Palace to make sure that unauthorised persons did not gain admittance, and that explosives could not be planted. From 8 a.m. on 26 May 1942, forty-eight police officers were posted in the Palace; sixteen constantly patrolled it, day and night, with night pistols for the night shift. One officer constantly patrolled the basement, another the attic, and still another was always stationed on the roof. One officer in the entrance hall had to check all persons entering and leaving the building in the four days before the speech; another at the door leading inside checked them again. All those helping with preparations had been given security checks, and only 'unobjectionable persons' were admitted. The other officers had to keep workmen and everyone else under close observation. After completion of preparations, all workmen had to leave the building, and the premises were searched 'for any objects that might have been left behind.'

From 7 a.m. on 30 May 1942, eighty officers were in the building, about half of them in uniform. 'This detail conducts a final general review, occupies all danger points, surveys all work still necessary, and observes all personnel.' The outside and the grounds around the building were patrolled twenty-four hours a day, in the last days before the speech, by patrols with police dogs. 'These patrols have to prevent unauthorised entry by persons climbing the outer walls.' From 8 a.m. on, the audience were being admitted, and the *Wehrmacht's* entrance controls were assisted by police officers in uniform. Five criminal-police officers in plain clothes had to patrol the attic constantly, as well as its entrance and the light switches located there. Ten officers were stationed on the roof of the building in order to watch the roof itself, and also the roofs, windows and balconies of houses around the Sports Palace. It is not clear what they could have done if someone with a telescopic-sighted rifle had taken aim from behind a gauze curtain at such a window; and there is no mention of their being armed with anything other than ordinary pistols, hardly weapons with which they could have intervened effectively from a rooftop and at a considerable distance. But their presence alone could have discouraged many a would-be assassin. Thirteen officers patrolled the upper levels of the Sports Palace audience areas which were not being used in this event, and they had to prevent all other persons from going there; two of them were instructed to watch the audience below, one of them had to occupy the stairs leading to the speaker's rostrum. In the main auditorium seventeen police officers in uniform were on duty guarding entrances and exits, stairs, and the rear of the speaker's platform where no one else was allowed to be. Twenty officers in plain clothes patrolled and guarded the entire basement area and its entrances, ten in uniform patrolled the outside of the building, concentrating on any attempts at climbing outer walls. One officer watched the balconies of the house at No. 168 Potsdamerstrasse; two each were stationed in the stairways of No. 36 Winterfeldstrasse and No. 1 Pallasstrasse, from which one had a direct view to the entrance area of the Palace, and they had to prevent strange persons from occupying the windows. Another fifty officers were detailed to occupy seventeen other houses on Potsdamerstrasse and Winterfeldstrasse from which there was also a direct view to the approach route and the entrance area of the Palace. Roofs and balconies of these houses had to be kept free of all persons, the roofs were occupied by officers with binoculars, and the residents were enjoined not to admit any strange persons to their apartments. All persons living in the immediate vicinity of the Sports Palace were registered in police files and subject to constant surveillance.

Shortly before noon on 30 May Hitler had himself driven from the *Reich* Chancellery to the Sports Palace, passing through Wilhelmsplatz, Leipzigerstrasse, Hermann-Göring-Strasse and Potsdamerstrasse with his usual motor convoy. In the Sports Palace he spoke to 'his young comrades' of struggle as the principle of all life, of constant selection of the stronger through struggle, and of the 'right' of the stronger to live. Afterwards he rode back to the Chancellery, and returned to 'Wolfschanze' by Special train.

At another semi-public event a year later, approximately the same precautions were in effect, on Heroes' Memorial Day, 21 March 1943. Here the *Führer's* assassination was, in fact, planned. One effort failed because of tight security; an alternative one failed because of erratic or purposely unpredictable behaviour on Hitler's part.

It was a follow-up plot, after a previous attempt (described in the Chapter on Travel) had failed, on 13 March 1943, when a bomb smuggled into Hitler's plane at Smolensk had not gone off. The conspirators in Army Group Centre High Command (Fieldmarshal von Kluge, C-in-C) who had made the abortive attempt saw a new opportunity at the opening of an exhibition of captured Soviet war material in the Berlin Zeughaus (Armoury and War Museum) on Heroes' Memorial Day.[28] Hitler usually gave a speech there, and then inspected an exhibition of captured weapons from one of the theatres of war every year, and thereafter reviewed a small parade. One of the conspirators, Colonel von Gersdorff, as head of the staff section (Ic/AO) that had prepared the exhibition, had a reasonable pretext for attending. He agreed to carry out the assassination when asked by Colonel von Tresckow, Operations Officer on Kluge's staff. The unexploded mines ('clams') left over from the unsuccessful 'bomb-in-the-aeroplane' attempt were to be used (Plate 14).

Gersdorff flew to Berlin on 20 March with Fieldmarshal von Model, C-in-C 9th Army, who also planned to participate in the ceremony in Berlin. Gersdorff still had to take over the 'clams' from Lieutenant Fabian von Schlabrendorff, Special Missions Officer attached to Tresckow, who had followed the bomb-in-the-aeroplane after its failure and had retrieved the material. During the night of 20 to 21 March he gave Gersdorff the 'clams.' Gersdorff wanted to plant them in the speaker's rostrum, if possible, to go off during Hitler's speech. For this he had to know exactly when the speech would be made, but this turned out to be highly classified information. Fieldmarshal von Model, however, wanted to visit Frau von Model in Dresden and to come back only in time for the ceremony, so Gersdorff and Model went to see Major-

General Schmundt, Hitler's chief *Wehrmacht* aide, and asked him. Schmundt hedged for a while, but finally divulged the information, saying Gersdorff and Model must not tell anyone else 'under penalty of death.' It developed that the speech was scheduled for 1 p.m. instead of the usual time, 12 noon. This was kept so secret that even Himmler seems to have been in the dark about the correct time, judging from a diary entry.

Gersdorff went to the Armoury during the afternoon of 20 March, pretending to inspect 'his' exhibition, and found conditions not at all favourable. Not only was the glass-roofed inner court where the speech took place very large and airy, so that an explosion might lose most of

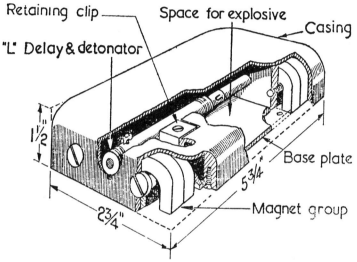

14. The Clam (adhesive mine)

its force; but all sensitive areas, where Hitler was going to go, sit or stand, were watched closely. Chairs and scaffolding were still being put up under the gaze of countless uniformed and plain-clothes SS and policemen. There was no chance of placing a bomb, and much less of setting a timer on the next day, shortly before the speech. Nothing as elaborate as Elser's bomb mechanism was available nor could it have been installed. The only timing devices available were chemical time-fuses that could be started ten or thirty minutes before the intended detonation.

This left only an attack on the *Führer's* life in which Gersdorff would blow himself up simultaneously with his victim. Shooting him was ruled out for a number of reasons: there were psychological difficulties in murdering someone face to face; there was the belief among the conspirators that Hitler wore bullet-proof clothes and that even his hat was fitted out with a steel inlay; and there was the very great likelihood that bodyguards and other bystanders would prevent the attack before it could succeed. It was thought best to use explosives. The only difficulty here was the lack of an instantaneous fuse. Gersdorff tried to find one, so he reports, but unsuccessfully. There was apparently not enough time, or not enough expertise readily available, in the few hours remaining, to rig up an ignition device with a flashlight battery. It was an odd and unlikely method of assassination for the assassin to set a fuse, and to wait ten minutes for his and his victim's death. But Gersdorff had gone on this mission with the promise of trying to kill Hitler, and he was going to try, even if the method was awkward and implausible.

The usual sequence of events was this: Hitler came in his open car from the *Reich* Chancellery through Wilhelmstrasse and Unter den Linden, both of which were cordoned off; at the Armoury entrance he was met by the Commanders-in-Chief of the *Wehrmacht* branches, including Himmler, by the Chief of OKW, and by other dignitaries; he walked into the inner court and took the first seat of the first row to the right of the aisle. The flags of the old and new *Wehrmacht* were displayed around the inner court. The orchestra played some solemn piece, Hitler made his speech, and then national anthems were played. After this, the guard of honour and the flags were moved outside for a wreath-laying ceremony and a parade. During this interval Hitler went to a wing of the Armoury where the exhibition was set up, and inspected it. The time allotted in the minute-by-minute schedules prepared in advance was ten minutes, after which Hitler left the exhibition and the building through the main entrance, walked past the guard, and then placed a wreath at the memorial next to the Armoury.

Gersdorff stood at the entrance to the exhibition with Fieldmarshal von Model, when Hitler came walking up. As Gersdorff remembers it, they were all saluting, and while his right arm was raised, he had his left hand in his overcoat pocket, pressing the thin metal tubing with the glass phial inside that contained the corrosive liquid of the chemical fuse. From now on, Gersdorff had to stay as close to Hitler as he could until the mine exploded. But to everyone's astonishment, the *Führer* virtually ran through the exhibition as if trying to escape from something, and there seemed to be no way of stopping him. If he left the exhibition too early, the whole ceremony would be thrown into confusion. But in *less than two minutes* from the time he had entered the exhibition Hitler was outside the building. There was nothing for Gersdorff to do but retire to one of the W.C.s and drop in the fuse, which had not yet reached the detonation point. He was unable to follow Hitler beyond the exhibition.

Several officials involved in the preparation and organisation of the ceremonies remember the confusion resulting from Hitler's deviation from the minute-by-minute programme. This also appears to be documented by the notes taken at the BBC Monitoring Service in London, where all German broadcasts were monitored, including the broadcast of the ceremony at the Armoury: 'Commentator: "The Fuehrer speaks," *Speech by Hitler* (Hitler spoke unusually quickly and hardly ever paused or raised his voice. The audience remained silent throughout).' There followed the transcript of Hitler's speech. Then the monitor recorded: 'At the close of Hitler's speech, orders were shouted and then "Deutschland ueber Alles" and "Horst Wessel" were played. Orders were again shouted, and the commentator said: "The Fuehrer salutes the flags, once again salutes the men of the three services gathered here, representatives of the State and of the Party, and goes down the central gangway into a special exhibition in the Zeughaus devoted to the fighting on the Eastern Front. All sectors of the Eastern Front are represented in this special exhibition and trophies captured in the fight against Bolshevism are shown, but in the centre stands a special memorial—the memorial of Stalingrad. The Fuehrer goes into the Exhibition. We shall come back to report on the placing of the wreath on the Memorial." Interval of a few seconds; shouting of orders; drums. At the Memorial in Unter den Linden we hear again orders shouted. Reporter says: "The Fuehrer has left the Zeughaus. Lt/Col. Jehreke [corr.: Gehrke], bearer of the Knight Cross, reports the guard of honour: the front of the four companies of the Army, the Navy, the Luftwaffe and the Waffen S.S. stand motionless: on the right wing is the Block of Honour, the Block of 60 flags, 27 flags of the old Army, three of the old Navy, and 30 flags of the new German Armed Forces. As the Fuehrer with his suite walks past the Battalion of Honour the band plays 'Deutschland ueber Alles,' on the Fuehrer's left is Reich Marshal Hermann Goering. The tune changes to 'Horst Wessel' as the Fuehrer approaches the Memorial. Four officers carry the wreath in front of him ...".'

The *Führer* may have had a close shave, but he had survived once again. Security precautions saved him from an attempt with a bomb hidden in the rostrum. Security had been defeated by an assassin's penetration into the immediate environment of the victim; but the assassin was handicapped by the inadequacy of his equipment, and defeated by Hitler's erratic unpredictability.

9 Travel

Adolf Hitler's restlessness is one of his most striking personality traits, and closely related to his lack of ordinary discipline and work habits. He had no lack of persistence in the pursuit of his goals, but there was a tendency to fill time with needless and irrational activity, such as giving free rein to incessant loquaciousness at all hours, or taking trips to every conceivable place, often at a moment's notice, and sometimes after tossing a coin to decide the destination.[1]

His military aide during the years 1934 to 1938, Colonel Hossbach, recalls that Hitler rarely failed to make a weekend jaunt south, to Munich or Berchtesgaden or both, and that as a result Saturdays and Mondays were lost for Government business. Many excursions were taken to Hamburg, Kiel, Weimar, Bayreuth, Hanover, or Dresden. During the 1930s Hitler never failed to attend the Bayreuth Wagner opera festivals for several days. Weimar, too, was often the destination of a trip.[2]

Hitler visited foreign countries if they were either friendly to or occupied by Germany. The friendly countries were represented before the war by Italy; during the war the only other non-occupied country Hitler visited was Finland. Before 1933 he would not have been welcome everywhere. Czechoslovakia, for example, arranged in October 1929 to have Hitler rejected at her borders as an undesirable alien when it became known that he might plan a motor trip to Czechoslovakia and Yugoslavia. From 1938 on, he travelled abroad more widely: Austria and Sudetenland in 1938; Bohemia and Moravia, and Poland, in 1939; Belgium, France and Italy in 1940 and 1943; Russia in 1941, 1942 and 1943; France in 1944. On his Russian trips he used the aeroplanes described earlier, escorted by a number of fighter planes, since long train journeys in Russia were not only time-consuming but dangerous, as Russian irregulars controlled large parts of the territory behind the Front. In the 1930s, and during the war within firmly-controlled territory (Germany, France, Poland), Hitler used his *Führersonderzug* quite often. If necessary he could order his plane to any point *en route*, or he could have cars requisitioned in an emergency. Few long-distance journeys were made by car, however.

In 1934 Austria was in ferment, and Hitler hoped to secure Mussolini's neutrality during a take-over by National Socialists there. On 14 June 1934 Hitler flew to Venice, accompanied by two other Ju 52 planes carrying officials of the Foreign Ministry. Hitler and his immediate entourage, including Brückner, Schaub, Sepp Dietrich and Otto Dietrich, stayed in the 'Grand Hotel' in Venice.[3] In the absence of massive security measures, Hitler was in considerable danger when he showed himself, with Mussolini, to the 70,000 milling about in St. Mark's Square, when he attended a concert in the Doge's Palace in the evening, or during a parade of Fascist organisations next morning, when the unit leaders saluted Mussolini and Hitler with drawn daggers. On 16 June Hitler flew back to Germany. The meeting had not been a great success. In fact Mussolini promised assistance to Austria against a possible German *coup* during the Dollfuss crisis, and he even moved some divisions up to the border.

Hitler's trip to Austria in March 1938 can hardly count as one to a foreign country: it was his homeland, and in the process of being occupied by the *Wehrmacht*. But although there was no Austrian military resistance, Hitler's trip to Linz and Vienna was, from a security point of view, much like one to a foreign country. The invasion began early in the morning of 12 March 1938, after the Austrian Nazi Party leader had 'asked for troops' in view of the danger of a civil war, and had 'legally' assumed government powers in Austria.[4] *Wehrmacht* troops had been concentrated along the Austrian border on 11 March, and Seyss-Inquart's 'request' was a mere formality.

SS-Standartenführer Rattenhuber commanded the combined *Führer-Begleit-Kommando*; *SS-Sturmbannführer* Gesche, commanding officer of the *SS-Begleit-Kommando*, was named Rattenhuber's deputy in command. The entire group was thirty-one strong and all wore SS uniforms so that RSD and *SS-Begleit-Kommando* were indistinguishable. Ten of them were drivers, including their leader, Kempka. Two, including Hitler's later SS Adjutant Otto Günsche, were responsible for the luggage. The rest were divided into three details under Gesche, Högl (deputy commander of RSD) and Schädle (of the *SS-Begleit-Kommando*). At least five cars were necessary to carry the entire crew of bodyguards and their weapons and luggage, and additional cars carried Hitler and such constant companions of Hitler as Linge, Bormann, Schaub, Brückner, Dr. Otto Dietrich, the personal physician Dr. Brandt, and Heinrich Hoffmann the photographer (officially, '*Reich* Photo Reporter'), as well as General Keitel, making up a convoy of more than twelve cars, all of them Mercedes-Benz. Hitler used a G4 three-axle cross-country Mercedes bearing an Army licence plate (WH-32290). The security details had some fourteen sub-machine-guns between them, with a total of 2,596 rounds of ammunition. Every man also carried two pistols. *SS-Sturmbannführer* Wernicke, one of the Personal Adjutants, was given two additional sub-machine-guns 'for special disposition,' with two loaded magazines each.

Hitler and his party covered the first leg of the trip in nine Ju 52 planes, leaving Berlin at 8.10 a.m. on 12 March, and arriving in Munich at 10.30 a.m.[5] The automobiles for the next part of the trip were stationed in Munich; the planes were ordered to await the party in Vienna. The party drove south to Mühldorf to VIII Army Corps headquarters. General von Bock commanded VIII Army Corps here. Soldiers and SS sealed off Bock's HQ in the Mühldorf Central School house upon Hitler's arrival and set up guards at all entrances. The Mayor of Mühldorf, Gollwitzer, a little man, slipped through, caught up with the *Führer* in a corridor, and introduced himself. He wandered around, trying to find out what was up. Finally he saw someone taking the *Führer's* standard off the black Mercedes and putting it on a G-4 Mercedes painted in Army drab. Someone in Hitler's suite said: 'The *Führer* is going to Braunau.'

He arrived there, at his birthplace, on the same day, 12 March, and went on to Lambach, Wels and Linz. The masses cheered endlessly, the delays were stupefying. The night was spent in Linz, and on 13 March the journey continued on to Vienna. Up to St. Pölten the average speed of the convoy was 40 kilometres per hour, and for the rest of the way to Vienna only 20 kilometres per hour. Hitler's progress through Austria was nothing short of triumphal, and much of the enthusiasm encountered was undoubtedly genuine, as such unimpeachable observers as the British Military Attaché in Berlin, Colonel Mason-MacFarlane, attest, although it was considerably less universal in industrial centres than elsewhere. At a crossroads between Linz and Melk, where the road turns off to Vienna, Mason-MacFarlane stopped for petrol at a garage and learned, on 13 March, that Hitler was about to pass by, and he decided to wait for the spectacle. Presently two Mercedes cars 'filled with SS bristling with tommy-guns and other lethal weapons, came by; they were closely followed by half-a-dozen super-cars containing Hitler and his immediate entourage and bodyguard.'

The trip was completed without serious incidents. In Vienna Hitler stayed at the Hotel 'Imperial' on Schwarzenberg Square and received the ovations of vast crowds there. On the afternoon of 14 March the visit ended with a parade of the German and Austrian armies.

Hitler's state visit to Italy was scheduled to begin on 3 May 1938. He left Berlin in his *Führer* Special on the afternoon of 2 May, accompanied by Ribbentrop, Hess, Schaub, Goebbels, Frank, Lammers, Bouhler, Amann, Dr. Otto Dietrich, Lieutenant-General von Stülpnagel, Rear-Admiral Schniewind, Sepp Dietrich and Major-General Bodenschatz.[6] Three Condor aeroplanes were flown to Rome empty by Captain Baur and his crews. At 8 a.m. on 3 May a cousin of the King, the Duke of Pistoia, met Hitler's train at the Brenner Pass. In the evening at 8.30 it arrived in Ostia near Rome, and Hitler was welcomed by King Victor Emmanuel III, Mussolini, Foreign Minister Count Ciano—and Fascist leaders in their black uniforms, with drawn daggers in their right hands raised for the Fascist salute. This was obviously customary, but it must have made German security men shudder to see these very sharp daggers only inches away from the *Führer's* face, on this and several other occasions during the visit. As Hitler and his hosts walked down the line of a guard of honour of the Italian Army, the King walked beside him, but Mussolini followed only behind the King, Ciano walked behind Mussolini, and then came the rest of the two entourages. Hitler and Victor Emmanuel then went off to the Quirinal Palace where Hitler was staying, riding in an open horse-drawn state carriage, flanked by Guards on horseback, without Mussolini, who was not a Head of State. Hitler smiled, but he was not pleased with what he called an antediluvian mode of transport. He was also completely alone in the carriage with the King, except for the driver and two footmen in top hats.

It was a problem to provide adequate security for Hitler and his party (which was more than twice as large as Mussolini's when he had visited Germany). The German authorities could not do very much by way of preparation except to ask the Italian authorities to collect information on Germans living in Italy, and they began these inquiries somewhat late, at the beginning of March 1938. But Mussolini 'solved' this problem in the grand style. He had 10,000 suspects, among them many Jews, arrested before the visitors arrived. A lone assassin not 'subject to suspicion' would still have had his chance at one of Hitler's public appearances, when he saluted disorderly crowds from the open window of his train coach, during wreath-laying ceremonies at the Tomb of the Unknown Soldier and at the memorial for the martyrs of the Fascist Movement, at one of the parades, or when Hitler spoke before some 6,000 Germans residing in Italy. But in carefully orchestrated instances, especially in the beginning of the visit, the reception given Hitler and his party by the crowds was magnificent, as only a dictatorship could produce it at will and regardless of weather or other factors. Mussolini of course had been given a splendid reception when he had been in Germany in 1937. Both dictators were aware of the contrived nature of such demonstrations, and the directives for them were straightforward and explicit, as when the Foreign Minister of Japan visited Berlin in March 1941. '600,000 populace are required to form the lane from Anhalt Station to Bellevue Palace ... Commercial and industrial enterprises will be informed as to when to give their employees time off without reduction of pay.'[7] This form of flattery was not ineffective despite its transparency.

In the evening of 4 May, after parades and reviews and wreath-laying ceremonies, Hitler took his Special to Naples. *En route*, whenever the train stopped, crowds gathered and people (mostly children) handed up flowers to Hitler, who showed himself at the window of his coach. In Naples Hitler and his suite reviewed naval demonstrations on 5 May from the battleship *Cavour*.

His mood suffered increasingly from witnessing the second-fiddle role his friend Mussolini had to play during this state visit,[8] and there had been an incident in Naples that had not helped. Hitler had been scheduled to make a brief appearance before some 200 German Nazis in Naples, and he had told Linge to take along a brown uniform coat and hat for this purpose. The review was to take place immediately after a banquet given by the Crown Prince, but when the moment came and Hitler wanted to slip into his brown jacket, Italian protocol officials told him there was not enough time to change, so he walked down the line of Germans in his tails—arm raised and coat-tails flying.[9] There is no evidence of any security surveillance of the German Nazis before or during this review.

The programme continued with ovations, more parades, receptions, exhibitions, and Air Force manœuvres near Civitavecchia on 8 May. A huge fireworks display concluded the visit to Rome. On 9 May Hitler took his Special to Florence, spent an afternoon and evening with Mussolini, and departed about midnight for Germany.[10]

In the autumn of 1938 Hitler demanded the 'return' of the German-speaking Sudetenland, while really intending to annex all Czechoslovakia. His directive of 30 May 1938 said: 'It is my unalterable decision to smash Czechoslovakia by military action within the foreseeable future.' He gave 1 October 1938 as the deadline.[11] A German invasion of Czechoslovakia would most likely have led to a European war. The underground Resistance to Hitler in Germany therefore became a conspiracy to unseat the dictator, and for the first time leading men in high government and military positions laid detailed and promising plans for a *coup d'état*. Hitler was to be arrested and put on trial as soon as he had given the expected order to march against Czechoslovakia. In a plot within the plot, Major F. W. Heinz and some of his friends of former Freecorps and *Stahlhelm* organisations, who were hand-picked to carry out the *Führer's* arrest, prepared to shoot him in the process, in the *Reich* Chancellery. Intervention of Hitler's friend Mussolini, hectic diplomatic activity by the British Government, and probably most of all the alerting of the British Navy and the calling up of French Army reservists, made Hitler accept a compromise at the Munich Conference on 28 September 1938: annexation of the Sudetenland in stages.

Hitler began to inspect his new acquisition on 3 October. He crossed the former border at Wildenau near Asch, in his familiar three-axle Mercedes G4, having taken his *Führersonderzug* from Berlin to Hof on 2 October.[12] He motored from Hof to Asch, Eger, and back to Hof via Wildstein and Schönbach. On 4 October he travelled via Falkenau and Karlsbad to Annaberg and then returned to Berlin to open the Winter Aid Programme campaign for 1938/39 on 5 October. He left Berlin again on the same day for Löbau in Saxony. On 6 October he continued his inspection of the Sudetenland, visiting Fugau, Schluckenau, Rumburg,

Kratzau, Friedland and some formerly Czech fortifications by car, and travelling on by train during the night. On 7 October he appeared in Neustadt in Upper Silesia, Schönwiese, Kohlbach, Jägerndorf, at some more Czech bunkers, and at Freudenthal. On 8 October he travelled from Patschkau in Silesia to Saarbrücken to inaugurate a new opera-house and attend a performance of Wagner's *The Flying Dutchman*. A further visit to the new territories took Hitler by car from Linz to Krumau on 19 October; on 25 October there followed Bratislava (back to Vienna for the night), and on 26 October a car trip from Vienna to Znaim. The Special had been brought up and was used as a hotel. On 27 October the Special took Hitler to Nicolsburg; then he went back to Vienna by car and attended a performance of the opera *Tiefland* in the evening.

Whatever the security arrangements looked like on paper for these trips, Hitler was by no means adequately protected *en route*. Secrecy and surprise make the work of the planning assassin difficult if he is alone. If he has a number of associates, and it is clear that an inspection tour is taking place, he can station his associates in places likely to be visited, and increase the chances of success considerably. Also, only very elaborate security precautions can provide a measure of protection against assassins stimulated by the sudden appearance of an opportunity. When Hitler passed through the various towns along his route, German troops had taken over the territory only two or three days before, in the first few instances. Cordoning off the streets through which the cars of Hitler's party travelled was often inadequate and at times haphazard. The troops employed were taken where they could be found; sometimes there were police troops, sometimes SS in nearly sufficient numbers, but at other times only signal corps troops were available, and there were stretches of crowded streets where no cordoning-off forces were present at all. On many occasions the crowds were not controlled and flooded the street, and they mobbed Hitler's car so that it could not move at all or only at a snail's pace. Then the *Führer-Begleit-Kommando* men had to get out and walk or trot alongside Hitler's Mercedes, three on each side, to try and put at least the distance of their own widths between the crowds and the car. The situation could get quite touchy; the faces of the body-guards and even of Hitler himself, standing up in his car and presumably enjoying the ovations, showed concern or anger at times. On one occasion, in Krumau, a large framed painting was handed up into the *Führer's* car by someone who wished to express his gratitude—this could easily have been a disguised bomb. Hitler also accepted many bunches of flowers, and even a basket of fruit. In another town one of the strings of little flags hung across the street at the third-storey level was dropped down in front of Hitler's car's windscreen, whether on purpose or by accident is not clear. If it had been strong cord or wire it could have prevented the car from proceeding for a few critical moments, and the possibility of this as part of an assassination plot could not be excluded.

In Schluckenau, on 6 October, Hitler reviewed the Sudeten German Freecorps, a bunch of irregular-looking characters with rifles slung over their shoulders. Flowers by the thousand were thrown in Eger and in Franzensbad—a very dangerous situation, since any general action of this kind makes it inconspicuous and easy for an assassin to toss a bomb and escape undetected. Even though secrecy was maintained as well as possible, if only by sometimes changing the route at short notice, there were often tell-tale signs of the *Führer's* imminent presence appearing in some of the larger towns hours in advance. Citizens could easily draw their conclusions when the main thoroughfares of their towns were suddenly cordoned off, and when film-camera operators took up positions with their cars and equipment in the market-place. There was also much private photography going on; a gun could be camouflaged as a camera, and an assassin could take aim without arousing suspicion.

On 14 March German troops began the occupation of the Czech part of Czechoslovakia.[13] On 15 March this was sanctioned by an 'Agreement' between the Czech and German governments, and the invasion began officially. In the night of 15–16 March Hitler got on his *Führersonderzug* and travelled south, as far as the border town Böhmisch-Leipa, where he arrived at 3 p.m. on 16 March. Captain Baur had to follow Hitler on the entire trip with several Ju 52 planes. He continued his trip in his customary three-axle Mercedes to Prague, where he arrived in the evening, held conferences with commanding generals in the Hradshin Palace, and then returned to his *Führersonderzug* where he spent the night.[14] On 17 March he went on by train to Brünn and Vienna, stayed overnight in the hotel 'Imperial,' and returned to Berlin by train on 18 March, arriving on 19 March in the evening.

Although Hitler faced an entirely new situation now, travelling in a country that definitely had not wished to be annexed, he still rode his open tourer through the streets of Prague and other towns. The crowds were apparently controlled more easily than in the Sudeten areas, but much of this control was self-control imposed by hostility. Hardly anyone seemed to have felt a desire to rush up to Hitler's car and give him flowers, and flowers were not thrown in his path here. The photographs taken by the *Reich* Photo Reporter and his crew show no instances of flower-giving or flower-tossing, and only once or twice is anyone seen rushing up to Hitler's car. In Prague there were, of course, a certain number of supporters of German occupation, among a total German-speaking population (many of them Jews) of some 40,000.

Security operations were more thorough than in October 1938. The *Führer-Begleit-Kommando*, in field-grey SS uniforms for the first time during an annexation (this time it was the closest thing yet to real war), commanded by *SS-Standartenführer* Rattenhuber, were less conspicuous; but cordoning-off was taken very seriously. There were few of the population in the streets, the lines of guards were dense, even along the river where there were no houses there were guards about every 10 to 20 yards. Where there were any onlookers, guards at two-yard intervals faced them rather than the passing motor convoy. Remarkably few of the onlookers smiled or waved, and Hitler took it in, sitting down most of the time. Only when he met a German Army column did he stand up occasionally and salute. His car was open, but all the windows (bullet-proof glass) were up. His car was preceded by two *Führer* Escort cars (open tourers)

15.   Hitler in Prague with Führer *Escort and military escort, 16 March 1939*

and then by two armoured cars, and followed by the cars of the suite and some more *Führer-Begleit-Kommando*. On 17 March in Bratislava, to which he made a detour, the reception was considerably more friendly, and more populace were on hand than in Prague, but security was still tight.

Many of the preparations for journeys up to this time still had been made *ad hoc* and often at very short notice. By January 1939 a schema was set up of what preparations must be made in what order, and who had to be informed of a forthcoming journey. First of all, in every case, those responsible for all three alternative forms of travel had to be informed. *Führersonderzug* schedules had to be either activated or worked out when required, and catering service had to be ordered; the government flight crews had to be informed through Captain Baur, and weather reports collected; chief driver Kempka had to be told, and it had to be decided whether open or closed cars were needed. In this way Hitler was always able to make his decision as to the mode of travel at the very last moment.

Next, the *SS-Begleit-Kommando* (Gesche) and the RSD detail (Rattenhuber) had to be alerted, and after that the personal adjutants (Brückner, Schaub, Wiedemann, A. Bormann, Wernicke, Bahls and Wünsche), and the secretaries Fräulein Wolf and Fräulein Schröder. Furthermore, the *Wehrmacht* aides, Press Chief Dietrich and his deputy, the physicians, the chief photographer, and appropriate persons at the place of destination had to be informed. On 29 May 1939 Rattenhuber made clear to Chief Adjutant Brückner in a letter that only the *Führer's* Adjutants' Office was authorised to inform anyone of a *Führer* expedition, and that only the minimum number of persons must be informed. Rattenhuber had always refused to inform police officials of non-public journeys the *Führer* took; if, nevertheless, streets, pavements and entrances were jammed with people on such occasions, it was up to the police and to the *Gestapo* to see to it that the *Führer* could come and go unhindered, and to find the information leaks.[15]

With the beginning of the war against Poland on 1 September 1939, travelling took another turn towards the dangerous for Adolf Hitler. Considering that he proposed (as he said in his speech to generals on 22 August 1939) to have many Polish men, women and children put to death by his SS Death's Head formations, to smash the Soviet Union after Stalin's (imminent) death, and then to rule the earth[16]—he was remarkably safe in Poland.

The *Führersonderzug* left Berlin on the evening of 3 September.[17] On such occasions the train was regularly accompanied from now on by members of the *Frontgruppe der FHQu. Truppen* commanded by Major-General Rommel. Nine or more personal adjutants and aides travelled on the train, at least two personal physicians, two secretaries, three or more press officials, several radio operators, 'guests' such as the chief photographer, a liaison officer of Himmler, a representative of the Foreign Office, three valets, the chief driver and a deputy, ten *SS-Begleit-Kommando* men and ten RSD men, fourteen officials and employees of the *Reich* Railway, thirteen railway catering service employees including waiters, cooks, kitchen maids and two silver cleaners, five railway-police officers, and three inspectors of the *Reich* Mail. Two motor convoys were directed wherever the *Führersonderzug* went, to be available at a moment's notice for a drive. A squad of aeroplanes, commanded by Captain Baur, also followed the *Führersonderzug*.

Hitler's Special, 'Amerika,' arrived in Bad Polzin, some hundred kilometres east of Stettin, at 1.56 a.m. on 4 September. At 9.30 a.m. the

Führer's motor convoy left for the first tour of the Front area. All cars were open Mercedes, still in glossy beige with black mudguards, but with licence plates and other insignia covered (by the time of the French campaign, the cars would be painted dull olive-grey).[18] Two groups were formed. In the first group there were Hitler's car, two *Führer-Begleit-Kommando* cars, a car for the aides, and a car for the Chief of OKW and some more aides. In Hitler's car, there were, besides the *Führer* (who now carried a gun on his belt) and the driver, Schaub, Schmundt, Captain von Below, Captain Engel, and Linge (with a machine-pistol). The next two cars carried *Führer-Begleit-Kommando* men and Brückner, with two machine-guns each mounted on several of the open cars. Usually the SS Escort car followed immediately behind Hitler's car, and the RSD car was next. In the adjutants' car sat M. Bormann, Major-General Bodenschatz, an SS aide of lower rank, and the *Reich* Photo Reporter. In the fifth car there were General Keitel and one of his adjutants, the liaison officers of the Army and Navy, and one of the Air Force. The second convoy consisted of two 'ministers' cars' with Ribbentrop and Lammers and their aides, one car for Himmler and his aides and bodyguard, one for *Reich* Press Chief Dr. Dietrich, one for other persons invited to accompany the *Führer*, a reserve car, a luggage car, a field-kitchen car and a petrol tanker.

The two groups of cars, already well armed, were surrounded by elements of the evolving *Führer-Begleit-Bataillon* (still known as *Frontgruppe der FHQu. Truppen*) under Rommel's command. Hitler's group was preceded by a squad of five soldiers on motorcycles and by two armed-reconnaissance vehicles, and five more motorcycle soldiers brought up the rear, followed immediately by the Headquarters Commandant's (Rommel's) car, five more motorcycle soldiers, a signal corps platoon and an anti-aircraft platoon with their guns. This intermediate column was called Column K (for *Kommandant*). It was followed at an interval of five minutes by elements protecting Group 2, known as Column M (apparently for military). They consisted of an anti-tank gun, followed by the cars of Group 2, after which there followed another anti-tank gun and parts of the signals platoon accompanying Group 1.

The first visit to the Front in this convoy took the *Führer* and his party as far as the Vistula where German troops were crossing at Topolno, and then back to a new location of the *Führersonderzug*. The journey took the convoy through Neustettin, Preussisch Friedland, Zempelburg and Komierwo, where Hitler was briefed about the situation by General von Kluge, Commander-in-Chief 4th Army. Usually on such occasions security was lax. There seems to have been the feeling that no attack could come from any of the soldiers by whom Hitler was surrounded, and that no outsider would dare make an attack in the face of all the soldiers—although Hitler's genocidal policies towards Poland were soon becoming obvious. During briefings, Hitler's eight or nine bodyguards just stood about looking on, or talking among themselves, but not, as they should have been, facing out from where Hitler was, watching the surroundings. There was always a good deal of private photography, too, carried on by soldiers who happened to be there. After lunch from the field-kitchen, the party left for Topolno. At one point the convoy was stopped because only minutes ago some Polish soldiers had ambushed a field-hospital company, but when there were no further signs of the Poles the journey continued. About 8 kilometres from Crone an oncoming lorry collided with one of the vehicles of the anti-aircraft platoon. But none of the drivers was at fault: the lorry driver had been shot through the chest by a Polish sniper just as he was going past the *Führer's* convoy. As the travellers pressed on through Crone and Brzezno to Pruszcz, the Fieseler Storch that followed them to provide aerial reconnaissance was shot at by mistake by German troops. Hitler then watched German troops crossing the Vistula at Topolno, and returned to Topolno to inspect some unfinished Polish bunkers. While he was there, Polish planes began dropping bombs only 2 or 3 kilometres away, whereupon the convoy began its retreat through Vandsburg and Flatow to Plienitz. The Special was waiting there; but it had to be moved approximately 15 kilometres south in the middle of the night after it was learned that some friendly soul in the Foreign Office had informed foreign diplomats of the location of the *Führer's* Special.

The next trip to the Front, on 6 September from Gross-Born (where the Special had been moved on 5 September) to Plewno where General Guderian commanded XIX Army Corps, and on to the Vistula bridge at Graudenz, was less eventful, as were the ones on 10, 11, 13 and 15 September. On 10 September Hitler and his suite made their first visit to the Front by air. Shortly after 9 a.m. a total of six Ju 52, which Hitler still considered more reliable than the Condor, carried them from Neudorf airfield to Bialaczow, where General von Reichenau commanded the 10th Army. The planes were accompanied, as usual, by six fighter planes. Hitler travelled in a plane marked D-AVAU, together with Colonel Schmundt, Brückner, Captain von Below, Captain Engel, Dr. Brandt, Kempka, Linge; six each of the SS escort and the RSD travelled in planes marked D-ARET and D-2600, respectively. Three other planes carried Keitel, Rommel, Bodenschatz, Ribbentrop, Dr. Dietrich, M. Bormann, Schaub, Wünsche, Himmler and others. A motor convoy as described above had been sent ahead to Bialaczow from where the party drove to Konskie and to Maslow. Security was again lax. In one of the photographs taken of the scenes Hitler can be seen walking across the airfield to his plane with Reichenau, three military aides, Rommel and Brückner, but without any bodyguards. At one point a woman ran up and clutched Hitler's hands; there were only Air Force men walking beside and behind him, and everyone including Hitler was smiling. Soon he was surrounded by several women and dozens of soldiers, without any bodyguards in sight, until finally Linge managed to elbow his way close to the *Führer*, and helped him get into his car. Only then the other bodyguards materialised. Hitler was still shaking hands as they gradually cleared a lane for his open Mercedes G4. Similar mob scenes occurred at many stops. In towns and even on the highway, the column often moved at a snail's pace along narrow streets and dusty roads congested with horse-drawn wagons and lorries full of prisoners-of-war going in

16.   Hitler on Front visit in Poland, 10 September 1939

the opposite direction. If any of them had reason and desire to kill Hitler, however, the chances were that they were not equipped when they met Hitler unexpectedly. But sometimes the *Führer* could be seen by many people long enough for considerable civilian crowds to gather round, and again and again he allowed himself to be surrounded and mobbed by soldiers, and to be isolated from his bodyguards. Almost every day during his visits to the Polish Front, and in every conceivable manner, Hitler got himself into situations in which his life was in great danger.

The planes had been flown to Maslow and the group flew back from here to Neudorf and arrived at 6.15 p.m. by car in Illnau, where the *Führersonderzug* and Ribbentrop's special train were stationed. On 11 September an almost identical journey was made to Boguslawice, west of Tomaszow, again by plane, and by car to Wola and back to Illnau.

On 12 September the Special was moved to Gogolin, and another visit to the Front followed, partly by air and partly by car. This time General von Blaskowitz south-west of Lodz, General Ulex north of Lodz, and General von Weichs at Bratoszewice had to brief their supreme warlord. The pace proved too much for the motor convoy; when on 15 September the *Führer's* party arrived in Pawlosiow at 10 a.m. by plane, there was no convoy there. It finally limped in at 11 a.m., after a twenty-two-hour drive, and after several vehicles had broken down. Hitler could not wait, and a makeshift convoy had been assembled for a look at troops

17.   Hitler on Front visit in Poland at Maslow, 10 September 1939; Rudolf Schmundt on Hitler's left

crossing the San River, but when the convoy arrived it was immediately put into service, and then sent on to Cracow the same afternoon. There it was to be ready for another trip on 16 September, but this was postponed to 17 September and finally cancelled.

Partly as a result of the past two weeks' experiences, it was concluded that the *Führer* Escort elements of the Army were insufficient. On 16 September Rommel flew to Berlin to persuade authorities there to let him organise a regular *Führer-Begleit-Bataillon* (*Führer* Escort Battalion).

At midnight on 18 September the *Führersonderzug* left Gogolin for Lauenburg (via Breslau, Frankfurt/O., Küstrin, Stargard) and Hitler's Headquarters was installed in the Goddentow-Lanz railway station. For 19 September two alternative plans were prepared; the *Führer* was to choose one of them shortly before departure time, 'depending on the situation at the Front or the weather.'[19] Neither plan was followed in every detail; the first plan, a trip to Danzig, was adopted with modifications.

The military escort came only as far as Zoppot, the border town, where *Gauleiter* Forster greeted Hitler and his party. Flowers were thrown— the streets were nearly covered with them in places—and great crowds filled the pavements and the windows and balconies. Only on 12 September the official Nazi Party newspaper *Völkischer Beobachter* had published this directive: 'Berlin, 11 September. The *Führer's* Adjutants'

18.   Hitler's motor convoy entering Oliva on visit to Danzig, 19 September 1939

Office says: The *Führer* will not accept flowers on his trips for the duration of the war. Any flowers intended for him should be given to the soldiers of the German *Wehrmacht*.' As Hitler walked past a guard of honour there were no SS or RSD men with him except Schaub. From Zoppot on, security and escort were provided by the police. In Zoppot, Oliva and Langfuhr, members of local NSDAP formations were stationed as a lane along the streets; between towns the police cordoned off the road. In the afternoon, reviews, receptions and speeches were put on in Danzig. A trip to Westerplatte by minesweeper, and from here by motor convoy via Zoppot to Gdingen, which was scheduled for 19 September was postponed to 21 September; a trip to Dirschau to see a blown-up bridge planned for 20 September was moved to 22 September. On this day the *Führer* observed the artillery bombardment of Praga, a suburb of Warsaw, and then went by car to Wyskow, from where the party flew back to Danzig to stay overnight in Zoppot's 'Casino Hotel' again. On 25 September his Special left Goddentow for Berlin, where he arrived at Stettin station at 5.05 p.m. His next trip to Poland, after a short visit to Wilhelmshaven on 28 September, took him to Warsaw by plane on 5 October for the great victory parade. He was met at the airport by his victorious generals, Brauchitsch, Milch, Rundstedt, Blaskowitz and

19.   Hitler in Warsaw, in Mercedes-Benz G4, Linge seated on folding hood, with Führer *Escort, 5 October 1939*

Cochenhausen, and was escorted by an Army detachment into Warsaw to the parade ground opposite the Dutch Embassy. The parade lasted for two and a half hours. Afterwards the *Führer* was to have an open-air lunch with the generals; but when he saw that 'elaborate' preparations had been made (white tablecloth) he displayed anger, walked out, and flew back to Berlin.

   Perhaps he had used the opportunity to vent his frustration at the resistance of 'the generals' to his plans for an immediate attack upon France. At any rate, he had other things on his mind, particularly the speech in the *Reichstag* on 6 October by which he hoped to talk Britain out of the war. During the speech, anti-aircraft batteries of the *Führer-*

Begleit-Bataillon were specially stationed around the *Reichstag* to make sure that perfidious Albion could not muffle the sound of the song of peace being sung there.

The next visits to the Front (discounting Christmas visits to a few garrisons) were taken in the Western Campaign. Until April 1940 and the occupation of Denmark and Norway, Hitler remained in Berlin. Security modifications for the Western Front tours consisted for the most part of needed improvements. One was designed to provide better secrecy. From the start of the campaign on 10 May 1940, every effort was made to prevent leaks about the movements and whereabouts of the *Führer* and his H.Q. The secretaries and others of the entourage were told to get ready for 'a journey' on 9 May; they were not told where they were going or how long they would stay. They were then taken by car to Staaken airfield so that they had to think they would travel by air, but the cars went on to the *Führersonderzug* at Finkenkrug, and it soon departed northward. Some asked Hitler: 'Are we going to Norway?' Hitler answered affirmatively. The word was that the train was bound for Kiel, from where the party was to fly to Oslo. But near Uelzen, in the middle of the night, the train suddenly changed direction and arrived at Euskirchen station at 4.25 a.m. on 10 May. *Führer* Escort Battalion details guarding stations where the *Führersonderzug* stopped had been ordered to take up their positions only half an hour before the train arrived. The *Führer* had himself driven to his 'Felsennest' HQ in Rodert at once.[20]

Three convoys were organised to accompany the *Führer* on his tours of the Front, so that they could be ordered quickly to distant places. A typical convoy, or *Frontgruppe*, of the *Führer-Begleit-Bataillon* in May 1940 consisted of elements of an infantry company, of a signal-corps unit, of a motor-cycle platoon, of an armoured-reconnaissance platoon including a radio car, a machine-gun car, two cars carrying 2-cm guns, two anti-aircraft platoons, two field-kitchens, two fuel tankers, parts of supply sections. This little army surrounded, preceding and following, fifteen cars of what was now known as a Grey Column, carrying Hitler and his party. The other two groups contained, in addition to two sets of essentially the same details as the first, nineteen Grey Column cars plus a Fieseler Storch and fourteen Grey Column cars, respectively. They and the rest of the *Führer-Begleit-Bataillon* (FBB) were commanded by the HQ Commandant. Major-General Rommel had been given a new post and had been replaced by Lieutenant-Colonel Thomas as *Führer* HQ Commandant. Many security regulations had been tightened after Elser's assassination attack. Dated 14 December 1939, the new directives aimed at preventing the inclusion of 'wrong or possibly dangerous items' in the *Führer's* and his suite's luggage. Luggage was henceforth picked up by three *SS-Begleit-Kommando* men in apartments or hotels where the *Führer* and members of his suite were staying; two had to fetch the luggage, and one always had to guard the pick-up car. The luggage was to be held ready, under guard, in a special room in Hitler's flat in the *Reich* Chancellery, or in the hotel or other residence, and it was never to be handed over to anyone but members of the *SS-Begleit-Kommando* who had to take it to cars, aeroplanes or the *Führersonderzug*. Anything brought there by others would not be transported. 'Luggage that did not have to be on hand at all times was to be stowed away in the car most distant from that in which the *Führer* travelled.'

It was a while before Hitler was able to inspect the conquests on the Western Front. During the first days of the campaign the roads in Belgium were still full of mines and not safe for travel. On 15, 16 and 18 May reconnaissance detachments of the *Führer-Begleit-Bataillon* sent out to collect information on the state of the roads reported the road west of Limburg was under artillery fire. One of Hitler's armoured Mercedes cars was being kept ready at Bastogne airfield, along with two three-axle cars for his *Führer-Begleit-Kommando* and two for the immediate military entourage plus one car in reserve. The leader of this small group was told to get in touch with Lieutenant-Colonel von Tresckow to find a good place for parking the Grey Column cars—the same officer who was to become the driving force behind the assassination attempts in 1943.

Hitler took his first trip to the Western Front on 17 May, when he flew to Bastogne to meet the staff of Army Group A (General von Rundstedt, Commander-in-Chief). A convoy of cars took him with his suite to Odendorf airfield; they flew to Bastogne airfield, motored about in a convoy sent ahead for this purpose, and returned to 'Felsennest' HQ the same evening.[21] A longer trip to the Front was taken on 1 and 2 June. Several *Führer-Begleit-Bataillon* detachments were sent ahead to Brussels airport and to Tournai. At the airport, three motor convoys were kept available from which the travel group was to be composed. They included a car for the *Führer*, two for his escort details, one for adjutants and one for Keitel, also a group of motor-cycle riflemen, an armoured personnel carrier with an anti-aircraft gun, a radio squad, a press-radio car, an armoured-reconnaissance-radio car, field-kitchen, and supply and luggage car. When the HQ Commandant went ahead to reconnoitre and find suitable quarters, fighting was still in progress in the south-west sections of Lille (30 May). Nevertheless, the Château de Brigode near Annappes, only 6 kilometres east of Lille, was considered suitable for the *Führer*—and the staff of a division commanded by General Kühne were given notice to move out by next morning. 'Inconspicuous occupation' (FBB war diary) of the château by members of the FBB was begun immediately.

At 9 a.m. Hitler and his party left 'Felsennest' HQ for Odendorf airfield, from where they flew off to Brussels at 10 a.m. on 1 June. At

20. *RSD detail during tour of the Front with Hitler in Belgium, 1/2 June 1940 (from left): Paul Leciejewski, Karl Weckerling, Hans Küffner, Josef Jörg, Peter Högl, Josef Hausner, Franz Grill*

21. *Hitler en route to Munich, near Wassertrüdingen, 18 June 1940*

Brussels airfield the travellers were met by General von Bock, Commander-in-Chief of Army Group B, who reported the situation to the *Führer*. Hitler went on through Brussels to Ghent, Courtrai and Bisseghem, in the customary order, with two carloads of his SS and RSD escort following him directly, and with Bormann, Dietrich, Brandt, Hewel, Morell, also adjutants, and finally Keitel and his aides following. At a distance of 1 kilometre there followed an anti-aircraft battery, radio cars, field-kitchen and supply cars. At Bisseghem airfield, General von Reichenau (C-in-C 8th Army) and General von Schwedler (Commanding General, IV Army Corps) reported. Dozens of Air Force men practised private photography, as usual. Then the party visited the battlefields and German military cemeteries at Ypres and Langemarck, and finally went to Château de Brigode for the night. Next day Hitler visited Avelin, Vimy, Arras, Douai, Bouchain and Cambrai, from where he took his plane to Charleville. Here General von Rundstedt (C-in-C 4th Army Group) reported to him. By 6.30 p.m. that day he was back in 'Felsennest.'

From a new Headquarters, 'Wolfschlucht' ('Wolf's Gorge') near Brûly-de-Pesche, where the *Führer* had moved on 6 June, he took a trip to Munich to meet the *Duce*. The French had asked for an armistice, through Spain; now the alliance partners had to discuss the conditions. Hitler flew from Gros Caillou airfield to Frankfurt-am-Main and took his Special from there to Munich on 17 June, arriving on 18 June, and returning on the 19th. Along the way, in the station of Wassertrüdingen, on the route Gunzenhausen–Nördlingen, the Special was mobbed by a crowd wedged up against the very coach where Hitler was looking out of the window. The thin security forces were unable, at least for some minutes, to cope with the multitude. Very large crowds also turned out in Munich and gave Hitler a triumphal reception as he rode through the streets in his open Mercedes to his apartment at Prinzregentenplatz, and to Prince-Carl-Palais to meet the *Duce*. After Hitler's return to 'Wolfschlucht,' the Special was moved to Heusenstamm, where it had been held in readiness before.[22]

Two days later, on 21 June, Hitler motored to the forest of Compiègne. Here the German armistice conditions were to be presented to the French High Command, in the same railway carriage in which the German Armistice Commission had received the Allied conditions in 1918. Hitler had the famous railway carriage taken out of its museum; a wall had to be knocked out first.[23] (The carriage was later taken to Berlin where it was destroyed in an RAF raid; the one now in the museum near Compiègne is a reconstruction.) In the presence of Hitler and of the C-in-Cs of the three *Wehrmacht* branches (Brauchitsch, Raeder, Göring), Keitel opened the negotiations by reading the preamble of the German conditions to the French representatives. Then Hitler and his suite left and returned to 'Wolfschlucht' the same evening. The armistice agreement was signed on 22 June; it went into effect on 25 June.

A great victory parade had been planned to be held in Paris after the defeat of France, and two attacks on Hitler's life were planned or considered for this occasion. Fritz-Dietlof Graf von der Schulenburg and Dr Eugen Gerstenmaier were the principal plotters in one of the plans; they hoped to shoot Hitler on the reviewing stand, but had to give up the idea when the parade was not held. In England, D. F. Stevenson, Director of Home Operations in the Air Ministry, had information that the parade was planned for 27 July; he wrote to the Deputy Chief of Air Staff on 13 July 1940: 'We could try to kill the Fuehrer. Doubtless the saluting base will be close to the Arc de Triomphe and no one can say what the effect of a few salvos of 40-lb and 250-lb bombs would be on an occasion of this kind . . .' But after having considered all aspects of the idea, including alternatives for bombing raids and the probable strength of German defences (which were not expected to be a major obstacle if there was a good cloud cover), Stevenson expressed himself against the plan: 'After considering these points, I am against the attack on Paris on this occasion. The triumphal march through Paris is in accordance with military custom—we did the same thing ourselves after the battle of Waterloo.' The parade was called off on 20 July, but Hitler paid a secret visit to Paris early in the morning of 23 June.[24]

For this sentimental visit (Hitler knew a great deal about the architecture of the world through the study of plans and photographs) he was accompanied by 'fellow artists' architect Albert Speer, sculptor Arno Breker and architect Hermann Giesler, in addition to the usual group of followers including Baur, Bormann, Schaub and Keitel. Speer had been given a uniform to fit him into the military environment. At 3.30 a.m. the party took off from Gros Caillou airfield and flew to Le Bourget. In five cars, with the usual SS and RSD escort, the group drove into Paris in the haze of the early morning. There was no cordoning-off, there were no visible security forces, except a solitary 'flic' at one or two corners of the deserted avenues. The party visited the Opéra, whose plans Hitler had studied so thoroughly that he could lead the group around without any help from the old caretaker, who merely had to unlock the doors for him. The representative of the Army occupation command who accompanied Hitler and his party through Paris from the Opéra was Colonel Speidel (involved in plots to assassinate or overthrow the *Führer* from February 1943 to July 1944). The tour now took the group down the Champs-Élysées, past the Madeleine to the Trocadéro, and to the Eiffel Tower, where they got out and walked a bit, then to the Tomb of the Unknown Soldier, and to the Dôme des Invalides where Hitler stood and mused at Napoleon's tomb. On to the Panthéon, Place des Vosges, the Louvre, the Palais de Justice, Sainte Chapelle, down the Rue de

Rivoli, and finally to the monstrosity of Sacré Cœur on Montmartre. By about 9 a.m. the entire visit was over, after no more than three hours. A number of people had recognised Hitler, but had ignored him or run away. A market woman had exclaimed 'C'est lui—oh, c'est lui!' before she fled. By 11 a.m. Hitler was back in 'Wolfschlucht' and soon began preparations for the invasion of Britain, and at the same time for an attack on Russia. As Halder noted in his diary on 22 July: 'Begin work on Russian problem.'[25]

Some more tours of battlefields in France followed, some from an HQ in the Black Forest, 'Tannenberg' (Pine Mountain), late in June and early in July 1940. Security was reduced to a minimum. It was fairly safe to count on secrecy and surprise, but there were anxious moments for the bodyguard when the *Führer's* small convoy of four or five open Mercedes cars passed a thinly-guarded column of thousands of French prisoners-of-war marching in the opposite direction.

Further trips took Hitler to a meeting with Mussolini at the Brenner Pass, to Hendaye for a meeting with General Franco in October 1940, and to Florence for another meeting with Mussolini. Hitler used his Special 'Amerika' on all of these occasions, always accompanied by Baur's three Condor FW 200, and by parts of the Grey Column. On 12 April 1941 Hitler took his train to a previously selected point near Mönichkirchen, some 35 kilometres south of Wiener Neustadt, just north of a long tunnel. He christened the location 'Frühlingssturm' (Spring Storm), and conducted here, from his train, the offensive against Yugoslavia until 25 April, which had become necessary to support the Italian campaign against Greece and which delayed the attack on Russia for about six weeks. The special trains of Göring, Keitel, Himmler and of the *Wehrmacht* Leadership Staff were also parked in the area.

On 25 April the Special departed with Hitler for Marburg in southern Styria. At Spielfeld-Strass he transferred to his motor convoy and then returned to Mönichkirchen. On 26 April the Special went to Marburg and Graz, and the *Führer* took a drive through Graz in his open Mercedes to the great merriment of crowds standing in the rain, and kept in check by a modest and mixed security force of Army, SS, Labour Service, and Air Force personnel. He even accepted a bunch of daffodils from some uniformed girls, and private photography was practised on a considerable scale here and at other stops. In Marburg, the *Führer-Begleit-Kommando* detail were forced to run alongside the *Führer's* car to keep the crowds at least an arm's length from it. Occasionally women and children managed to hand flowers to Hitler.[26] The train was parked for the night at Maria-Saal. Next morning it took Hitler to Klagenfurt, and by evening it was on its way back to Berlin, where it arrived on 28 April at 6.30 p.m. During most of May Hitler stayed at his 'Berghof' retreat, and then spent two weeks in Berlin before a new and decisive epoch was begun.

The offensive against the Soviet Union was begun on 22 June 1941 at 3.05 a.m., in a simultaneous attack with Finnish, Roumanian, Hungarian and Slovakian armed forces. Hitler took up his new HQ 'Wolfschanze' (Wolf's Redoubt, usually translated Wolf's Lair) on 24 June, having left Berlin by Special at 12.30 p.m. the previous day, and gave the installation its new name. It had been known as 'Chemische Werke Askania' (Chemical Works Askania) during the construction period.[27]

Preparations for visits to the Front were not made until 17 July. On 21 July at 3.30 a.m. Hitler flew to Army Group North and conferred with Fieldmarshal Ritter von Leeb, returning to 'Wolfschanze' by 10.30 a.m. On 4 August at 4 a.m. he visited Army Group Centre HQ at Borissow, to confer with Bock, Guderian and Hoth, returning on the same day. A complete Grey Column had been sent there, although there can be no doubt that the Army Group command could have found enough cars to take Hitler and his suite around. The same procedure was followed for a Front tour to Berdichev on 6 August to visit Army Group South (Rundstedt).

Special security measures were taken when the *Duce* visited the *Führer* on 25, 26, 27 and 28 August. Heavy anti-aircraft guns were brought up, and when the *Führer* and the *Duce* took the local shuttle train to 'Mauerwald' some 18 kilometres away, where the Commander-in-Chief of the Army and the General Staff were quartered, there were guards posted all along the tracks. On 26 August both dictators flew in Hitler's plane from Rastenburg airfield to Terespol and met Fieldmarshals von Bock, von Kluge and Kesselring. *Führer-Begleit-Bataillon* Front Groups to transport and escort the party had been sent ahead. They returned via Göring's temporary HQ near Rostken airfield, arriving back in 'Wolfschanze' by 4 p.m. The Front Group was sent on to 'Installation South,' another HQ rarely used, between Frystak and Krosno, where the two dictators went by their respective specials. The *Duce's* train went to 'Installation South,' the *Führer's* Special was parked at Strzyzów, from where Hitler took his cars. The train was later brought up, and after a talk in the tea-house, the dictators and a small group from their respective suites had dinner in Hitler's Pullman car. Next morning they flew to Uman where a Front Group plus an anti-aircraft platoon and half an armoured reconnaissance platoon awaited them. They were met by Fieldmarshal von Rundstedt, and were driven some 40 kilometres south to review an Italian division. Due to poor road conditions (as the *Führer's* HQ Diary recorded) the division had not arrived at the appointed place, and *Führer* and *Duce* travelled 20 kilometres further to meet the division. Then they returned to Uman, flew back to Krosno, and were driven back to 'Installation South.' At 8 o'clock that evening the *Duce's* Special left for Rome. Hitler returned by train to 'Wolfschanze.'

Throughout the year Hitler travelled mainly by Special or by aeroplane. He visited Marienburg and the Tannenberg Monument on 10 September, and Army Group Centre HQ at Borissow on 24 September. Occasionally he took his train to Berlin one evening to give a speech on the next day, as on 3 October, and returned on the evening of that day to 'Wolfschanze.' He found time for the commemorative observances in Munich on 8 and 9 November 1941 and was back on 10 November. On 20 November Hitler rode his *Führersonderzug* to Berlin for the state funeral of General Udet, and he was back on 22 November. On 26

22.   *'Anlage Süd' HQ with artificial tunnel and Mussolini's Special train, August 1941 ;*
on far left Linge, in foreground Mussolini and Hitler

November he made the same journey again, this time for the state funeral of Colonel Mölders, the most successful German Air Force fighter pilot. Hitler was back in East Prussia on 30 November, flew to Kiev, Poltawa and Mariupol on 2 December, and took his Special to Berlin on 8 December to give a speech in the *Reichstag* on 11 December which contained the declaration of war against the United States. He left Berlin on 15 December and arrived in 'Wolfschanze' on 16 December, where he remained for the rest of the year.[28]

In the first six months of 1942 Hitler took seven trips to Berlin from 'Wolfschanze,' with two follow-up trips to Munich and Berchtesgaden, all by *Führersonderzug.* He also flew to Finland once, and twice to Poltawa (1 June and 3 July), to Army Group South HQ.[29] On one of the flights to Poltawa, Hitler's Condor had a close call, although he was not in it at the time. His pilot Baur reports that the plane was suddenly being shot at by Russian planes above Nikolayev airfield, immediately after take-off, and several shots went through the wings. Baur opened the throttle wide, gained altitude, and turned as if to attack the Russians, whereupon they departed.

A really dangerous situation developed on a visit to Army Group Don (Fieldmarshal von Manstein, C-in-C) at Saporoshe, about three weeks after the fall of Stalingrad. Suddenly, after a late situation conference, the *Führer* decided that he must go and see Manstein and his staff. About 2 o'clock in the morning of 17 February 1943 the *Führer* and his immediate staff, including Zeitzler, Jodl and others, flew from Rastenburg via Vinnytsa to Saporoshe.[30]

This was the time when the conspirators in Army Group Centre HQ near Smolensk were trying to lure Hitler there in order to do away with him. At another HQ, in Walki near Poltawa (Army Group B, Field-marshal von Weichs, C-in-C), a visit by the *Führer* had also been expected, and here, too, preparations had been made for his demise. The chief conspirators here were General Hubert Lanz and Major-General Dr. Hans Speidel, his Chief of Staff. Lanz commanded a group of units called Army Detachment Lanz, consisting of SS Corps Hausser, elements of *Leibstandarte SS 'Adolf Hitler'* under Sepp Dietrich, *SS-Division 'Reich'* under Keppler, *SS-Division 'Totenkopf'* (Death's Head) under Theodor Eicke (formerly Inspector General of Concentration Camps), parts of *Panzer-Division 'Grossdeutschland'* (Greater Germany), and some other units. Lanz was to try to stabilise the situation in the Kharkov area after the collapse of the Italian 8th Army there, but this was an almost impossible task, and it turned out soon that the commanding officer of a *'Grossdeutschland'* Tank Regiment, Colonel Graf von Strachwitz, was of the same opinion. It further developed that Lanz, Speidel and Strach-witz shared the opinion that Hitler was a criminal and must be done away with. It was agreed that he was to be arrested on his next visit to the Poltawa area. If there was any resistance—and what else could be expected from the SS and RSD bodyguards?—force was to be used. Indeed, the conspirators fully expected to kill Hitler there and then. But instead of visiting Poltawa where so many of his favourite SS troops were fighting, he chose to fly to Saporoshe. The 'Lanz Plan' never came off. But there were also other dangers for Hitler.

Baur and his pilots landed their planes at about 6 a.m. on the larger of two airfields, one located east of the city. The Front was not far, and while Baur and the other pilots and crews were waiting at the airfield, they suddenly learned that Russian tanks were approaching from Dnje-popetrovsk on the highway at which the airfield was situated. Some twenty tanks were reported, and fighter planes sent to fight them off could not operate because of low clouds and fog. The situation was generally under control, but a few of the tanks got through and appeared near the edge of the airfield, whereupon Baur requested permission to transfer the Condor planes to the southern, smaller airfield. But Hitler sent word that this would not be necessary as he would be ready to take off shortly. Preparations were made to defend the airfield. Then Hitler arrived, chauffeured by Kempka, and the three Condor planes took off, just as Gigant transport planes were flying in with anti-tank guns and other weapons and supplies.

It was subsequently learned that the Soviet tanks had taken up defensive positions in a nearby *Kolkhos* (collective farm) rather than attack the airfield—because they had run low on fuel. They could have found enough at the airfield if they had risked a small battle; but the several hundred planes parked there must have signalled to them the likelihood of a very stiff resistance.

The next Front visit was made at Army Group Centre HQ on 13 March 1943. A week earlier, Admiral Canaris, Chief of Intelligence (*OKW/Amt Ausland/Abwehr*), had flown there, on 7 March, with his Chief of Central Section, Major-General Oster, with his Head of Section II, Colonel Lahousen, and with Dr. von Dohnanyi, one of Canaris' closest collaborators and, like Oster, a leading member of the conspiracy against Hitler. The purpose was a general conference, but Canaris had also brought along with him a case of explosives. The preparations were very extensive, ranging from plans to seize central government strongholds in Berlin and throughout the *Reich*, to the procurement of explosives, so it is not unlikely that some information about them reached the *Reich's* chief policeman, Heinrich Himmler, perhaps in garbled form.[31]

There were a number of assassination attempts reported. On 16 February a telegram from the German Consulate in Lausanne warned of a planned assassination attempt against Göring within the next two weeks, and the information was immediately relayed to *SS-Standartenführer* Schellenberg at Section VI (SD, Foreign Intelligence) RSHA. On 7 March Kaltenbrunner at Section IV (*Gestapo*) RSHA informed all *Gestapo* offices and other appropriate authorities that small parcels containing bombs and addressed to various German government agencies had been posted as registered mail at a Warsaw post office on 3 March. The parcels consisted of wooden boxes $21 \times 9 \times 8$ cm, filled with solid pioneer explosive rigged to be detonated upon opening by electric ignition, and, in case they were not opened, for detonation by a delay fuse of British origin. There was widespread concern, and Himmler made sure that not only all appropriate SS authorities were warned, but also Frau Himmler. With pedantry and with understandable concern, Himmler checked up on Rattenhuber's RSD and discovered that this agency, primarily concerned with the prevention of assassination attempts against the highest *Reich* leaders, had not functioned well. Himmler discovered that his personal RSD detail stationed in Gmund am Tegernsee, where his home was, had not been informed of the threat by 9 March, although Himmler's first teleprinted communication dealing with the case was dated 6 March. On the same day he had been on the telephone to Kaltenbrunner concerning the escape of British R.A.F. officers in Poland, ordering an 'aeroplane with specialists and dogs' to Poznan, and he expressed concern to Kaltenbrunner about special border controls, and about car thefts in Warsaw. On 10 March he also telephoned Rattenhuber who was at 'Wehrwolf' HQ near Vinnytsa in the Ukraine with Hitler at the time. On 11 March Rattenhuber instructed appropriate RSD agencies to exercise special caution: It must be anticipated that the assassins would vary colour, size, form and sender of the parcels. Therefore they must immediately be turned over to the RSD untouched. The same procedure must be followed, Rattenhuber's instructions continued, with parcels whose sender was unknown, or of whose arrival no advance notice had been received. Special couriers were to be used in transporting suspect parcels if any turned up.

Himmler seems to have taken the necessary steps to meet the new threats. But nothing has come to light to indicate that security measures around the *Führer* were intensified, although the air was buzzing with assassination threats. Since this was Rattenhuber's responsibility, and Himmler had informed him, the evidence does not warrant suspecting the *Reich* SS Leader of any intentions, let alone overt acts, in these incidents. But it may be noted that this was approximately the time when Himmler himself began making contacts with opposition circles in Germany, contacts which continued at least until autumn 1943, and it was the time when the RSHA competitors of the military intelligence service (*OKW/Amt Ausland/Abwehr*) were ready to deal lethal blows to their arch-enemies around Admiral Canaris. At a time when plots against the *Führer* were hatched all over the *Reich*, and at all Fronts, and when assassination plots were coming to the attention of the *Gestapo*, Himmler was well informed about the opposition, but made little use of his knowledge. In any case, the very least in stepped-up security one would have expected in connection with the *Führer's* journeys would have been a general prohibition of parcels on his aeroplanes.

Hitler arrived near Smolensk on 13 March 1943, on his way back from Vinnytsa to East Prussia. He wanted to talk over the offensive at Kursk. Again, he came with his entourage in three Condor aeroplanes, accompanied by several fighter aircraft. After landing, they were met by Field-marshal von Kluge, C-in-C Army Group Centre, and by his Operations Officer, Major-General von Tresckow. Hitler, looking old, bent and tired, used only his own Grey Column cars that had been brought all the way to Smolensk for the visit, and he had himself chauffered by his own driver Kempka. On his way to the HQ compound, his convoy had to cross a railway track; all rail traffic was suspended for the entire duration of the visit. The greatest possible secrecy was observed, and the route from airfield to HQ compound was carefully sealed off by troops especially brought in for the purpose.[32] Bodyguards in field-grey SS uniforms were seen with sub-machine-guns ready to shoot, on the way to the conference room, and after the conference during the half-kilometre walk to the dining hall. All around the HQ, a wide security cordon had been established, and along Hitler's path lanes of soldiers guarded his safety.

But not all of them did. Several squadrons of 'Cavalry Regiment Centre' were deployed in the security operation; the regiment was under the command of Lieutenant-Colonel von Boeselager, who was in the conspiracy. Boeselager's brother, also one of the conspirators, was Special Missions officer to Fieldmarshal von Kluge. A group of officers and non-commissioned officers of Boeselager's regiment had agreed to assassinate Hitler by shooting him collectively as he passed their security cordon.

Originally the plan had been to shoot Hitler at lunch, but objections had been raised to this. Fieldmarshal von Kluge, who was informed of the plot, suggested that 'one could not just shoot the man at his meal.' It would have been nearly inevitable that others, including Kluge himself and visiting C-in-Cs of armies who were there for the conference, would be hit or at least endangered. On the other hand, the conspirators themselves thought they could not do without Kluge, who would be needed to help hold the front and stabilise the internal military and domestic situation while negotiations for an armistice would proceed. So the idea of the lunch assassination was given up.

It is less clear why the shooting attack along one of the paths was not made, either while Hitler walked from his car to the HQ conference building, or on his way from there to lunch. On his way back to his car, the chances were poor; the cars were parked in front of the door. It appears, however, that the plan had been just this: to shoot Hitler as he walked back to his car. Major König who commanded No. 1 Squadron of 'Cavalry Regiment Centre,' and who personally led the men guarding Hitler's path inside the HQ compound, later hinted that Hitler had not followed the paths that had been planned for him. It has been observed more than once that Hitler was given to seemingly capricious changes of plans as a means of increasing his security. But it is equally plausible that Major-General von Tresckow, the king-pin in the conspiracy at Army Group Centre, had decided the use of explosives was both more likely to succeed and less likely to burden the Army with a stigma. An inexplicable plane crash in Russia seemed preferable. Tresckow's contact in Berlin, Captain Ludwig Gehre, had obtained through Otto John (who worked for Lufthansa) a complete description of Hitler's four-engine Focke-Wolfe 200 Condor; the description must have arrived with Canaris, Oster, Lahousen and Dohnanyi on 7 March.

Tresckow's plan was to smuggle a bomb with the fuse activated on to Hitler's plane so that it would crash *en route*. He had prepared two pairs of 'clams' and wrapped them to look like a parcel of two bottles of brandy to anyone who was told that such it was. A fuse for thirty-minute delay ignition was installed so that it could be pressed shortly before it was put on the plane. During the lunch, Tresckow asked a member of Hitler's entourage, Colonel Heinz Brandt from the General Staff who was expected to have his place on Hitler's plane, if he could take along a 'present', or 'betting debt', for Major-General Stieff back at General Staff HQ in East Prussia, and if he could put it on Hitler's Condor. Brandt agreed.

Hitler had a special meal prepared by his cook who had been brought along. Before he started eating, Dr. Morell had to taste the food. This of course looked like the manifestation of suspicion of being poisoned, characteristic of oriental despots, but the correct explanation may well be that given by one of Hitler's personal SS aides, *SS-Sturmbannführer* Schulze-Kossens: Hitler's stomach was so weak and so easily upset that he could not tolerate anything with even slightly too much spice or salt. Schlabrendorff and Gersdorff, however, would not consider this a likely story. They believed they had proof of Hitler's overriding fear of assassination attempts after they had had a chance, in an unguarded moment, of handling Hitler's military-style hat, and had found that it was 'heavy as a cannonball' because it was lined with some $3\frac{1}{2}$ lb of protective metal plate (this is denied by Linge and Kempka).

When Hitler and Kluge drove back to the airfield, Schlabrendorff went there in another car and brought along the package. As Hitler started to get into his plane, Schlabrendorff pressed the fuse capsule, and at a sign from Tresckow he handed the package to Brandt. According to Schlabrendorff, Brandt then boarded Hitler's plane with the package, immediately after Hitler himself. Then the planes took off, escorted as usual by several fighter planes. The fuse was one for a thirty-minute delay, so that the crash would have occurred shortly before the planes reached Minsk. It was assumed that one of the fighter planes would radio to one of its ground contacts reporting the mishap and that the conspirators waiting near Smolensk would soon get the news. But nothing happened until after about two hours, the conspirators learned that Hitler had landed safely at Rastenburg airfield. It only remained for Schlabrendorff to gather up the remains of this abortive attempt. He had to travel back to East Prussia under a military pretext, and retrieve the package by explaining that a mix-up had occurred and sacrificing two bottles of brandy to exchange the bombs for the genuine article. Upon examination of the fuse he found it had functioned correctly until the striker pin, driven forward by a compressed spring released by a retainer wire consumed by the corrosive acid, had struck the detonator cap—but the detonator cap had not ignited the explosive. The best guess why the detonator cap had not detonated the plastic explosive is that the temperature where the parcel was had dropped very low. The pilot's cabin and the luggage compartment of the Condor had no heat, and the warm-water heating system in the passenger cabin also failed to function at times, as Hitler's pilot recalls.[33]

It was not security precautions which had foiled this attempt, so it is hardly surprising that precautions were not adapted to prevent further attacks of this nature.

The *Führer* continued to travel here and there, from 'Wolfschanze' to Berlin and Munich, and back again, and to points near the Fronts. On 27 August 1943 he flew to 'Wehrwolf' HQ for the last time, and on 8 September to Saporoshe.[34] With the bombing of German cities, and with the increasingly less successful war efforts, Hitler's rare public appearances became less triumphal. He refused to visit bombed cities, and although he was always fully and accurately informed about the number of people killed in air raids and about the destruction of buildings, he never showed concern for the suffering population, only for theatres, bridges or other pieces of architecture that had been lost or damaged.[35] He took part in the ceremonies commemorating the 1923 *putsch* on 8 November 1943 and gave a speech in Munich's 'Bürgerbräu' Beer Hall, after a long public silence. He left 'Wolfschanze' by Special on 7 November at 4.10 p.m. and arrived in Munich at 4.10 p.m. on 8 November. He gave his unusually aggressive speech in the 'Bürgerbräu' Beer Hall at 5 p.m., drove to his Prinzregentenplatz apartments at 6.30, and had dinner with the *Gauleiter* and other Party dignitaries in the *Führer* Building at Königsplatz at 8 p.m. By midnight he was back in his apartment, and on 9 November he paid a visit to Professor Troost's architecture studio, held a situation conference at 1 p.m., and had lunch at the 'Osteria Bavaria' at 3. At 4.30 p.m. he left on his Special for 'Wolfschanze,' where he arrived the next day at 6.50 p.m. On 19 November he took a trip to Breslau, where he gave a speech on the 20th, shrouded in great secrecy; during the night of 20 to 21 November, he was back in his HQ again, one day before a particularly heavy air raid on Berlin.

As late as 1944, when the Allies enjoyed almost full control of German airspace, Hitler still travelled by aeroplane. He took a brief trip to 'Wolfschanze' from Berchtesgaden (where he had moved in February) on 20 March 1944, and he flew there again on 9 July 1944.[36]

In June 1944, after the successful Allied invasion of Normandy, Hitler visited one of his HQ in France, 'Wolfschlucht II' near Margival. He travelled by Condor to Metz on 16 June, and drove the rest of the way in the early hours of 17 June in order to confer with Fieldmarshals von Rundstedt and Rommel, C-in-Cs of the western theatre and Army Group B, respectively. All *Luftwaffe* fighter planes were grounded along Hitler's route and the anti-aircraft batteries were forbidden to fire during the flight in order to prevent any errors. During lunch, on 17 June, Hitler had his food tasted before his eyes, and two SS bodyguards stood behind his chair. Shortly before the *Führer's* arrival, SS troops had sealed off the HQ installation hermetically, in an obvious affront to the Army units stationed in the area. It was, all things considered, an unpleasant encounter. Hitler abused the military men in ways that were by now becoming familiar, reproaching them for retreats, and Rommel retorted that it was easy to order operations from behind a desk instead of visiting the Front to see what the realities were. An air-raid alert interrupted the conference and the participants had to withdraw to the air-raid shelter attached to Hitler's bunker. There Rommel told the *Führer* the entire Normandy Front would soon collapse, the Allies would invade German territory, the Front in Italy would collapse too, and Germany would be completely isolated. It was necessary to end the war now. But Hitler told him to mind the Normandy Front and nothing else.

A visit to the Front HQ of Army Group B at La Roche-Guyon was scheduled for 19 June. But when Speidel, Rommel's Chief of Staff, wanted to talk over the arrangements with Rundstedt's Chief of Staff, General Blumentritt, he 'received the unbelievable information that Hitler had returned to Berchtesgaden during the night of 17 to 18 June.'

On 12 June the rocket-driven V1s were first launched against London, two days ahead of schedule, and before they were ready. Ten were launched, of which four failed at once, two disappeared without trace, three only reached the general target area, and one destroyed a railway bridge in London. On 14 June 244 bombs were launched, causing numerous fires in London, and 500 were launched on 15 June; by 22 June 1,000 had been launched. On 17 June one of them fell and detonated near 'Wolfschlucht II,' causing Hitler and his entourage to disappear in great haste back to the 'Berghof.'

On 14 July 1944 Hitler took his train to 'Wolfschanze,' where he stayed throughout the collapse of Army Group Centre under the attacks of the Red Army, throughout the near-successful assassination attempt by Colonel Graf von Stauffenberg, throughout the collapse of the Front in France and the loss of Paris. On 20 November 1944 he left his East Prussian HQ for Berlin, never to return.

Hitler left Berlin once more to move to his Western HQ 'Amt 500' near Bad Nauheim on 11 December 1944. From here he directed the Ardennes Offensive, and returned to Berlin on 15 January 1945, arriving at 9.40 a.m. on 16 January, after it had failed. Only once more did he venture forth from the capital, on 11 March 1945, when he visited the HQ of an Army Corps at the Oder Front. He never left Berlin again after this.[37]

10 Residences

Reich Chancellery

The first impression a visitor to the old Chancellery received at the main entrance at No. 78 Wilhelmstrasse was the presence of several police and SS or *Wehrmacht* sentries. Special guard rooms were installed in 1934 for the *Wehrmacht* (then still called *Reichswehr*) guards on the ground floor of the south wing of the old Chancellery. In 1936 the State Secretary and Chief of the Chancellery Dr. Lammers, the commander of *Leibstandarte-SS 'Adolf Hitler'* (LSSAH) Sepp Dietrich, Lammers' security officer Police Captain Deckert, and Police Captain Koplien of 16th Police Precinct Berlin clarified the various assignments: the police sentries had 'full responsibility for police matters, most of all for regulating traffic and for identity checks;' 'the SS guard supports [them] in these functions, and otherwise is in charge of matters inside the old Chancellery.'[1]

At the main entrance, No. 78 Wilhelmstrasse, where a police sentry (Post I) was stationed day and night, only 'inconspicuous surveillance' of strangers was required, but no identity checks; these were made inside by the receptionist. Post II was stationed at the gate to the inner court and to Hitler's apartments, No. 77 Wilhelmstrasse, day and night, and had to ascertain that persons entering were properly authorised. Persons without passes had to be sent to the main entrance to receive special permission through the receptionist. Delivery men, for instance, would be referred by Post II to the receptionist at the main entrance, where they would receive a metal tag that identified them as authorised to Post II. But Post II would have to remember exactly whom he had sent over and recognise whomever he saw coming back with a tag. The fact that a visitor was outside the security control of the Chancellery between being admitted and entering the building represented a gap. Post III had to check identity and authorisation to enter of all persons arriving in cars at the main gate and to regulate traffic with the assistance of the SS guard. The gate was closed from 9 p.m. to 7 a.m., and it was to be closed also when large crowds gathered nearby. In the Chancellery gardens, police guards with dogs patrolled the grounds from 10 p.m. to 5 a.m.

Members of RSD and *SS-Begleit-Kommando* were expressly permitted to use any entrance, but if they were not personally known to police sentries their identities had to be established before they were allowed to pass. The *Führer-Begleit-Kommando* had quarters in a hut in the Chancellery gardens, near the gardener's house.

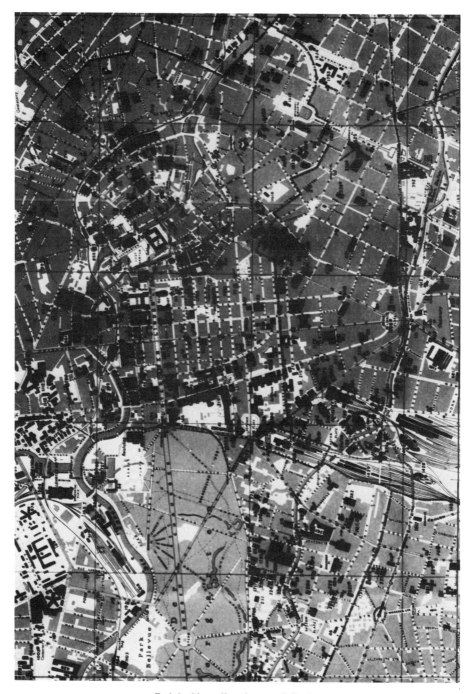

23a.   Reich *Chancellery in central Berlin, 1944*

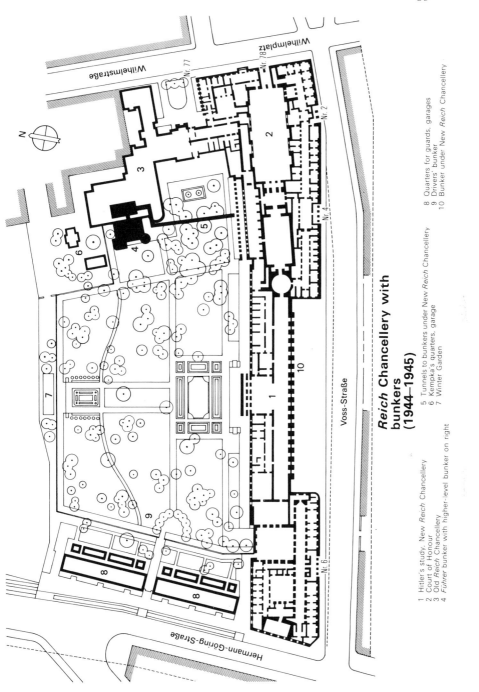

Reich Chancellery with
bunkers
(1944–1945)

1 Hitler's study, New *Reich* Chancellery
2 Court of Honour
3 Old *Reich* Chancellery
4 *Führer* bunker with higher-level bunker on right
5 Tunnels to bunkers under New *Reich* Chancellery
6 Kempka's quarters, garage
7 Winter Garden
8 Quarters for guards, garages
9 Drivers' bunker
10 Bunker under New *Reich* Chancellery

Wilhelmstraße
Wilhelmplatz
Voss-Straße
Hermann-Göring-Straße

Nr. 77
Nr. 78
Nr. 2
Nr. 4
Nr. 6

23b.   Reich *Chancellery and bunkers, 1944–5*

SS guards were increasingly in evidence inside and outside as the years passed. A temporary regulation for LSSAH sentries on duty at the Chancellery of 10 August 1938 stated: 'When the *Führer* is present, the SS guard consists of 1 commanding officer, 3 non-commissioned officers, and 39 men; when he is absent, the figures are 0:3:33.' Of these, 13 and 11 guards were constantly on post, respectively. From 15 September 1938 a new temporary guard regulation for the SS guards was issued for a total guard 1:2:12 strong: Post 1 was stationed at the Adjutants' Office, armed with a pistol; Post 2 at the kitchen anteroom (pistol); Post 3 along the garden front (carbine); Post 4 at the garage entrance on Hermann-Göring-Strasse (pistol).

The connecting hallways between the *Reich* Chancellery on the one side and Presidential Chancellery and offices of the SA Chief of Staff, Lutze, on the other side of the first and second storey, were sealed off by SA guards to all persons who wished to enter the *Reich* Chancellery from there. Such persons were to be told they must use the main entrance at No. 78 Wilhelmstrasse. Here the receptionist made the first identity check; strangers and visitors had to be escorted to appropriate offices in the Chancellery. During peak business hours two receptionists had to be on duty, and additional ones had to expect to be called upon. The receptionists were warned not to give any information on the presence or absence of the *Führer*, of the Chief of the *Reich* Chancellery or of any of the other officials.

Personal protection of the *Führer* inside the *Reich* Chancellery was the task of the *SS-Begleit-Kommando*, RSD and LSSAH guards. There was still another security service operating inside the Chancellery called *Sicherheitsdienst* (SD, Security Service, not to be confused with Heydrich's SD of the SS), and its members were held personally responsible for the prevention of all criminal acts and dangers. At first this *Sicherheitsdienst* was provided by a few criminal-police officers and four gendarmes; on 1 October 1935 the gendarmes were replaced by civil servants of the Chancellery (*Ministerialamtsgehilfen*) in order to avoid frequent change of personnel, which Hitler objected to. As with other security services, Rattenhuber had authority to give directives to the SD of the Chancellery. At night, two of its men were posted, three in daytime. On special occasions, such as *Führer's* Birthday on 20 April 1936, its strength was doubled. A daytime regular crew consisted of nine men who took turns in threes. Post 1 was stationed in the ground-floor entrance hall near the lift; he had to watch entrance and hall, and the passage to the inner courtyard. He was responsible for sending persons back to the receptionist if they were not properly admitted, and making sure that visitors handed over their tags on leaving the premises. Post 2 was responsible for the ground-floor hallway along which offices were located. Unlike Post 1 he was not stationary but patrolling, so that he could watch entrances and passages, and make sure that all persons he did not know were properly authorised to be where they were. Post 3 patrolled the first storey, where he had in the main the same functions as his colleagues downstairs. He also had to watch the stairs leading up to the third story. The anterooms of the Chancellor's offices, and of the State Secretary and Chief of the *Reich* Chancellery, had to be guarded '*most strictly*,' and the most meticulous identity checks for all visitors were required.

At night SD men took over the duties of the receptionists from 10 p.m.; at this time all doors and gates had to be locked. Post 1 was now stationed inside the receptionist's office and had to answer the telephone as well as open and lock the doors when required. A bell signal from the police sentry outside would tell him when he had to open the door. Post 2 patrolled the ground floor and occasionally the upper storey. Strangers without valid passes had to be arrested on the spot. They were to be taken to 16th Police HQ by police officers. In case of any incidents, Captain Deckert was to be informed by telephone at once.

The above security measures were insufficient if many people were milling around in the *Reich* Chancellery. Yet the directives for Hitler's birthday on 20 April 1936 provided for only three additional RSD men in the building. In the cramped space of the old *Reich* Chancellery surveillance was extremely difficult when many people were there. The security men themselves then did not have enough room to move about as needed. On 30 January 1937, eighty-four foreign diplomats were invited to view a torch-light procession with the *Führer* from within the Chancellery. Scores of Hitler's associates, aides, friends and hangers-on were on hand, too, on such occasions. The potential dangers are perhaps best illustrated by the fact that at least one admission card was sent out without a name on it (it was sent to the Dutch Legation). But when, as during Admiral Horthy's state visit in August 1938, there were 100 additional orderlies from the LSSAH on duty in the Chancellery, the impression an outsider had was one of comprehensive vigilance and control.

A closer look at the security regulations reveals weaknesses and gaps, many of which are recorded in the watch logs and in *Reich* Chancellery correspondence. 'Aryan' ancestry, Party membership and general loyalty did not of themselves produce a high level of reliability and vigilance, particularly among the LSSAH men. Ordinary methods of control, based on principles of reward and punishment, were found indispensable. The SS guards at the *Reich* Chancellery were controlled by a *Sicherheits-Kontrolldienst* (Security Control Service) established in 1939, after Elser's assassination attempt, in addition to all the existing security forces, and every few hours officers of their own regiment came to see if they were doing their jobs properly.[2] More often than one might expect, they were not.

There were other difficulties, all traceable to a certain irresponsibility and juvenile interpretation of what it meant to be part of an élite corps. The *Reich* Chancellery found it necessary to write to Sepp Dietrich, Commander of the LSSAH, that SS guards had taken to riding up and down in the lifts to pass the time, and that for two years the hooks on the clothes-racks in an anteroom leading to Hitler's offices were frequently being torn off at night. To top it all off, the SS men were playing the radio in their guard room at full volume with the windows open, at all hours. Lammers sent a letter of complaint to Hitler's Personal Adjutant, Brückner (October 1935).

In June 1936 one of the SS guard officers on duty at the *Reich* Chancellery complained that there were only five rounds of ammunition per rifle, while the *Wehrmacht* guard had two whole boxes of ammunition. Furthermore, there were no keys available to the SS guards for the Wilhelm-strasse gate, while a temporary wooden gate was unnecessarily open day and night. A few days later, the commanding officer of the *Reich* Chancellery SS guard reported that the wall separating a neighbouring garden from the Chancellery garden was unguarded although the neighbouring garden was on higher ground and it was easy to climb over the walls. In fact two women were arrested on 8 June after they had climbed into the Chancellery garden.

A more serious matter was dealt with in a report by Captain Deckert, Lammers' security adjutant, to Rattenhuber and to *SS-Sturmbannführer* Wernicke, one of the *Führer's* personal aides. An unemployed salesman had managed to scale a construction fence on Vossstrasse unnoticed by any of the guards on 11 January 1937 about 2.30 p.m., in broad daylight, and had climbed into the *Reich* Chancellery through an open toilet window. He wanted desperately to see the *Führer* (as he later revealed), perhaps hoping to get a job. He had been out of work for five years, and he had repeatedly asked for work at the office of the Ministerpresident of Prussia. But on the day he slipped into the Chancellery to see the *Führer*, he carried a gas pistol. A maid noticed the strange man and alerted a Security Service (SD) guard, a retired police sergeant. The intruder was taken to another guard, who checked the stranger's identification card and decided, after brief questioning, that the man had no evil intentions. He let him go. Only then Captain Deckert was informed; it was after 3 p.m. Deckert managed to summon the intruder to his office and had him rearrested. An additional SS guard was subsequently posted at the construction fence.[3]

On 14 February 1937, shortly before 9 a.m., a thirty-three-year-old butcher, Franz Kroll, appeared in the Chancellery and tried to push his way through to Hitler's rooms; he was restrained by a security man. He had the smell of alcohol on his breath and said the police had robbed him of 135 Reichsmarks. He was turned over to 16th Police HQ.

A bookbinder named Walter Zeitler, apparently a religious crackpot, wrote to the Chancellery on 17 March 1937 saying that he intended to come to see Hitler on Palm Sunday at 9 a.m. and tell him about his, Zeitler's mission as Divine Saviour. He was not admitted.

A mentally ill man named Josef Thomas from Elberfeld, carrying a gun, travelled to Berlin to see Hitler and Göring in November 1937. He was arrested by the *Gestapo* on 26 November 1937.

The danger from careless guards may at times have been greater than that from mentally-disturbed people. On 8 December 1937, twenty minutes before midnight, one of the SS guards on the first storey was playing with his gun and accidentally fired a shot into a wall.

On 23 January 1938 an SA guard in the lobby of No. 1 Vossstrasse played with his pistol and accidentally fired a shot. The shot went through the back of a chair that had been vacated only a few moments earlier. This was the third time within a short period (there had been still another incident) that accidental shots were fired by guards in the Chancellery.[4]

The old Chancellery was a far cry from the fortress the *Führer* envisioned in his plans for a completely new Government quarter in post-war Berlin. The only modest beginning pointing in that direction had been made in 1935: a new balcony was added to the Chancellery, at a total estimated cost (including bronze doors) of 28,360 Reichs-marks, so that the *Führer* might show himself to the masses. It was re-inforced with 8-mm steel plate.[5] A magnificent new chancellery was built in 1938 as a temporary, makeshift official residence, to be used only until Berlin could be completely rearranged according to the *Führer's* ideas.

The New *Reich* Chancellery that Albert Speer built for Hitler in record time was completed on 7 January 1939, less than a year after planning had begun and the decision to build had been taken. Hitler had told his 'Building Inspector-General' Speer in January 1938: 'I shall have extremely important conferences in the near future, and I need huge rooms and halls with which I can impress especially the smaller poten-tates. You can use the entire terrain along Vossstrasse, and I don't care how much it costs.'[6]

Visitors who were received ceremoniously entered the grounds by car, through a huge double-gate. They were led up some stairs to a 'small' reception hall, through another double-door 5 metres high into another hall, then up a few more stairs, through a round room with a high cupola, and then they began their long march of 145 metres through a gallery more than twice as long as the Hall of Mirrors at Versailles. After a march of a total of 220 metres the visitor finally reached Hitler's recep-tion hall. As Hitler put it: 'They will get an idea of the might and great-ness of the German *Reich* on their long way from the entrance to the reception hall.' At the end of the march, the visitor was led into Hitler's oversized office with its huge desk.

At least some forty or fifty people were free to enter the New Chancellery if they wished to have lunch with the *Führer*. They only had to telephone the aide on duty and tell him they were coming.[7] Most of them were *Gauleiter* and *Reich* Leaders in the Party, some were Cabinet Ministers, and some were other members of Hitler's inner circle, such as his architect Speer. With the exception of the *Führer's Wehrmacht* adjutants, military men did not belong to this category of privileged visitors. But someone like Speer could simply drive up in his car to the gate on Wilhelmstrasse where two SS sentries in black uniforms stood motionless with carbines, and where a policeman would recognize him and open the gate without further ado. Speer would then park his car in the courtyard and enter Hitler's private apartments next to the New Chancellery. Now Speer would encounter a member of the *SS-Begleit-Kommando*, but he was usually allowed to enter Hitler's rooms unaccompanied. Here, in a lounge and some sitting-rooms, he would find Hitler's guests of the day standing around talking and waiting for Hitler, some fifteen minutes before lunch, and presently Hitler would emerge from his rooms upstairs or from the adjoining New Chancellery. He would talk with his guests for a few minutes or read some news summaries, and then all would go into the dining-room. This freedom of movement for a privileged few, the opportunity to walk around unaccompanied in Hitler's rooms wherever they were, existed throughout the war. After 20 July 1944 the privileged visitors still only had to have their briefcases examined.

Certain other persons, too, perhaps some fifty of them, had at least the opportunity of coming within a few feet of Hitler's person almost any time they wished. Dr. Erich Kordt, head of Foreign Minister Ribbentrop's personal secretariat, was one of them. When he prepared his plans to assassinate Hitler on 11 November 1939, the day before the scheduled offensive against France was to begin, he made a point of showing up frequently in the large anteroom where people used to wait for Hitler. The attempt was never made, partly because the offensive was postponed, and partly because security was tightened after Elser's attack in Munich on 8 November.[8]

Outsiders would have had greater difficulties in entering the New Chancellery, but there were gaps in security. The receptionists were warned not to tell anyone whether Hitler was in the Chancellery or not. The RSD were required to keep strictly secret all of Hitler's unofficial departures and returns from and to the Chancellery. Even the men who had to accompany Hitler, say, to the opera, were told only minutes before departure. But in the New Chancellery, the *Führer's* standard on the Chancellery roof was raised by two LSSAH men at the precise moment when Hitler's car passed through the main gate, and the standard remained up, for all to see, for as long as Hitler was there, coming down as soon as he left the premises.[9]

A few days after the inauguration of the New Chancellery building, on 18 January 1939, a *Wehrmacht* double sentry from *Wachregiment Berlin*, later known as *Wachregiment 'Grossdeutschland'* (Berlin Guard Regiment) was posted at the No. 4 Vossstrasse entrance (Presidential Chancellery). The full crew was one non-commissioned officer and six men, with three carbines. This arrangement was less than cosy. There were at first not enough bunks for the off-duty shift, and in May 1939 repeated complaints had to be lodged by the Guard Regiment about bedbugs.[10] From the guard room, an alarm signal could be transmitted to the *Führer's* apartments. The main drive-in-gate was also guarded by a *Wehrmacht* sentry, and at least one policeman was always on hand there.

The lines of responsibility between *Wehrmacht* and SS in matters of guarding the *Führer* and *Reich* Chancellor were fairly well established by 1939, but fluctuations did occur. *Wehrmacht* and SS sentries were not always posted at the same entrances, perhaps as part of an effort to avoid any permanent arrangements that assassins or other conspirators might be able to rely on. In March 1939 Hitler decided that on tours members of the *SS-Verfügungstruppe* (SS Special Task Troops), which in most cases meant from LSSAH, should be sentries outside his hotel or other residence; that on *Wehrmacht* Day in Nuremberg they were to be replaced by *Wehrmacht* guards of honour; that in other extraordinary circumstances *Wehrmacht* guards might also be posted; and that when the country was mobilising (i.e. in time of war) the *Wehrmacht* provided the guards of honour from the *Wehrmacht* unit organised to guard the *Führer's* HQ.

Besides the *Wehrmacht* sentries, there were police and SS guards outside the New Chancellery at the other entrances, and RSD men constantly patrolled the grounds.

At times this got to be a nuisance: the SS guard outside the winter garden had to be told repeatedly not to pass too close to the windows and entrance so as not to disturb conferences in the winter garden. Only seven days after this admonition, one of the *Führer's* aides again complained to LSSAH that one of the SS sentries had been pressing his nose against the winter garden windows.[11] There was also an SS guard at Hitler's private entrance, and there were two at the entrance to the new building in the Court of Honour, during daylight hours; there were two in the Great Hall in front of Hitler's office, with carbines (pistols at night), one at the entrance to the cupola hall, one at the side-entrance, from No. 6 Vossstrasse, to the Great Hall, or Marble Gallery (these last two guards were later replaced by RSD men); there were, finally, two sentries (SS or *Wehrmacht*) each in front of the No. 4 Vossstrasse entrance and No. 6 Vossstrasse entrance. No. 2 Vossstrasse was guarded by an

SA double sentry. For special events, one additional SS guard was placed at the entrance to the Marble Gallery and one at the entrance of the Great Reception Hall. In addition to these conspicuous SS men, there were always RSD men around, usually in uniform, wherever Hitler was near, and some patrolled the buildings and grounds constantly.

It was unlikely that anyone could enter unnoticed, unless one of the sentries was asleep, as happened occasionally. The watch log of the LSSAH details records for 19 March 1939, while the *Führer* was in the Chancellery: 'At 0.45 a.m. the guard officer on duty, *SS-Obersturmführer* Nothdurft, found *SS-Rottenführer* Nowotzek sleeping at post 16.'[12]

Passes, like sentries, were meant to increase security, but again exceptions to the rule could defeat the purpose. The passes required for entering the New Chancellery were a constant source of difficulties and potential security breakdowns. In January 1939, a few days after the New Chancellery had been inaugurated, Hitler's Chief Personal Adjutant, Brückner, ordered Rattenhuber to prepare new passes and identification cards with photographs for all persons whose duties required their presence in the Chancellery.

But there were so many types of passes that they often caused more confusion than control. Sometimes old Chancellery hands refused to co-operate, or too much deference was shown by guards to higher-ranking personalities. At times, in April 1939 for instance, persons who had valid passes were allowed to take in persons without any passes; this practice was based, according to the guard log, on an oral order from Wernicke.[13] Several types of old passes dating back to the time before the inauguration of the new building were still honoured by the guards, and they also honoured two types of passes issued for the 'Berghof' which said that the bearer was authorised to enter Hitler's rooms. In July 1939 one of the SS guards discovered that the police sentry on Post 8 frequently left his position, so that the gate in the old courtyard (No. 77 Wilhelmstrasse) remained unguarded. When an SS sentry stationed there during the night of 13 July and the following morning did not allow anyone through without a currently valid pass, so many persons were excluded and could not get to work that there was nothing to do but declare a variety of seven or more types of passes temporarily valid in addition to the officially current ones. Thus outdated passes for accompanying Hitler, passes for photographers and passes for workers were temporarily revalidated. By the beginning of August 1939 a satisfactory situation still did not exist; when this was brought to the attention of *NSKK-Oberführer* A. B. Albrecht by members of the bodyguard, he could only reply that a change was not likely before September. The officials who had to prepare the new regulations were not expected back in Berlin before then. But the imminence of war seems to have speeded up the proceedings.

A new regulation went into effect on 1 September 1939 governing passes to enter the *Führer's* apartments, the New Chancellery, the Chancellery of the *Reich* President, and the Chancellery of the Leader of the NSDAP and of the Supreme SA Leadership. To enter Hitler's rooms one needed a stiff grey linen identity card with the bearer's photograph and with a golden seal on the outside, and a yellow diagonal bar on the inside. The card also had to have the signature of the *Führer's* Chief Personal Adjutant, *SA-Obergruppenführer* Brückner. The identity cards were prepared by the RSD. Persons seeking admission to Hitler's rooms without proper identity cards were to be taken to the commander of guards in the anteroom of Hitler's apartment by an SS or policeman.[14]

Passes to enter the other buildings and offices of the Chancellery were issued by the Chancellery, and signed by either Lammers or Brückner. The RSD had a list of all of them. The passes looked like the ones for Hitler's rooms, but without the yellow diagonal bar.

A third type of pass, for labourers, was also issued by the Chancellery. It was made of white half-linen and signed by Lammers. Again, the RSD had a list of the passes, and they were responsible for having *Gestapo* and criminal-police offices run security checks on the workers. If workers had to enter the grounds and buildings without delay in an emergency (a broken water pipe, for instance), security officers had to accompany them as long as they were there.

Persons wishing to tour the New Chancellery had to have permission from either Brückner or his deputy, *SS-Sturmbannführer* Wernicke, or from Chancellery Office Director Ostertag or his deputy Police Major Deckert. The RSD had to be informed.

The garage on Hermann-Göring-Strasse could be entered only by persons possessing an additional pass of green colour and signed by *SS-Sturmbannführer* Kempka. It was guarded by an SS sentry.

Loss or theft of passes had to be reported to the RSD Command office immediately. Construction workers and other workmen who had to enter the Chancellery had to give up their passes after they had finished their jobs, but the RSD administrative offices or the Chancellery repeatedly had occasion to try to trace unreturned passes. If these could not be recovered they had to be declared invalid and all security personnel had to be informed. But the only effective way of preventing unauthorised use of passes without impeding the operation of the Chancellery unduly was to change the passes periodically.[15]

In June 1939 Hitler's Chief Personal Valet, Heinz Linge, lost his pass and apparently neglected to tell the authorities. In November Rattenhuber wrote to the LSSAH to which Linge belonged, to the Berlin police, to all RSD offices, to the *Gestapo*, the *Wehrmacht Wachregiment Berlin*, the Supreme SA Leadership, and to the Chief of the *Reich* Chancellery, saying that Linge's old pass was invalid. There is a note of resignation in Rattenhuber's letter: the pass was lost 'under circumstances which are no longer known'—Linge must have said he could not remember what had happened to his pass. Rattenhuber reminded everyone in the *SS-Begleit-Kommando* that losses of passes must be reported at once.[16]

By the end of 1940 the numbers for passes to enter the Chancellery or Hitler's rooms ran to more than a thousand, and there must have been at least several hundred in circulation at any given time. It is difficult to see how abuse through loss, theft or issuing passes to unworthy characters could be avoided. The security gap could not be closed, however, without isolating the *Führer* almost completely from anyone but the 'Palace Guard.'

After the introduction of new passes (with photographs of the bearer) for entering Hitler's apartment and the *Reich* Chancellery, eight were reported lost or stolen within six months, and none of the eight was recovered. As Rattenhuber remarked, there 'existed the danger that the passes might be used for purposes of assassination attacks.' A new system was introduced to establish controls at shorter intervals: the RSD issued stamps of approbation every month which it sent to a specified group of agencies—the *Führer's Adjutantur* (Adjutants' Office), the Chief of the *Reich* Chancellery, the Chief of the Presidential Chancellery, the Chancellery of the Leader of the NSDAP, and the Supreme SA Leadership. The stamps were then distributed by the agency for which the bearers of the passes worked, and everyone had to sign for his stamp. This new rule went into effect on 1 March 1940.[17]

Even Eva Braun got a pass and a monthly stamp. But Sepp Dietrich never signed for his stamp in March, April or May, and Albert Bormann signed for him once. Dietrich's stamp was not picked up for April and May 1940. Fräulein Schroeder, one of Hitler's secretaries who eventually awaited the end with him in the Chancellery bunker, signed for Gerda Daranowski, Johanna Wolf and Albert Bormann, once each; Gerda Daranowski once signed for Christa Schroeder. Another example of potential loopholes: in 1940 a teleprinter was installed on the third floor of the Chancellery for the duration of the war, and it was manned by alternating female postal officials who happened to be available at the Main Telegraph Office. The woman who arrived each evening at 8 o'clock to stay until 7 a.m., and who carried a personal pass with photograph issued by the Main Telegraph Office, was to be given a Chancellery night pass which had to be turned in in the morning.

With the beginning of the war, security was again intensified. On 21 September an order prohibited the use of the pavements along the New Chancellery building in Vossstrasse and Wilhelmstrasse by any pedestrians. Especially after dark, persons entering the Chancellery on foot could do so only by approaching the correct entrance at a right angle from the pavement across the street. Rattenhuber soon added more details: several more policemen were posted, with two stationed twenty-four hours a day at two wrought-iron gates leading to the *Führer's* apartments (no. 77 Wilhelmstrasse after the New Chancellery had been finished), and the doors were to be kept locked during the hours of darkness; one of the two policemen had to patrol inside the iron-stake fence, the other outside. The great bronze gate leading to the Court of Honour (No. 78 Wilhelmstrasse) was also manned day and night by a policeman; it could be opened only with special permission by the *Führer's* adjutants. Changes of the guards had to be made through the south gate of the Old Chancellery. An additional policeman at the corner of Wilhelmstrasse and Vossstrasse had to keep pedestrians from the pavements and send them to the other side of the street after dark. The emergency exit of the air-raid shelter could not be locked without defeating its purpose, but it was guarded twenty-four hours a day by a policeman. SA, *Wehrmacht* and SS sentries guarded the entrances at Nos. 2, 4 and 6 Vossstrasse day and night, and an SS sentry patrolled the Marble Gallery.[18]

Two *Gestapo* officers patrolled the southern pavements on Vossstrasse day and night. A policeman at the corner of Vossstrasse and Hermann-Göring-Strasse had to send pedestrians to the opposite pavement after dark, and one had to keep his eye on the Chancellery front facing Hermann-Göring-Strasse. At night, this front was put under surveillance by two more *Gestapo* officers.

In the Chancellery garden, two SS patrols were responsible for the east and west sections. Six SS men guarded the eastern, northern and southern sections of the garden after dark, while the western section was further secured by a police officer with a dog. Finally, the subway tunnel running from Potsdamerplatz north-east under Leipzigerplatz to Vossstrasse, and then under Vossstrasse east to Wilhelmstrasse and Kaiserhof stations, was specially guarded to prevent acts of sabotage against the New Chancellery.

Security measures around the Chancellery were so comprehensive that an attempt like that by Georg Elser in Munich's 'Bürgerbräu' was highly unlikely. But when the news of the explosion of 8 November 1939 reached Berlin, security-conscious officials were shaken and concerned.

Among the first to react with intensified vigilance was Minister of State and Chief of the *Reich* President's Chancellery Meissner. The revised regulations there, most of them basically the same as those applying to the New Chancellery (*Wehrmacht*, SS and SA guards outside, SS and RSD inside, especially at the connecting hallways leading to the *Reich* Chancellery), emphasised that no visitor must *ever* be allowed to walk around unaccompanied.[19]

Two days later, SS Adjutant Max Wünsche issued new directives for the *Reich* Chancellery.[20] Some guard positions not manned by RSD or *SS-Begleit-Kommando* men, or not manned by such guards during Hitler's absence, were now manned at all times by RSD or SS Escort men; other positions were manned day and night when they had not been before. The SS man at Post 3, the entrance to Hitler's rooms, was instructed not to make a report when the *Führer* came out or in, but, if the *Führer* greeted him, he had merely to reply with '*Heil, mein Führer!*' Furthermore, the garden was patrolled thoroughly at all times, and the gardeners especially had to be checked carefully to see that only authorised ones came in. All of these intensified measures were necessary 'for reasons known to you,' as Wünsche put it: to prevent another attack like Elser's.

In the weeks following Elser's attack, the great overhaul of security regulations was undertaken, and the new regulations were eventually issued over Heydrich's signature, clarifying and intensifying many procedures. But it could hardly surprise anyone that security also suffered from the flood of directives. The war added to the flood in many ways. It was more difficult to keep the population under surveillance when cities were being emptied of schoolchildren and mothers to protect them against enemy air raids; when hundreds of thousands of men were in the armed forces, uprooted and away from their homes, often on the move, going on leave and coming back, in great numbers; when millions of Germans were wearing uniforms, and when uniforms often shielded their wearers against identity checks; and when millions of foreigners— forced labourers, prisoners of war, refugees and *émigrés*, people in the process of resettlement, volunteers from other countries—were milling about in the *Reich*. But still more directives and adjustments of security precautions in the *Reich* Chancellery and at other residences of the *Führer* seemed indicated precisely by the worsening war conditions.

It turned out, for example, that the air-raid shelters in the *Reich* Chancellery had to be reached through the anterooms of Hitler's apartments, after passing through a dining room and a sitting room. All *Wehrmacht* guards not on post at the time of a raid had to take this route to the shelter. An RSD officer in the entrance hall to Hitler's rooms had to direct them through the proper doors. All but one of the SS, *Wehrmacht* and SA guards posted had to stay where they were during air raids.

This rule also applied to the RSD guards. Air raids, of course, were excellent opportunities for desperate would-be assassins to plant their bombs or to take up positions from which to waylay their prey—if security were relaxed in the least.[21] The RSD men were instructed to lock up one gate, and to send two men to the shelters. The others had to stay, and only when the anti-aircraft battery on the Chancellery roof was firing were they allowed to seek some protection against falling shell-fragments; but they had to be able to spot incendiary bombs at once and to make sure they were put out immediately. The guards were to be changed every half-hour during air raids.

At the beginning of February 1942 a newly-constructed tower for an anti-aircraft battery was manned by men of No. 1 *Flak Division*. Its command staff was moved into the upper floor of the *Reich* Chancellery at the No. 2 Vossstrasse entrance. This involved a total of 154 men including orderlies, runners, etc., who had to enter the Chancellery every day, and it developed that 'satisfactory control was no longer possible, and that there was great danger for the security of the *Reich* Chancellery and the *Führer's* apartments.' Now—after this situation had existed for a month, to be sure—certain adjustments had to be made. First of all, the command staff was to be removed from the Chancellery so that the number of No. 1 *Flak Division* men who must enter the Chancellery was reduced to those actually manning the guns. A list of their names had to be kept at the guard position at Supreme SA Leadership offices at No. 2 Vossstrasse, and unlisted *Flak* men had to be identified by their unit commander and conducted in and out of the Chancellery individually. No one except *Flak* men was allowed on the roof of the Chancellery; visitors were not under any circumstances allowed into the anti-aircraft area. The military identification book was declared the pass for entering and leaving; the RSD Chief decided against special passes such as workers received because these permitted people to enter all rooms of the Chancellery, and this would be 'thoroughly undesirable.' Moreover, the constant expansion of the group of people allowed to enter, and the frequent turnover of individuals belonging to the *Reich* Chancellery *Flak* detachment, would increase the dangers for the Chancellery complex. More passes would be lost, etc.[22]

By the end of December 1940, in order to foil any assassination attacks that might occur, the RSD had decided that gifts for the *Führer*, flowers and the like, must no longer be taken directly to his rooms in the *Reich* Chancellery or on Obersalzberg. Until then they had usually been received by a member of the household (servant, cook, maid, etc.) or of the *SS-Begleit-Kommando* detail in the small entrance hall at No. 77 Wilhelmstrasse.[23] Letter mail, dispatches of the German News Service, newspapers and films were still to go to the SS Escort detail in the small entrance hall. But gifts, packages, flowers of unknown origin and the like had to be taken to No. 4 Vossstrasse, and the guard there then had to call over an RSD officer on duty in the *Führer's* apartments. The RSD officer had to examine the package or other item in the presence of either *SS-Sturmführer* Wernicke or *SA-Sturmführer* Rotte, in a room specially set aside for this purpose. It was important, said the directive, to use a room far away from Hitler's quarters for this examination. Rattenhuber rejected any responsibility for incidents in cases in which the procedure was not followed, and he instructed his RSD men to record every examination of packages with date, contents, sender and time. Similar precautions existed for Hitler's birthdays. In a later directive signed by Högl as Chief of RSD Bureau No. 1, and by Hitler's Personal Adjutant Albrecht, this regulation appears somewhat relaxed by the provision that an RSD man had to be consulted on items delivered for Hitler 'if necessary.'

If deliveries of any kind, including railway parcels and mail (excepting letters), arrived for persons other than Hitler, they were to be stored by the guard at the kitchen until the recipient could be reached. He had to be questioned whether he had expected the shipment, and whether he agreed to have it examined by an RSD officer. Letter bombs were apparently not known or feared.

These methods were too cumbersome for daily deliveries of supplies to the kitchen. Therefore all suppliers had to submit lists of the names of their delivery men, and the RSD had to run security checks on them. In cases of urgent deliveries made by unknown persons dispatched by a supplier, the firm had to telephone in the name and an RSD man would then examine the man's identity papers and perhaps make sure he was dealing with the right man by a telephone call to the supplier. The same rules were to apply to Hitler's 'Berghof' retreat. Food, wines and similar items of unknown provenance must be kept from Hitler's or his guests' tables 'as they could not be examined by the officials to see if they were harmless or not,' except in unusual cases when special reasons required this. Finally, Martin Bormann had to give his consent to the commissioning of any new suppliers.

On 30 July 1944, ten days after Stauffenberg's assassination attempt, Martin Bormann wrote to Heinrich Himmler a letter classified 'top secret', 'personal,' and for Himmler's hands only. He reported that he had had a complete review made of all items purchased for use or consumption at Hitler's residences—'Berghof,' Munich, Berlin, *Führersonderzug* and 'Wolfschanze' HQ.[24] The review had shown that changes in the handling of such matters were necessary, and he, Bormann, was going to attend to them. Vegetables, fruit, potatoes and so on needed in Hitler's diet kitchen were either home-grown under Bormann's control, or purchased in such large quantities that dangers could be presumed not to exist. But some items were very scarce and had to be bought wherever there was a supply, usually in small quantities, and often from suppliers who had stopped selling these items to anyone except those buying for the *Führer's* diet kitchen. 'With a view to the *Führer's* security, the one is as intolerable as the other.' Therefore, a new arrangement was being made, similar to the one governing Dr. Morell's medicine supplies: in future, the SS quartermaster's office for medical supplies would buy large quantities of the needed items, examine them, keep them stocked, and send the required quantities to wherever they were ordered for the *Führer's* consumption. All conceivable security precautions and checks must be used, Bormann said further, in selecting the personnel for handling the items, and in devising procedures. In general terms, the procedure described above had been personally approved by the *Führer*—a clear sign not only of Hitler's personal concern with the details of his security, but also of the atmosphere of increasing fear and suspicion, and of the gradual breakdown of reliable and safe conditions in the last months of the war. Whereas formerly such items as cornflakes, wheat germ, endocrinal whole salt, or dried hip had simply been picked up as needed by kitchen employees who were sent to market, elaborate procedures were now introduced which could hardly be expected to work smoothly in the worsening conditions.

Despite all the precautions there were incidents which affected security. Generally, a decree of the *Reich* Chamber of Audits dating back to March 1922 prohibited all persons not on official business, including members of other *Reich* agencies, from entering the Chancellery; Lammers had specifically referred to it in January 1939: all maintenance and services, including refuse removal, cleaning of buildings, courtyards and pavements, servicing and supplying of the heating system, chimney-sweeping, extermination of insects and rodents, were entirely and exclusively within the competence of the Chancellery administration. Thus these tasks were not, as in the case of all other buildings belonging to the *Reich*, part of the competence of the *Reich* Ministry of Finance. Nevertheless, incidents of persons entering the Chancellery without pass or authorisation occurred again and again, and memories had to be refreshed periodically as to what regulations applied.[25] On 11 March 1942 two labourers working on telephone cables in front of the Chancellery, wearing blue working clothes, simply walked into the Chancellery and claimed they were looking for a fellow worker. They talked to two of the guards, who directed them to other entrances without accompanying them, so that the two labourers roamed the basements of several parts of the building until they were finally stopped by a third guard in an inner court. Rattenhuber was frustrated by the recurrence of such incidents, which demonstrated to him how relatively easy it was, in spite of all the elaborate security precautions, to get into the Chancellery and near the *Führer*. He could only threaten to report any further such incidents to Bormann, and announce that he refused to accept responsibility if his directives were not obeyed.

During the war years, security services in the *Reich* Chancellery deteriorated, at times to the point of neglect. Hitler came only for short stays in the later years, before he left his East Prussian HQ. Those exercising supervision over *Reich* Chancellery security services were away from Berlin most of the time, too, and some authority was delegated to the Chancellery's Personnel Department. Major Deckert (who had been promoted) was no longer in charge, a new man had taken over, Police Lieutenant-Colonel Rauch, who expressly retained his right to issue directives but who could himself seldom be there to supervise their implementation.

Newly-issued regulations for daily *Sicherheitsdienst* (Security Service) duties, dated 30 September 1944, do not contain anything new. They re-emphasised the rule that no one from the outside must be allowed to walk around the *Reich* Chancellery unaccompanied. It is clear from the reduced number of guards and from the reduced number of entrances the Security Service guarded, that few visitors and much less traffic were expected now; Berlin, having been subjected to saturation bombing, was no longer the lively capital it had been in 1939 and in 1940. Slightly more attention was required in the directive for times when Lammers would be there; but no reference is made in this context to Hitler. The *Sicherheitsdienst* men were merely told to give vague, non-informative answers if anyone asked whether the *Führer* was there. The RSD still had a detachment in the Chancellery, of course, and so did *Wehrmacht* and SS.

In the final stage of the Third *Reich*, the Chancellery once more became the command centre and HQ of the *Führer* and of what had been one of the mightiest war machines. Those final scenes will be looked at later.

Munich

Adolf Hitler moved to Munich from Vienna in May 1913 to avoid military service in the Army of Habsburg Austria-Hungary, an international state he did not think worth serving. At first he rented a room from a master-tailor, Josef Popp, at No. 34 Schleissheimerstrasse. In 1914 Hitler volunteered for service in a Bavarian regiment. He remained in the Army until the end of March 1920 and lived in Munich barracks (*Max-II-Kaserne*) except for a short tour of duty outside Munich. From 1 May 1920 he was registered as living at No. 41 Thierschstrasse, on the first floor, in two sublet rooms.[26]

In September 1929 Hitler, who described himself as a 'painter and writer,' and as having come to Munich for professional reasons, applied to the Munich city authorities for larger quarters. He wanted nine rooms plus kitchen, bathroom, etc. But this was a formality; the city was really asked to consent to the lease of the second-storey flat at No. 16 Prinzregentenplatz by Herr Hugo Schühle, a merchant, to Herr Adolf Hitler. Hitler and Schühle had signed the lease on 10 September, and the application to the city was dated 13 September.[27] Permission was duly granted on 18 September, 'in consideration of the political and social position of the applicant,' and from 1 October 1929 until the end of World War II, Hitler had the apartment at his disposal. It was larger than described in his application: nine rooms, two kitchens, two storage rooms, two bathrooms, etc. The rent was set at 4,176 Reichsmarks per annum. The 1931, 1932 and 1933 editions of the Munich city directory list Hitler as living at No. 16 Prinzregentenplatz: 'Hitler, Adolf, writer.' The 1934 edition lists him as *Reich* Chancellor, along with the 'kitchen-master' Ernst Zaske, a member of the Party since February 1923 and now with the RSD, and the 'merchant, Dietrich, Jos.'—none other than the chief of Hitler's LSSAH. Zaske was still listed in the 1935 edition, but there was no more listing of Hitler or Dietrich, and after 1935 neither Hitler nor anyone belonging to his immediate entourage was listed in the directory as living at No. 16 Prinzregentenplatz. But the list of other tenants in the house grew shorter from year to year.[28]

When Hitler came to stay at his Munich apartments, the RSD posted fourteen of its officers to make the street safe from 'Friedensengel' to No. 16 Prinzregentenplatz. Other RSD officers had to make sure the pavements were cleared so that Hitler could step out of his car and into the house unhindered. They were required to do this gently and politely, but occasionally an unpleasant incident forced Rattenhuber to remind them that there was not to be any shoving, pushing or other rough handling of the public, and to threaten penal transfers for violators. He demanded that all RSD officers be able to distinguish immediately in cases when they had to intervene 'whether they were dealing with an enemy of the state who must be kept away from the *Führer* by every available means, or with a harmless person who merely wishes to cheer, and who out of spontaneous enthusiasm tries to get close to the *Führer*.' The RSD must not swoop down on harmless passers-by as in a raid, for often people had no idea that the *Führer* was near. It never looked good to use force in Hitler's presence.[29] Sometimes the rumour of Hitler's arrival spread quickly enough for a crowd to gather; he might have been spotted at the railway station or on the *autobahn* at the outskirts of the city, or somewhere *en route*. But some people did not mind waiting for hours and days to catch a glimpse of the *Führer*, and once it was known that he was inside the chances of success were improved.

Whether Hitler was there or not, there were security men inside and outside the house keeping it under surveillance. There were fourteen RSD officers permanently assigned to this object, seven of them always on duty at any given time. When Hitler was in the house or in Munich, one Munich policeman and one *SS-Begleit-Kommando* man stood guard in front of the house. When the *Führer* was not in Munich, only plainclothes men patrolled the site, partly with dogs. The roof could be reached from the neighbouring roofs and had to be watched. In the chimneys, bars and grates were installed to prevent the dropping of explosives. An RSD officer occupied the attic constantly and watched the roof, while another RSD officer in civilian clothes patrolled the streets around the house. From a guard room on the ground floor the street and hallway could be observed, and no one could enter or leave the house unnoticed and unchecked. Non-residents had to identify themselves and give proof that they were expected before they were allowed to come in. From 1939 the guards could ring any apartment in the house and have the tenant confirm that he expected the person at the door. When Hitler was in the house, tenants were expected not to receive visitors except in cases of great urgency. There was no precise regulation to this effect, but the 'recommendation' was unmistakable. Residents of the house could use their own keys until November 1939, though they still had to be seen and recognised by the guards. After Elser's attack they had to ring the doorbell to be admitted by the guards.

Hitler's 'official home' in the Capital of the Movement, the 'Führerbau' on Arcisstrasse, whose construction north of the Brown House was begun in 1933 and completed in 1937, was also subject to constantly increasing security measures.[30] Duty regulations for porters, doormen and night-watchmen were updated as the war situation required, for example in November 1941. An RSD detail for the 'Führerbau' operated under regulations of which the most detailed versions were issued on 16 January 1943 and 24 June 1944. There were still passes in two different colours permitting bearers to enter either only during office hours (white) or at any time (red). A few members of the Party Chancellery had red passes, by permission of M. Bormann, also the employees of the House Inspectorate. Every month a new stamp had to be placed in the passes to validate them for the next month. RSD identification cards were a third category of passes permitting bearers to enter the 'Führerbau.' SS guards functioned under directives from the Inspectorate; one SS patrol guard was on duty in the courtyard of the administration building, and two with dogs constantly patrolled the north and south sides of the 'Führerbau', whose ground-floor windows did not have bars. Porters, doormen and nightwatchmen were reliable Party and SS members. They were given the usual instructions: meticulous scrutiny of all visitors and their papers; precise controls of the time visitors spent in the building, which included an escort to the office to be visited, and a visitor's pass containing name, address, occupation, purpose of visit, time in, time out, time spent at the visited office, with signature of the receiving official; passes lacking a current stamp had to be confiscated and instructions concerning the fate of the bearer had to be requested from the In-spectorate; the correctness of deliveries had to be checked, items had to be examined, suppliers had to be contacted to confirm the shipment and the delivery man's identity, greater quantities had to be examined by RSD officers; maintenance and repair workmen had to be constantly supervised by RSD officers and doormen; four rounds every night were prescribed, but at different times each night; any unauthorised persons discovered on the premises were to be arrested and turned over to the

RSD; any unlocked doors or fires had to be reported (during air-raid warning periods an additional crew of ten air-raid fighters were brought in, as well as additional SS guards); and when Hitler was in Munich the 'Führerbau' had to be accessible at all times, for: 'During his presence in Munich, the *Führer* always unexpectedly visits the "Führerbau."' If Hitler *was* in Munich, three groups of specialists employed by the Central NSDAP administration and directed by an *SS-Sturmbann-führer* had to search all storeys of the building, then station eight additional guards throughout basement and ground storey so that all access routes were guarded and sealed, including the underground walk connecting the 'Führerbau' with the Supreme Party Court; when Hitler was in the building, security was under the overall direction of the Chief of RSD or his Deputy. Increased guard strength and security precautions were required equally when official events were held in the 'Führerbau;' most administrative activities were then suspended and most employees were instructed to leave the building. RSD officers then had to assist the security forces of the Inspectorate, especially in identity controls of guests; one RSD officer was assigned to assist the porter to ensure 'that persons in the *Führer's* entourage were not denied entry,' another had to examine all deliveries, a third had to patrol the entire building to see to it that no unauthorised persons were present (this was a somewhat unrealistic assignment during an 'official event' with the many guests who had passed the entrance controls). The *Gestapo* provided an official for liaison with the RSD. Outside, cordoning-off was carried out similarly as described in the Chapter on Public Appearances. Under the new regulations issued in 1944, an RSD officer was in the lobby and on patrol in the house at all times from half an hour before until an hour after office hours, whether the *Führer* was in Munich or not, and the RSD officer was given authority over porters, doormen, orderlies and others regarding all security activities, as outlined above, particularly with regard to visitors. During Hitler's presence, additional RSD officers (exclusive of those in his *Begleit-Kommando*) were stationed in the lobby, at the doors and gates. It would have been possible to bring in unwelcome items such as time-bombs only with collusion of insiders, or alternatively through very clever deception. Luggage is specially mentioned, reflecting the increasing dislocations and disruptions brought on by the war, when people carried their most valued belongings with them to save them from destruction in air raids, unwilling to leave them at the particularly endangered railway stations. Thus all luggage that was to be delivered for an employee of the building had to be received by him in person, or by a colleague on condition that the owner informed porter and colleague in advance of the details of the delivery. Mail parcels were examined by a criminal-police officer in the mail-room. In cases of doubt, parcels had to be opened *outside* the 'Führerbau,' either in the mailroom or in an air-raid shelter.

Obersalzberg

Hitler became familiar with the Berchtesgaden area through Dietrich Eckart in the winter of 1922–3 when Eckart was in flight from the authorities and went into hiding there. Through the years, Hitler often stayed at inns in the village of Salzberg on the Obersalzberg, a mountain near Berchtesgaden, actually making it the closest thing to a permanent residence in the 1920s, particularly after his release from Landsberg prison in 1924.[31]

In 1928 Hitler rented a small country house 'Haus Wachenfeld' in Salzberg near Berchtesgaden, later known as the 'Berghof.'[32] A few years later, Hitler owned the house.[33] Security was difficult in the wild, hilly environs of 'Haus Wachenfeld.' In 1933 a man in an SA leader's uniform tried to assassinate Hitler; he was arrested when his uneasy manner and his peculiar behaviour aroused suspicion. A gun was found on him.[34] Down to 1936 (approximately) Hitler regularly used public paths through the forests, accompanied by his guests (such as Speer, Bormann, Göring, Dr. Dietrich, Eva Braun) and three or four RSD officers. He did not like strenuous walks, so he tended to walk downhill, or only one way to the tea-house at Mooslahnerkopf, and then to have himself driven up or back again, usually in a Volkswagen. Hitler used to walk at the head of the small column with only one of his guests or aides, talking to him or listening to him, more likely the former. Every half-hour or so he would tell his conversation partner: 'Get me the Press Chief!' or 'Send Bormann up!' Then the latest partner knew that he had been relegated to the rear, and someone else was honoured by walking with Hitler alone.[35]

On these outings the *Führer* could very well have been waylaid by an attacker, from behind a tree or from the bushes at a distance. Bodyguards were there, both near the *Führer* and at some distance away to patrol the terrain. But if they were effective in preventing attacks it was less through any ability to foil an attempt in progress than by deterring attackers, who ran a high risk of being caught before or after their attack. Hitler did not want security men constantly scurrying around in front of him. If security was to be provided it was not to be obvious, and only a wide and tight ring of guards and fences around the entire area could be the solution. By the late 1930s security was still poor on many occasions, but it was gradually improved by the setting up of more and more guard- and fence-perimeters.[36]

Often the walking party with Hitler in the early years encountered hikers, who would stand back and greet the *Führer* deferentially. Sometimes they would say something to him and he would react with a friendly

24a. 'Berghof' with guard house, 1938

word or two. On some outings large groups of people were encountered, and once Hitler barely escaped into a café from the enthusiastic crowd that threatened to wedge him in completely.[37] He had to stay inside until one of his cars and some more RSD and SS Escort men had been fetched, and afterwards, he stood up in his car as it slowly wound its way through the crowds, with two security men walking in front and three on each side. Hitler still carried his whip, but of course he could not think of using it unless physically and maliciously attacked. He did always carry a gun, just in case, and so did his valets as well as the security guards.

Hitler's public appearances at his 'Berghof' became routinely orchestrated rituals over the years. Until at least 1937 and, with more and more restrictions, still in the early years of the war, Hitler allowed as many as two thousand people per day to gather within the security perimeters to see him. They came from all parts of the *Reich* to get a glimpse of the *Führer*, and it became customary for him, whenever he was at the 'Berghof,' to walk past the waiting throngs after his lunch, between 3 and 4 p.m., when he went for his walk, or, alternatively, to have the visitors file past him. He would smile for a few minutes, drop a word or two, perhaps put his hand on the head of a little blonde girl, or on the arm of one not so little, while the *Reich* Photo Reporter's crew were busily taking pictures. Those responsible for Hitler's security believed that the risks in such relatively predictable appearances were greater than those involved in the unpredictable walks. But someone stalking his prey with patience, determination and skill could pose a greater threat than someone mingling with the admiring crowds outside the fence of the 'Berghof,' cordoned off and well mixed with black SS uniforms. At any rate, security was really not satisfactory on the Obersalzberg during the 1930s.

Rattenhuber was worried in November 1937 after Hitler had ordered a number of *Leibstandarte* sentries on Obersalzberg to be withdrawn, and he urgently pointed out to Bormann and Brückner that it was now possible for anyone to drive around on Obersalzberg when Hitler was there.[38] Many SS men of LSSAH patrolled the grounds around the 'Berghof,' but this activity was largely ineffective because of three entrance points guarded by workmen who did not have sufficient authority. These points were Post 1 at the 'Platterhof' barrier; Post 2 at 'Hintereck;' and Post 3 at the access road to the new farm. The 'Platterhof' check-point was particularly important because visitors gathered there and often became witnesses to verbal fights between labourers or soldiers and workmen's guards. Therefore Rattenhuber requested that the three guard positions be taken over by SS men.

When Maurice Bavaud, the Swiss theology student, was looking for a suitable gap in the security rings in October 1938, in order to assassinate Hitler, he could not find one. But he was able to stalk Hitler for several days (though not for three months, as Hitler exaggerated in retrospect) without ever being stopped.[39] He had arrived in Berchtesgaden on 25 October and taken a room at the Hotel 'Stiftskeller'. RSD Bureau 9 (formerly 7b), charged with checking all strangers, 'for the security of the *Führer*,' did not find any cause for suspicion. From the hotel Bavaud went off for long walks in the environs, and to practise target-shooting in the forests, taking shots at trees from 7 to 8 metres' distance. He used up at least twenty-five rounds of ammunition, and he did not have a silencer for his gun. Once he asked a policeman how he might get closer to the 'Berghof,' but he was told that no one was allowed through the fences and gates. Bavaud did not test this at the time. Visiting cafés in Berchtesgaden, he struck up an acquaintance with Police Major Deckert, Lammers' security officer currently at the vacation Chancellery in nearby Bischofswiesen, and Deckert suggested Munich as a good place to get near the *Führer*.

Bavaud returned after his attempt to shoot Hitler in Munich had failed (as described in the chapter on Public Appearances), arriving back in Berchtesgaden by train on 10 November. He took a taxi to Obersalzberg, but could not go further than Schiessstättbrücke check-point. He told the guard he carried a letter to Hitler from an important French political personage, coming directly from Paris, and that he must hand over the letter personally. The guard telephoned and then told Bavaud the *Führer* was not on Obersalzberg. This was true, but the information was given in violation of rules. Bavaud went straight back to Munich, found that Hitler had left there, and returned again on 12 November, this time to Bischofswiesen, hoping to arrange an interview through the vacation Chancellery as had been suggested to him at the Brown House in Munich. He had really reached the end of his line, with his financial resources reduced to some 5 Reichsmarks, as he set out on foot on his desperate last attempt to see the *Führer*. Darkness fell, and then it occurred to Bavaud that it was Saturday evening, that all the offices were probably closed, and he gave up his plan.

Meanwhile Martin Bormann, in charge of all administration on Obersalzberg, was buying up the land around 'Haus Wachenfeld,' often using considerable pressure to force owners of centuries-old farms to sell. In 1935 Hitler decided to remodel and enlarge his chalet into the impressive 'Berghof,' and ten years of practically uninterrupted construction began on Obersalzberg. The interior of the house was now dominated by the great room with the breath-taking view of Berchtesgadener Land through the large window that could be lowered totally out of sight. This first phase of construction was completed on 6 July 1936. An annexe was finished in April 1938.[40] There were adjoining apartments for Hitler and Eva Braun which could be entered only from the two far sides. The terrace on which teas were held was enlarged, too. Also on the terrace, and also at considerable risk to his life, Hitler received the congratulations of the Berchtesgaden New Year's Shooting Club who banged away with ancient fire-arms to usher in the New Year.[41]

More and more buildings were modelled or erected above the 'Berghof,' including garages, SS barracks, gate-houses, guest houses, and houses for potentates like Göring, Bormann and Goebbels. The former Hotel 'Türken' was turned into quarters for the RSD. There were also

OBERSALZBERG AREA

0　　　　　500　　　　　1000 m

24b.　Obersalzberg area with Berchtesgaden, 1939–45

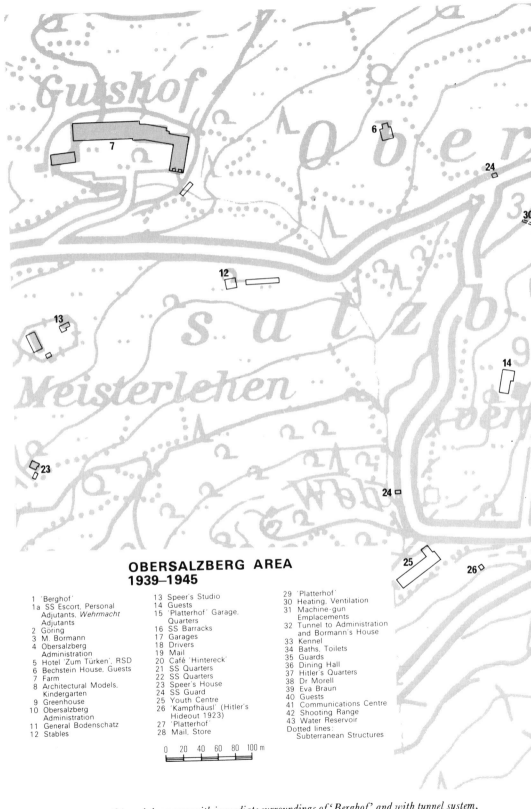

OBERSALZBERG AREA
1939–1945

1   'Berghof'
1a SS Escort, Personal
    Adjutants, *Wehrmacht*
    Adjutants
2   Göring
3   M. Bormann
4   Obersalzberg
    Administration
5   Hotel 'Zum Türken', RSD
6   Bechstein House, Guests
7   Farm
8   Architectural Models,
    Kindergarten
9   Greenhouse
10 Obersalzberg
    Administration
11 General Bodenschatz
12 Stables

13 Speer's Studio
14 Guests
15 'Platterhof' Garage,
    Quarters
16 SS Barracks
17 Garages
18 Drivers
19 Mail
20 Café 'Hintereck'
21 SS Quarters
22 SS Quarters
23 Speer's House
24 SS Guard
25 Youth Centre
26 'Kampfhäusl' (Hitler's
    Hideout 1923)
27 'Platterhof'
28 Mail, Store

29 'Platterhof'
30 Heating, Ventilation
31 Machine-gun
    Emplacements
32 Tunnel to Administration
    and Bormann's House
33 Kennel
34 Baths, Toilets
35 Guards
36 Dining Hall
37 Hitler's Quarters
38 Dr Morell
39 Eva Braun
40 Guests
41 Communications Centre
42 Shooting Range
43 Water Reservoir
Dotted lines:
    Subterranean Structures

0 20 40 60 80 100 m

24c.   *Obersalzberg area with immediate surroundings of 'Berghof' and with tunnel system,*
1944–5

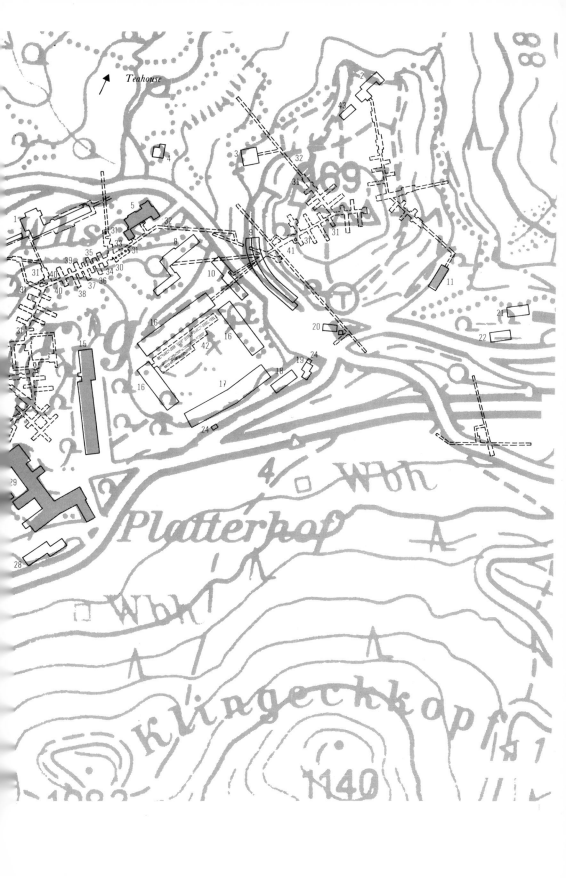

a new farmhouse, a large greenhouse and a mushroom plantation, and new roads cut through what had once been a romantic alpine landscape. The land under Bormann's control around the 'Berghof' eventually included some 7 square kilometres.

The entire area under immediate control of Hitler's Obersalzberg Administration (Bormann) was enclosed by chain-link fences and barbed wire. It was divided into *Bezirke* (districts): *Bezirk* I immediately around the 'Berghof' (red passes); *Bezirk* II (green passes) included all territory including *Bezirk* I but excluded the Kehlstein area, which was *Bezirk* III.[41a] Additional fences here and there sectioned off construction sites or minor, secondary zones. *Bezirk* I had three gates manned by RSD men, sentries from *SS-Wachkompanie-Obersalzberg*, and, when Hitler was present, also by SS Escort men; the outer gates of *Bezirk* II (Teugelbrunn, Klingeck and Au) were manned by RSD people only when Hitler was on the Obersalzberg, and in his absence by workmen's guards (*Arbeiterposten*). There was only supply, maintenance and guard-shift traffic into and out of *Bezirk* III since the Kehlstein tea house was almost never used.

Bezirk II, especially, was filled to the brim with noisy trucks and dust, with the roar of construction machinery, with the blasts of explosions for excavation and tunnelling. The beautiful mountainside was covered with stores of pipes, boards, insulation material, scaffolding, stones, cement, sand and other construction materials, and with countless ugly hutments housing thousands of labourers. On some sites construction work and noise did not stop day and night. Bormann was not bothered by the infernal noise of blasts and excavators, by the ear-splitting screech of cement-mixers, even if it was near his own house; on the contrary, if it stopped, be it in the middle of the night, he had his head out of the window in a minute, demanding an explanation for the 'outrageous delay of the work.'[42]

Hitler would occasionally remark that when it was all finished he would build himself another little chalet in a quiet, secluded valley. But he also said that Bormann was in charge of all this building, and that he would not interfere with it. It was never finished; Bormann always thought of something else to build, and, after the war had begun, money and concrete in unprecedented quantities were poured into underground shelters, living quarters and offices. The *Führer* was Supreme Commander of the Armed Forces, after 19 December 1941 also Commander-in-Chief of the Army, and when he moved to Obersalzberg, most of his HQ moved with him, including aides, office personnel, signal-corps troops, *Führer-Begleit-Bataillon* troops and *Leibstandarte-SS 'Adolf Hitler'* troops. They all needed quarters and office space. Great vistas of never-ending construction programmes opened in Bormann's mind. Part of the alpine infantry barracks at Strub near Berchtesgaden was used, and a new camp was built near Winkl, on the Bad Reichenhall–Berchtesgaden road, for that part of the Army General Staff which moved from East Prussia with Hitler. One forest camp 'Beseler,' near Winkl, was finished only in February 1945.

In March 1942, at Speer's request, Hitler ordered a stop to all construction on Obersalzberg (excepting what was almost finished). Speer, now in charge of all war production, had argued that all men and all material must be used only for what would directly contribute to the military effort. Bormann, within days of Hitler's decision, secured another *Führer* Order allowing him to continue with the vast and largely unnecessary construction programmes. In June 1944 a total of 28,000 workers were building HQ installations, including the ones on Obersalzberg. Speer went to Hitler again and got a *Führer* Order suspending all construction work on Obersalzberg. But work was never suspended until the very last weeks of the war.[43]

In the summer of 1943 underground bunker-building got under way on a vast scale. Underground bunker systems were built for Hitler and his immediate suite (aides, Eva Braun, valets, household personnel), and for Bormann, his family and his aides. There were plans for a system for Göring, but Göring, having lost the Battle of Britain in 1940, had had a bunker constructed for his needs as early as 1941 with steel-and-concrete walls 3 metres thick. Other bunkers were built, complete with drainage, heating systems, gas and air-pressure chambers, for the inhabitants of 'Platterhof,' the SS barracks, for greenhouse workers, and finally for the workers building the bunkers. Simplicity had been the principle initially, but soon all sorts of requests had to be met. Architects wanted marble, wood panelling, air-conditioning, carpets; and the security people said that there must be machine-guns installed at the entrance chambers (the emplacements can still be seen). The caretakers needed broom-cupboards, the dog-handler needed a room for Hitler's dog, the cooks needed kitchens, etc. When everything was almost finished, the anti-aircraft command centre demanded a bunker of its own, and all the communications cables had to be reconnected underground, the cable tunnels had to be dug up again; they were extended and shifted with every change of plans. The total length of the seventy-nine underground tunnels ('bunkers') is estimated at 2.775 kilometres, and 4,120 square metres in area.

The security provided by all these efforts was open to doubt. Protection against air raids offered short-term security at best. The vast numbers of guards and labourers decreased security at the same time they were working to increase it. The more people there were around, the greater the chance that enemy agents, saboteurs or assassins were among them. Only some 30% of the labour force on Obersalzberg were Germans in 1943; the others were mostly unskilled labourers, Czechs and Italians.

Employment of Russian prisoners-of-war was prohibited in both the wider *Führerschutzgebiet* (*Führer* Protection Area) and in the narrower *Hoheitsgebiet* (Sovereignty Zone). Prisoners-of-war, however, were an indispensable labour source as German manpower resources were drained and depleted by the call-up, and the available French and other prisoners-of-war were not enough for the many *Wehrmacht* construction projects, for railway building, and for the *autobahn* in the environs of Hitler's 'Berghof.' Up to November 1941 the *Führerschutzgebiet* was not very large and consisted mainly of the *Bezirk* (administrative district) of Berchtesgaden and of Hallein. But in November 1941 the Chief of the *Gestapo* bureau in Salzburg declared the *Führerschutzgebiet* expanded to include the entire city of Salzburg, the larger *Gerichtsbezirk* (judicial district) of Salzburg and *Gerichtsbezirk* Thalgau within *Landkreis* (rural administrative district, approximately equivalent to county) Salzburg, furthermore *Gerichtsbezirke* Hallein and Golling with *Landkreis* Hallein.[44] Now the *Führerschutzgebiet* boundaries also extended west as far as Reichenhall, several kilometres south beyond Golling, almost to Mondsee and Wolfgangsee in the east, and to Seekirchen and Freilassing in the north. The President of Alpenland Provincial Labour Office protested against a consequence of this expansion, namely the ban of Soviet-Russian prisoners-of-war in it. It was impossible, he wrote to the *Reich* Labour Ministry, to replace all currently employed Soviet-Russian prisoners-of-war in the area by French ones, and on the contrary he was forced to bring in more Russian prisoners-of-war for the projects under way—military barracks, the Salzburg–Vienna *autobahn*, railway work, etc. The Ministry negotiated with the *Reichssicherheitshauptamt* (RSHA), a personal decision of the *Führer* was obtained, and finally, the *Gestapo* bureau in Salzburg transmitted to the President of Alpenland Provincial Labour Office, on 1 December 1941, the following directive: 'By order of the *Führer* it is now permissible to employ Soviet-Union prisoners-of-war within the *Führerschutzgebiet*, provided they are adequately guarded. In so far as the intent of this directive is observed, there is no longer any objection to employment of prisoners-of-war of other nationalities within the *Führerschutzgebiet* in Gau Salzburg. Soviet-Union civilian labourers, however, must not be employed within the *Führerschutzgebiet*.'

From 16 July to 1 November 1942 and from 19 February to 13 March 1943 Hitler resided in his Ukranian HQ 'Wehrwolf' near Vinnytsa; in the time between these moves he resided at 'Wolfschanze,' also taking trips to Munich, Berlin and Berchtesgaden. When Hitler returned to Obersalzberg for a longer stay (interspersed with trips) on 22 March 1943 (he stayed until June), 'Berghof' security was improved. New regulations were issued for the nineteen-man team of the RSD Bureau at 'Haus Türken.'[45] One RSD officer (SS uniform, pistol) always patrolled in front of the 'Berghof' on a three-hour shift; another (pistol, key-ring) patrolled the immediate vicinity of the building; two more (pistols, key-rings) patrolled area sectors from 8 a.m. to 8 p.m.; one was always at the bureau telephone, either in the office or in his quarters.

An RSD guard was always on duty at a Berchtesgaden hotel known as 'Haus Emma,' in six-hour shifts. He was instructed to dress in 'proper' civilian clothes (no Bavarian-style jackets), and to carry pistol and torch. Here, on the first floor, sixteen shorthand typists were at work; they lived here, and transcribed stenographic records of everything that was said at all military situation conferences in which Hitler partici-pated.[46] The RSD officer had to make certain that only the shorthand typists and fifteen other persons named on a list could enter, and that no one else could get close enough to hear what was spoken as the short-hand writers dictated their notes to the typists. Electronic listening devices with a range of several hundred metres were not known then. The windows had to be kept closed. The guard had to stay in the hall on the first floor where four rooms were used as work-rooms, so that he was able to see all the rooms all the time, and he was strictly forbidden to leave his post. In case of emergency or sudden illness, he had to have the chief shorthand writer, Dr. Peschel, telephone the RSD Bureau. It was all right to sit down, even to consume non-alcoholic beverages, as the surveillance was to be as inconspicuous as possible, but surveillance had to be constant and without any gaps. The officer was also strictly forbidden to talk to hotel guests or hotel personnel. The list of those authorised to enter the work-rooms contained the names of the Bor-mann brothers, Schaub, Colonel Scherff (special *Führer's* aide for the history of the war), Dr. Brandt or his deputy, Professor Morell, Section Chief Kronmüller, Lieutenant-Colonels Engel and von Below, *SS-Haupt-sturmführer* Schulze (-Kossens) and Pfeiffer, valets Linge and Junge, *SS-Sturmbannführer* Günsche (aide) and *SS-Sturmbannführer* Darges (aide).

Added to the new regulations were, finally, directives substituting a sixteen-man RSD Special Bureau Obersalzberg for the workmen's guards at the outer check-points (Teugelbrunn, Antenberg, Klingeck, Au), thus closing some of the worst security gaps around the 'Berghof' residence.[47]

These RSD officers had to check all passes authorising entry to make sure that the bearer was identical with the person for whom the pass was issued, that the pass was in fact genuine, and that it bore the necessary weekly stamp. Day passes could be issued upon instructions from RSD Bureau 1, or, for visitors to 'Landhaus Göring,' from an RSD Bureau 2 official who was always on duty at Göring's house. Records were kept to show entry and exit times of all visitors.

The days of Hitler's benevolent contact with the public were over, after the set-backs in the summer of 1942, and after the fall of Stalingrad on 31 January 1943. 'Gatherings of hikers (holiday-makers from Berch-

tesgaden and its environs) at the gates must be prevented in all circumstances,' said the instructions for the RSD. It was undesirable to have
'curious inquirers' constantly surrounding the RSD guards, and to have
bystanders searching (with their eyes) every car that came or went. Such
persons were to be sent away politely but firmly. Certain persons specially listed were allowed to travel by car, or to have their cars come or
go, via the road from Schiessstättbrücke to Obersalzberg: cars belonging
to the 'Berghof,' to Göring's house, Bormann's house, Speer's house, the
Reich Press Chief's office, Minister Hewel, the *Reich* Photo Reporter, Dr.
Brandt, Speer, Obersalzberg Administration, RSD; furthermore, the
duty cars of the SS Guard Troop, of the 'Platterhof' field-hospital
detachment, of the anti-aircraft detachment, of the *Reich* Mail (the school
bus); the food vans of hotel 'Platterhof' and of Camp Antenberg, service
vans of Berchtesgaden power plant, of the road and river office, of the
veterinary surgeon who had to come to the farm; cars of people who
lived along the road were allowed in, and in emergencies cars of physicians, midwives and first-aid services. All persons who desired or were
ordered to visit someone or some official agency on the Obersalzberg
could do so only if the visit was first communicated and verified to the
RSD, and they could use the Obersalzberg road only if this was so specified by the appropriate authority. But even cars looking like those of,
say, Bormann, Göring, or the *Führer* himself, must not be let through
without further inspection, as a directive of 21 February 1942, in typical
Bormann prose, made clear: 'If the gate guards open the gates upon
the sounding of a horn, then this is the most outrageous carelessness,
because sounding a horn is not identification. All cars will in future have
to stop outside the gates so that the guards can check the passes of any
persons they do not know, and make certain that the cars are to be
allowed through. Guards who open the gates before a thorough check,
merely because a car of our sort is coming up, are worthless and must
be relieved from duty at once. A uniform is no identification, either, regardless of whether it is that of an *SS-Obergruppenführer*, of a *Gauleiter*,
or of a *Reich* minister.'[48] Only a perfect double with authentic pass and
car could have got in, other than authorised persons.[49] Despite all precautions, assassination attacks could have been made easily enough by
insiders. Three efforts are on record, although none got beyond the initial
stage of an assassin bringing his weapon into the vicinity or presence
of Hitler's person.

Captain von dem Bussche, a member of the military conspiracy
around Tresckow, volunteered to lead a display of new uniforms and
field equipment that Hitler was to view in December 1943. Great care
was taken by the RSD and SS Escort people to make certain that the
fire-arms being shown to the *Führer* were not loaded. But Bussche intended
to carry on his person a prepared explosive charge with a four-and-

a-half second hand-grenade fuse. He would start it in his pocket, rush up to Hitler, hold him, and be blown to bits with him. The showing was postponed, however; Bussche, who had been waiting in 'Wolfschanze' for a few days to be summoned there or elsewhere, had to return to the Russian front—and lost a leg in combat. Another officer, Ewald von Kleist, volunteered, but the display was postponed again. It was finally held on 7 July 1944, at Klessheim Palace near Salzburg, but none of the officers willing to make the attack was able to participate.[50] Major-General Stieff, one of the conspirators, attended the show, but he did not want to carry out the assassination attack.

Captain von Breitenbuch, serving as aide-de-camp to Fieldmarshal Busch who commanded Army Group Centre in Russia, agreed in March 1944 to try to assassinate Hitler. On 11 March Busch came to confer with Hitler at the 'Berghof.' Breitenbuch, also a member of the conspiracy around Tresckow, preferred to use a pistol and to take his chances, including almost certain death by a bullet fired by a bodyguard, SS adjutant or servant. He carried a small Browning pistol in his trouser pocket. But Breitenbuch was not allowed into the conference room and had to abandon his plan.

The third effort, really two attempts, was made by Colonel Count von Stauffenberg, Chief of Staff to General Fromm, C-in-C Home Army, on 6 and 11 July 1944, when he came to the 'Berghof' for conferences. On 6 July Stauffenberg brought along a package of explosive with fuses in his briefcase, apparently hoping that Major-General Stieff would carry out the attack at the uniform and equipment display on the following day. Stieff declined. On 11 July Stauffenberg was back at the 'Berghof' with his briefcase and the explosive, this time intending to place the explosive in the briefcase with fuse running next to Hitler, then to leave the room on some pretext, and depart in the car that his aide was keeping ready in order to return to Berlin to lead the follow-up *coup d'état*. Since the conspirators still believed Göring and Himmler must be killed at the same time as Hitler and they were not there, Stauffenberg did not carry out the attack.[51] On 14 July Hitler and his HQ moved back to East Prussia; the next two attempts, therefore, will be dealt with in the 'Wolfschanze' context.

While in Breitenbuch's case security operations may have interfered with the assassination attempt, this was probably not so for Bussche and Kleist, and certainly not for Stauffenberg on 11 July. Security had been defeated through an impenetrable 'disguise:' entry into Hitler's presence on official duty. There were in fact at least a handful of conspirators who had relatively easy access to Hitler—General Fellgiebel (C-in-C Signal Troops), General Wagner (Quartermaster General and Deputy Chief of the General Staff of the Army), Colonel Meichssner, Major-General Stieff, Admiral Canaris, Fieldmarshal Rommel (who joined the

conspiracy in 1944), and of course Stauffenberg from 1 July 1944 after
he had become Chief of Staff to General Fromm. All but Stauffenberg
were unwilling to exploit their opportunities. Tresckow, on the other
hand, who tried very hard to gain access to Hitler's presence and who
did not lack will or capability for an assassination attack, never succeeded—for ordinary military and administrative reasons.

There were other 'security measures' at work, too, that were more
subtle and more effective than barbed-wire perimeters and black-uni-
formed bodyguards, although they obviously had no effect on a man
like Stauffenberg.

In 1938, when the Sudeten Crisis was brewing, Captain Wiedemann,
Hitler's Personal Adjutant, told a friend, Dr. von Dohnanyi, some of
the statements the *Führer* had made on the beneficial effects of war as
an educational experience desirable for every generation. Wiedemann
concluded: 'Only a revolver can help against that man! But who shall
do it? *I* am in a position of trust!'[52] The *Führer* cynically relied on this
sort of mentality. Perhaps similar considerations kept *Reichskabinettsrat*
Killy in the *Reichskanzlei* administration from passing on his inside knowledge to conspirators with whom he was in contact and in sympathy.

The *Führer's* valets were instructed to carry guns at all times. They
had training in target practice, like RSD and SS Escort men, periodically, at Wannsee, Lichterfelde in the SS barracks, or in police facilities
near their posts. The valet Wilhelm Schneider claims that personal valets
who served at table did not actually carry their guns, but this implies
a serious violation of *Führer's* orders—an unlikely story.[53] Linge and
Kempka agreed, however, that in case of danger the only thing they
could do was to throw themselves between the *Führer* and the attacker.
They could not rely on their guns; more likely than not they would be
unable to use them without endangering Hitler as much as an attacker.

Insiders such as cooks (including a Jewish cook for a number of years),
valets, and SS bodyguards had every chance of assassinating the *Führer*.
But it so happened that none of them felt motivated to do so. They benefited from their association with Hitler, they believed in him, they were
attached to him uncritically, they did not see the impending disaster
or did not feel responsible to the rest of the nation. No case is known
of one of them losing his sanity. Fear was probably the least of the factors
providing security in this inner circle. Hitler never tired of personally
looking after the well-being of his servants, making certain that they received generous pay and the same food as that served at his table, that
each of his employees had his own room and that quarters were provided
for married servants. He gave them substantial gifts on weddings and
other family occasions; he had the children and wives of his immediate
entourage over for coffee, chocolate and cake on his own birthday; he
talked with everyone; he cultivated their loyalty and love. Even the low-

liest of his servants could always feel himself in the *Führer's* favour as long as he was not lackadaisical or insubordinate.

Hitler was almost as safe from his military foes as he was within the inner circle of his aides and servants. Allied intelligence services knew the locations of his major HQ, in the case of 'Wolfschanze' at least from January 1942,[54] and of course the exact geographical locations of the 'Berghof', of the apartment in Munich and of the *Reich* Chancellery had never been secret. Yet neither the Chancellery nor the 'Berghof' were specific targets of bombing attacks until the very last weeks of the war, and the house at No. 16 Prinzregentenplatz remained nearly untouched throughout. 'Wolfschanze' was never bombed, nor were any of the several western HQ installations. As late as 30 June 1944 SS Anti-aircraft Command Obersalzberg were able to report: 'Direct raids upon the object have so far not occurred. In several cases of overflight, fire was opened. The hit situation was generally good.'[55]

A mixture of tactical, strategic and political considerations at various levels of responsibility appears to have forestalled Allied bombing attacks upon any of Hitler's most-used residences. Some of these considerations indicate a certain success of security precautions. But only vague outlines of Western Allied thinking on the subject have so far become visible, and the mystery of why the Russian Air Force never bombed 'Wolfschanze', only a few hundred miles or less west of the Russian Front by 1944, is not likely to be solved soon.

Although intelligence on the location and buildings of such sites as 'Wolfschanze' was available, there remained questions of the reliability of the information, of Hitler's presence there at a given time, of the strength of the air-raid shelters and anti-aircraft defences. In the case of 'Wolfschanze' HQ in East Prussia, the distance from the nearest Western Allied bomber bases in England was so great that only long-range heavy bombers, without fighter escorts, could have been employed. Flying over the Baltic Sea would have minimised the dangers of interception.

The United States Army Air Forces did conduct bombing missions against targets approximately as far from their English bases as 'Wolfschanze,' and some of the targets were only about a hundred miles short of Hitler's main eastern HQ. On 9 October 1943, 352 heavy bombers of the American Eighth Air Force based in England struck industrial objects at Anklam (Arado plants), Marienburg (Focke-Wulf FW-190 airframe plant), Danzig (U-boat yards) and Gdingen (port area).[56] Twenty-eight heavy bombers were lost on these missions. Marienburg and Gdingen/Rahmel aircraft plants were targets of 138 heavy bombers of the Eighth Air Force on 9 April 1944, when the bombers again flew without fighter escorts because of the great distance (shorter-range missions on this day also operated without fighter escorts because of bad weather). A total of 399 B-17s and B-24s of the Eighth Air Force were engaged and thirty-two bombers were lost on this day.

It was obviously possible to bomb 'Wolfschanze', too. It was really a question of whether or not the target was considered important and worth the effort. There was indeed a 'debate among Allied strategists on the possibilities and the wisdom of dropping a blockbuster on the Fuehrer's field stronghold,' whose geographical details were known.[57] Arguments raised against such an undertaking in 1943 and 1944 were military and political ones. It was argued that an attack on Hitler's HQ would be too costly in terms of losses because of distance, danger of interception and heavy defences; but these risks were accepted in the bombing of Berlin, Danzig and Dresden, or in air-supplying the Warsaw Uprising of 1944. A very different factor is suggested by the reasons given for abstaining from an attack on Hitler at his planned victory parade in Paris, and again by a remark of the British Prime Minister to Major-General Ira C. Eaker in 1943, then commanding the U.S. Eighth Air Force based in Britain, after the general had raised objections to a proposal by Churchill to bomb a certain hotel in France where Hitler had been reported to be staying: ' "Upon consideration, I share your doubts about that mission. That would be like anarchy." '[58] Nevertheless, British military authorities again came forward, in June 1944, with a similar suggestion, 'to wipe out Hitler's sanctuary at Berchtesgaden' (Operation 'Hellhound'), and the objections were again similar. The United States Army Air Forces command sidetracked this plan on the grounds 'that it would prove too costly and would probably increase rather than diminish German support of the Fuehrer, who would surely survive it.'[59] Analogous considerations were applied to the German Army General Staff HQ near Zossen, about 15 miles south of Berlin, until very late in the war. This installation was 'long regarded as invulnerable to bombing even with the heaviest explosives, and for that reason not systematically attacked.' Only on 15 March 1945 was an attack launched in which American Air Force planes dropped 14,000 tons of bombs, destroying 'most of the buildings above the ground,' but not the vast underground bunkers.[60]

In February 1945 a plan to bomb selected targets in the Berchtesgaden area was proposed by the United States Fifteenth Air Force, as Operation 'Doldrum.'[61] It was rejected by the American Strategic Air Forces in Europe command, partly on the grounds that the small targets required ideal bombing conditions (clear weather), and that the project would cost the entire Fifteenth Air Force 'one visual bombing day.' But several weighty reasons cited against the project were not tactical: Hitler's blunders in conducting the German military effort 'have been to the great advantage of the Allies;' Hitler's death in a bombing attack would make him a martyr in the eyes of the German people; 'Hitler and his like can only be irrevocably discredited if he is at the helm when the final collapse comes;' an unsuccessful attack would be exploited by Goebbels to ridicule the Allies for a large bombing effort against a target of no importance; if Hitler's home is destroyed, this 'will bind him even closer to those Germans who have been bombed out;' 'an unsuccessful attack would enhance the reputation of Hitler in the eyes of the German people;' Goebbels would argue that the Allies were obviously mortally afraid of Hitler if they went to such pains to kill him.

One instance is known in which an effort was made, nevertheless, to kill Hitler through aerial bombing. This is reported by the Mediterranean Allied Tactical Air Force for 4 November 1944: Four P-47s of 27th Fighter Group flew a special mission to attack a Milan hotel where Hitler was reported to be stopping. Upon their return (without any losses) they reported three direct hits with 500-lb bombs on the roof of the hotel, and two hits in the street immediately in front of the hotel.[62] Hitler was thousands of miles north-east of Milan at the time, in 'Wolfschanze.'

The contradictions of the evidence may reflect simply the variations of opinion at various command levels. However the central importance of Hitler in the German war effort was assessed—as a danger, or as an asset to the Allied conduct of the war—there can be no doubt that systematic and concentrated raids on Hitler's known abodes would have caused great disruption to the German military leadership, through damage to communications, railways, roads, car pools, security systems. Most of the personnel in 'Wolfschanze' and in 'Mauerwald,' and equally in the Berchtesgaden area, were not housed in bunkers; there were no underground structures at 'Wolfschanze' and 'Mauerwald;' if the *Reich* Chancellery and the above-ground structures on Obersalzberg had been in ruins and rubble, Hitler would probably have avoided them, and he would have become a fugitive after the Russian advance had forced his departure from 'Wolfschanze' in the autumn of 1944. Moreover, it would have been possible to kill Hitler with aerial bombs, given the will and the intention.

There was never any real danger of Allied troops occupying the Obersalzberg area in a *coup de main*, until the very last weeks of the war. The territory was too mountainous to land airborne troops. Precautions were taken, nevertheless, in good time. Anti-aircraft batteries were installed near the 'Berghof' as early as 1935. From 1940 *Waffen-SS* units were kept in alert-readiness at all times around the 'Berghof,' and periodically they were given new instructions and admonitions. When Hitler moved to the 'Berghof' for a longer stay in 1944 (February to July), during the third phase of major construction at 'Wolfschanze,' new readiness tests were run at Obersalzberg. '*Ente*' (duck) was the code-word for practice alerts; '*Geier*' (vulture) would signal a real attack. Within five minutes the units had to be armed and ready to fight with all their fire-arms and hand grenades, in steel helmets and gasmasks.[63]

From approximately 1943 onwards Allied bomber formations could fly over German territory relatively unhindered, and Hitler expected concentrated air raids on his Headquarters and required appropriate precautions. As in the case of the *Reich* Chancellery air-raid shelters, Hitler paid out of his private funds for a great deal of the construction and camouflage work on Obersalzberg. Of RM 931,900 which were required, Martin Bormann furnished RM 430,544 from the funds of the Obersalzberg Administration. An SS Smoke-making Detachment was deployed to make the area invisible during air-raid alerts. It turned out in 1944, however, that some anti-aircraft batteries were also fogged up completely during the operation, and they had to be moved to higher locations. This made life difficult for their crews in the winter. Only mules could take supplies up to some of the batteries.[64] By July 1944 there were twelve 10.5-cm anti-aircraft guns stationed on and around Obersalzberg, eighteen 8.8-cm guns, twenty-seven 3.7-cm guns, six 2-cm guns, and another six 2-cm quadruple guns. The largest of the batteries, on Rossfeld, was manned by some 500 *Waffen-SS* soldiers.

The bombs finally came on 25 April 1945, with devastating accuracy, when 375 R.A.F. Lancasters and Mosquitos, escorted by 98 Mustangs of the U.S. Eighth Air Force and 13 Mustang squadrons of R.A.F. Fighter Command, flew low, taking cover from anti-aircraft fire behind mountains, until they were almost over the target, and then dropped their bombs. On 26 April 1945 *The Times* reported on the attack that twelve 1,000-lb bombs, fused for deep penetration, were used against the 'Berghof' chalet, and large numbers of 4,000-lb and 1,000-lb bombs were dropped on the SS barracks. After the second run, and with two of the Lancasters missing, the anti-aircraft batteries had been silenced. When it was all over, most of the buildings on Obersalzberg were smoking ruins. What was left was pillaged first by the local population in the hours between departure of the last German troops and arrival of the American troops on 4 May 1945, and then by the American troops, more or less systematically.[65]

11 Military Headquarters

From Bad Polzin to Mönichkirchen

Hitler's first wartime Headquarters was a railway station where his *Führersonderzug* 'Amerika' stopped: Bad Polzin. The station was guarded by troops from Infantry Regiment 'Grossdeutschland', with garrisons in Berlin, to which the Berlin Guard Battalion also belonged.[1] Guard troops included the staff; a signal-corps platoon from the Army signal school in Halle; a security company with two motorcycle platoons, an armoured reconnaissance platoon, an anti-tank platoon, two guard platoons, a supply section; and two railway anti-aircraft units. Only the two guard platoons and the supply section originally belonged to Infantry Regiment 'Grossdeutschland;' other units came from Army training centres and from Regiment 'General Göring.' In anticipation of the attack against Poland on 26 August 1939, the *Frontgruppe der FHQu. Truppen* (Headquarters Front Units) were mobilised on 23 August, but most of them did not move out until 31 August, when they took up positions in and around Bad Polzin. They were commanded by Colonel Erwin Rommel, the later Fieldmarshal, who was promoted to Major-General by Hitler himself, on 25 August. The troops were divided into three sections: Security Group 1 to guard the train station and an outer security perimeter; Security Group 2 in reserve; a Front Group (one motor-cycle platoon, half an armoured reconnaissance platoon, one signal platoon, one anti-aircraft platoon, half an anti-tank platoon, and part of the supply section), organised to accompany the *Führer* and the *Reich* ministers on visits to the Front. Soon the troops were considered not strong enough. Police forces of at least company strength were required for the outer perimeter. On the eve of the attack, a company of military police (100 men) and a company of regular police (fifty men) were added to the Headquarters troops. The military police were soon exchanged for a Provincial Police unit.

Outer security was provided by anti-tank batteries, by anti-aircraft batteries, by a squadron of fighter planes, and by auxiliary forces from the military police and later from the Provincial Police. The police cordoned off a security area with a 500-metre radius around the railway station, but people who lived within it were merely told not to approach the special trains or the station except on normal access streets. Travellers could still use the railway station, though gatherings of many persons

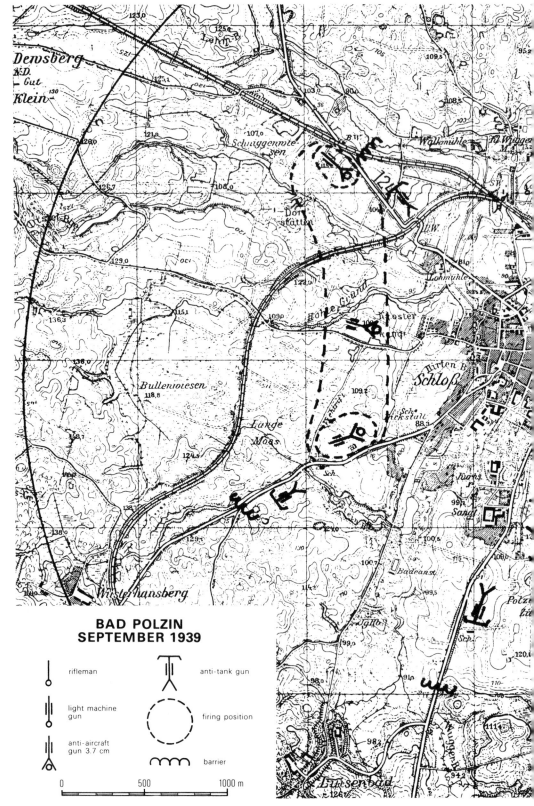

**BAD POLZIN
SEPTEMBER 1939**

rifleman	anti-tank gun
light machine gun	firing position
anti-aircraft gun 3.7 cm	barrier

0   500   1000 m

25. *Bad Polzin, September 1939*

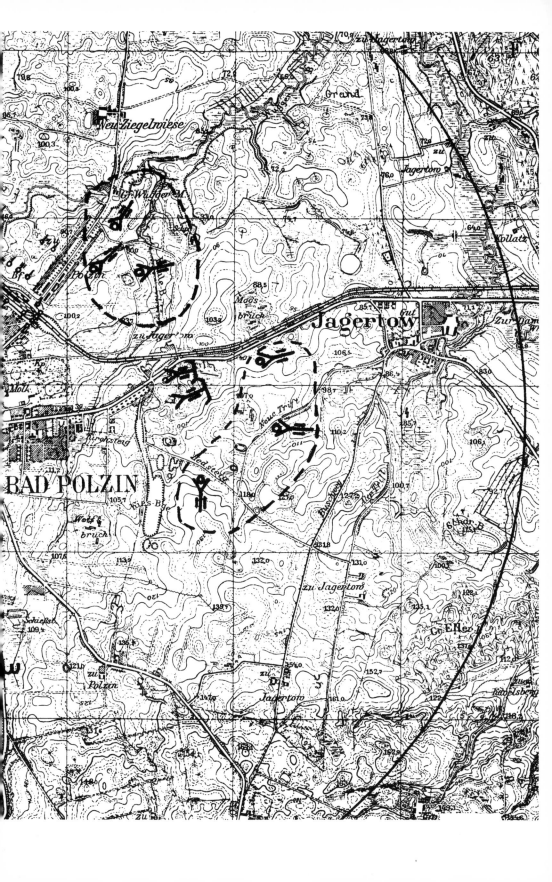

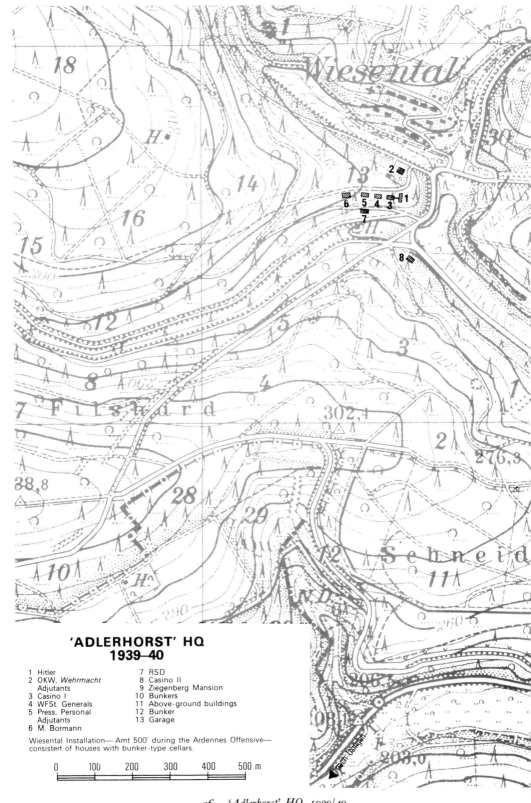

**'ADLERHORST' HQ
1939–40**

1 Hitler
2 OKW, *Wehrmacht*
   Adjutants
3 Casino I
4 WFSt. Generals
5 Press, Personal
   Adjutants
6 M. Bormann

7 RSD
8 Casino II
9 Ziegenberg Mansion
10 Bunkers
11 Above-ground buildings
12 Bunker
13 Garage

Wiesental Installation— Amt 500' during the Ardennes Offensive—
consisted of houses with bunker-type cellars.

0   100   200   300   400   500 m

26. *'Adlerhorst' HQ, 1939/40*

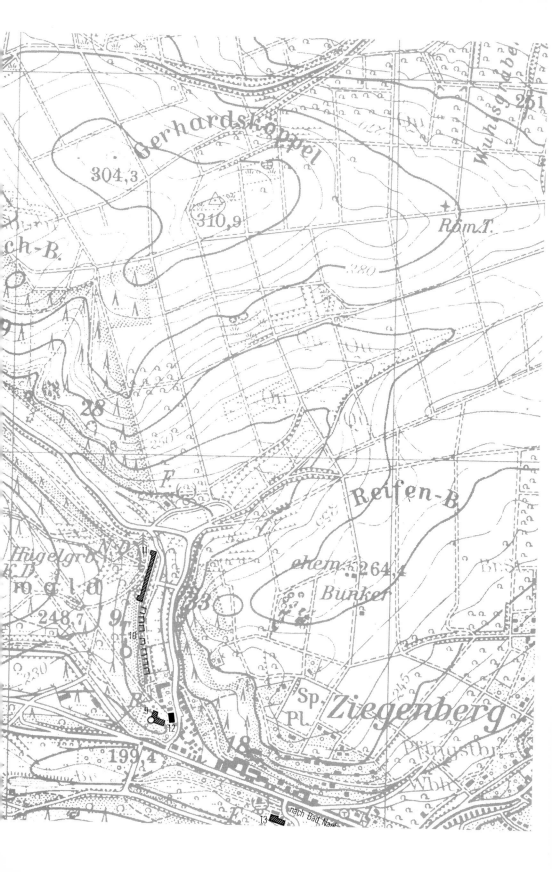

were prohibited. Platoons of Infantry Regiment 'Grossdeutschland' guarded the trains, and they cordoned off Hitler's path from train to car or vice versa. Within the inner circle formed by 'Grossdeutschland' troops, the RSD were in charge; only HQ members could pass through the inner ring and approach the trains, unless accompanied by an RSD officer.[2]

The *Führer* Headquarters at Bad Polzin was meant to be temporary, and makeshift. Soon the Polish campaign made Bad Polzin a place far behind the Front, and buildings were not put up there; a station waiting room was used as HQ command centre.[3]

Preparations to form a permanent battalion to accompany the *Führer*, the *Führer-Begleit-Bataillon* (FBB, *Führer* Escort Battalion), were begun by Major-General Rommel on 14 September 1939. On 28 September the FBB was an accomplished fact, and it received a special standard from Hitler. Cuff-bands that said *Führerhauptquartier* (*Führer* HQ) were added and worn from 3 September, by all members of the battalion. On 15 January 1941 all FBB members were ordered to wear on the right arm, above the wrist, the cuff-band saying *Führerhauptquartier* only when they were not actually serving at the HQ, as when on leave. Had they worn the cuff-bands while on HQ duty they might have given away its location if they appeared outside the security perimeter. By an order of the C-in-C Home Army dated 19 September 1940, those parts of the FBB belonging to the Army had to wear a cuff-band on the left arm that said *Grossdeutschland*.[4]

Hitler arrived in Bad Polzin on his train on 4 September. A second train, the 'ministers' train,' arrived a quarter of an hour later.[5] While Hitler and his suite left for a visit to the Front by car the same morning, the trains were moved to Plienitz, where they were to be boarded again. But at midnight Hitler's train had to be moved about 15 kilometres south because the new location had been leaked by the Foreign Office. Both trains went on to Gross-Born on 5 September, about 30 kilometres south-east of Bad Polzin, and a new Headquarters was set up there, largely with the same security arrangements as before. On 9 September the Headquarters trains were moved south to Illnau, near Oppeln in Silesia; on 12 September to Gogolin about 30 kilometres south of Oppeln; on 18 September they arrived at Goddentow-Lanz, near Lauenburg, about 40 kilometres north-west of Danzig. Hitler stayed at the 'Casino Hotel' in Zoppot for a few days. On 26 September the *Führersonderzug* left Goddentow-Lanz for Berlin. Now the *Führer* HQ was in the *Reich* Chancellery; a platoon of HQ troops, *Wache Führer*, were stationed there.

Hitler ordered the preparation of the offensive against France before the Polish campaign was completely over. On 10 October 1939 he sent Rommel to look for a suitable HQ location in the West. While HQ troops were training and practising attacks against bunkers, hand-to-hand combat, and anti-aircraft fire against flying targets, Rommel and some members of his staff looked at railway stations in the West.

Hitler's adjutants Schmundt, Captain Engel, Captain von Below, Naval Captain von Puttkamer, Dr. Todt and Speer also scouted around, in civilian attire, inspecting sites. Todt and Speer had instructions to modernise Ziegenberg mansion near Bad Nauheim; some bunkers were also built around the mansion. The installation was called 'A,' for 'Adlerhorst' (Eagle's Nest). But after millions of Reichsmarks had been spent, hundreds of kilometres of telephone cables and the best in communication equipment installed, Hitler said such an HQ was too luxurious for him. In time of war, he must live in simple style; his reputation as a leader with the most modest personal requirements was at stake, and those making pilgrimages to the *Führer's* former HQ after the war would never understand it. A new installation was built near Wiesental, about a mile north.[6] Hitler did not use this HQ until the Ardennes offensive in December 1944, when he stayed in the bunkers near Wiesental, now called 'Amt 500,' while Fieldmarshal von Rundstedt resided in Ziegenberg mansion.

At Rodert near Münstereifel, approximately 65 kilometres south-west of Bonn, about 45 kilometres from the Belgian border by road, there were some anti-aircraft gun emplacements, with hutments for the troops. The nearest airfield was at Euskirchen, about 15 kilometres north. These installations were to be converted into a *Führer* Headquarters. The attack in the West, initially scheduled for 12 November, had been postponed a few days earlier; the next scheduled date was 15 November, then 19 November, then 3 December, then 17 January. On 14 November 'Rodert,' also known as Installation 'R,' later as Installation 'F,' and finally as 'Felsennest' (Mountain Nest), was taken over by elements of the FBB. A month later, on 16 December 1939, Installation 'F' was considered finished by the construction supervisors in Bonn.[7]

There were still many details to attend to. Although it was to be a modest HQ, it proved necessary to build catwalks between the bunkers and hutments so that the *Führer's* entourage would not have to wade through mud. Fences were put up around the installation between December and February. Camouflage was added, water-pipes and other plumbing were put in, air conditioning was installed in the bunkers, and an air-raid shelter had to be constructed. Assorted guard details had to be borrowed from locally-stationed units at first, until 4 March 1940—clearly a gap in security precautions, but it was closed, more or less, in good time. Gun emplacements were built, and the troops received training.

Hitler's quarters were in a tiny bunker and consisted of one working room, one bedroom, a few small rooms for aides, and a kitchen and bathroom. Hitler and his entourage spent a good deal of the time out

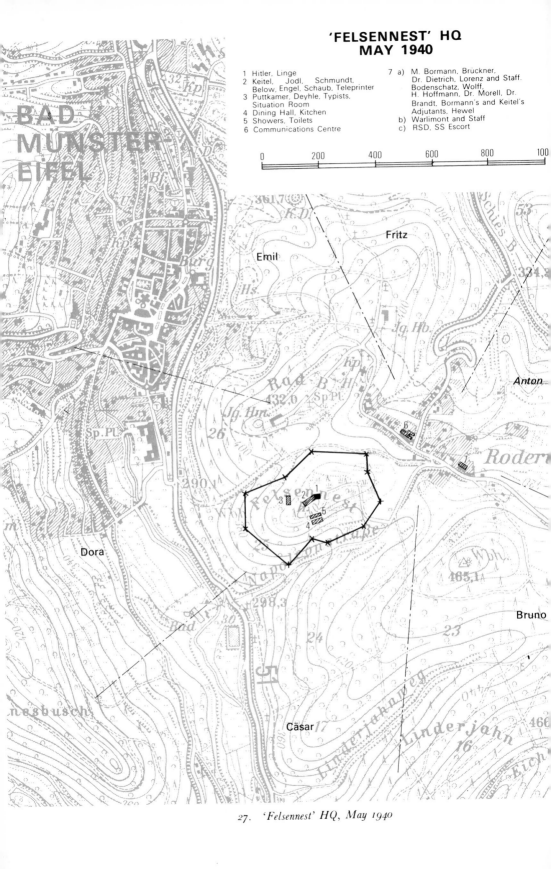

'FELSENNEST' HQ
MAY 1940

1 Hitler, Linge
2 Keitel, Jodl, Schmundt, Below, Engel, Schaub, Teleprinter
3 Puttkamer, Deyhle, Typists, Situation Room
4 Dining Hall, Kitchen
5 Showers, Toilets
6 Communications Centre

7 a) M. Bormann, Brückner, Dr. Dietrich, Lorenz and Staff. Bodenschatz, Wolff, H. Hoffmann, Dr. Morell, Dr. Brandt, Bormann's and Keitel's Adjutants, Hewel
   b) Warlimont and Staff
   c) RSD, SS Escort

27. 'Felsennest' HQ, May 1940

of doors when they used the place in May and during a few days in June.

On 19 December 1939, *SS-Standartenführer* Rattenhuber issued new orders 'to secure the *Führer* Headquarters and environs' near Bad Nauheim.[8] This may have been done merely to protect a valuable installation that might one day be used (as it was during the Ardennes offensive in 1944), or to keep a facility available until the complex at 'Rodert' was finished. But the preparations there were extensive, and in retrospect one has the impression that they were part of an effort to mislead spies. Nineteen RSD men, 103 regular policemen and three gendarmes were detailed to patrol the area near Bad Nauheim in six security districts, covering more than twenty communities around Bad Nauheim. Everything was apparently set up in expectation of the Western Offensive in January, preparations had to be finished by 15 January, and the RSD had to report for duty. Criminal-police Commissar Friedrich Schmidt was in charge of operations until Rattenhuber himself would arrive, presumably with Hitler. RSD men had to bring with them 7.65-mm and 6.35-mm pistols with fifty rounds of ammunition for each pistol, as well as civilian clothes and field-grey uniforms.

RSD tasks were as usual: generally, all aspects of security of the *Führer* and of other high-ranking personalities; their protection; inconspicuous escort service; prevention of unauthorised entry into security zones; supervision of other security organs; security checks on landlords who put up members of the *Führer* Headquarters; surveillance of railway stations and hotels; identity checks of uniformed persons to make sure they had a right to wear uniform; surveillance of all neutral military attachés, other foreign military officers, and German war correspondents and photographers; collection and confiscation of enemy propaganda material; counter-espionage against railway espionage or parachute drops of agents or materials; reporting systematic-looking flights of pigeons and small balloons. The possibility of small balloons carrying lethal gas into the *Führer* HQ also had to be kept in mind; nor could light-signals be overlooked, or any other sort of illicit, illegal and irregular transmission of information. The RSD had to make sure that no prisoners-of-war or other foreigners were employed or lived in the near vicinity of the Headquarters. Passes admitting persons to the Headquarters were modified on 20 November 1939 by stamping a green diagonal bar into them to prevent misuse. Brückner and other appropriate officials were requested to have all passes of persons in their sphere of authority brought over to Commissar Högl at No. 40 Kanonierstrasse, Berlin W8, for stamping.[9]

The air was thick with expectation of the *Führer's* arrival in his Western Headquarters in the first days of May 1940— at Rodert, not at Ziegenberg. A code-word for the event was arranged: 'Whitsuntide leave approved' would signal the arrival of the *Führer* Special at Euskirchen station, where Hitler was to be met by his Headquarters motor convoy.[10] Lieutenant-Colonel Thomas was now HQ Commandant; Rommel had been given command of the 7th *Panzer* Division on 15 February 1940. The code-word came through on 9 May 1940 at 1 p.m., by telephone. At 4.38 p.m. Hitler's train left Berlin. A *Führer-Begleit-Bataillon* front group took up positions under cover near Euskirchen station shortly before 1 a.m., and moved out to the square in front of the station at 4.25 a.m.—the exact moment when the train pulled in. At 4.30 a.m. the *Führer's* convoy of cars left with the *Führer* for 'Felsennest.' Meanwhile, the Special and the anti-aircraft detachment were sent via Bonn, Mainz, Frankfurt-on-Main to Heusenstamm, where the train was parked. At 5 a.m. on 10 May 1940 the *Führer* was in his 'Felsennest,' touring the entire installation and inspecting every detail of it. At 5.35 a.m. the German armies attacked in the West.

It occurred to the security authorities in Hitler's HQ, perhaps after the spectacular successes of German parachute troops in the Netherlands, that the French and the British might attempt an airborne assault against the HQ. On 23 May 1940 precautions were ordered.[11] A guard company of ten officers and 224 men, and including two separate assault groups, was designated. They were quartered in Rodert, Münstereifel, Kreuzweingarten, and the *Führer* HQ itself. They were armed with heavy and light machine-guns, rifles, hand-grenades and pistols. The object for all units was clearly stated: 'Total annihilation of the enemy. Prevention of penetration into fenced territory, into guest house, and into hutment L.' (Hutment L housed part of OKW.) Defence outside the fence was to continue as long as an enemy had not penetrated inside. 'The guard platoon riflemen at the five gates of the fence have keys to the gates. They only unlock them to allow the fighting troops in or out under orders of the nearest officer; otherwise the keys must not be in the locks.' If an airborne assault was likely or expected, the precautions were clearly inadequate. There is no mention of mine-fields, outer fences or perimeters, or of tanks and other heavy weapons which were to become characteristic of HQ installations in later years.

Air-raid warning systems were ordered to be set up west of Ziegenberg HQ as early as October 1939, along a line running north and south. Similar arrangements were made for 'Felsennest.' There were a number of overflights by enemy planes, but never any serious raids.[12] Shortly after midnight on 25 May 1940 an HQ anti-aircraft battery took nineteen shots at a plane flying past (over Flammersfeld). During the next night 'intense enemy activity in the air space over Installation "F"' was reported, and 384 rounds were fired by HQ anti-aircraft batteries. Anti-aircraft group Münstereifel reported 'several enemy planes,' including bombers and small fighter aircraft. They fired 570 rounds of machine-

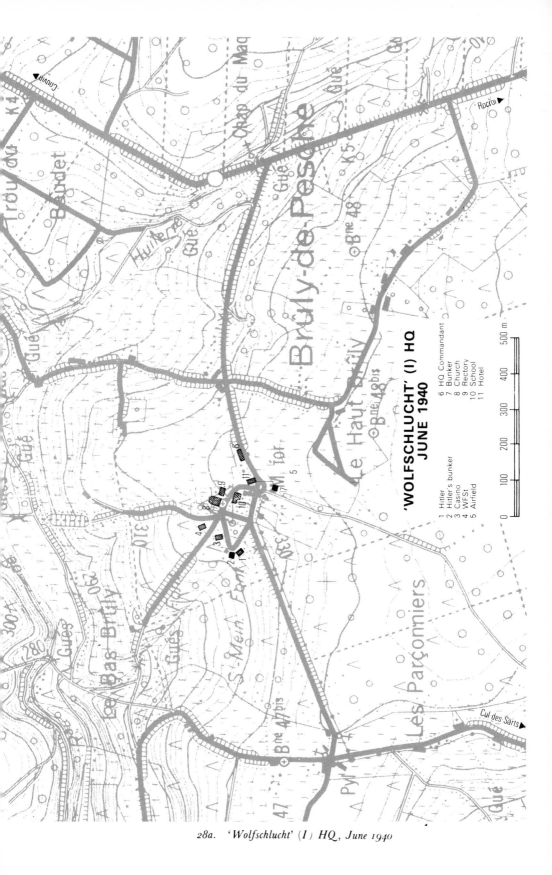

'WOLFSCHLUCHT' (I) HQ
JUNE 1940

1 Hitler
2 Hitler's bunker
3 Casino
4 WFSt
5 Airfield
6 HQ Commandant
7 Bunker
8 Church
9 Rectory
10 School
11 Hotel

28a.   'Wolfschlucht' (I) HQ, June 1940

gun ammunition, forty-one rounds were fired from 2-cm guns. At least one aircraft received an engine hit, whereupon another dropped some bombs without causing damage. During the next night 640 machine-gun rounds and thirty-two 2-cm rounds were fired. Bombs were apparently not dropped, but one of the bombers was shot down by a neighbouring 8.8-cm battery. Shortly after midnight on 27 May, HQ batteries fired 249 rounds at enemy planes; one was hit. Enemy leaflets were dropped over 'Adlerhorst' at Ziegenberg during the night of 10

28b. 'Wolfschlucht' (I) HQ, aerial view, June 1940

to 11 August 1940, and collected by RSD officers the next day. About 1 a.m. on 12 August enemy planes dropped phosphorus incendiary bombs on an airfield near 'Adlerhorst.' There were overflights of the same site on six more occasions in August, and on at least five occasions in September, when 2,638 rounds were fired at enemy aircraft.[13]

Hitler wanted to move his HQ westwards soon after he had come to 'Felsennest.' An FBB detail was sent to the Maginot line east of Avesnes, and Dr. Todt was there, too, inspecting the bunkers. But they were judged inappropriate.[14] On 22 May Lieutenant-Colonel Thomas picked a spot, together with Colonel Schmundt, Captain Engel and Dr. Todt: Brûly-de-Pesche, 6 kilometres south-west of Couvin, in Belgium. Three hutments were to be built—one for the *Führer*, one as a dining hall, and one for OKW Section L. The installation was to be called 'Waldwiese'

28c. '*Wolfschlucht (I) HQ, Hitler's quarters, June 1940*

28d. '*Wolfschlucht' (I) HQ (from left): Heinz Lorenz, Willy Deyhle, Albert Bormann, Hans Rattenhuber, Karl Bodenschatz, Hitler, June 1940*

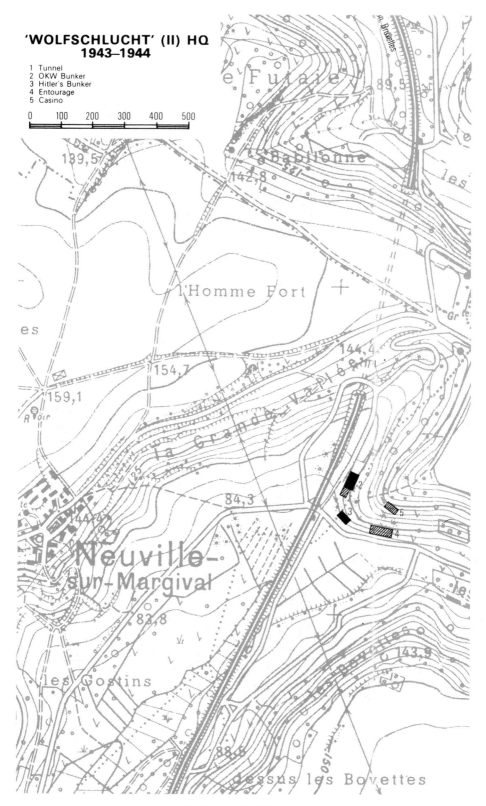

'WOLFSCHLUCHT' (II) HQ
1943–1944

1 Tunnel
2 OKW Bunker
3 Hitler's Bunker
4 Entourage
5 Casino

0   100   200   300   400   500

29. *'Wolfschlucht' (II) HQ, 1943/44*

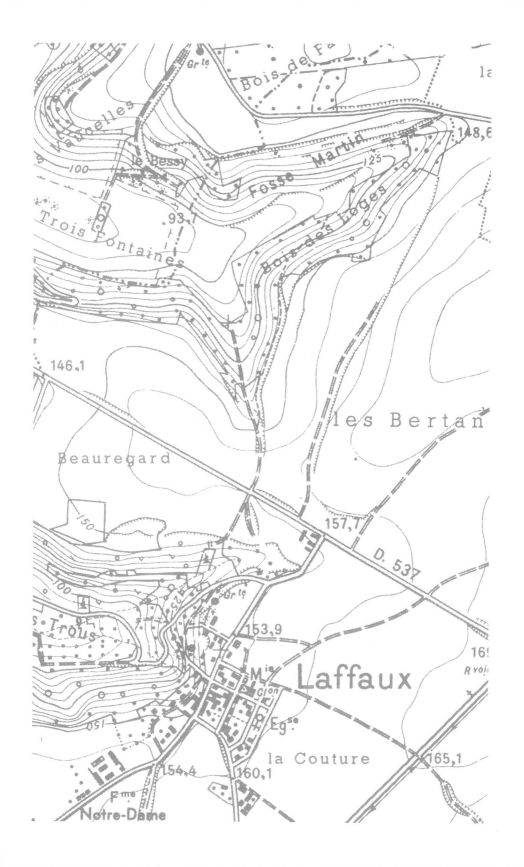

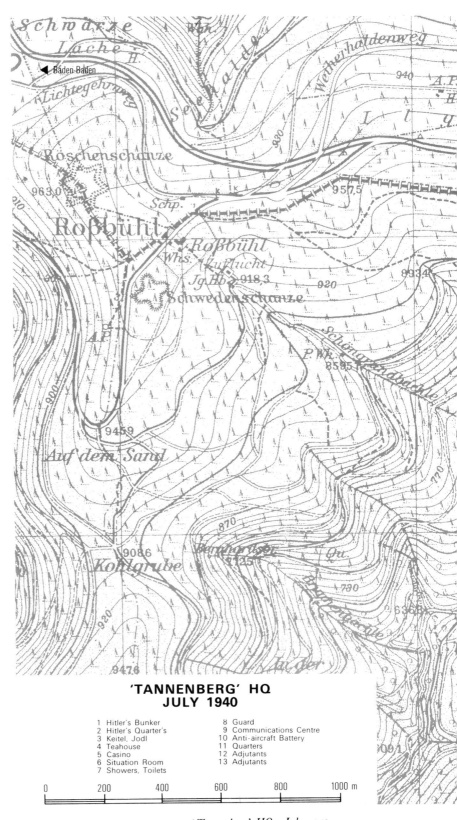

**'TANNENBERG' HQ
JULY 1940**

1 Hitler's Bunker
2 Hitler's Quarter's
3 Keitel, Jodl
4 Teahouse
5 Casino
6 Situation Room
7 Showers, Toilets
8 Guard
9 Communications Centre
10 Anti-aircraft Battery
11 Quarters
12 Adjutants
13 Adjutants

0   200   400   600   800   1000 m

30a. 'Tannenberg' HQ, July 1940

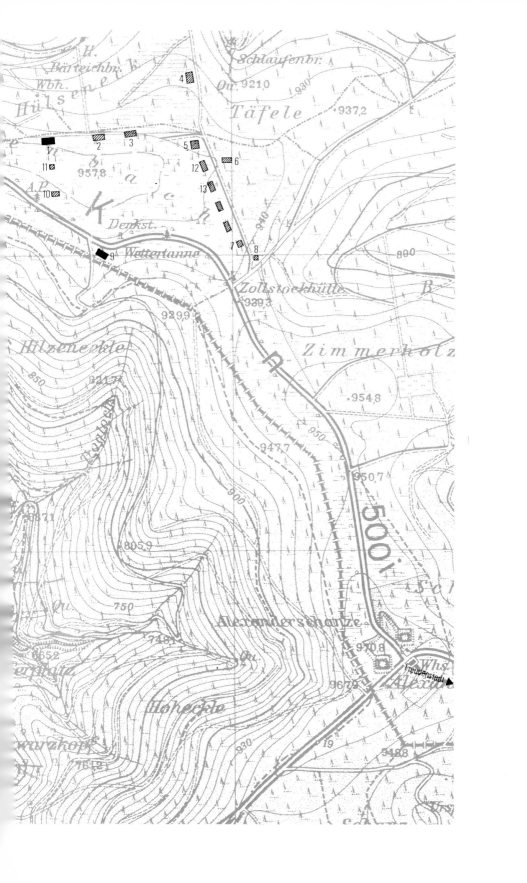

(Forest Meadow). The FBB and barbed-wire barriers and fences, as well as field-guns and anti-aircraft batteries (including No. 604 Reserve Fortress Anti-aircraft Detachment), were to protect it. The village and an area around the Headquarters site were evacuated. On 6 June Hitler moved in, and he re-named the place 'Wolfschlucht' ('Wolf's Gorge') upon his arrival. Names incorporating 'Wolf' were chosen, as Hitler told one of his secretaries, in reference to a cover name he had used during the Years of Struggle.[15]

This new HQ was modest in the extreme. Although staff and security forces used the buildings of the village, including the little church, Hitler himself occupied a very simple hutment; an air-raid shelter was quickly built for him by Dr. Todt's construction crews, but he never used it despite frequent overflights by enemy aircraft, and although in one instance incendiary bombs fell on buildings housing *SS-Begleit-Kommando* and *Reichssicherheitsdienst* details. Hitler preferred to stay out in the open during these dangerous moments.[16]

One other Headquarters installation was prepared in France, near Margival, and later known as 'Wolfschlucht II' (Wolf's Gorge II), or 'W2.' It had a very strong bunker, and steel doors sealed a tunnel nearby in which the *Führer* Special could be parked. It was built only in 1943/44 and was not used until after the invasion of Normandy by Allied troops when, on 17 June 1944, Hitler came there for one day to confer with his field commanders.[17]

The next move of the *Führer's* Headquarters was to Installation 'T,' or 'Tannenberg' (Pine Mountain), in the Black Forest on the Kniebis mountain, near Freudenstadt. On 28 June the *Führer* and his suite flew from Gros Caillou airfield to 'T,' after most of the personnel had left the day before. The few bunkers there were damp and not really habitable. Hitler spent much of his time outdoors and on trips to the Alsace to visit Strasbourg and some World War I battlefields. There was an open space of several acres, partly containing a three- or four-year growth of pines, adjoining an area in which buildings—bunkers, hutments, a porch—were placed among high mature trees. Surrounding the opening was a very dense pine forest, which could not be completely cordoned off by the wooden rail fence and barbed wire outside it, and by the sparsely-placed FBB guards, and RSD and *SS-Begleit-Kommando* patrols.[18] On the day Hitler arrived in 'Tannenberg,' preparations were begun for him to move to the Headquarters complex near the one at Ziegenberg. It was now known as Installation 'A,' or 'Adlerhorst' ('Eagle's Nest'). After Hitler had moved to 'Wolfschlucht', 'Felsennest' had been turned over to a guard company of VI Army Corps; after the move to 'Tannenberg,' 'Wolfschlucht' was passed on to *Organisation Todt*. On 5 July 1940, when Hitler finally returned to Berlin, all field headquarters units were moved to 'Adlerhorst,' leaving at 'Tannenberg' only

30b. 'Tannenberg' HQ, inner security perimeter, July 1940

a small guard unit of FBB which was soon replaced by a guard unit from V Army Corps in Stuttgart. At 'Adlerhorst,' however, the majority of HQ troops remained, keeping the installation ready for use, until 25 November 1940, when almost all were finally brought back to the barracks of Regiment 'General Göring' just outside Berlin. On 12 December 'Felsennest' was turned over to VI Military District Command. It was used again briefly to prepare for Hitler's Christmas visit in December

30c. 'Tannenberg' HQ, Hitler's bunker, July 1940

1940, but on 31 January 1941 Schmundt and Thomas conferred about turning over the installation to the NSDAP, and it was never used again by Hitler.[19]

The next HQ location was a length of railroad track, south of Wiener Neustadt, outside a tunnel, near Mönichkirchen, between 12 and 25 April 1941. Here the *Führer* Special was parked, with the locomotive constantly under steam so that the train could pull into the tunnel at any time. This location was known as 'Frühlingssturm' ('Spring Storm').[20]

'Wolfschanze'

As the German military machine was being geared up for the attack against Russia, the most famous of Hitler's Headquarters, 'Wolfschanze' ('Wolf's Redoubt' or 'Wolf's Lair'), was being set up 8 kilometres east of Rastenburg in East Prussia (now Kętrzyn in Poland). During the initial construction stage, the project was code-named Chemische Werke 'Askania' (Chemical Works 'Askania'), also 'Anlage Nord' ('Installation North'), ostensibly a bomb-proof war production plant. The location, surrounded by lakes, swamp areas and mixed forest, had been selected in November 1940 by a special order of Hitler who had sent out Dr. Todt, his Army Adjutant Lieutenant-Colonel Engel and other HQ staff officers and construction specialists to look for three suitable sites with

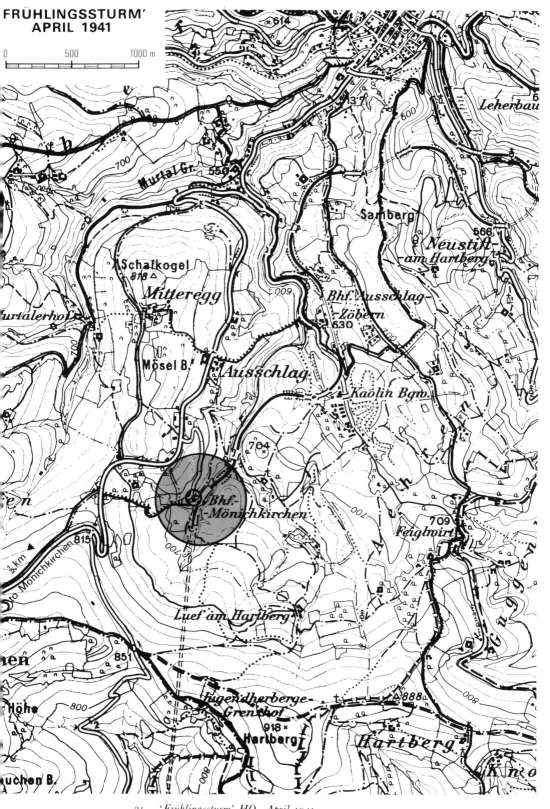

31. 'Frühlingssturm' HQ, April 1941

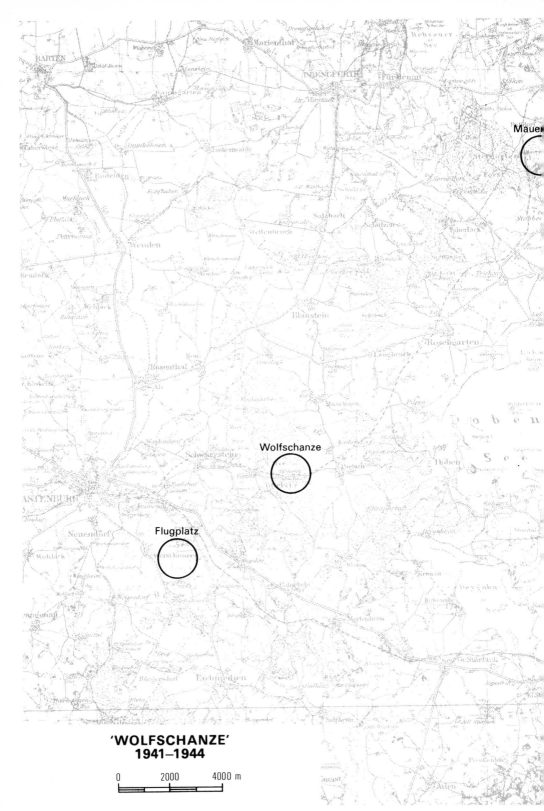

'WOLFSCHANZE'
1941–1944

0   2000   4000 m

32a.   'Wolfschanze' HQ and other HQ, 1941–4

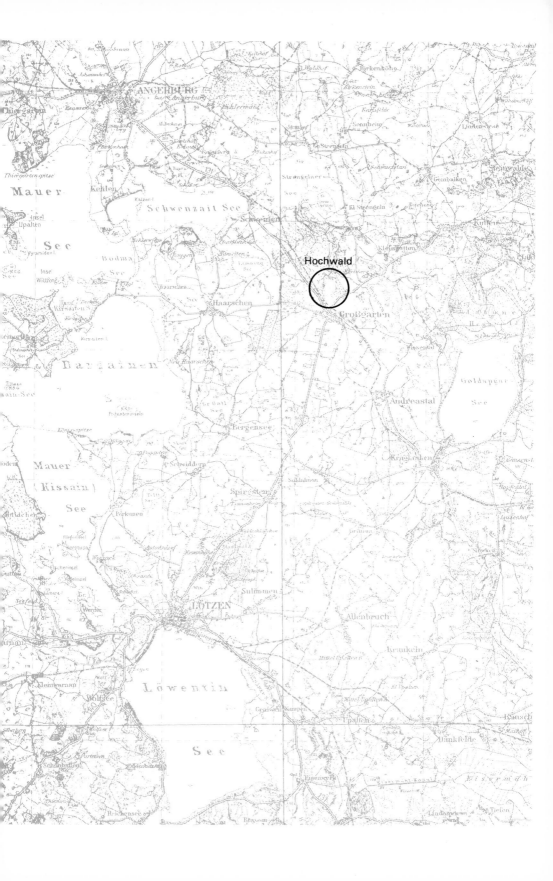

'WOLFSCHANZE' HQ AREA
WITH AIRFIELD, 1941–1944

1 Commandant, Air Traffic Control, Weather Station
2 *Führer* Squadron, OKW Squadron, *Führer* Courier Squadron Telephone Exchange, Teleprinter, Kitchen Command
3 Hangars
4 Water Tower
5 Officers' Quarters

6 Casino
7 Ground Personnel
8 Ground Personnel
9 Wilhelmsdorf Farm
10 Radio Guidance Signals
11 Kitchen, Mess
12 Guards

32b. '*Wolfschanze*' *HQ area with airfield, 1942*

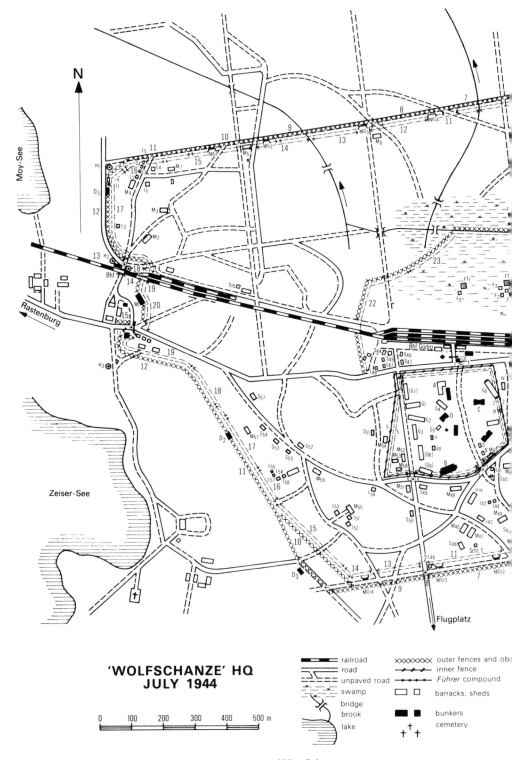

**'WOLFSCHANZE' HQ
JULY 1944**

▬▬▬ railroad	✕✕✕✕✕✕	outer fences and ob
▭▭▭▭ road	◦↙◦↙◦	inner fence
‑‑‑‑‑‑ unpaved road	•–•–•–	*Führer* compound
swamp	▭ ▢	barracks, sheds
bridge		
brook	◼ ◼	bunkers
lake	† ††	cemetery

0   100   200   300   400   500 m

32c. 'Wolfschanze' HQ, July 1944

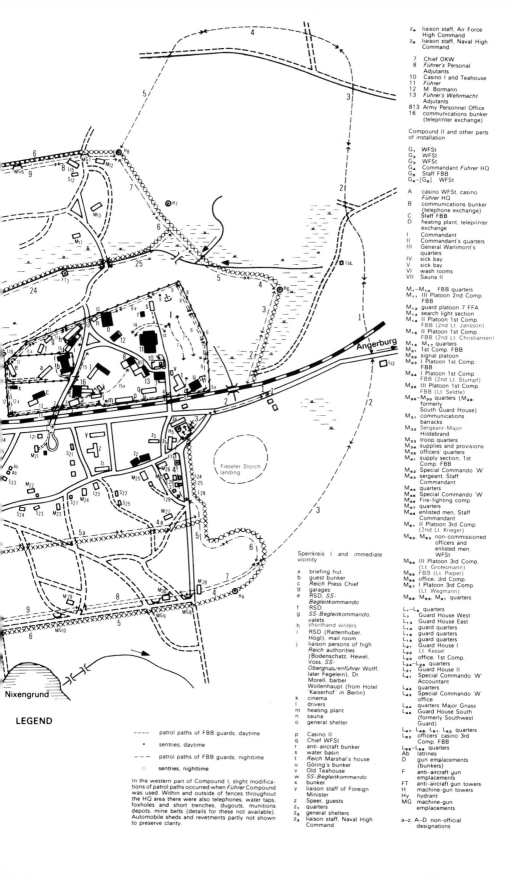

z₄ liaison staff, Air Force High Command
z₅ liaison staff, Naval High Command
7 Chief OKW
8 *Führer's* Personal Adjutants
10 Casino I and Teahouse
11 *Führer*
12 M. Bormann
13 *Führer's Wehrmacht* Adjutants
813 Army Personnel Office
16 communications bunker (teleprinter exchange)

Compound II and other parts of installation

G₁ WFSt
G₂ WFSt
G₃ WFSt
G₄ Commandant *Führer* HQ
G₅ Staff FBB
G₆–[G₉] WFSt

A casino WFSt, casino *Führer* HQ
B communications bunker (telephone exchange)
C Staff FBB
D heating plant, teleprinter exchange
I Commandant
II Commandant's quarters
III General Warlimont's quarters
IV sick bay
V sick bay
VI wash rooms
VII Sauna II

M₁–M₁₀ FBB quarters
M₁₁ III Platoon 2nd Comp. FBB
M₁₂ guard platoon 7 FFA
M₁₃ search light section
M₁₄ II Platoon 1st Comp. FBB (2nd Lt. Jansson)
M₁₅ II Platoon 1st Comp. FBB (2nd Lt. Christiansen)
M₁₆, M₁₇ quarters
M₂₁ 1st Comp. FBB
M₂₂ signal platoon
M₂₃ I Platoon 1st Comp. FBB
M₂₄ I Platoon 1st Comp. FBB (2nd Lt. Stumpf)
M₂₅ III Platoon 1st Comp. FBB (Lt Seldte)
M₂₆–M₃₀ quarters (M₂₆, formerly South Guard House)
M₃₁ communications barracks
M₃₂ Sergeant-Major Hildebrand
M₃₃ troop quarters
M₃₄ supplies and provisions
M₃₆ officers' quarters
M₄₁ supply section, 1st Comp. FBB
M₄₂ Special Commando 'W'
M₄₃ sergeant, Staff Commandant
M₄₄ quarters
M₄₅ Special Commando 'W'
M₄₆ Fire-fighting comp.
M₄₇ quarters
M₄₈ enlisted men, Staff Commandant
M₅₁ II Platoon 3rd Comp. (2nd Lt. Krieger)
M₅₂–M₅₃ non-commissioned officers and enlisted men, WFSt
M₅₄ III Platoon 3rd Comp. (Lt. Grotesmann)
M₅₅ FBB (Lt. Pieper)
M₅₆ office, 3rd Comp.
M₅₇ I Platoon 3rd Comp. (Lt. Wegmann)
M₅₈, M₅₉, M₆₁ quarters

L₁–L₆ quarters
L₇ Guard House West
L₁₃ Guard House East
L₁₄ guard quarters
L₁₆ guard quarters
L₁₉ guard quarters
L₂₁ Guard House I
L₂₂ Lt. Kessel
L₂₃ office, 1st Comp.
L₂₄–L₂₉ quarters
L₃₁ Guard House II
L₄₁ Special Commando 'W' Accountant
L₄₂ quarters
L₄₃ Special Commando 'W' office
L₄₄ quarters Major Gnass
L₄₅ Guard House South (formerly Southwest Guard)
L₄₇, L₄₈, L₅₁, L₅₂ quarters
L₅₃ officers' casino 3rd Comp. FBB
L₅₅–L₅₈ quarters
Ab latrines
D gun emplacements (bunkers)
F anti-aircraft gun emplacements
FT anti-aircraft gun towers
H machine-gun towers
Hy hydrant
MG machine-gun emplacements

a–z, A–D non-official designations

Angerburg

Fieseler Storch landing

Nixengrund

LEGEND

- - - - patrol paths of FBB guards, daytime
• sentries, daytime
– · – patrol paths of FBB guards, nighttime
○ sentries, nighttime

In the western part of Compound I, slight modifications of patrol paths occurred when *Führer* Compound was used. Within and outside of fences throughout the HQ area there were water taps, telephones, water taps, foxholes and short trenches, dugouts, munitions depots, mine belts (details for these not available). Automobile sheds and revetments partly not shown to preserve clarity.

Sperrkreis I and immediate vicinity

a briefing hut
b guest bunker
c *Reich* Press Chief
d garages
e RSD, SS-*Begleitkommando*
f RSD
g SS-*Begleitkommando*, valets
h shorthand writers
i RSD (Rattenhuber, Högl), mail room
j liaison persons of high *Reich* authorities (Bodenschatz, Hewel, Voss, SS-*Obergruppenführer* Wolff, later Fegelein), Dr. Morell, barber Wollenhaupt (from Hotel 'Kaiserhof' in Berlin)
k cinema
l drivers
m heating plant
n sauna
o general shelter
p Casino II
q Chief WFSt
r anti-aircraft bunker
s water basin
t *Reich* Marshal's house
u Göring's bunker
v Old Teahouse
w SS-*Begleitkommando*
x bunker
y liaison staff of Foreign Minister
z Speer, guests
z₁ quarters
z₂ general shelters
z₃ liaison staff, Naval High Command

a view to security against parachute-troop attacks, among other requirements. At the same time when 'Wolfschanze' was being built, two other HQ sites were prepared, 'with utmost speed;' they were known as 'Anlage Mitte' ('Installation Centre') near Tomaszow in Poland, and 'Anlage Süd' ('Installation South'), near Krosno in Poland. These two installations were merely artificial tunnels of reinforced concrete for the

32d. '*Wolfschanze*' *HQ, bunkers camouflaged, 1942*

Führer Special, with platforms and a few wooden huts. 'Anlage Nord,' however, was earmarked by Hitler to serve as a permanent HQ for his forthcoming campaigns. A railway line (one track) and a road went through 'Wolfschanze,' connecting Rastenburg with Angerburg and Lötzen where other staffs were quartered. The railway line was closed to non-military traffic.

At first, a few bunkers were built, and also some huts. Only enough trees were cut to make space for the buildings; a Stuttgart landscaping firm was hired to install artificial trees, camouflage nets and artificial

'moss' on top of the buildings, over the concrete roads inside the installation, and wherever man-made structures might be visible from above.
Aerial photographs were taken to make certain that the camouflage was
effective. The *Führer* Special, too, was kept under cover of camouflage
trees and nets when it stopped at Bahnhof Görlitz, the 'Wolfschanze'
railway station.[21]

Serious efforts were made to keep secret the exact location of the HQ.
But aerial photographs could not have withstood close scrutiny and

32e. '*Wolfschanze*' *HQ, aerial photograph to test camouflage, 1942*

analysis; up to the start of the attack against the Soviet Union, the daily
Russian passenger plane between Moscow and Berlin passed over
'Anlage Nord' regularly, and the construction activity could hardly have
escaped aerial reconnaissance; in a small cemetery inside the installation
there were burials of local inhabitants at least as late as 4 January 1942,
as headstones still show today. The pretence of a chemical plant was
kept up as long as possible, partly by giving HQ personnel civilian pass-
ports during the months of initial preparation, but these efforts at secrecy
were, on the whole, in vain. Hitler had no illusions about keeping the
secret of German military preparations for the attack against Russia;
in fact he reckoned with detection and wanted to make certain decisions

dependent upon Russian reactions to his preparations. Equally, the construction of 'Wolfschanze' could not remain secret. In an American compilation of information on the German Armed Forces of October 1942, one reads: 'The war station of the OKW is known as the *Fuehrerhauptquartier* (i.e. Hitler's GHQ). During the Polish campaign it was situated between Berlin and the Polish frontier, moving to the Rhineland for the campaign of 1940 and to East Prussia for the early stages of the attack on the U.S.S.R.' And in the February 1944 edition of the same work, entitled 'Order of Battle of the German Army,' the following is recorded: 'The field headquarters of the OKW, which includes the principal sections of the Armed Forces Operations Staff, is known as the *Fuehrerhauptquartier*. During the Polish campaign it was situated between Berlin and the Polish frontier, moving to the Rhineland for the campaign of 1940, and to East Prussia for the early stages of the attack on the U.S.S.R. It is now (January 1944) probably near Rastenburg in East Prussia.' The Swiss intelligence service, too, was informed of the precise location of 'Wolfschanze' by the spring of 1944 at the latest, and Allen Dulles in Berne received precise data on 'Wolfschanze' at the same time.[22]

Hitler took up residence at the new headquarters on 24 June 1941 and named the place 'Wolfschanze.'[22a] He stayed, with many interruptions, until 20 November 1944. He spent days, sometimes weeks, in Berlin, in Munich, at the 'Berghof,' and from 16 July to 1 November 1942 and 17 February to 13 March 1943 at an installation called 'Wehrwolf' that was located a few miles north of Vinnytsa in the Ukraine, on the road to Berdichev.[22b] As the contemporary information available on this HQ is very limited, it can only be mentioned in passing.

Around 'Wolfschanze' there was a wide security zone patrolled mainly by elements of FBB. A visitor might arrive by train at Görlitz station (every night a pair of courier trains left from the Silesian Station in Berlin and from Angerburg in East Prussia, respectively, to arrive at their opposite destinations the next morning); by aeroplane at Rastenburg airfield south-west of the HQ installation; by road from the west, south or east; or by rail trolley (which commuted between 'Wolfschanze' and Army High Command at 'Mauerwald' camp near Angerburg), stopping either at Görlitz station or at the eastern entrance to the complex, near Göring's *Luftwaffe* liaison offices. By this time, the visitor had passed at least one check-point in order to enter through a 50-metre belt of thousands of mines into the fenced area of the HQ installation—either the West Guard, South Guard or East Guard. But he was not yet inside the inner compound in which Hitler's quarters were located. There were three inner security zones, known as *Sperrkreis* I, *Sperrkreis* II, and *Sperrkreis* III (Restricted Zone I, etc.), each complete with check-points and guards. A visitor thus passed at least two or three, and up to four check-points on his way to Hitler's *Sperrkreis* I, and another one inside. On

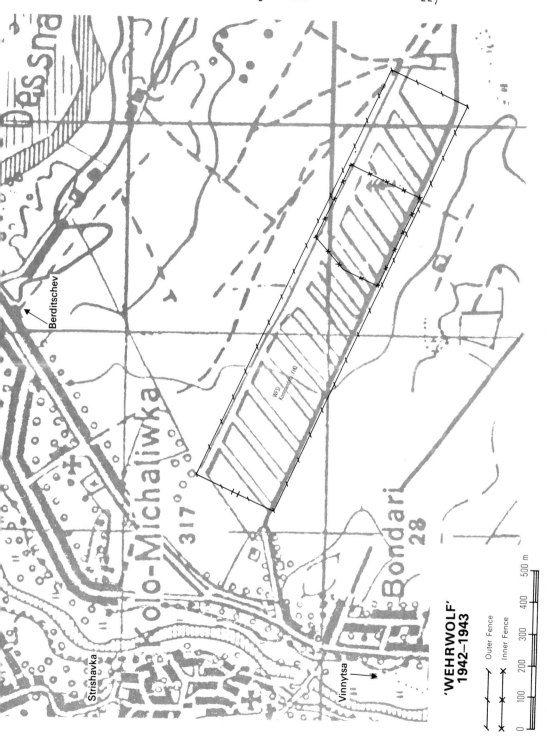

33a. 'Wehrwolf' HQ, 1942–3

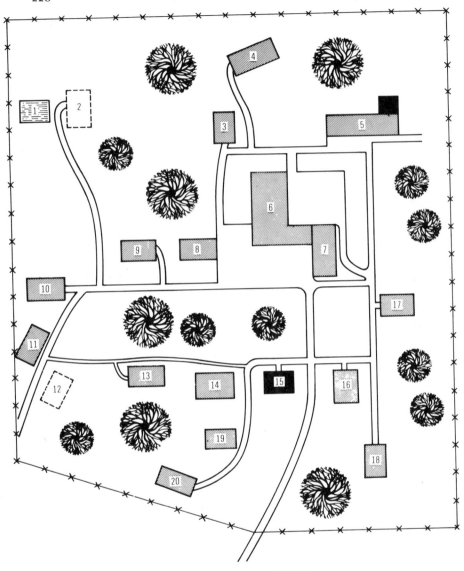

**'WEHRWOLF' HQ
1942–1943**

1 Swimming Pool	11 Press
2 Cinema	12 Guests
3 M. Bormann	13 Communications Centre
4 Shorthand Writers	14 Bath, Sauna, Barber
5 Hitler	15 Common Bunker
6 Casino	16 *Wehrmacht* Adjutants
7 Teahouse	17 Keitel, Jodl
8 Personal Adjutants	18 Chief, Army Staff
9 Generals	19 RSD
10 Guests, Secretaries	20 Servants, Orderlies

33b. 'Wehrwolf' HQ, schematic lay-out of buildings, 1942–3

9 July 1942, a Polish labourer had apparently left his place of employment without permission and wanted to take a short-cut on his way
home. He was shot dead immediately he came inside the outer fence
of 'Wolfschanze.' He had carried a knapsack with some meat and bread,
and a jackknife.[23] In August 1943 a Polish woman entered the security
perimeter at *Wache Ost* unnoticed by any guards, during the changing
of day-time and night-time guard details. She walked westwards, following the railroad, and she was arrested only when she arrived at *Wache
West*, after having traversed the entire length of 'Wolfschanze' HQ. This
incident must have contributed to the introduction of tighter security
precautions in September 1943, of which more will be said below.

Security Zone II was a fenced area north and south of the Rastenburg–
Angerburg road, inside the larger fenced area. It contained, within a
further fenced enclosure south-west of Security Zone I, the concrete-
and-brick one-storey houses of *Wehrmachtführungsstab* (WFSt, *Wehrmacht*
Leadership Staff), and of the HQ Commandant and his staff. There
were two messes; heating plants; and a communications centre (teleprinter exchange). East of these buildings, still south of the road, there
were concrete-and-brick houses for the Navy and Air Force liaison
offices, a two-storey building for the drivers, with garages at the ground-
floor level; in later years, there were two tall bunkers for the general
population of the HQ to be used in case of air raids, barracks for the
elements of FBB manning and patrolling the outer perimeter with its
machine-gun and anti-tank gun emplacements, and barracks for the
Führer-Flak-Abteilung (*Führer* Anti-Aircraft Detachment) manning the
anti-aircraft batteries throughout the installation. North of the road
there were a few buildings housing guard troops, and the heart of the
installation, *Sperrkreis* I. Here were Hitler's own bunker, Keitel's bunker,
a press bunker (Dr. Dietrich), Bormann's bunker, another communications centre (telephone exchange), concrete-and-brick houses for Jodl,
Göring, the Army Personnel Office and the Adjutants' Office, for guests,
for Hitler's personal physicians, for the RSD, for Kempka's motor pool,
and for the shorthand writers. There were an officers' mess and a mess-hall,
a teahouse, a sauna, a heating plant, a general air-raid shelter. Only
a few buildings, like the mess with its wine-cellar, had basements, and
there were a few basement-deep dug-outs; otherwise there were no
underground structures in the swampy area, all bunkers were above
ground; and there were no tunnels or 'secret' passages.

There were essentially three construction periods of 'Wolfschanze:'
1940–1, 1942–3 and 1944.[24] During the first period, concrete-and-brick
houses were built, with windows with steel shutters (in *Sperrkreis* I: *Reich
Press Chief*, guests, RSD and *SS-Begleit-Kommando*, personal servants,
Bormann, Hitler, communications, generals' quarters and barber's shop,
personal adjutants and *Wehrmacht* adjutants, garage, heating plant,

34a.   *'Wolfschanze' HQ, Hitler's bunker and annexe from second construction period, after autumn 1942*

34b.   *'Wolfschanze' HQ, Hitler's bunker with security guards during Ciano's visit, 25 October 1941*

officers' mess and Keitel), and a number of wooden buildings, including the Old Teahouse and a sauna. During the second period, wooden hutments were put up which were later covered with brick walls and concrete ceilings to protect them against incendiary bombs and shell fragments. These included buildings for guests, stenographers, the New Teahouse, Navy liaison offices, a second officers' mess, Jodl's offices, Göring's offices, a cinema, and wooden annexes to Hitler's bunker, the Army Personnel Office, Keitel's building, Dr. Dietrich's building. South of the road, there were some more such buildings, including one for Foreign Minister von Ribbentrop's liaison man, one for Dr. Todt and

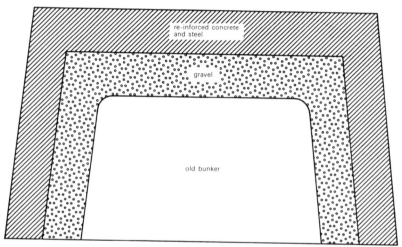

34c. 'Wolfschanze' HQ, schematic diagram of reinforced bunker, 1941–4

later Speer, two for the Navy High Command liaison office, and one for the Air Force High Command liaison office. Thus, the Commanders-in-Chief of Navy and Air Force had their own liaison offices, and their respective command staffs had their own liaison offices here, too. Himmler had his own liaison man in Hitler's HQ, at first *SS-Gruppenführer* Karl Wolff and later *SS-Gruppenführer* Fegelein. Spartan simplicity dominated at 'Wolfschanze' HQ as in the other HQ installations, in Hitler's own quarters as elsewhere, according to his detailed instructions, and in calculated contrast with the display of marble, costly rugs, tapestries and art treasures in the New *Reich* Chancellery.[25]

In the final construction period, a number of existing bunkers were reinforced, and some new ones were built. The old ones received additional shells of at least 4 metres of steel and concrete, making them completely windowless, including Hitler's own bunker and wooden annex (work on this project was not completed until autumn 1944); the guest bunker; the communications bunkers in *Sperrkreis* I and *Sperrkreis* II; Bormann's bunker; general air-raid shelters in *Sperrkreis* I. Hitler's bunker depended entirely on artificial oxygen supply when the several doors and air intakes (fitted with gas-protection chambers) were closed.

At Hitler's bunker the shell ceiling alone measured 5 metres thick, bringing the total thickness of the two ceilings to at least 7 metres. This was considered more than enough protection against direct hits of the heaviest known aerial bombs. The intermediate layer of gravel would have provided a cushioning effect and prevented the cracking of the inner bunker shell. Extended bombing with 10-ton bombs would eventually have destroyed the bunkers, nevertheless. Hitler fully expected 'massive daylight [aerial] attacks on headquarters,' as he told Speer on 14/15 October 1943, when he ordered the third construction period to increase the strength of existing bunkers and to construct new ones. When in the autumn of 1944 the Red Army was only about 100 kilometres east of 'Wolfschanze,' there was even more cause for concern. Allied planes frequently flew over 'Wolfschanze' in 1944, though there was never a serious attempt at bombing the installation. Once some Russian planes dropped just a few bombs in the outer security zone.[26]

Potentially, security was defeated by the very efforts to increase it, just as on Obersalzberg, through the presence of thousands of labourers of *Organisation Todt*; hundreds were brought into *Sperrkreis* I every day during construction periods to work on the *Führer* Bunker. In June 1944 a total of 28,000 labourers were engaged in construction work in the various *Führer* HQ installations. As Goebbels put it on 20 July 1944: 'Then what is the use of all security precautions?' It must have been easy, he said, when Hitler himself suspected that one of the labourers had planted the 20 July bomb, to penetrate into the best secured area of the world.[27]

There were several other HQ installations in the general area, between 18 and 70 kilometres away; Hitler's men had worked successfully to keep Ribbentrop, Himmler and others out of the *Führer* HQ; decentralisation was safer, too. The other installations served the needs of the Army High Command and its General Staff; of Göring and his staff; and of Ribbentrop and his staff. Göring's HQ 'Robinson' was in Rominten Forest north-east of Goldap and consisted of little more than a place for his special train; the Air Force High Command had its HQ in Goldap. In June and July 1941, at the beginning of the Russian campaign, Himmler's railway carriage (from his special train 'Heinrich') was parked on a modest railway siding near Grossgarten (now Pozezdrze), and Ribbentrop's and Lammers's railway carriages were also parked here. In addition to a platform there were only five bunkers, which were air-raid shelters but otherwise not habitable and very small,

34d.   'Wolfschanze' HQ, Hitler's bunker, ruin, from northwest, 1974

34e.   'Wolfschanze' HQ, Hitler's bunker, ruin, reinforced roof, 1974

34f. '*Wolfschanze*' *HQ, Restricted Zone I, communications bunker, 1974*

whilst working conditions in the hot railway coaches were all but intoler-able.[28] In July Ribbentrop managed to obtain a place away from his railway carriage and soon afterwards Lammers did, too. Ribbentrop liked great mansions; in 1939, Kransberg Castle near 'Adlerhorst' had been prepared for him, and now he soon made his headquarters in Steinort Manor which belonged to Graf Lehndorff, approximately 8 kilo-metres north-east of 'Wolfschanze,' and 10 kilometres south of the Army High Command HQ 'Mauerwald.' In August Himmler decided to move out; on 16 September he took up residence in a farm-house, and in the autumn of the same year the construction of 'Hochwald,' Himmler's *Feldkommandostelle* (field command post), began, with barracks, garages, a central kitchen, etc., at the site of his original railway siding. The site, in a dry high pine forest about a kilometre north of Grossgarten, was considerably healthier, more comfortable and more attractive than the site chosen for the *Führer* in its breezeless, fetid swampland. Even 'Mauer-wald,' between a lake (Mauersee) and the Rastenburg–Angerburg rail-way, in a thick mixed forest, was less swampy than 'Wolfschanze.'

'Mauerwald' Camp was divided into two sections, 'Fritz' and 'Quelle,' separated by the Rosengarten–Angerburg road. General Staff offices were all in 'Fritz,' except for the supply section, which was in 'Quelle,' together with administrative offices. The bunkers and hutments were all built into the forested area; but it was considered advisable not to concentrate all facilities there. Some were quartered in barracks at Angerburg, Lötzen and other towns nearby, as a precaution against air attacks. Some 1,500 persons worked in 'Fritz' and 'Quelle,' and for weeks running they got no further than the shore of the lake for an occasional hour after duty. A guard battalion was there mainly for outer security, usually composed of field forces on rotation. Later in the war, two companies of older men not fit for Front Line duty performed security services. The work of General Staff section chiefs was protected inside the camp by a tight screen of secret-field-policemen (a group of about sixty) and intelligence agents, patrolling quarters and offices day and night.

The HQ installations, particularly 'Wolfschanze,' were integrated into the early-warning system of Air Fleet '*Reich*,' land forces under the control of No. I Military District Command in Königsberg were integrated into the defensive planning of the various camps. 'Wolfschanze,' however, was more heavily protected than any of the others. There was a *Führer-Luft-Nachrichten-Abteilung* (FLNA, *Führer* Air Intelligence Detachment) with observation posts to give advance warning of any single aeroplane entering the airspace within a radius of between 80 and 100 kilometres of the HQ. If a plane penetrated this airspace, an alert list of key persons was immediately activated. There was also the FNA, a *Führer-Nachrichten-Abteilung* (FNA, *Führer* Signal Detachment), and, of course, a greatly strengthened *Führer-Begleit-Bataillon* (later *Führer-Begleit-Brigade*).

The firepower of these various forces fluctuated. From May until September 1941 there were usually thirty 2-cm anti-aircraft guns deployed in and around 'Wolfschanze;' from October 1941 until March 1942, twenty-two or less, and thirty-one by July 1942. From May 1941 till July 1942 the number of light machine-guns No. 34 increased from 70 to 110; from June till August 1941 there were between twenty-nine and thirty-two light machine-guns No. 38, between twenty-one and sixteen 3.7-cm tank guns No. 38, and two 5-cm anti-tank guns No. 38. There were throughout the period from May 1941 to July 1942 two or three heavy machine-guns; seven to nine 2-cm tank guns No. 38; between four and nine anti-tank rifles No. 39. Until September 1941 there were also four 3.7-cm anti-tank guns, afterwards replaced by thirteen 5-cm tank-guns, four 5-cm long-barrelled tank guns, and four 5-cm anti-tank guns No. 38. Tanks ready to fire were stationed inside and outside the outer perimeter. In September 1944, with the Russian Front coming ever closer, Hitler personally ordered the following items to be added to the 'Wolfschanze' arsenal: 200 sub-machine-guns No. 44 with 300,000 rounds of ammunition, 250 pistols No. 08 with 250,000 rounds

35. 'Mauerwald' HQ, 1943

**'MAUERWALD' HQ
1943**

of ammunition, 250 combat daggers, 250 brass knuckledusters or lead rods, eight flame-throwers of the latest model, 500 bazookas, 550 parachute-troop helmets, twenty-five telescopic sights of the latest model Z4, 200 mines, forty field compasses, sixty flashlights, fifty hand-carried spotlights, ammunition for 2-cm anti-aircraft guns, 2,700 12-cm grenades for mortar No. 42, 900 12-cm smoke grenades, 100 bunker lights, and a total of 25,200 grenades for a variety of tank guns.

Troop strength rose, after a tank company was added in May 1941, from 1,277 to 1,567 officers and men. Security and guard duties along the fences of Restricted Zones I (*Sperrkreis* I) and II of 'Wolfschanze' were the primary responsibility of FBB units. They were billeted partly inside and partly outside the HQ area. One entire platoon of the three guard companies was on active guard duty at any given time.

Inside, especially in *Sperrkreis* I, the principal security forces were RSD and *SS-Begleit-Kommando*. Rattenhuber and his deputy, Högl, were still in charge of Hitler's personal security inside his HQ, but there was by the end of 1942 a slight shift toward greater SS control here. Bureau I of RSD was declared responsible for the immediate security of the *Führer*, that is, for the police aspects of providing personal security, 'in cooperation with the *SS-Begleit-Kommando*.' An SS officer was responsible for punctual changes of guards and patrols of both services, for the guards at the cinema, for arms and equipment of guards and patrols, for giving out passwords, and for supervising the presence of guard details of both services in their quarters during the period of readiness before they went on their duty shifts.[29] The following permanent guards were posted (apart from those escorting Hitler around *Sperrkreis* I whenever he left his bunker for a walk): one *SS-Begleit-Kommando* sentry in front of the *Führer* Bunker day and night (primarily for military sentry duty); one RSD officer (armed with a 7.65-mm pistol, at night with tracer-ammunition pistol and flashlight) in constant patrol around the *Führer* Bunker day and night; one RSD guard (armed like his colleague) in front of the shorthand writers' hut day and night; and one RSD patrol (7.65-mm pistol) throughout *Sperrkreis* I from 10 a.m. to 6 p.m.

The RSD officer patrolling the territory immediately around Hitler's bunker had to watch all entrances and the entrance to the coal storage room; he had to prevent disturbances of any kind, particularly noise, and the entry of any unauthorised persons into the bunker. He had to supervise the work of the heating man, and of all craftsmen and repairmen in or around the bunker. He was required not to leave his post at all when the second entrance to Hitler's bunker, through the wooden annexe, was open during the situation conferences that were held there; during fog or darkness; or when work had to be supervised. Otherwise Hitler's personal adjutants (Schaub, Albert Bormann, Schmundt, Schulze-Kossens, Günsche) were empowered to use the RSD guard for small errands and runner services. In such cases, the RSD officer had to inform the *SS-Begleit-Kommando* guard. He also had to make sure that unauthorised persons, including persons on duty or quartered in *Sperrkreis* I, did not walk about unnecessarily in the vicinity of the *Führer* Bunker. One of Keitel's orderlies remembers that he had to have permission to go from Keitel's bunker to the *Führer* Bunker in every single instance.[30] Persons found wandering about and not familiar to the RSD guard had to be asked 'in polite form' for their identification papers, which had to be most thoroughly examined, and the the persons had to be helped on their way to whatever person or office they had been looking for when presumably they had become lost. This might include escorting them, or having them escorted by someone else from the office the person wanted to visit, if the RSD officer could not leave his post. A person found without a pass that authorised him to be in *Sperrkreis* I was to be 'identified by someone who knew him, with observation of all precautions, or he was to be taken to the leader on duty at once.' In all such cases, Rattenhuber or his deputy had to be informed immediately.

Such cases did occur. Some military officers tried to play one-upmanship by contriving to get an assignment that would allow them to visit the supreme sanctum, Hitler's HQ, and some succeeded, in the earlier years of the war. It was also possible to get into the *Führer's* HQ by mistake. In 1942 a colonel got off the local train (connecting Rastenburg– 'Wolfschanze'–'Mauerwald'–Angerburg) near *Sperrkreis* I, thinking he was in 'Mauerwald,' wandered into *Sperrkreis* I, sought out the officers' mess, and was having breakfast there when Hitler's Navy Aide, Rear-Admiral von Puttkamer, discovered him. He refused to believe that he was in 'Wolfschanze' until Puttkamer pointed out to him Hitler, exercising his dog.[31]

Up to September 1942 Hitler had been accustomed to eating lunch with a rather large group of some twenty persons who were regaled with a vegetarian meal, and with Hitler's monologue. The guests included such fixtures as Bormann, Schaub, Baur, Schmundt, Dr. Dietrich and Hewel, but also members of the FBB, of the *SS-Begleit-Kommando*, and visitors. After an angry exchange of words between Hitler and Jodl in the first days of September 1942, at 'Wehrwolf' HQ near Vinnytsa, Hitler ate his lunch alone, or with his secretaries, for a while.[32] He became bored and wanted company, but the list of those lunching in the same room with Hitler was a reduced one. Hitler also felt that either his oral orders given in situation conferences were often twisted, or that his views were too often simply ignored. To remedy this, he got Bormann to set up a stenographic service by which every word he or anyone else spoke during the conferences would be faithfully recorded. Hitler had strictly forbidden any note-taking at his lunch table, and Bormann had arranged to have some notes taken secretly. The result was the *Secret Conversations 1941–1944*. A reading of these 'table-talks' makes clear that Hitler was wise in trying to prevent the recording of the revealing pseudo-intellectual mish-mash he usually spewed forth. But for the official shorthand writers, those transcribing what had been spoken at military situation conferences, a special concrete-and-brick building was set up, with a barbed-wire fence around it, and an RSD guard, within *Sperrkreis* I of 'Wolfschanze' after the HQ had moved back from Vinnytsa in the Ukraine on 1 November 1942. This building was strictly out of bounds to everyone except the shorthand writers who had been sworn in on 12 and 14 September, to Martin and Albert Bormann, Schaub, Dr. Brandt or his deputy, Morell, *SS-Obersturmbannführer* Dr. Heim (a shorthand writer and art expert), *SS-Obersturmbannführer* Dr. Bankert, Major Engel, Major von Below, the SS adjutants Schulze-Kossens, Günsche and Pfeiffer, and the valets Linge and Junge. These staff members were required, if they had been present at a situation conference, to read over and correct the transcript in the shorthand writers' building. The RSD sentry had to make certain that no one came close enough to overhear what was spoken in the building. It was not so much that even members of the inner circle of the HQ could not be trusted to be completely loyal, but that the atmosphere among this inner circle, as in most such groups, was one of casual camaraderie. The sort of people Hitler liked to have around, and his own standards of decency, ethics and discretion, all tended to produce many violations of regulations. Rules against private long-distance telephone conversations were constantly broken, and leaks of secret information often occurred. It was unclear how members of spy-rings such as *Rote Kapelle* (Red Orchestra) and the Rado-Rössler group (based in Switzerland) obtained their highly secret material. Presumably, their sources were in the *Führerhauptquartier* itself.

Hitler knew full well that dangers lurked even in his inner HQ circle, not merely from his declared enemies. When Marshal Antonescu sent him caviare and sweets he ordered them to be destroyed. At home, too, Hitler remarked to Schmundt, Jodl and Engel in November 1942, there were 'groups busy trying to destroy him and his work, and he also knew that there were designs against his life; so far, he had managed to make life miserable for those who were out to get him. What was particularly sad about it all was that they were by no means fanatical Communists, but in the first place members of the intelligentsia, so-called priests, and also high-ranking officers.'[33] Thus even in the innermost circles of the seemingly monolithic power-machine of Hitler's *Reich*, constant vigilance was of the essence, and it had to be revived by ever-renewed directives, as it flagged again and again.

The RSD guards had general instructions not to stand or walk together, not to talk unnecessarily to anyone, nor to enter the *Führer*

Bunker except in order to supervise the work of the heating man or a craftsman. Any messages or packages for the *Führer* Bunker must be handed over to an orderly there; during the night they were to be placed inside a window that was left open for this purpose. And: '*It is forbidden under any circumstances to open the steel door to the former bedroom of SS-Gruppenführer Schaub!*'—probably because it contained Hitler's safe to which only Hitler and Schaub had keys.[34] If the *Führer* was outside or near the Bunker, the RSD guard had to withdraw far enough to be able to keep other persons away from the *Führer*, and so that he himself would not disturb the *Führer* and his conversation.[35]

On 31 July 1943 Schmundt wrote to all offices in *Sperrkreis* I and II (Chief OKW, Chief WFSt, Chief Army Staff, General Bodenschatz, Rear-Admiral Voss, Colonel Scherff, Lieutenant-Colonel Sander, M. Bormann, the personal adjutants of the *Führer*, *Reich* Press Chief, Ambassador Hewel, and Rattenhuber); the order was also sent to Morell, Brandt, Baur, *Führer* dentist Blaschke, the *Reich* Photo Reporter, Frentz and other photographers; all forty-five members of a special SS commando had to sign that they knew the contents, and so did all orderlies and personnel in Mess No. I and in *Sonderzug* 'Brandenburg' (the *Führer* Special). The document said: 'The *Führer* has ordered that topics dealt with in the *Führer's* situation or other conferences must not be conversation topics in the mess. Furthermore, the *Führer* wishes that the special need for secrecy, particularly in the military and political sectors, be pointed out again to all gentlemen present in the *Führer's* HQ. Please note and communicate this *Führer* Order to all gentlemen in the respective realms of duty.'[36]

In January 1944 the two main telephone numbers of 'Wolfschanze' were changed, to be effective on 1 February 1944, in order to prevent unauthorised persons from obtaining telephone connections into the HQ exchanges. This had happened, and, especially in the weeks before this change, an alarming number of people had requested the telephone numbers by telephoning Rastenburg Post Office. Fifteen offices in the HQ had to be informed of the change, but their chiefs were asked to see to it that knowledge remained restricted to those who definitely had to know.[37]

On 20 September 1943 Major-General Schmundt and *NSKK-Gruppenführer* Albert Bormann issued new directives aimed at increasing security and secrecy within *Sperrkreis* I (Restricted Zone I).[38] A new *Sperrkreis* A (Restricted Zone A) was created within *Sperrkreis* I. It included the bunkers and annexes of Keitel (No. 7), of the personal adjutants (No. 8), of Mess No. 1 and Teahouse (No. 10), of the *Führer* (No. 11), of Bormann (No. 12), and of the *Führer's Wehrmacht* Adjutants' Office, Army Personnel Office, etc. (Nos. 13 and 8/13). This was the basis for the new arrangement: 'The *Führer* has ordered: The secrecy of events, intentions, conferences, etc. in his presence and near him in the *Führer's* HQ must be guaranteed by all available means. The *Führer* has directed that persons who speak to others of secret matters about which the others do not need to be informed shall be reported to him personally for disciplinary punishment. Besides secrecy, the security of the person of the *Führer* is decisive in creating Restricted Zone A. The *Führer's* orders force strict measures which may bring hardship to the one or the other. The requirement of increased security and secrecy must take precedence over all personal wishes.'

Only persons serving with Hitler directly, and those who had their offices in *Sperrkreis* A and who lived there, were now allowed in regularly. New passes were issued for persons allowed to enter the Zone regularly because they worked or lived there; additional passes could be issued by the HQ Commandant but only with permission of the Chief *Wehrmacht* Adjutant, Schmundt, or his deputy, and in consultation with *SS-Obergruppenführer* Schaub or his deputy. Day passes could be issued by the guard only after permission had been given by a personal or military adjutant of the *Führer*. No one was allowed to enter *Sperrkreis* A without a pass, not even in the company of a person with a pass, except in urgent cases when they could be accompanied by one of the RSD officers on duty at the gates, who alone had the authority to make such exceptions. They had to take the visitor where he was going, and either bring him back afterwards, or see to it that a pass was issued. If anyone was found alone without a pass in *Sperrkreis* A (how could he possibly have got in except by climbing over a fence?), he had to be arrested or ordered out. Motor traffic in *Sperrkreis* A was restricted to cars of 'personalities from *Reich* ministers, *Reich* leaders, and Fieldmarshal up;' these and their drivers and other accompanying persons had to have valid passes. Supply cars and those of persons with officer rank living in *Sperrkreis* A could also be brought in. All others had to be left outside. The three gates, at Keitel's, the adjutants' and Bormann's buildings, were each manned by one non-commissioned officer of the *Führer-Begleit-Bataillon* and one RSD officer. Passes were checked by the Army officer; the RSD officer had to assist, especially in cases of doubt. For press and teleprinter runner services, always the same soldiers had to be used, and they had to have passes. One RSD officer constantly patrolled within *Sperrkreis* A. The list of permanent lunch guests in Mess No. 1, Dining-room 1, was limited to the *Führer's* immediate suite in accordance with his orders. Other guests for luncheons or meals in the Teahouse could come only if asked by Schaub or Schmundt after permission or request from the *Führer*; applications had to be made in good time. Persons ordered to come to the *Führer* or to an agency in *Sperrkreis* A had to wait in Mess No. 2 in Restricted Zone I and were treated as guests of the *Führer*.

The list of lunch guests (of whom a few at a time could come to Dining-room No. 1) included Keitel, the brothers Bormann, Dr. Dietrich, Hewel, Jodl, Bodenschatz, Schaub, General Buhle, Schmundt, Rear-Admirals Voss and Puttkamer, Major-General Scherff, Dr. Brandt, Dr. von Hasselbach, Dr. Morell, the *Reich* Photo Reporter, Staff Leader Sündermann (Propaganda Ministry), *SS-Oberführer* Rattenhuber, Colonel Baur, Colonel Gaim (pilot), Lieutenant-Colonels Sander, Engel, von Below and Doldi (pilot), Major Weiss, Major Betz (flyer), Major John von Freyend (Keitel's adjutant), Major Waizenegger (Jodl's adjutant), *SS-Sturmbannführer* Darges, Högl, Kempka, Captain Fuchs, Captain von Szymonski, *SS-Hauptsturmführer* Pfeiffer, Judge Müller, District Leader Lorenz, Lieutenant Frentz—a total of 38. In Dining-room No. 2, there lunched 23 aides, valets and typists, and 10 shorthand writers and their typists—a total of 43.

A few days later, the HQ Commandant issued new directives for various types of alerts. There were four levels: alert readiness; alert, gas alert; fire alert.[39] Alert readiness was communicated without any sirens, only by telephone or runner, to order preparedness to defend the HQ against an expected attack—by aeroplanes, parachute troops, airborne-troop landings, or saboteurs. Defence positions had to be manned, guards and patrols doubled, general attention increased. All outside lights were switched off centrally. Grey Column vehicles and the cars of WFSt had to move out to designated shelters. Cars were not allowed to enter Restricted Zone I during an alert. This alert level applied only to the HQ troops. The next level was 'Alert, signalled by siren, telephone, anti-aircraft fire, or falling bombs;' the same signal was used for air raids and for parachute-troop landings. A (full) alert, of course, could be sounded without any preliminary stages. In case of full alert, everyone had to go into an air-raid shelter; at every wooden structure two orderlies or other soldiers had to man the foxholes and watch for fires, and report them or put them out. Everyone had to know the watchword of the day, and how to wear his armband (the method for this was changed frequently). After dark, armbands had to be put on immediately: 'Whoever moves about out of doors without an armband after the siren has sounded will be regarded as an enemy and will be shot!'

Gas alerts were given by gong, telephone, whistle blasts, or by shouting 'Gas!' The proper response was: 'Keep calm! Immediately put on gas-mask.' Otherwise, ordinary alert procedures were to be followed. Fire alerts required mainly that fires be reported and put out. The signals were telephone calls or shouts of 'Fire!'

From 5 May 1944 the directives were slightly modified in that another alert level was added.[40] 'Silent alert readiness,' only for HQ troops, and signalled by telephone or runner, meant that parachute drops or airborne-troop landings were taking place in the wider environs of the HQ, or that shots were heard nearby or inside without their cause being immediately apparent, or that mines were detonated and it was not immediately clear whether this was due to 'natural' causes such as game or falling trees. Any shot fired within the outer perimeter automatically produced an alarm. Alert readiness was now signalled by siren in accordance with regulations followed in the entire *Reich*, just as 'end of alert' (three high-pitched sounds in one minute for preliminary end of alert; one-minute tone on the same pitch for final end of alert). No distinction was made between alerts for air raids and those for airborne-troop landings: there was no way of telling what would be dropped before it occurred, so that the troops had to be ready for both. Trains had to pull out of 'Wolfschanze' when a preliminary alarm (now level 2) was sounded or telephoned.

It might have been difficult to drop troops in summer on the few solid open spaces between forests, swamps, lakes and the many thousands of mines distributed over large areas around the HQ installations. But in the winter they could be landed on frozen lakes, and concern over this possibility was so great in the winter of 1943–44 that anti-aircraft batteries were installed that could fire point-blank at such troops, possibly punching holes in the ice for them. In case of parachute-troop attack, HQ troops were instructed to alert everyone by shouting 'Parachute troops!' and by shooting off violet flares. German aerial defences were obviously not being relied on to keep enemy planes away from 'Wolfschanze:' 'In case of parachute-troop drops in the centre of the installation, defensive weapons will also be aimed inwards. Therefore do not leave shelter before "end of alert" is sounded! Danger!!' The warning was repeated against moving about without an armband after an alert. In cases of gas alert, the gas-protection chambers in the bunkers had to be closed. In Goldap, some 70 kilometres north-east, a battalion of airborne troops was stationed, to be flown and dropped into the *Führer's* HQ if enemy troops got in, be they guerrilla bands, airborne or parachute troops, or fast-moving front troops. Later, a battalion of parachute troops was stationed at Insterburg for the same purpose.[41] On 15 July 1944, in a conference with Hitler, Himmler brought up the subject of 'attack on F.H.Qu. by parachute troops' as a potential danger. In a situation conference on 17 September 1944 Hitler expressed his concern about the protection of the HQ area and environs, and about the danger of a *coup de main*: 'If something goes wrong here—here I sit, here is my entire Supreme Command, here sits the *Reich* Marshal, here sits the Army High Command, here sits the *Reich* SS Leader, here sits the *Reich* Foreign Minister! Well, this is the *coup* that would pay most of all, that's quite obvious. I would not hesitate to risk two parachute divisions here, if I could capture the entire Russian leadership at one stroke. Keitel: The entire German leadership!'

On 23 July 1944, unrelated to the 20 July assassination attempt, alert procedures were further modified and supplemented.[42] Three officers or their deputies were constantly informed of the air situation: the HQ Commandant, the Air Force adjutant with the *Führer*, and the General Staff officer of the Air Force with WFSt. Sirens would be sounded by the duty officer in the HQ Commandant's office directly upon being informed by the regional anti-aircraft command, Anti-aircraft Group Masuren. Preliminary alerts were sounded if reconnaissance planes, nuisance raiders (no more than three, and not approaching the object concentrically) or individual fighter planes (up to nine) approached within 50 kilometres. Full alerts were sounded if more than three or more nuisance raiders approached concentrically to within 50 kilometres; if a fighter formation approached from the east to within 70 kilometres or a bomber formation to within 200 kilometres, or to within 150 kilometres without bombs. In cases of sudden attacks by low-flying planes, alerts were given directly by *Führer* Anti-aircraft Detachment. The same applied if communications broke down between Anti-aircraft Group Masuren and 'Wolfschanze.' The sirens of 'Wolfschanze,' of Ribbentrop's HQ at Steinort, and of Himmler's *Feldkommandostelle* (Field Command Post) 'Hochwald' (which could also be alerted by Anti-aircraft Sub-group Lötzen) were connected to the Masuren warning system. The sirens of Göring's HQ 'Robinson' and of his Special train 'Asien' were sounded from Anti-aircraft Sub-group Goldap.

All the security measures described above, internal and external, designed to foil an overt enemy attack, or 'sabotage,' or an underground attack, could not prevent the near-successful assassination attempt made on 20 July 1944 by Colonel Claus Graf von Stauffenberg.

Stauffenberg, who had served in the Ib (Supply) Section of the Army General Staff from 1940 through 1942, much of the time at 'Mauerwald' camp, had been assigned to a divisional staff in Rommel's Africa Corps in February, March and April 1943. He was wounded and all but given up by the physicians, but he recovered by August, having lost one hand and two fingers on the other, an eye and a knee-cap. It appears that it was during his pain-filled hours in hospital that he decided to try to do something to save Germany from ruin. He joined friends and brother officers in their active preparations for assassination and a *coup d'état*.[43] In June 1944 Stauffenberg became Chief of Staff to the Commander-in-Chief of the Home Army, Colonel-General Fromm; thus he had an opportunity to come into direct contact with Hitler. As Stauffenberg had only one hand, a shooting attempt was not considered safe enough, and anyway, Stauffenberg would be needed in Berlin to direct the coup. The plan was to deposit in Hitler's presence a briefcase full of explosive timed to explode within about five minutes after it was deposited. One could never be sure if Hitler would stay where he was long enough for this purpose, but the situation conferences seemed to provide the most useful opportunities.

The conspirators back in Berlin believed that Himmler and Göring should be killed at the same time as Hitler, and at least two opportunities to kill Hitler were missed because of Himmler's and Göring's absence. One effort was abandoned at 'Berghof,' on 11 July, and one at 'Wolfschanze,' on 15 July (the HQ had moved back there on 14 July), for this reason. But it is worth noting that Stauffenberg entered and left

36. *'Wolfschanze' HQ, between guest bunker (b) and situation hut (a) (from left): Stauffenberg, Puttkamer, Bodenschatz, Hitler, RSD officer, Keitel, 15 July 1944*

Hitler's HQ several times with a briefcase full of explosives without encountering any difficulties.

On 20 July Stauffenberg was scheduled to confer with General Buhle and Fieldmarshal Keitel at 'Wolfschanze,' and afterwards to report on new reserve units at Hitler's midday situation conference. Immediately after a conference with General Buhle in Jodl's house in *Sperrkreis* I, all participants, including Stauffenberg, went over to Keitel's bunker and annexe for a further conference which lasted up to the time scheduled for Hitler's situation conference. When it was about 12.30 p.m. and Keitel's adjutant reported that Lieutenant-General Heusinger (who was to report on the Eastern Front) had just arrived on the trolley from 'Mauerwald,' Keitel leaped up and said it was high time to go to the situation room near the Guest Bunker. Stauffenberg was expected to come along at once, but he needed a few minutes to prepare the bomb. He excused himself and said something about wanting to wash, or change his shirt, and Keitel's adjutant, Major John von Freyend, showed him to his private room. But Stauffenberg came out again and looked for his aide, Lieutenant von Haeften, and the explosive.

Haeften had been shown into a sitting-room, where he waited for Stauffenberg. The explosive, wrapped in oiled paper and canvas, had been deposited on the floor in the hallway, just outside the sitting-room. An orderly had noticed it and had asked Haeften about it. Haeften had replied that this was material that Stauffenberg needed later on for his report at the situation conference. This had been at about 11.45 a.m.; when the orderly looked down the corridor again, he did not see the canvas package any more.[44]

In the interval between Keitel's conference and the situation conference, the participants of the former had walked out of Keitel's building and were standing in front of the entrance, waiting for Stauffenberg. Stauffenberg had found his way to the sitting-room and, with a pair of pincers bent so that he could use them with his three fingers, he squeezed and broke the fuse capsule on one of two 2-lb packages of explosive he had brought along and Haeften had been keeping for him; Haeften was now holding the package. At this moment the door opened and the orderly, standing at the door looking in, said that Keitel wanted Stauffenberg to hurry up. Stauffenberg reacted very nervously and abruptly. Then Keitel's adjutant called from the entrance: 'Stauffenberg, *do* come along now!' The orderly was still standing there in the corridor; the door of the sitting-room was still open.

Stauffenberg must have felt he had been discovered. Whatever he was thinking, he went off with only one of the two explosive packages in his briefcase. All indications are that he planned to use both at the same time: a plausible reason for bringing the second one cannot otherwise be found, and the experts later agreed that double the amount used would probably have killed everyone in the room, including Hitler.

By the time Stauffenberg had rejoined the group, Keitel had gone on ahead to the situation hut, and the rest now followed. *Sperrkreis* A no longer functioned, as Hitler did not live there. Only the construction site of his bunker was fenced off from the rest of *Sperrkreis* I. But a fence and gate sealed off the Guest Bunker and the situation hut in a separate compound, the *Führersperrkreis* (*Führer's* Restricted Zone), within *Sperrkreis* I. There were SS and RSD guards at the gate, in front of the bunker, and patrolling inside the Zone. New pass procedures had apparently not been set up in the short time since the HQ had been moved back from

'Berghof' on 14 July. The rule that had applied to Zone A still applied, however, that only a very small number of persons were allowed to enter, and only on legitimate business; the number of such people was in fact smaller, as Zone A had five buildings and the *Führer* Zone only three.

Keitel's adjutant had offered to carry Stauffenberg's briefcase, and the one-handed Colonel had energetically refused. But near the entrance to the hut, he handed Major John von Freyend the briefcase and asked him to place him close to the *Führer* because of his impaired hearing, and so that he could be up-to-date when it would be his turn to speak. John placed Stauffenberg to Hitler's right only about two persons away from him, near the large map table around which all the conference participants were standing, and put the briefcase down on the floor in front of Stauffenberg.

There was an SS guard standing outside the hut, and an RSD patrol was not far away. Inside, there was a sergeant operating a small telephone switchboard, and in the conference room there were two SS officers; one of them was Hitler's personal aide Günsche, the other Himmler's liaison man Fegelein. All but three of the other twenty, not counting Hitler and Stauffenberg, were military men. There were two shorthand writers, Berger and Buchholz, and Ribbentrop's liaison man (in the absence of Hewel) Minister Sonnleithner.

No one thought of asking Stauffenberg to show his briefcase—it was customary to bring briefcases. Nor were conference participants searched for weapons, although it seems to have been proper to leave hats and belts (with or without pistols) on a rack outside the room. Stauffenberg, of course, had a perfect disguise: he was really the man who had been summoned to this conference on official business. It was just as a team of investigators from RSHA stated in their report dated 26 July 1944: 'Any failure of security measures *provided* against an assassination attempt cannot be discovered, since the possibility had never been taken into consideration that a General Staff officer who was summoned to the situation conference would lend his hand to such a crime.'[45]

After he had been present for a minute or two, Stauffenberg excused himself, mumbling something about a telephone call, and left the room, having deposited his briefcase under the great map table. He walked over to building 8/13, where his aide and General Fellgiebel were standing, and waited. At approximately ten minutes before 1 p.m., a great explosion was heard. Stauffenberg and his aide got into a staff car that had been ordered there, ostensibly to take them to lunch with the HQ Commandant. They rode past the situation hut where they saw a huge black cloud of smoke and dust, and first-aid personnel and other people running to and fro. Stauffenberg had the impression—so he told his fellow-conspirators back in Berlin a few hours later—that no one could possibly have survived the blast in the conference room.

His 'disguise' helped Stauffenberg to get through the two check-points. At the *Sperrkreis* I check-point he bluffed his way through, saying something about '*Führer's* Orders' and highest urgency; the guards (FBB and RSD) should not have allowed him through, having heard the explosion, but they did. At *Wache Süd* (southern guardhouse), at the outer gate, the difficulties were considerable. The gate was closed, obstacles had been placed in the roadway, and the military guard refused to let anyone through. Stauffenberg went into the guardhouse and telephoned to one of the HQ Commandant's officers (Möllendorf) whom he knew

37a. 'Wolfschanze' HQ, situation room after explosion of Stauffenberg's bomb, 20 July 1944

and whom he had seen at breakfast in the morning; Möllendorf ordered the guard to let Stauffenberg and Haeften pass. They proceeded to the airfield, got on a plane with engines running (it had been provided by the Quartermaster-General, General Eduard Wagner, who was in the plot), and took off for Berlin.

In the situation room, the explosion was experienced by the participants as a bright yellow flame and a deafening thud. They were thrown down, burned, bruised, pierced by splinters of wood. Most of them scrambled to their feet and stumbled out as fast as they could; some climbed through windows. A shorthand writer died in the afternoon, three officers died on 22 July and on 1 October. The others sustained more or less light injuries. Hitler was shaken, but not seriously injured. His

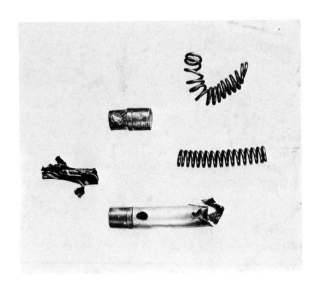

37b. Remains of Stauffenberg's briefcase, fuse, and pliers, and discarded explosive

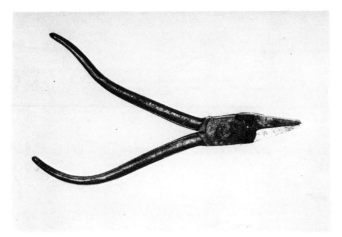

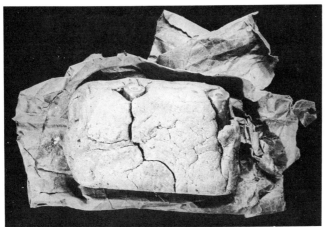

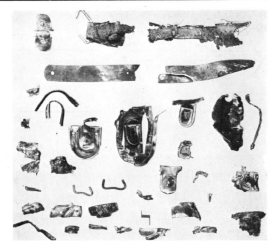

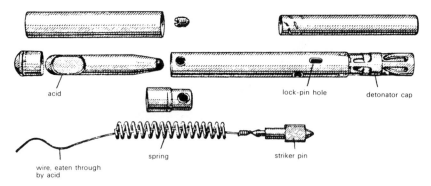

acid   lock-pin hole   detonator cap

spring   striker pin

wire, eaten through
by acid

37c.   Fuse of the type used by Tresckow, Gersdorff and Stauffenberg

eardrums were perforated, he had bruises on one hand, and a haemor-
rhage in the elbow with which he had been leaning on the map table.
'I am invulnerable, I am immortal!' Hitler kept saying to Dr. Morell,
who treated his injuries. The *Führer* declared that his survival was a
miracle. A few days after the attempt he told General Koller, Chief of
the General Staff of the Air Force; 'I came back from the First World
War unharmed, I've had quite a few difficult flights and dangerous car
trips, and nothing has happened to me. But this is the greatest miracle.
It really is a miracle.'[45a]

There would have been ample grounds for cancelling Mussolini's visit:
Hitler's condition, and the necessity to review and perhaps change
security procedures. Nothing of the sort was done. RSD officers came
and sealed off the situation hut, the bunker Hitler lived in was carefully
searched for more explosives, and alert conditions were applied at the
compound and outer security-zone gates. At first, *Organisation Todt*
labourers working on the *Führer* Bunker were suspected by Hitler and
by others of having planted the bomb. General Fellgiebel (another con-
spirator, but one not willing to kill Hitler personally, despite ample
opportunities) was standing in front of the Guest Bunker after the
explosion to ascertain whether the *Führer* was dead or alive. Some witnesses report that Fellgiebel immediately congratulated Hitler on his survival, when the *Führer* had emerged from the Guest Bunker after a change
of clothes and first-aid treatment. When Jodl came up, Fellgiebel
remarked: 'You see, this comes from being so close to the Front Lines;'
Jodl replied angrily: 'No, this comes from the HQ being a construction
site.' The only reasonable explanation seemed to Jodl to be that a Communist had infiltrated the OT and had planted the bomb.[46] Later he
wondered why Fellgiebel had not finished Stauffenberg's work by shooting the *Führer* then and there.

Soon Stauffenberg's disappearance was noticed, and the telephone switchboard operator remembered and reported that the Colonel had left without his briefcase. It soon became clear that he was the assassin. The RSHA investigation team came to the conclusion: 'The incident makes it mandatory to take into consideration even the ultimate possibility [such as a General Staff officer being an assassin] in providing protective measures for the *Führer*. Concerning these, proposals will be submitted in consultation with the *Reich* Security Head Office.'[47] There are indications of what measures were taken. During the night of 20 to 21 July, elements of *Leibstandarte-SS 'Adolf Hitler'* arrived, occupied all important points inside the installation, and sealed off *Sperrkreis* I; SS guards were added to every *Führer-Begleit-Bataillon* post inside and outside the *Führer* HQ. An entire SS alert unit was stationed in *Sperrkreis* I, which led to friction with regular troops. Finally HQ Commandant Streve and Schmundt (from his hospital bed) succeeded in persuading Hitler to have the SS withdrawn, at least from inside the restricted zones, after about a week. After another two weeks, they were withdrawn completely.[48] The regular Army's role in Hitler's protection was nevertheless reduced in the long term. A list of active SS units as on 13 November 1944 showed two companies designated as *Führer* escort units: Nos. 1 and 2 *SS-Panzer-Grenadier-Führer-Begleit-Kompanie 'LSSAH.'*

Everyone entering the presence of the *Führer* now had to have his briefcase checked, and more. Warlimont recalled that this made him so angry that he no longer brought a briefcase. Military officers who had to appear before Hitler in regulation uniform had to come without the weapons that were part of this uniform. However, there were usually no RSD or *SS-Begleit-Kommando* men present at situation conferences, only SS personal adjutants and aides, as before. There was still no X-ray screening device, though the installation of one was now being considered.

There was considerable excitement one day, some time after the practice of searching briefcases had been instituted, when the briefcase of Foreign Minister von Ribbentrop's Adjutant, Captain Ötting, was checked.[48a] There existed a rarely-followed regulation according to which bearers of secret *Reich* documents were required to carry with them at all times the means for the destruction of such papers. Thus Captain Ötting always carried, in his briefcase, with his secret and top-secret papers, one hand grenade and a bottle of petrol. The *Führer* HQ guards were greatly shocked by this discovery, and Ötting had to leave his briefcase behind; in future he adjusted to the common disregard for the regulation concerning destruction of secret papers.

On 22 July Dr. Giesing, an otorhinolaryngologist stationed in Lötzen Reserve Hospital, was suddenly summoned to Hitler to treat him for earache and ear-bleeding.[49] Dr. Brandt, a Personal Physician, took Giesing to the *Führer* Zone in *Sperrkreis* I, where SS and RSD officers guarded

the situation hut and the Guest Bunker in greater numbers than had
been seen before. Behind the Guest Bunker there was a tent into which
Dr. Giesing was escorted by one of the guards for a thorough search.
His briefcase was emptied, every instrument was looked at, even the bulb
of his ear-examination lamp was taken out, examined, and screwed back
in. Two bottles with liquids (2% pantokain solution for local anaesthetic
and sterilised physiological salt solution) were set aside. Dr. Giesing had
to leave his hat and dagger (he did not carry a gun), and he had to
empty his coat and trouser pockets and turn them inside out. He was
given back his handkerchief and keys, but not his fountain pen, pencil
and pocket-knife, which remained on a table. There followed a search
of Dr. Giesing's person. Dr. Brandt came back from the Guest Bunker
where he had gone, and took Dr. Giesing with him. Dr. Giesing said
he needed the bottles; Brandt told the guards it was all right, and an
RSD officer took the doctor's briefcase and the bottles and carried them
into the bunker, following Giesing and Brandt into a room where Linge
and two other men in SS uniforms were waiting. Linge took over the
case and the bottles, led Giesing into the dining-room, and went away,
still carrying the case and bottles. After a few minutes he reappeared
with only the briefcase, and wanted to know if the bottles were really
needed. Dr. Giesing said he might need them if the examination caused
the *Führer* pain. Linge said if that happened he would fetch the bottles.
As it turned out, they were not needed and remained in the anteroom
throughout the consultation. After the examination, Dr. Giesing was
escorted out again and his identity was carefully noted at every check-
point.

On the next day Dr. Giesing had to see Hitler again. This time a day
pass had been prepared for him and it was ready at the West Guardhouse. It was handed over after Dr. Giesing's own identification papers
had been compared with it. The pass and personal identification had
to be presented at a check-point inside *Sperrkreis* II, then again at the
entrance to *Sperrkreis* I, and again to Zone A (as the *Führer* Zone was
also called now). There followed the same procedure in the tent and
in the bunker as on the day before; only the bottles did not present a
problem this time—Dr. Giesing had not brought them.

These comprehensive precautions are in contrast to a relative lack of
security on other occasions. When Hitler visited those injured in the 20th
of July bomb explosion in Rastenburg Reserve Hospital at Carlshof
(between 20 and 29 July), he came with his motor convoy apparently
unannounced, and special precautions had not been taken.[50] As he got
out of his open car, he was instantaneously surrounded by patients who
had been taking walks in the hospital grounds, some of them on crutches.
Hitler stopped and talked to them; several had cameras and took pictures
of Hitler, who turned and smiled at the photographers several times.

Any one of the maimed soldiers, some of whom may have cursed the *Führer* only minutes earlier, could have killed the dictator there and then. But they cheered him.

During September 1944 Hitler felt very ill. On 19 September he had himself driven to Rastenburg Reserve Hospital for an X-ray examination. This time, SS and RSD guards were posted, an hour in advance of his expected arrival, outside the hospital entrances as well as inside at the door to the department of surgery. Other RSD officers searched the X-ray room and adjoining rooms for hidden explosives. Hitler arrived at approximately 6.30 p.m., sitting in his car next to Kempka, with Günsche, Schulze-Kossens, Linge and Hasselbach behind him. Some other aides and SS and RSD bodyguards followed in two more cars. The examination proceeded without a hitch.[51]

On 1 October Dr. Giesing was summoned once again to examine Hitler. On the *Führer's* night-table he saw a pistol. When Linge noticed that Dr. Giesing was looking at it, he took it away and put it into a cupboard.

Security procedures were as contradictory as ever, and a good deal more paranoiac, in the last few months of Hitler's régime. On 11 October 1944, officials of the RSD (Rattenhuber and *SS-Untersturmführer* Münkner), of OT (Engineer Welker and Inspector Krause) and of the Institute of Criminal Technology at RSHA (*SS-Sturmbannführer* Dr. Widmann and *SS-Untersturmführer* Sachs) held a conference at 'Wolfschanze.'[52] It was suggested that X-ray examination methods be used to detect 'bombs, explosive charges and the like' in parcels arriving at the *Führer's* HQ and at the Obersalzberg residence. Widmann also sent Rattenhuber a sample of a British explosive charge that was designed to go off at a certain altitude. It was mainly a piece of rubber hose containing explosive.

On 1 September Colonel Remer, who had been prominent in beating down the *coup d'état* in Berlin on 20 July, was appointed Combat Commandant of *Führer's* HQ. Colonel Streve was now merely Camp Commandant of the HQ, no longer HQ Commandant, and he had to turn over to Remer command authority over all HQ troops.[53] Remer was given the disciplinary powers of a brigadier, and he was declared responsible for internal and external military security of the HQ. The additional arms and ammunition referred to earlier were incorporated in the HQ arsenal in consultation with Remer.

In October 1944 the problem of oxygen supply for the *Führer* Bunker at 'Wolfschanze' was not yet solved satisfactorily. Construction on the bunker had finally been completed; but on 11 October the experts mentioned above found that a submarine-type oxygen-circulation system, installed in case the gas-filtering system broke down, constituted a danger because the steel containers of compressed air and oxygen had not been filled and checked in the presence of RSD personnel; for this they had to be taken to the Danzig Wharf, because the nearest facilities, at Oster & Co. in Königsberg, had been destroyed by enemy air raids.[54] The experts also discovered that the gas flow could not be adjusted to the required amount. A separate oxygen system for the *Führer's* study showed leaks, indicating that a new valve was needed; also certain parts required for the system had not yet been procured. In other words, the bunker inhabitants would have been helpless victims if the contingency against which all these measures were taken had occurred at this time. Worse still, the air-conditioning system for the situation-conference room in the *Führer* Bunker was based on a new and untested liquid-chemical method and led Dr. Widmann to comment that it would have to be determined 'whether harmful gases will be produced in the chemical cleansing fluid through the release of the cooling substance Frigen (difluorchlormethane)' from possible leaks in the cooling pipes. It was not clear if all Frigen would be removed in the chemical bath through which the air passed subsequently, because the composition of the cleansing fluid was a company secret. It was pointed out, however (presumably to hint at how the company secret might be obtained), that the financial soul of the company (La Pureza, Paul Rummel & Co., Kommanditgesellschaft, Berlin-Friedrichsfelde, Alt-Friedrichsfelde 10a) was Wilhelm Streve, a brother of the HQ Camp Commandant, and that Herr Rummel himself had worked in South America for thirty-eight years (the relevance of this last point is obscure).

On 22 October 1944 Dr. Widmann's associate Sachs was finally able to report that all pressure containers had been checked and found to be in proper working order. On 2 November another conference was held at *Führer's* HQ. The oxygen-supply system was found in good order, except for a small leak. It was advisable, however, to increase the stock of oxygen containers from six to thirty so that the supply would last more than about thirty days.

Now the gas-filtering system was found defective: the only sure way to tell exactly when a filter was used up was to employ an expert nose, or canaries, which would die before humans. 'Since it cannot be assumed that the *Führer* wishes to keep canaries in his rooms, the information supplied by the producer is very deficient; for it must be assumed that by the time a smell of gas is noticed serious gas-poisoning will have occurred.' It was therefore suggested that the producer firm be prevailed upon to furnish gas-detectors with which to check the gas filters, and to put up charts on which the times of operation of the gas filters could be entered. The company (Drägerwerk in Lübeck) responded on 28 November 1944 and suggested posting 'a person with good smelling ability who is also reliable as a sniffing post.'

Nor was the air-circulation system quite satisfactory: the operating instructions were not clear either to the people manning the bunker or to the visiting experts, and there were no tools available for changing pressure bottles. Certain valves to control pressure in the gas-protection chambers were still missing. And the air-conditioning system, while found 'not dangerous' on 10 November 1944, was vulnerable in case of power failure: it would stop completely. Tests run at Dr. Widmann's Institute with the Frigen produced some good news and some bad. The bad news was that Frigen could escape if pipes broke, and that it had a very weak smell and might not be noticed; the good news was that Frigen was apparently unchanged after contact with the cleansing fluid (though not enough was known in Germany about the properties of Frigen); and that the highest conceivable Frigen concentration in the bunker air, if all the Frigen escaped, would be 0.15%—and two white mice had survived 0.3% for 105 minutes and 5.0% for forty-five minutes. There was little chance that the *Führer* would be poisoned by Frigen.

On 20 November 1944 Hitler left 'Wolfschanze.' He never returned, but this was not yet taken for granted. By 22 November 1944, and 'in view of the present situation at the Eastern Front,' Keitel had seen to it that all preparations had been made so that 'Wolfschanze' would not fall into enemy hands undestroyed. A detonation calendar for all bunkers and huts was drawn up, and within twenty-four hours of the final order the destruction could be carried out. The code-word was 'Inselsprung.' But on 4 December 1944 Keitel also gave precise orders to keep 'Wolfschanze' and 'Mauerwald' intact and ready for use at any moment, until further notice.[55] Thus the gas experts had to continue worrying about Hitler's bunker at 'Wolfschanze.' On 9 January 1945 Dr. Widmann noted that the gas-protection system was still deficient, and that the same had been discovered in Hitler's 'Berghof' bunker. But a few days after Widmann's note pioneer troops blew up the 'Wolfschanze' bunkers.

Several other *Führer* HQ installations had been or were being prepared. There appear in the contemporary documents such names as 'Riese' for an installation near Bad Charlottenbrunn, 'Hagen,' 'Lothar,' 'Wolfsturm' near Friedrichsroda, 'WO' (formerly 'Felsennest') near Bad Münstereifel, 'Brunhilde' near Diedenhofen, 'Rüdiger' near Waldenburg in Silesia, 'Siegfried' in Pullach south of Munich, 'Amt 600' in the Giessen–Bad Nauheim area, and 'Wolfsberg' at Herrenhof.[56] The OKH (Army High Command and General Staff of the Army) was to be housed in 'Olga' near Ohrdruf, and parts of OKH moved there in the last days of February 1945. But Hitler never used any of the new installations. He did use, finally, during the Ardennes Offensive, the Wiesental HQ that had been built for him near Bad Nauheim. The rest of the time he stayed in the *Reich* Chancellery. The General Staff remained in 'Zeppelin' at Zossen, and eventually its heads moved into Berlin for the last days of the war.

Chancellery Bunker

After his return to Berlin from 'Wolfschanze,' Hitler left the city again only twice.[57] He moved to a military HQ once more, leaving on 10 December 1944 at 5 p.m. by his *Führer* Special 'Brandenburg' for 'Adlerhorst.' He left his train east of Giessen to travel the rest of the way by car. He arrived at 7.30 a.m. on 11 December, and addressed commanding generals at the Western Front on 12 December. Here at 'Amt 500,' as the small group of bunkers was called while he used them, 2 kilometres from the Ziegenberg mansion he had rejected as too luxurious, Hitler once again lived in a field headquarters of bunkers, hutments, fences, security perimeters, complete with SS and FBB troops, *SS-Begleit-Kommando*, RSD officers, passes, identity checks, and frisking. Here he directed his last-chance offensive against the Western Allies, while the Red Army was about to overrun Germany's eastern provinces and the *Führer's* long-time HQ 'Wolfschanze' (their offensive began on 12 January).

On 15 January 1945, two weeks after a ghostlike New Year's Day with well-wishing and a festive luncheon, Hitler left 'Adlerhorst,' arriving on his train in Berlin-Grunewald at 9.40 a.m. on 16 January. From here he took his motor convoy to the Chancellery where he arrived at 10 a.m. At 11 a.m. he received Colonel-General Guderian for the situation conference; at 1.20 p.m. he awarded a medal to *SS-Gruppenführer* Krüger, took forty minutes for lunch, and then gave a medal to Colonel-General Schörner. During the afternoon, he watched the weekly newsreel, as he had been doing frequently in these weeks.

Very little reliable information and almost no contemporary documents have come to light on which to base a description of Hitler's last weeks from a security point of view. The following comments therefore must be brief.

Upon his return from 'Adlerhorst,' Hitler had lived in his apartments in the Old Chancellery until about mid-February; afterwards he made his permanent residence in the bunker that had been built under the Old *Reich* Chancellery and under the garden beyond it, beneath an 8-metre roof of steel and concrete. Construction of air-raid shelters under and adjoining the buildings at No. 77/78 Wilhelmstrasse and No. 1 Vossstrasse had started in 1935. The New Chancellery also included air-raid shelters when it was completed in January 1939. The bunker under the Chancellery garden was built in 1942 and 1943 at a cost of 1.4 million Reichsmarks. Until about mid-March Hitler still took his meals in his old rooms, and the situation conferences were held upstairs in Hitler's study in the New *Reich* Chancellery; the long hallway with the study had not yet been destroyed, though most of the valuable paintings and tapestries were soon taken away. But the constant air raids and air-raid

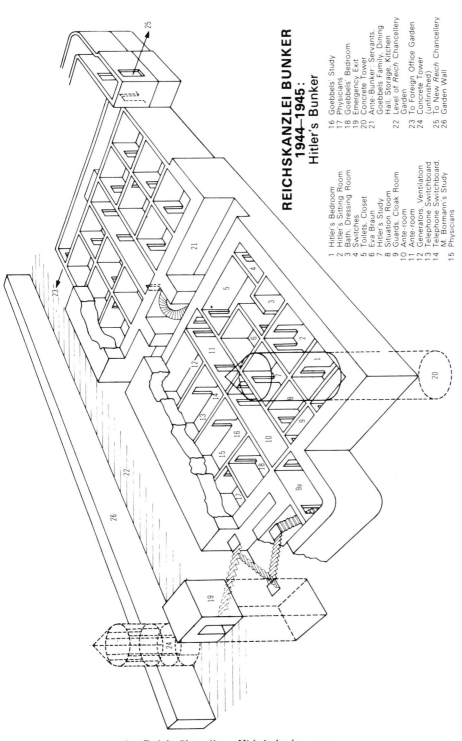

**REICHSKANZLEI BUNKER
1944–1945:
Hitler's Bunker**

1 Hitler's Bedroom
2 Hitler's Sitting Room
3 Bath, Dressing Room
4 Switches
5 Toilets, Closet
6 Eva Braun
7 Hitler's Study
8 Situation Room
9 Guards, Cloak Room
10 Ante-room
11 Ante-room
12 Generators, Ventilation
13 Telephone Switchboard
14 Telephone Switchboard.
15 Physicians
16 Goebbels' Study
17 Physicians
18 Goebbels' Bedroom
19 Emergency Exit
20 Concrete Tower
21 Ante-Bunker. Servants.
   Goebbels Family. Dining
   Hall. Storage. Kitchen
22 Level of *Reich* Chancellery
   Garden
23 To Foreign Office Garden
24 Concrete Tower
   (unfinished)
25 To New *Reich* Chancellery
26 Garden Wall

38. Reich *Chancellery, Hitler's bunker, 1944–5*

alerts were too much of a nuisance, and soon all activity was shifted to the bunker.[58]

Here Hitler had a bedroom, sitting-room, bathroom and situation-conference room. There were rooms also for Eva Braun, Goebbels, the valets, a few of the bodyguards, one of the personal physicians, and some offices (Bormann, Goebbels), a telephone switchboard room and an engine room. Hitler's sitting-room (also referred to as his study) was dominated by a large painting of Frederick the Great.[59] The Chancellery complex also included, under the New Chancellery, air-raid shelters for guards and children, who were brought in every night, since Hitler had ordered in September 1940 that some of the Chancellery underground shelters be used in this way, at his expense. Gradually the place became a delivery station and a field hospital, and finally, in April, the head-quarters of the forces for the immediate defence of the Chancellery, *Kampfgruppe Mohnke*, was installed here. Such members of Hitler's entourage as M. Bormann, Lieutenant-General Burgdorf, Dr. Nau-mann, Hewel, Rear-Admiral Voss and others also had quarters here.

Building and construction were still continuing. As late as April, bunkers, gun emplacements and other defensive structures were made from steel and concrete. The *Führer* Bunker was also provided with gas-protection chambers, although these were not without their weaknesses and malfunctions. Speer related after the war how he had wanted to assassinate the *Führer* with gas, in mid-February, after Hitler had given orders to destroy all power plants, bridges, factories and other vital in-stallations so that neither the enemy nor the German people would be able to exist.[60] But he missed the opportune moment when the bunker's air filters were being changed, and then Speer found that he would have been unable to carry out his plan in any case: when he examined the situa-tion in the garden again, he saw SS and RSD guards everywhere, at the bunker exits, in the observation towers, on the roofs of the entire Chancellery complex, and there were large spotlights installed all around. Just in case these should fail, there were four-barrelled flare pis-tols installed at every corner of the building; they could have illuminated building and grounds for several minutes. Where there had been small air-intake shafts, there were now large concrete chimneys to make the shafts invulnerable to objects that might fall in and obstruct the passage, and most of all to protect them against heavier-than-air war gases that could creep along the ground and sink down into the shafts. Hitler had ordered these changes, and his fear of poison gas was understandable. At the end of World War I he had been temporarily blinded by poison gas, and the Front was coming closer and closer now. Hitler did not have much faith in the gas filters and protection chambers, and he feared that the Russians might use a gas that incapacitated people for only twenty-four hours, so that he might be captured alive. The gas-filtering system did turn out to be unreliable: on 25 April the ventilators of the upper bunker had to be shut off for fifteen minutes because they sucked in more smoke, sulphurous fumes and dust than air, as Russian artillery grenades kept hitting the Chancellery area.

Speer admits that he had ample opportunities, as so many others did, to shoot Hitler with a pistol; but he explains that even at this late date Hitler's suggestive control and power over him were too great. There is some evidence that Speer's relations with Hitler had cooled, but no more, when he made his farewell visit to the bunker in April. Speer could still come and go without being searched, and he could well have brought with him explosives to kill Hitler.[61]

Although Hitler knew that his days were numbered, he grew constantly more suspicious of assassination plots, and he grew ever more fearful of losing control over his own life and person. When Berlin was raided by enemy bombers almost every day, and even the Army General Staff HQ at Zossen was attacked heavily for the first time on 15 March, Hitler developed a phobia that he might be caught in bed during a raid. Allied Air Force commanders had considered the underground bunker system near Zossen invulnerable, and only the above-ground structures were destroyed in the raid of 15 March. But the *Führer* Bunker was surrounded by groundwater, and Hitler thought that, if a bomb hit the bunker-wall at an angle, the water might gush in and drown him. Therefore, he always got up and dressed quickly when there was an air raid, often at about 11 a.m., although he ordinarily would not have risen before noon.[62]

Captain Boldt regularly accompanied, as an aide, Colonel-General Guderian, the Chief of the Army General Staff, together with Major Freytag von Loringhoven, the Adjutant, to situation conferences in the *Reich* Chancellery, beginning in early February; he gave a description of the procedures, though not without some exaggeration.[63] Guderian and the two other officers were allowed to proceed after their names and papers had been checked against log-book entries; but much of the Chancellery had been heavily damaged by bombs so that long detours had to be taken to Hitler's study, the conference room. At every passage there were SS guards, and every time the visitors had to identify themselves. At the anteroom, the visitors met several officers in field-grey SS uniforms, and heavily armed SS men. Here the Colonel-General and his assistants put down their weapons. Two of the SS officers took their briefcases from them and examined them. They were not actually frisked, but even if they had been, they could probably still have brought knives stuck in their boots, or plastic explosive. Again, a gap appeared in the thinking of the security-conscious. As it had not occurred to them before 20 July 1944 that a General Staff officer might be an assassin, it did not occur to them now that an assassin might use a knife. After the examination, the visitors were allowed into the anteroom. Here there were three SS orderlies, waiting to serve refreshments, and at the door to Hitler's study stood more SS guards in field-grey uniforms. Hitler's Personal Adjutant, Günsche, emerged from the study and said that it would be a few more minutes. Finally Freytag von Loringhoven and Boldt were shown in. They laid out the maps on the desk, Günsche stayed and sometimes helped with the maps. Then they returned to the ante-room where others were waiting to take part in the conference—Keitel, Jodl, Dönitz, M. Bormann, their aides, also Himmler and Fegelein, Kaltenbrunner (Chief, RSHA), Dr. Dietrich's deputy, Lorenz, and M. Bormann's aide, Zander, as well as Göring, Generals Koller and Christian (Air Force) and Lieutenant-General Burgdorf (successor to Schmundt).

Finally, Burgdorf went inside, reappeared, and said the *Führer* was ready to receive the gentlemen. Göring walked in first; Keitel, Guderian, Dönitz and the rest followed according to rank and pre-eminence. When the conference was over, Guderian and his assistants took the long walk back through the *Reich* Chancellery, past all the guards and check-points, examined at every turn, and drove back to Zossen.

The Front was moving in closer and closer, and preparations were made to defend the Chancellery. A 'Combat Commandant of the *Reich* Chancellery' was appointed, at first Lieutenant-Colonel Pick; from the beginning of March until 22 April *SS-Sturmbannführer* Günsche was Combat Commandant. The *Führer-Begleit-Bataillon* had grown to a division, but it was deployed on the Western Front.[64] A company of it had remained in the Lichterfelde barracks and Günsche now moved it to the Chancellery. The *SS-Begleit-Kommando* was also increased in strength; *Wache Reichskanzlei* of LSSAH was still here, too. With these troops, the outside of the Chancellery complex could be patrolled reasonably well. But the grounds were becoming constantly less controllable through destruction of walls and fences, and the general chaos; only the most uncompromising vigilance could ensure timely discovery of any intruders. When Hitler's secretaries complained about rough treatment by guards, Hitler told Günsche that he did not need all that much protection, his protection was 'in other hands.' On 22 April the position of *Kampfkommandant* was abolished. A *Kampfgruppe Mohnke* was formed under *SS-Brigadeführer* Mohnke, for the defence of the government buildings—even though Hitler himself now openly declared the war lost.[65] The Combat Group consisted of: the Guard Battalion of LSSAH under *SS-Sturmbannführer* Kaschula (it had been billeted in Lichterfelde until 22 April); the Training and Replacement Battalion of LSSAH brought into Berlin from Spreenhagen, under *SS-Obersturmbannführer* Klingemeier; the *Führer-Begleit-Kompanie* mentioned above; and soldiers who had become separated from their units and now happened to be in Berlin. Mohnke had previously commanded the 1st *SS-Panzer-Division 'Adolf Hitler;'* at that time, in February 1945, his division was judged the least qualified of the SS tank divisions, and he himself was thought to be a morphine-addict.

Hitler prolonged the battle for Berlin until Russian troops were no more—and probably less—than 500 metres away from the Chancellery, and until he had sacrificed even more thousands of soldiers and of mere children dragged into the war as Hitler Youth in these last days. Finally, on 30 April, deep underground, where he could not hear the screams of tortured women and children, and of the soldiers who were dying to prolong his life, he shot himself, sitting on a sofa in his 'study.' His wife of twenty-four hours, Eva Hitler, sat next to him and bit her cyanide capsule.[66]

12 Conclusions

Efforts to make Hitler's life safe reflect the basic contradictions of his existence. Almost everything he did proved self-defeating in the end. He set out to remove or destroy the German Jews; throughout the 1930s he was satisfied to have every conceivable government agency including *Gestapo* and SD pursue a policy of Jewish emigration.[1] But all this time he planned, and in 1939 began, the conquest of territories whose Jewish populations were so large that their emigration would have taken more than a century and a half at the emigration rates achieved in the 1930s and which depended on quotas set by countries accepting immigrants. Hitler believed in struggle as a Darwinian principle of human life that forced every people to try to dominate all others; without struggle they would rot and perish. In case of success the victorious people would have to become divided against itself to be able to continue the struggle so vital for human existence. Alternatively, and realistically, victory was not expected and the prospect of defeat was viewed with indifference. Even in his own defeat in April 1945 Hitler expressed his faith in the survival of the stronger, and declared the Slavic peoples to have proven themselves the stronger.[2] Self-defeat, in a sense, was really the principle. Hitler's speeches are full of dark references to his own defeat, from the earliest years in the 1920s down through the greatest triumphs to the final defeat.[3]

Hitler's faith in what he called Providence is similarly threaded through with contradictions. It was to him an 'iron necessity' of Providence that he must fulfil his Mission—Germany's greatness and expansion, *Lebensraum*, her rule over all the Earth, the destruction of the Jewish people. But Providence might desert him suddenly and then there would be no one to fulfil his Mission, so he said: 'I may at any time be done away with by a criminal, an idiot.'[4] There was an element of gambling in Hitler's faith in Providence. He was aware of this, and he applied this consideration to his personal security as to everything else. It was, as he remarked in May 1942, referring to Bavaud's and Elser's assassination attacks: 'In the two really dangerous attempts made to assassinate me, I owe my life not to the police, but to pure chance.' And on 20 August 1942: 'I have risked my own life a thousand times, and I owe my preservation simply to my good fortune.'[5] Most of the attempts on Hitler's life failed only after security had already been defeated. Hitler himself took a keen interest in measures for his personal security, and he ordered and authorised ever vaster efforts to provide it. But he himself frequently and needlessly defeated security by acting contrary to what he knew were vital security maxims, by carelessness, and by his irresistible urge to play *va banque* for the highest stakes.

On the other hand, the security that could be provided was limited even if it was not defeated by the object of protection. There was a limit beyond which the general effectiveness of the ruler was so impaired by a further increase of security that security became worthless. Efforts to provide the utmost security led to its potential defeat by the methods employed, such as vast construction projects with thousands of foreign labourers, and the proliferation of security forces with their rivalries, duplication and mutual paralysis. Any increase of security now seemed to contain its own negation.

Linge, Schulze-Kossens, Kempka and others tend to describe security measures around Hitler as negligible, insufficient and even amateurish, nor do they regard this as a reflection upon their own security functions. Especially before the war, so they argue, Hitler rejected extensive security precautions because he needed and sought immediate contact with his masses, because he believed in surprise as the best precaution, and because he believed that virtually the entire people felt nothing but enthusiasm and admiration for him, while precautions could not foil the few determined enemies and maniacs who might wish to kill him. Precautions were necessary and useful not so much against assassination attempts as against uncontrolled enthusiasm. In all this there is a good deal of truth, but it is not the full story.

The extensive security precautions and directives described in the present study, Hitler's involvement through personal orders, and his personal control over his bodyguards, are proof that whatever Hitler may have said on various occasions about his unconcern, he was in fact deeply and morbidly if irrationally concerned with his own security. Every time there had been an attack on his life, such as after 8 November 1939 or after 20 July 1944, security was intensified; it has been seen that this was done with Hitler's approval. At the same time, Hitler continued to expose himself to danger. Hitler was worried enough about Maurice Bavaud's efforts to murder him to talk about it and to discuss the reasons for his escape on several occasions. While his hypochondriac anxieties increased with every attack, his assertions that security was useless also became more frequent, and he preferred to attribute his survival to Providence.

The contradictory conclusion is that Hitler was usually well guarded and protected, and it cannot be denied that a good handful of the conspirators who sincerely wished Hitler dead could have murdered him had they been psychologically capable of such an act. On the other hand, those who did try failed less because of security measures than due to bizarre accidents.

Hitler's own thinking about his security in Berlin in 1939 is revealing in more than one respect. When he talked to Speer about building his future capital, he said he 'might be forced to take unpopular measures, and then there could be an insurrection.' One had to be prepared for this possibility: all buildings on the square where the new *Führer* Palace was to stand were to have heavy steel shutters and doors, all bullet-proof, and the entire square was to be closed off with steel gates. The Palace itself would have no windows at all, the only openings being a huge heavy steel door and a door on to a small balcony, five storeys above the crowds, from which Hitler could receive ovations. The barracks of *Leibstandarte-SS 'Adolf Hitler*,' the bodyguard regiment, were to be moved close to the Palace, but the Army's Berlin Guard Battalion barracks were to be located even closer.[6] Hitler's mentality was that of one living in a fortress under siege, and determined to have the fortress defended to the last drop of blood of the defenders. It was also the mentality of the gambler who does not give up as long as he can breathe and gamble. And Hitler never stopped gambling whether he refused to despair when the Party was low in funds, or when he sat in his *Führer* Bunker, knowing that every hour his life and his war continued caused untold suffering, death and misery to his own people; he preferred to hope for a miracle like the one that saved Frederick the Great.[7]

Hitler was profoundly indifferent to his chances of success, in the last resort. At the end of March 1945 he told Speer: 'If the war is lost, the people too will be lost. It is not necessary to take into consideration the basic things the German people needs for its continued existence. On the contrary, it is better to destroy these things. For the people has shown itself to be the weaker one, and to the stronger Eastern people alone belongs the future. What remains after this struggle are only the inferior types, in any case, since the good ones have fallen!'[8]

On 30 April 1945 Hitler summoned his faithful pilot, Hans Baur, and told him: 'I still have two possibilities: I could go into the mountains or join Dönitz in Flensburg. But in two weeks I would again be where I am now, I would be facing the same alternative. The war is ending with Berlin—I stand or fall with Berlin. One must have the courage to draw the consequences—I am making an end! I know that tomorrow millions of people will curse me—Fate willed it thus.'[9]

As if to create a final, absurd contradiction in his own 'security,' Hitler had the executions of those who tried to kill him for years continue almost to the last hour of his own life, even while he was preparing for his suicide. The machine which had protected him so long, RSD, *Gestapo*, SS, and the entire perverted judicial system of the Third *Reich* still operated, still killing his enemies. On the *Führer's* birthday, on 20 April 1945, twenty-eight people were executed in the prison at Brandenburg-on-Havel. On 23 April 1945 Johannes Albers (trade-union leader, sentenced to death), Kurt Sorge (engineer), Captain Dr. Paul van Husen and Wilhelm Schmidt were taken from Berlin's Lehrterstrasse prison to Plötzensee prison to be executed. They were saved at the last minute by the arrival of Red Army units. But sixteen other political prisoners, also from Lehrterstrasse prison, were led off by SS and shot in the back of the neck a few blocks away, in the early hours of 23 April.[10]

Down to his own end Hitler mocked all men and what they believed in, including himself and his leadership. While men, women and children died so that he might live a few hours longer, he took his own life, in an ultimate self-defeat of his personal security.

Assassination Attempts and Plots

Year	Place	Assassin	Page
1940	Paris	Fritz-Dietlof Graf von der Schulenburg, Eugen Gerstenmaier	145
1943	Walki	Hubert Lanz, Hans Speidel, Hyazinth Graf Strachwitz	149
1943	Smolensk	Friedrich König	152
1943	Smolensk	Henning von Tresckow, Fabian von Schlabrendorff, Rudolf-Christoph Freiherr von Gersdorff	151–4
1943	Berlin	Rudolf-Christoph Freiherr von Gersdorff	122–5
1943	'Wolfschanze'	Axel Freiherr von dem Bussche-Streithorst	190–1
1944	'Wolfschanze'	Ewald Heinrich von Kleist	190
1944	Obersalzberg	Eberhard von Breitenbuch	190
1944	Obersalzberg	Claus Schenk Graf von Stauffenberg	190
1944	'Wolfschanze'	Claus Schenk Graf von Stauffenberg (two attempts)	245–54
1945	Berlin	Albert Speer	260–1

The line is fluid between a 'plot', and mere thoughts. The list was kept short to avoid inflation with plans that may not have been serious. Thus it is possible, on the other hand, that some plans were omitted which were made in earnest. For instance, the proposals to kill Hitler through aerial bombing were not included; see these in the Index, under 'assassination.'

Comparative Table of Ranks

German Army	SS	Police	British Army	U.S. Army
Generalfeldmarschall	Reichsführer-SS		Field Marshal	General of the Army
Generaloberst	SS-Oberst-Gruppenführer	Generaloberst	General	General
General	SS-Obergruppenführer	General	Lieutenant-General	Lieutenant-General
Generalleutnant	SS-Gruppenführer	Generalleutnant	Major-General	Major-General
Generalmajor	SS-Brigadeführer	Generalmajor	Brigadier	Brigadier-General
	SS-Oberführer		Senior Colonel	Senior Colonel
Oberst	SS-Standartenführer	Oberst	Colonel	Colonel
Oberstleutnant	SS-Obersturmbannführer	Oberstleutnant	Lieutenant-Colonel	Lieutenant-Colonel
Major	SS-Sturmbannführer	Major	Major	Major
Hauptmann, Rittmeister (Cav.)	SS-Hauptsturmführer (SS-Sturmführer until 18 July 1933; SS-Sturmhauptführer from 18 July 1933 to 15 Oct. 1934)	Hauptmann	Captain	Captain
Oberleutnant	SS-Obersturmführer	Oberleutnant	Lieutenant	First Lieutenant

Leutnant	*SS-Untersturmführer (SS-Sturmführer from 18 July 1933 to 15 Oct. 1934)*	*Leutnant, (Ober-Meister)*	Second Lieutenant	Second Lieutenant
Stabsfeldwebel, Stabswachtmeister	*SS-Sturmscharführer*	*Hauptwachtmeister*	Regimental Sergeant-Major	Sergeant-Major
Hauptfeldwebel, Oberfeldwebel	*SS-Hauptscharführer, SS-Stabsscharführer*	*Zugwachtmeister*	Sergeant-Major	Sergeant-Major
Feldwebel, Wachtmeister	*SS-Oberscharführer*	*Oberwachtmeister*	Quartermaster-Sergeant	Technical Sergeant
Unterfeldwebel	*SS-Scharführer*	*Wachtmeister*	Staff Sergeant	Staff Sergeant
Unteroffizier	*SS-Unterscharführer*	*Rottwachtmeister*	Sergeant	Sergeant
Stabsgefreiter, Obergefreiter	*SS-Rottenführer*	*Unterwachtmeister*	Corporal	Corporal
Gefreiter	*SS-Sturmmann*		Lance-Corporal	
Oberschütze, Obergrenadier, etc.	*SS-Oberschütze*		Senior Private	Private 1st Class
Schütze, Grenadier, etc.	*SS-Mann*	*Anwärter*	Private	Private

Note: Ranks given in the text, notes and index are linguistic translations but not necessarily equivalents of German ranks. British style was used in cases such as second lieutenant, lieutenant.

Notes

(Unless otherwise stated, originals or copies of un-
published documents cited in the Notes are in the possession of the author. The phrase 'for the following' at the
beginning of a note or citation means that the material
cited covers the text to the next note—never less, sometimes more. Shortened references are used when full
details have been given earlier.)

Chapter 1

1. Werner Maser, *Adolf Hitler: Legende, Mythos, Wirklichkeit* (Bechtle Verlag:
Munich and Esslingen, 1971), pp. 141–2; Werner Maser, *Die Frühgeschichte der
NSDAP: Hitlers Weg bis 1924* (Athenäum Verlag: Frankfurt/M., Bonn, 1965),
pp. 287, 458–61; *Documents on British Foreign Policy (DBFP)*, Third Series, vol.
VII (H.M.S.O.: London, 1954), No. 314; *Akten zur deutschen auswärtigen Politik
(ADAP)*, Series D, vol. VII (Imprimerie Nationale: Baden-Baden, 1956), No.
192.

2. *Trial of the Major War Criminals before the International Military Tribunal Nuremberg 14 November 1945 – 1 October 1946*, vol. XXVI (International Military Tribunal: Nuremberg, 1947), p. 339; Max Domarus, *Hitler: Reden und Proklamationen
1932–1945*, 2 vols (paginated continuously) (Selbstverlag des Verfassers: Neustadt a. d. Aisch, 1962–3), vol. II, pp. 1056–8; cf. Maser, *Adolf Hitler*, pp. 253–
4, 265–6.

3. Otto Dietrich, *12 Jahre mit Hitler* (Isar Verlag: Munich, 1955), pp. 183–
4; NA Record Group HL–242, on film rolls ML 941, 942, containing a selection
of photos taken by *Reich* Photo Reporter Heinrich Hoffmann and his assistants
(cited hereafter as NA RG HL–242); *Völkischer Beobachter (VB)*, 10–12 Nov.
1933–8.

4. Elisabeth Hannover-Drück and Heinrich Hannover, *Der Mord an Rosa Luxemburg und Karl Liebknecht: Dokumentation eines politischen Verbrechens* (Suhrkamp
Verlag: Frankfurt/M., 1967), *passim*; E. J. Gumbel, *Vier Jahre politischer Mord*
(Verlag der Neuen Gesellschaft: Berlin-Fichtenau, 1922), p. 81; Bruno Gebhardt, *Handbuch der deutschen Geschichte*, vol. 4 (Union Verlag: Stuttgart, 8th ed.
1961), pp. 97–9.

5. M[atthias] Erzberger, *Erlebnisse im Weltkrieg* (Deutsche Verlags-Anstalt:
Stuttgart, Berlin, 1920), p. 383; see also Ernst von Salomon, *The Outlaws* (Cape:
London, 1931), pp. 228–42, 272–82; Ernst von Salomon, *Der Fragebogen*
(Rowohlt Verlag: Hamburg, 1951), pp. 129–39; Ernst Röhm, *Die Geschichte eines
Hochverräters* (Verlag Franz Eher Nachfolger: Munich, 1928), pp. 125, 136–7;
Hans Langemann, *Das Attentat* (Kriminalistik: Hamburg [1956]), pp. 140–73,
237–41.

6. Walter M. Espe, *Das Buch der N.S.D.A.P.: Werden, Kampf und Ziel der N.S.D.A.P.* (G. Schönfeld's Verlagsbuchhandlung: Berlin, [1934]), pp. 327–34; cf. Hans Volz, *Daten der Geschichte der NSDAP* (Verlag A. G. Ploetz: Berlin, Leipzig, 11th ed. 1943), pp. 141–5:201 dead from 1923 up until 1933; Maser, *Frühgeschichte*, p. 350.

7. Ernst Deuerlein, 'Hitlers Eintritt in die Politik und die Reichswehr,' *Vierteljahrshefte für Zeitgeschichte (VfZ)*, 7 (1959), pp. 177–227, esp. 178–81.

Chapter 2

1. Gebhardt, pp. 128–30; Deuerlein, 'Hitlers Eintritt,' pp. 219–22; *VB*, 9 Nov. 1921; Adolf Hitler, *Mein Kampf*, 3rd ed. (Verlag Frz. Eher Nachf.: Munich, 1930), pp. 563–7, 610–11, 613; Maser, *Frühgeschichte*, pp. 301–6; *Reichsgesetzblatt, Teil I* (hereafter *RGBl.*), *1922*, hrsg. vom Reichsministerium des Innern (Verlag des Gesetzsammlungsamts: Berlin, 1922), p. 585; Staatsarchiv München St. Anw. 2386 and Pol. Div. 6803 containing police reports and a court sentence concerning the battle, dating from October 1921 to February 1922; cf. *VB*, No. 85, 9 Nov. 1921, p. 3; David Irving, *Hitler's War* (Hodder and Stoughton: London, Sydney, Auckland, Toronto, 1977, p. 805 (on Hitler's habit of carrying a 6.35-mm pistol), also [Heinz Linge], 'Kronzeuge Linge,' *Revue* [Munich], (1955–6), *16. Folge*, p. 14.

2. Hitler, *Mein Kampf*, pp. 614–18; Volz, p. 10; Maser, *Frühgeschichte*, pp. 357—9.

3. Hitler, *Mein Kampf*, pp. 391–2; Maser, *Frühgeschichte*, pp. 223, 254–6; Michael H. Kater, 'Zur Soziographie der frühen NSDAP,' *VfZ* 19 (1971), pp. 124–59; Röhm, pp. 100–1; Deuerlein, 'Hitlers Eintritt,' pp. 178–84, 187–90, 201–5.

4. Röhm, pp. 13–74, 88–114, 122–3, 161, 163–4, 239, 283–89.

5. Membership list of NSDAP in Bundesarchiv Koblenz (BA) NS 26/230. This makes Röhm member No. 123, not one with a number below 70 as Röhm recalled in his memoirs (Röhm, p. 107); cf. Maser, *Frühgeschichte*, pp. 167, 192. According to the list of meetings published by Deuerlein, 'Hitlers Eintritt,' p. 188, the date would be 16 January 1920. Röhm, pp. 107–8; the Armed-Forces Law of 23 March 1921 (*RGBl.* I, p. 329) forbade membership or participation by soldiers in political associations and meetings.

6. Röhm, pp. 140–3, 150–1, 154–8, 164–6, 175, 191–202. The RKF had split away from the *Reichsflagge*, whose remnants sided with Kahr; Heinrich Bennecke, *Hitler und die SA* (Günter Olzog Verlag: Munich, 1962), p. 81; Röhm, pp. 212–16 and photograph at appendix; Bradley F. Smith, *Heinrich Himmler: A Nazi in the Making, 1900–1926* (Hoover Institution Press: Stanford, Calif., 1971), pp. 131–6.

7. Hitler, *Mein Kampf*, pp. 549–50; Röhm, p. 221; Gunter d'Alquen, *Die SS: Geschichte, Aufgabe und Organisation der Schutzstaffeln der NSDAP* (Junker und Dünnhaupt Verlag: Berlin, 1939), pp. 6–7; Ernst Hanfstaengl, *Zwischen Weissem und*

Braunem Haus (R. Piper & Co. Verlag: Munich, [1970]), pp. 50–2, 232–3; Maser, *Frühgeschichte*, pp. 287, 303. Schreck died in 1936; Hess was sentenced at Nuremberg to life-long imprisonment and is still serving his sentence at Spandau prison in Berlin. *Abschrift der Liste der Ordnungsmänner der N.S.D.A.P. 1919/20*, Hoover Institution NSDAP *Hauptarchiv* Roll 1, No. 215; Berlin Document Centre (BDC) SS Officer (SSO) files on Maurice, Schreck, Graf, Weber, Amann, Hess.

8.   Hitler, *Mein Kampf*, pp. 40–2.

9.   Hitler, *Mein Kampf*, p. 551; cf. *VB*, 9 Feb. 1921, cited by Maser, *Frühge schichte*, p. 288; Bennecke, pp. 30–3.

10   Röhm, pp. 108–9; Volz, pp. 119–20; Ernst Deuerlein (ed.), *Der Hitler-Putsch: Bayerische Dokumente zum 8./9. November 1923* (Deutsche Verlags-Anstalt: Stuttgart, 1962), pp. 706–7; Hanfstaengl, p. 123; Bennecke, pp. 28–31; Maser, *Frühgeschichte*, pp. 307–9, 363.

11.   Harold J. Gordon, Jr., *Hitler and the Beer Hall Putsch* (Princeton University Press: Princeton, 1972), p. 36.

12.   Röhm, pp. 108–9, 141; Maser, *Frühgeschichte*, pp. 307–8, 363; Johannes Erger, *Der Kapp-Lüttwitz-Putsch* (Droste Verlag: Düsseldorf, 1967) *passim*; Bennecke, p. 29; Hanfstaengl, p. 123; Gabriele Krüger, *Die Brigade Ehrhardt* (Leibniz-Verlag: Hamburg, 1971), pp. 105–8.

13.   Röhm makes this point throughout his memoirs; cf. Bennecke, *passim* and esp. pp. 28–75, 84, 109.

14.   See note 2 above; Hitler, *Mein Kampf*, pp. 562–7, 613–17; Volz, pp. 9, 119; Bennecke, p. 32, shows that Hitler's figure of up to 800 enemy combatants at least doubles the true figure.

15.   Hitler, *Mein Kampf*, pp. 564–5; [Erich] Ludendorff, *Auf dem Weg zur Feldherrnhalle* (Ludendorffs Verlag: Munich, 1937), p. 68; d'Alquen, p. 7; *VB*, 9 Nov. 1921; and see below, pp. 38, 45.

16.   [Adolf Hitler], *Hitler's Secret Conversations 1941–1944* (Farrar, Straus and Young: New York, 1953), p. 176; Bennecke, pp. 45, 78; Maser, *Frühgeschichte*, pp. 412–14; Hanfstaengl, p. 52.

17.   Röhm, p. 162; Bennecke, pp. 45, 63; d'Alquen, p. 6; Volz, p. 120; Shlomo Aronson, *Reinhard Heydrich und die Frühgeschichte von Gestapo und SD* (Deutsche Verlags-Anstalt: Stuttgart, 1971), pp. 48, 264–5 note 57; Gordon, pp. 63–4.

18.   Stadtarchiv Munich, Zim. 116; Röhm, pp. 100, 109, 118, 158, 160, 170; Gordon, p. 363; Ordnungsmänner (note 7 above).

19.   Röhm, pp. 221–2; [Alfred Rosenberg], *Das politische Tagebuch Alfred Rosenbergs aus den Jahren 1934/35 und 1939/40* (Musterschmidt-Verlag: Göttingen, 1956), p. 88; Ludendorff, pp. 61, 75; Hanfstaengl, pp. 131–3; Gordon, pp. 285–6, 353.

20.   Gordon, pp. 353–65.

21. Gordon, pp. 364, 464; Hanfstaengl, pp. 147–8; Philipp Bouhler, *Kampf um Deutschland* (Zentralverlag der NSDAP, Frz. Eher Nachf.: Berlin, 1938), p. 68; Volz, p. 14.

22. For this and the following: Röhm, pp. 272, 289–325, 334–41; Maser, *Frühgeschichte*, p. 455; see photograph in Maser, *Hitler* (3rd ed.), after p. 320; *Hitler's Secret Conversations*, p. 138; Volz, pp. 20, 121; Bennecke, pp. 114, 119, 125; d'Alquen, pp. 6–7.

23. Volz, p. 122; Bennecke, pp. 128–31, 214.

24. Charles Drage, *The Amiable Prussian* (Blond: London, 1958), p. 69; Bennecke, pp. 137, 140, 154, 213–14.

25. Bennecke, pp. 141–2; Thilo Vogelsang, *Reichswehr, Staat und NSDAP* (Deutsche Verlags-Anstalt: Stuttgart, 1962), p. 116; cf. Drage, pp. 69–70; Dietrich Orlow, *The History of the Nazi Party 1919–1933* (University of Pittsburgh Press: Pittsburgh, 1969), pp. 211–12.

26. Bennecke, pp. 147–9; Orlow, pp. 211–12; Drage, pp. 72–6; Peter Hüttenberger, *Die Gauleiter* (Deutsche Verlags-Anstalt: Stuttgart, 1969), pp. 221–4; Karl Dietrich Bracher, Wolfgang Sauer and Gerhard Schulz, *Die nationalsozialistische Machtergreifung* (Westdeutscher Verlag: Köln, Opladen, 2nd ed. 1962), pp. 848–9; Volz, p. 124; Vogelsang, p. 116.

27. Bennecke, p. 149; Orlow, p. 212; Drage, pp. 74–7; Volz, p. 124.

28. *Hitler's Secret Conversations*, p. 138; Volz, p. 122; SS *Inspekteur für Statistik* to Himmler 1 March 1943, NA T–580 Roll 88; d'Alquen, p. 7; Edgar Erwin Knoebel, *Racial Illusion and Military Necessity* (Ph.D. Thesis: University of Colorado, 1965), pp. 1–18, 376; Maser, *Hitler*, p. 296; Bracher-Sauer-Schulz, p. 838; Himmler, order 18 May 1936 (on Schreck's death), NA T–354 Roll 194.

29. Bennecke, pp. 239–40, reprints the order; Bracher–Sauer–Schulz, p. 850; Heinz Höhne, *Der Orden unter dem Totenkopf* (Siegbert Mohn: Gütersloh, 1967), pp. 28–30, also for what follows.

30. Höhne, pp. 30–1.

31. Röhm, p. 216; Volz, p. 122; Höhne, pp. 43–5; cf. Bennecke, p. 54; Smith, pp. 131–6, 152, 167.

32. For this and the following: Höhne, pp. 34–8, 40, 41, 44–8; Smith, pp. 20–34, 47–9, 77–129. Cf. the list of a collection of Himmleriana in Hermann-Otto and Elfriede Winiarski, *3. Tradition Auktion* (Törwang über Rosenheim, [1973]), No. 2368; *Hitler's Secret Conversations*, p. 138; Knoebel, pp. 11–16; Röhm, *SA-Befehl Nr. 3* and *SA-Befehl Nr. 4*, Munich, 25 Feb. 1931, BA Slg. Schumacher O. 462; Bennecke, p. 153; Volz, pp. 124, 128.

33. Knoebel, pp. 15–16, 376; Himmler to OSAF 2 Oct. 1931, NA T–580 Roll 88.

34. Höhne, pp. 60, 62; Bracher–Sauer–Schulz, pp. 848–9; Drage, p. 74; Aronson, pp. 51–2.

35. Drage, pp. 70, 72, 81–9; Stennes, letter 3 Apr. 1974; Höhne, p. 66, gives Stennes a more active part in this new revolt; cf. *VB*, 1–4 Apr. 1931; Vogelsang, *Reichswehr*, pp. 119–20; Bracher–Sauer–Schulz, pp. 852–3.

36. Stennes, letter; Drage, 90–104; Rudolf Diels, *Lucifer ante Portas. Zwischen Severing und Heydrich* (Interverlag: Zürich, n.d.), pp. 184–5.

37. Volz, p. 124; Höhne, p. 67.

38. Volz, p. 125; Aronson, p. 55 (who dates Heydrich's appointment August 1931).

39. Hans Baur, *Ich flog Mächtige der Erde* (Pröpster: Kempten, 1956), p. 81; Otto Dietrich, *Mit Hitler in die Macht* (Verlag Frz. Eher Nachf.: Munich, 1934), pp. 52–3, 83–4, 109; Joseph Goebbels, *Vom Kaiserhof zur Reichskanzlei* (Zentralverlag der NSDAP, Frz. Eher Nachf.: Munich, 1934), pp. 64, 135.

40. Baur, pp. 84, 88–9, 91; Dietrich, *Mit Hitler*, pp. 77, 169; Hanfstaengl, pp. 262, 279; Hildegard Kutzke, Dr. Julius Lippert, Josef Berchtold, Gunther d'Alquen [*et al.*], *Wir fliegen mit Hitler* (Verlag Deutsche Kultur-Wacht: Berlin-Schöneberg, [1934]), pp. 31, 46–7, 68; *Mainzer Tageszeitung* No. 251, 12 Sept. 1933; *VB*, 15 June 1932, p. 1.

41. *Grieben Reiseführer Band 19: München und Umgebung* (Grieben-Verlag: Berlin, 1936), p. 59; Bouhler, p. 81; Volz, pp. 30, 32; Karl Fiehler, *München baut auf* (Franz Eher Verlag: Munich, n.d.), p. 63 and photo; Adolf Dresler, *Das Braune Haus und die Verwaltungsgebäude der Reichsleitung der NSDAP in München* (Zentralverlag der NSDAP, Frz. Eher Nachf.: Munich, 2nd ed. 1937), pp. 10, 13.

42. *Vorschrift für den Sicherheitsdienst im Braunen Haus (S.D.V.)*, signed by Röhm, 1931, OSAF-Befehle Qu. Nr. 114/32, *Stabsbefehl (Neuregelung des Sicherheitsdienstes im Braunen Haus)*, BA Slg. Schumacher O. 434; Erich Czech-Jochberg, *Wie Adolf Hitler der Führer wurde* (Verlag Philipp Reclam jun.: Leipzig, [1933]), p. 68.

43. Volz, pp. 29, 37, 42, 125; cf. Julius K. von Engelbrechten, *Eine braune Armee entsteht* (Zentralverlag der NSDAP: Munich, 1937), pp. 129–31, for examples of marks of identification worn during periods when uniforms were forbidden.

44. Höhne, pp. 71–3, also for what follows.

45. Orlow, p. 282; cf. Vogelsang, *Reichswehr*, pp. 308–9. Rosenberg, p. 47, makes reference 'to those of the Brown House guard who were to shoot NSDAP Treasurer Schwarz, Buch and others;' 'those' were shot during the Röhm Affair. Höhne, pp. 71–3. Also: [Ernst Röhm, *Briefe an Dr. Heimsoth*] (als MS. gedruckt: Berlin, 1932); Röhm, *Geschichte*, pp. 236–7; Drage, pp. 81–2; Stennes, letter 3 Apr. 1974; Bennecke, pp. 149–52; Orlow, p. 213 (with an error concerning Röhm's stay in Bolivia) and p. 215 (complaints of Party functionaries about Röhm's homosexuality); *Erlass Nr. 1* of OSAF (Hitler) 3 Feb. 1931 in Bennecke, pp. 160, 162; Vogelsang, pp. 117–19.

46. Dresler, pp. 14–15.

Chapter 3

1. *Polizeipräsident* [*von Berlin*], *Richtlinien für die Sicherung der Reichskanzlei* 25 Sept. 1923, Chancellery conference minute 1 Aug. 1922 (partic.: *Staatssekretär* Dr. Hemmer, *Reichskommissar* Kuenzer, *Staatskommissar* Weismann, *Oberregierungsrat* Weiss, *Geheimer Regierungsrat* Wever), instructions for police officers on duty at Reich Chancellery Sept. 1923, *Schutzpolizei* Berlin, *Abänderung der Erweiterung der Wachtvorschrift* [*sic*] *für die Reichskanzleiwache vom 27.9.1923*, BA R 43 II/990.

2. *Polizeipräsident/Abt. IA* to *Reichskanzlei* 27 Apr. 1931, BA R 43 II/990.

3. *Staatssekretär der Reichskanzlei to Polizeipräsident* 25 Nov. 1932, BA R 43 II/990.

4. BA R 43 II/990; *Hitler's Secret Conversations*, p. 367; Diels, p. 51.

5. BA R 43 II/990.

6. For this and the following: Diels, pp. 51–4, 176–9; cf. Goebbels, *Vom Kaiserhof*, p. 272; Fritz Tobias, *Der Reichstagsbrand* (Grote: Rastatt/Baden, 1962), pp. 132–8, 626.

7. See Tobias, *passim*; Hans Mommsen. 'Der Reichstagsbrand und seine politischen Folgen,' *VfZ* 12 (1964), pp. 351–413; *RGBl.* I, 1933, p. 83; *Strafgesetzbuch für das Deutsche Reich mit Nebengesetzen*, 29th ed. (W. de Gruyter: Berlin & Leipzig, 1930), para. 44.

8. *Oberreichsanwalt* to *Reichsminister der Justiz*, 1 June 1933, BA R 43 II/1519; Domarus, pp. 216–17.

9. BA RG 1010/3183, R 43 II/990, R 43 II/991, NS 29/vorl. 435.

10. Cf. Bracher–Sauer–Schulz, pp. 830–55, 897–966; Diels, pp. 277–8; Bennecke, *Hitler*, p. 216; Heinrich Bennecke, *Die Reichswehr und der 'Röhm Putsch'* (Günter Olzog Verlag: Munich & Vienna, [1964]), pp. 31–5, 42–4, 48–9; cf. Hermann Mau, 'Die "Zweite Revolution"—der 30. Juni 1934,' *VfZ* 1 (1953), pp. 119–37.

11. Diels, pp. 51, 252–5, 279, 282; cf. Bracher–Sauer–Schulz, p. 961. *Rede des Reichskanzlers Adolf Hitler vor dem Reichstag am 13. Juli 1934* (M. Müller: Berlin, [1934]), pp. 22–3.

12. Bracher–Sauer–Schulz, pp. 959–66; cf. the list printed in Bennecke, *Reichswehr*, pp. 87–8.

13. Cf. Rosenberg, pp. 44–9; Kempka, statement 24 Aug. 1974; Gesche, statement 12 Nov. 1974; *Das Archiv*, June and July, 1934, pp. 327, 470; Höhne, pp. 108–9; Bennecke, *Reichswehr*, pp. 56–8; Bracher–Sauer–Schulz, p. 961; on LSSAH activities during the Röhm purge see also James J. Weingartner, 'Sepp Dietrich, Heinrich Himmler, and the Leibstandarte SS Adolf Hitler, 1933–1938,' *Central European History* I (1968), pp. 276–8; Goebbels noted under 9 March 1943: 'After all, Sepp Dietrich once before beat down a revolt during the Stennes

Revolution; how much better would he do now!' [Joseph Goebbels], *The Goebbels Diaries 1942–1943* (Doubleday: Garden City, New York, 1948), p. 288.

14.   Rosenberg, pp. 45–6; *Das Archiv*, July, 1934, p. 470; cf. Baur, pp. 118–22; Höhne, p. 109.

15.   Rosenberg, p. 46; Aronson, p. 193; Bracher–Sauer–Schulz, p. 961; Eicke to Himmler 10 Aug. 1936, NA T–580 Roll 88.

16.   Bennecke, *Reichswehr*, p. 58; Volz, p. 128; Bracher–Sauer–Schulz, pp. 960–5; Fritz Wiedemann, *Der Mann der Feldherr werden wollte* (Blick & Bild Verlag für politische Bildung: Velbert-Kettwig, 1964), pp. 64–5.

17.   For this and the rest of the chapter: Peter Hoffmann, *The History of the German Resistance 1933–1945* (Macdonald and Jane's: London; M.I.T. Press: Cambridge, Mass., 1977), pp. 251–6; cf. Wolfgang Abendroth, 'Das Problem der Widerstandstätigkeit der Schwarzen Front,' *VfZ* 8 (1960); pp. 186–7; BA RG 1010/3183, R 43 II/1101b; *Auswärtiges Amt/Politisches Archiv* 83–69 A.g.; BA NS 29/vorl. 435; cf. Wolfgang Diewerge, *Der Fall Gustloff* (Verlag Frz. Eher Nachf.: Munich, 1936), *passim*; David Frankfurter, 'I kill a Nazi Gauleiter: Memoir of a Jewish Assassin,' *Commentary* 9 (1950), pp. 133–41; *Auswärtiges Amt/Politisches Archiv* 83–69g 21.4. (111g); *SS-Hauptscharführer* [Adolf] Eichmann, *Bericht über die Palästina-Ägyptenreise von SS-Hptscharf. Eichmann und SS-O'Scharf. Hagen 4 Nov. 1937*, IfZ, *Eichmann-Prozess-Beweisdokumente; SS-Sturmbannführer* [Dr. Franz] Six, *Bericht 17 June 1937*, NA T–175 Roll 411/2936189ff.; Alexander Foote, *Handbook for Spies* (Museum Press: London, 1953), pp. 30–3; Johann Georg Elser, *Autobiographie eines Attentäters* (Deutsche Verlags-Anstalt: Stuttgart, 1970), *passim*; Anton Hoch, 'Das Attentat auf Hitler im Münchner Bürgerbräukeller 1939,' *VfZ* 17 (1969), *passim*.

Chapter 4

1.   The appellation IA dated from 1921: Bracher–Sauer–Schulz, p. 537; Hans Buchheim, *Die SS—das Herrschaftsinstrument. Befehl und Gehorsam* (Deutscher Taschenbuch Verlag: Munich, 1967), p. 35.

2.   For this and the following: Buchheim, pp. 36–9, 42–3, 49; cf. Stennes, letter; Cuno Horkenbach, ed., *Handbuch der Reichs- und Staatsbehörden, Körperschaften und Organisationen* (Presse- und Wirtschaftsverlag: Berlin, 1935), p. 99; Bracher–Sauer–Schulz, pp. 439–42, 601–3; Höhne, pp. 82–3, 86–9; Diels, pp. 187–212, esp. 187–90; cf. Bracher–Sauer–Schulz, p. 862.

3.   For this and the following: Gesche; Kempka; NA T–354 Roll 196/3855273; Himmler to Lammers 31 May 1934, BA R 43 II/1103; *Der Chef des Reichssicherheitsdienstes* [Himmler], *Die Deutsche Polizei*, 1 Sept. 1944, RSD files, Hoover Institution Ts Germany R 352 f; '*Abschrift aus einem Bericht des Pol. Rats u. Personalreferenten Paul Kiesel über den RSD an das Bayer. Staatsministerium für Sonderaufgaben*,' [Nov. 1945], papers of *Krim. Dir.* F. Schmidt; Rattenhuber to *Reichskanzlei* 15 Dec. 1938, Himmler to Lammers 13 June 1940, BA R 43 II/1104; Rattenhuber to Schwerin von Krosigk 19 March 1940, and minute by Schwerin von Krosigk 29 March 1940, BA R 2/12160; Frick to Lammers 13 July 1934; Pfundtner to

Schwerin von Krosigk, Lammers and Brückner 13 and 22 Dec. 1934, 6 Feb. 1935, and Erbe to the same 8 Jan. 1935, BA R 43 II/1103; cf. Domarus, p. 463; Aronson, pp. 102–3; minute 29 Jan. 1935, BA R 43 II/1103; minute 16 Feb. 1935, BA R2/12159; on Rattenhuber and Högl cf. BDC/SSO file, BA R 43 II/1104, Frau Rattenhuber, statement 25 May 1973, *Dienstalterliste der Schutzstaffel der NSDAP, Stand vom 1. Oktober 1938*, NAT–175 Roll 205, and *SS-Personalbefehl Nr. 13*, 4 May 1934, Munich, NA T–354 Roll 212; *Schutz- und Wachkommandos des Führers und Reichskanzlers und der Reichskanzlei, c.* 13 Dec. 1934, BA R 43 II/1103; according to Pfundtner on 13 Feb. 1935, the *Führerschutzkommando* was being paid primarily 'from funds of the Bavarian Political Police,' minute 16 Feb. 1935; cf. Buchheim, pp. 35–49; Daluege, General of Provincial Police, was head of Dept. III (Police) in the *Reich* and Prussian Ministry of the Interior—Horkenbach, p. 58.

4. [Martin Bormann], *Daten aus alten Notizbüchern*, 18 Oct. 1940, Hoover Institution, NSDAP *Hauptarchiv*, Roll 1.

5. Minute 16 Feb. [1935], BA R2/12159; conference minute 15 Feb. 1935, and minutes by Wienstein and St[einmeye]r 13, 16, 18 March 1935, 20 Apr. 1935, 20 October 1935, BA R 43 II/1103; Rattenhuber's rank is incorrectly given as *SS-Sturmbannführer* in the conference minutes, actually his *Rangdienstalter* as *SS-Obersturm bannführer* was as from 4 July 1934: *RDA-Liste*, NA T–175 Roll 205 fr. 4041946; cf. Domarus, p. 490; budget for RSD 1935, BA R 2/12159; Himmler to Schwerin von Krosigk 8 March 1937, BA R 2/12159; Lammers to Himmler 22 Oct. 1935, Himmler to Lammers 29 Oct. 1935, BA R 43 II/1103; [Himmler], *Die Deutsche Polizei*.

6. Himmler to Hitler 13 Nov. 1935, Lammers to Himmler 14 Nov. 1935, Lammers to Hess 1 Nov. 1935, Grauert, minute 30 March 1936, Lammers to Himmler 22 Oct. 1935, 13 and 14 Nov. 1935, BA R 43 II/1103.

7. This was reaffirmed on a number of later occasions. E.g. Lammers to Schwerin von Krosigk [2 May 1936], draft, BA R 43 II/1103: '... the *Führer* and *Reich* Chancellor has reserved it to himself to make the final decision and to carry out single-handedly the appointments of all officers of the *Reichssicherheitsdienst*.' Himmler to Lammers 30 Oct. 1935, Lammers to Himmler 1 Nov. 1935, BA R 43 II/1103; *RGBl.* I, 1935, p. 1203; Horkenbach, p. 129; Hess's adjutant Winkler to Lammers 5 Nov. 1935, BA R 43 II/1103; cf. Hans Mommsen, *Beamtentum im Dritten Reich* (Deutsche Verlags-Anstalt: Stuttgart, 1967), pp. 182–202.

8. Rattenhuber, *Befehlsverhältnisse*, Feb. 1935, BA R 2/12159; Högl to Brückner 20 Nov. 1939, BA NS 10/136; BA NS 10/55, 10/124; Friedrich Schmidt, letters 8 Feb. 1966, 6 Oct. 1966, 4 Oct. 1967. Neither official records nor other evidence indicate that Himmler's authority was anything more than formal and administrative, although the *Befehlsverhältnisse* were described by Rattenhuber in 1935 thus: 'The *Kommando z.b.V.* is subordinated to the *Reichsführer SS* Himmler. His deputy is *Gruppenführer* Heydrich. *Reichsführer SS* Himmler, with the approval of the *Führer*, charges *SS-Obersturmbannführer* Rattenhuber with the leadership [of *Kommando z.b.V.*]. The personal security service with the *Führer* is combined with the leadership of the entire *Kommando z.b.V.*' James Leasor, *The Uninvited Envoy* (McGraw-Hill: New York, Toronto, London, 1962), *passim*; BDC Bormann file.

9. BDC Bormann file; *RGBl.* I, 1941, p. 295; Horkenbach, p. 129; Albert Bormann, letter 15 Nov. 1964; Albert Speer, *Erinnerungen* (Propyläen-Verlag: Frankfurt/M., Berlin, 1969), pp. 273, 280, 287, 289–90, 301, 340–1; Diels, pp. 184, 255; Lammers to Supreme *Reich* Authorities 8 May 1943, BA NS 6/159; cf. Speer, p. 301; Hitler's order read: '*Reichsleiter* M. Bormann bears, as my personal assistant, the title "Secretary of the *Führer*",' dated 12 April 1943, BA NS 6/159. Cf. Erich Kempka, *Ich habe Adolf Hitler verbrannt* (Kyburg Verlag: Munich, [1950]), pp. 39–55. On Bormann's permanent membership of Hitler's entourage: M. Bormann to Chief SS Personnel Chancellery 2 Sept. 1938, BDC/SSO file Darges.

10. For this and the following: Cf. above, pp. 5–6, 9–10; Rattenhuber to Lammers 14 Nov. 1935, BA R 43 II/1103. The date on appointment forms had to be 9 November. *RGBl.* I, 1933, p. 1017; *RGBl.* I, 1934, p. 785 (Law of 20 Aug. 1934); Robert J. O'Neill, *The German Army and the Nazi Party, 1933–1939* (Cassell: London, 1966), pp. 54–61; Hitler to Lammers 17 Jan. 1936, BA R 43 II/1103. Himmler could not administer this official oath because he was not yet a *Beamter*; Wienstein, note for Lammers 17 Jan. 1936, Rattenhuber to Wienstein 23 April and 18 June 1936 and Wienstein, minute 18 June 1936, BA R 43 II/1103; Lammers, minutes 3 and 16 Jan. 1942, BA R 43 II/1104; [Himmler], *Polizei*.

11. Rattenhuber, *Befehlsverhältnisse* Feb. 1935; [Schwerin von Krosigk], minute May 1937, BA R 2/12159; [Himmler], *Polizei*; correspondence concerning RSD bureau in Berchtesgaden, *Staatsarchiv* Munich LRA 31931.

12. *Ibid.*, also for the following; Heydrich to Schwerin von Krosigk 8 March 1937, BA R 2/12159; on Bavaud, see below, pp. 102–05, 180–1.

13. RSD correspondence 1935, and appointments list for 1936, dated 6 May 1936, BA R 43 II/1103; Rattenhuber, draft budget 1937 for RSD 28 Feb. 1937, BA R 2/12159; Kiesel; Rattenhuber to *Persönlicher Stab* RF SS 22 Oct. 1943, BA Slg. Schumacher O. 462, counted '176 officers and officials' in RSD, exclusive, apparently, of RSD members without officer rank or government-official status.

14. Minute 16 Feb. [1935], BA R 2/12159.

15. Friedrich Schmidt, letters; Kiesel; Kempka, pp. 28–9; Himmler, appointment proposals 30 Oct. 1935, BA R 43 II/1104; Rattenhuber to Wienstein 14 Nov. 1935, Himmler to Lammers 13 Nov. 1935, 27 Feb. 1936, 9 Apr. 1936, 13 March and 13 June 1940, Himmler's appointment proposals 5 March 1936, 31 March 1936, 28 March and 13 June 1940, BA R 43 II/1103 and BA R 43 II/1104; cf. *Der Chef der Sicherheitspolizei und des SD*, circular No. 79/41 of 1 July 1941, BA Slg. Schumacher O. 434.

16. Göring to Lammers 31 May 1934, Himmler to Lammers 13 Nov. 1935, Rattenhuber to Wienstein 14 Nov. 1935, BA R 43 II/1103; *RGBl.* I, 1933, pp. 175–7; Mommsen, *Beamtentum*, pp. 166–79; *RGBl.* I, 1936, pp. 893–6; cf. Peter Hoffmann, 'Hitler's Personal Security,' *Journal of Contemporary History* 8 (1973), No. 2, pp. 25–45; *RGBl.* I, 1933, p. 175 (7 Apr. 1933); *RGBl.* I, 1935, pp. 1145, 1333.

17. Correspondence of *Reich* and Prussian Ministry of the Interior with

Regierungspräsidenten, presidents of police, and all *Land* ministries for internal affairs, Oct. 1934, StA Oldenburg 136 Nr. 2835.

18.   NA RG 242-HL ML 941, 942.

19.   Keitel, directives *re* RSD 31 Aug. 1939, and to Rattenhuber 6 Nov. 1939, BA R 2/12160; Rattenhuber, *Betrifft: Sicherung des Führerhauptquartiers* 19 Dec. 1939, BA NS 10/136; Kiesel.

Chapter 5

1.   For this and the following: see Chapter 2, note 17; BDC/SSO and RuSHA (*Rasse- und Siedlungshauptamt*) files on Dietrich; NA T–354 Roll 195; also James J. Weingartner, *Hitler's Guard: The Story of the Leibstandarte SS Adolf Hitler 1933– 1945* (Southern Illinois University Press: Carbondale and Edwardsville, [1974]), pp. 4–19 (Weingartner says nothing about the SS Escort and its connection with LSSAH).

1a.   In the last weeks of the war, Hitler expressed rage and disappointment when Dietrich could not keep the Russians out of Austria. After the war Dietrich was accused of responsibility for illegal executions of prisoners-of-war; he was sentenced to life imprisonment in a procedurally questionable trial by a Nuremberg military tribunal in 1946 (Malmedy Trial), released in 1955, and tried and convicted in Munich in 1957 for his participation in the Röhm massacre of 1934. He was finally released in 1959 after having served his sentence, and he died in 1966. See Weingartner, *Hitler's Guard*, pp. 135–7, 146–7.

2.   LSSAH files, NA T–354 Rolls 205, 206, 208; Kempka, statement; Heinz Linge, statement 14 Aug. 1974; cf. below, pp. 76–7.

3.   For this see below, Chapter 11; Speer, p. 173; NA T–78 Roll 351/6310661.

4.   [Göring] to [Levetzow *et al.*] 22 Sept. 1933, BA R 43 II/1103; cf. Buchheim, p. 32; Volz, pp. 125–6; LSSAH files, NA T–354 Roll 195.

5.   Helmut Heiber (ed.), *Reichsführer! ... Briefe an und von Himmler* (Deutsche Verlags-Anstalt: Stuttgart, 1968), pp. 51, 56; cf. below, p. 53; Richard Schulze-Kossens, letter 4 March 1974; NA T–175 Roll 204; Weingartner, 'Sepp Dietrich,' pp. 271–5; Weingartner, *Hitler's Guard*, pp. 7, 9, 23.

6.   Volz, pp. 119–20; *RGBl.* I, 1933, p. 1016.

7.   Göring (note 4 above).

8.   For this and the following: Grauert and some of his correspondents still referred to the *Leibstandarte* as *Stabswache*; Grauert, decree 22 Dec. 1933 and Lammers to Schwerin von Krosigk 4 Jan. 1934 (draft), BA R 43 II/1103; Hsi-hue Liang, *The Berlin Police Force in the Weimar Republic 1918–1933* (University of California Press: Berkeley, 1970), p. 172; Höhne, p. 82; Weingartner, *Hitler's Guard*, pp. 5–7; Roger James Bender, *Air Organisations of the Third Reich* (R. James Bender Publishing: Mountain View, California, 1967), p. 44.

9.   See note 8.

10.   BA R 43 II/1103.

11.   Daluege, *Die Ordnungspolizei nach dem Stande vom 1. Dezember 1938*, NA T–175 Roll 241; Himmler, circular No. 79/41, 1 July 1941, BA Slg. Schumacher O. 434; [Himmler], *Polizei*.

12.   LSSAH *Abt. Sippenforschung* to Stab 28 Jan. and 17 March 1937, NA T–354 Roll 208; Himmler, circular No. 79/41; Heiber, *Reichsführer*, p. 75; Weingartner, *Hitler's Guard*, pp. 153, 157, notes.

13.   BDC files on Dietrich; *Statistisches Jahrbuch der Schutzstaffel der NSDAP*, 1937, 1938, p. 83, NA T–175 Roll 205; LSSAH files, NA T–354 Roll 195; BDC, NSDAP membership files; Schulze-Kossens, letter 2 Apr. 1974.

14.   For this and the following: Gesche, statement; BDC/SSO and RuSHA files on Gesche and Gildisch; Volz, p. 45.

15.   *Organisationsbuch der NSDAP*, ed. by *Reichsorganisationsleiter der NSDAP* (Zentralverlag der NSDAP, Frz. Eher Nachf.: Munich, 3rd ed. 1937), plate 51.

16.   For this and the following: Rosenberg, pp. 44–7; Aronson, pp. 193–4; Liang, pp. 92, 166, 172; *Das Archiv*, July 1934, p. 470; Buchheim, pp. 18–19; NA T–354 Roll 213; BDC/SSO files on Chr. Weber, Graf, Maurice, Dietrich, Gildisch; *Nachtrag zum Reichstags-Handbuch der V. Wahlperiode 1930* [Reichstagsdruckerei: Berlin, 1932]; Horkenbach, pp. 128–30; Kutzke, pp. 80–1; Georg Franz-Willing, *Ursprung der Hitler-Bewegung 1919–1922* (Verlag K. W. Schütz: Preussisch Oldendorf, 2nd ed. 1974), pp. 200–1.

17.   Adolf Hitler, *Mein Kampf* (*My Struggle*) (Hurst & Blackett: London, 1934), p. 202; BDC/SSO and RuSHA files on Maurice and Weber; de-nazification proceedings files on Maurice, 1948, *Amtsgericht*, Munich, *Registratur* S; Gordon, p. 619. On the Maurice–Geli–Raubal affair see also Albert Zoller, *Hitler privat: Erlebnisbericht seiner Geheimsekretärin* [Christa Schröder] (Droste Verlag: Düsseldorf, 1949), pp. 87–91; [Joseph Goebbels], *Das Tagebuch von Joseph Goebbels 1925/26* (Deutsche Verlags-Anstalt: Stuttgart, n.d.), p. 105; Heinrich Hoffmann, *Hitler wie ich ihn sah* (Herbig: Munich, [1974]), p. 216; *Neue Zeit*, 26 May 1948; Albrecht Tyrell (ed.), *Führer befiehl . . . Selbstzeugnisse aus der 'Kampfzeit' der NSDAP* (Droste Verlag: Düsseldorf [1969]), pp. 211–13.

18.   BDC/SSO and RuSHA files on Gesche and Gildisch; sentence of *Schwurgericht bei dem Landgericht Berlin* [on Gildisch] of 18 May 1953/(500) 1 Pks. 4.51 (6.53).

19.   *SS-Untersturmführer* Hammersen to I Battalion LSSAH 5 June 1936, NA T–354 Roll 20; Friedrich Schmidt, letters; Gregor Karl, letters 18 May 1966 and 17 Feb. 1968; BDC/SSO files on Gesche; Otto Günsche, statement 6 Nov. 1972.

20.   *Der Politische Polizeikommandeur München, Personalkarte* No. 211, 3 May 1934; Gesche, *curriculum vitae* [c. 1935]; questionnaire completed by Gesche 1936; data provided by Gesche after Oct. 1939; *SS-Stammkarte, Personalkarte* and *SS-Stamm-*

rollenauszug of Gesche 1934; all in BDC/SSO and RuSHA files on Gesche, also
for the following.

21. SS Group South to Himmler 20 Oct. 1932; SS Office to Gesche 31 Oct.
1932; Himmler to Brückner 31 Oct. 1932; Brückner to Himmler 9 Nov. 1932;
all in BDC/SSO and RuSHA files on Gesche; Domarus, p. 139.

22. Gesche, statement 12 Nov. 1974; BDC/SSO and RuSHA files on Gesche,
Kempka.

23. For this and the following: BDC/SSO files on Gesche: Rattenhuber to
Himmler 1 July 1935; *Reichsführer SS/SS-Personalkanzlei* to *Begleitkommando des
Führers* c/o Rattenhuber 14 Sept. 1938; Gesche, *Erklärung* 26 Sept. 1938; *Reichs-
führer SS/Persönlicher Stab* (RFSS/PSt) to *SS-Personalhauptamt* (SSPHA) 26 Sept.
1939; RFSS/SSPHA to *SS-Führungshauptamt/Kommandoamt* (SSFHA/KA) *der
Waffen-SS* 14 Apr. 1942; RFSS/PSt to SSFHA/KA *der Waffen-SS* 13 Apr. 1942;
SSFHA/KA *der Waffen-SS* to *SS-Panzer-Jäger-Ersatz-Abteilung* Hilversum 27 Apr.
1942; Gesche, *Erklärung* 30 Apr. 1942; SSFHA/KA *der Waffen-SS* to *Begleitkommando des Führers* 23 Apr. 1942; SSFHA/KA *der Waffen-SS*, minute 5 Aug. 1942;
Wolff, teleprinter message to SSFHA/KA *der Waffen-SS* 11 Dec. 1942; SSFHA
IIa to PSt RFSS 29 Nov. 1944; Himmler to Gesche 20 Dec. 1944. Gesche was
made *SS-Obersturmbannführer.* Cf. Heiber, *Reichsführer, passim*; Günsche, statements 6 Nov. 1972 and 12 Nov. 1974; Gesche, statement; RFSS, directive 21
Dec. 1937, NA T–354 Roll 200; *Führer* Order 22 Dec. 1942, NA T–175 Roll
42; Schulze-Kossens, letters 16 Jan. and 4 Mar 1974; correspondence of Schulze-
Kossens, Gesche, A. Bormann Jan. 1943, NA T–175 Roll 43/2554962–83; cf.
Helmut Heiber (ed.), *Hitlers Lagebesprechungen* (Deutsche Verlags-Anstalt: Stuttgart, 1962), p. 36; Schulze to Gesche 12 Jan. 1943 (in Schulze-Kossens' files).

24. BDC/SSO files on Gesche.

25. *Ibid.*; Gesche, statement; Günsche, statement 12 Nov. 1974.

26. BA NS 10/134 and R 43 II/967b.

27. For this and the following:BDC/SSO files; Günsche, statements 6 Nov.
1972, 12 Nov. 1974; Schulze-Kossens, statements 24 July 1975 and letters 20
Nov. 1973, 16 Jan. 1974; Rattenhuber to Brückner 29 Nov. 1939, BA NS 10/
136; Schmundt, *Folgende Wageneinteilung ...* 3 Sept. 1939, BA NS 10/126; KTB
FHQ Nr. 1–6, NA T–77 Rolls 857, 858 and T–78 Roll 351; Wünsche to *Ers.
Btl.* LSSAH 18 Nov. 1939, BA NS 10/83; Rattenhuber, *Ergänzung zur Dienstvorschrift für die Dienststelle 1 für die Dauer der Verlegung des Führerhauptquartiers auf den
Obersalzberg* 26 March 1943, Hoover Institution Ts Germany R 352 kb; LSSAH
Standartenbefehl 5 Feb. 1938, NA T–354 Roll 213/3877097; 2 Sept. 1938, NA T–
354 Roll 214/3878655; 21 May 1938, NA T–354 Roll 213/3876947; 5 Dec. 1940,
NA T–354 Roll 203/3864732; [Bormann], *Daten* 18 and 21 Oct. 1940, NA T–
84 Roll 387/000503; also BA NS 10/55, R 43 II/1103, R 43 II/967a, R 43 II/
967b (*Reichskanzlei/Adjutantur* files); Günsche, letter 7 Sept. 1977.

28. At the end of 1943 Himmler wrote to Darges that he was firmly convinced
that Darges would get married in 1944; there are allegations of affairs involving,
among others, Gretl Braun, Eva Braun's sister and the later Frau Fegelein. The
incident that finally caused Darges' transfer, however, involved a fly: according

to most versions, it had irritated Hitler during a situation conference, as it kept coming back to the spot on the map from which Hitler tried to shoo it away: when he looked up he saw Darges grinning, he took him aside and told him to have himself transferred. BDC/SSO files; Günsche, statement 6 Nov. 1972; Schulze-Kossens, statement 24 July 1975; Puttkamer, statement 5 March 1964.

29.   For this and the following: Linge, statement; Kempka, statement 24 Aug. 1974; BDC/SSO and RuSHA files on Linge, Krause, Schneider, Junge, Meyer.

30.   Bormann correspondence Nov. 1944, NA T–175 Roll 28/2353008–15.

Chapter 6

1.   BDC/SSO files on Gesche and Kempka; cf. below, pp. 132–3.

2.   [Heinz Linge], 'Kronzeuge Linge,' *Revue*, Munich (1955/56), *4. Folge*, p. 46.

3.   D[eckert], *Dienstanordnung für den Sicherheitsdienst (SD) in der Reichskanzlei*, Lammers to Meissner [*et al.*] 28 March 1935, BA R 43 II/1105; list of names and weapon numbers in *Sicherheitsdienst* files, initialled by Deckert 14 July [1940], BA R 43 II/1104; Lammers to Schwerin von Krosigk 12 Dec. 1939, Rattenhuber to RSHA 28 Feb. 1940, Dr. Best (on staff of RFSS) to Schwerin von Krosigk 18 March 1940, BA R 2/12160; Deckert to ret. police *Oberwachtmeister* Erich Niedich, Walter Teske, Willi Peter, Arthur Steinicke, 22 Dec. 1939 and 9 Jan. 1940, and Ostertag, *Bescheinigung* 6 Feb. 1940, BA R 43 II/1104. Weingartner, *Hitler's Guard*, p. 4, erroneously thinks only the LSSAH was used to provide security at the *Reich* Chancellery.

4.   Baur, p. 124; Rattenhuber to Lammers 4 March 1942 and Lammers to Schwerin von Krosigk 6 Apr. 1942, BA R 2/12160.

5.   Helmuth Spaeter, *Die Geschichte des Panzerkorps Grossdeutschland*, Vol. I (Selbstverlag Hilfswerk ehem. Soldaten für Kriegsopfer und Hinterbliebene e.V.: Duisburg-Ruhrort, 1958), pp. 44, 60; Ronald Lewin, *Rommel as Military Commander* (Batsford: London; Van Nostrand: Princeton, N.J., 1968), p. 9. Cf. below, Chapter 9 on *Travel*, note 18; *Wehrmacht-Fernsprech-Verzeichnis Gross-Berlin Teil I u. II* (1941–3), NA T–78 Roll 355/6315760.

Chapter 7

1.   Hanfstaengl, p. 131; Höhne, p. 64.

2.   *Trial* XXI, p. 414; Linge, statement; Linge declared the alleged attribution by him of the statement to Hitler as erroneous (cf. Linge, 'Kronzeuge,' *2. Folge*, p. 41, and *3. Folge*, pp. 42, 44). Also BDC/SSO file on Linge (Linge's *curricula vitae* vary in some details and do not seem to account for the years 1928–30). Günsche told the author on 12 Nov. 1972 that Hitler's remark had not referred to Gesche but to Schaub, whose hands were usually shaking.

3.   *Hitler's Secret Conversations*, pp. 366–7; cf. Baur, p. 106; Picker, pp. 306–7, 505–12; Zoller, p. 33; Speer, letter 5 Nov. 1973.

4. Himmler to Lammers 31 May 1934, BA R 43 II/1103; photo-album given to staff members of command staff Army Group Centre by Fieldmarshal Günther von Kluge (n.p., n.d.), Boeselager Family Archive, Schloss Kreuzberg/Ahr; Linge, statement; Kempka, statement 24 Aug. 1974.

5. Inventory and Commission Books in Daimler–Benz A. G. Archive; NA RG 242–HL ML 941, 942; Hoffmann, *Hitler*, p. 64; also for the following.

6. NA RG 242–HL ML 941, 942; *Hitler's Secret Conversations*, pp. 367, 415; Gesche, statement 12 Nov. 1974; Günsche, statement 12 Nov. 1974; Linge, 'Kronzeuge,' *2. Folge*, p. 41; Speer, letter 5 Nov. 1973; Rudolf Semmler, *Goebbels— the man next to Hitler* (Westhouse: London, 1947), p. 61. Kempka, p. 61, gives these measurements from memory: 45-mm armour glass, 3.5 to 4-mm specially hardened steel side-plates, 9- to 11-mm floor plates (tested and found safe against a 500-g charge of dynamite).

7. Kempka, statements 19 Aug. 1965 and 24 Aug. 1974; Kempka, pp. 18, 20–1, 138; Daimler-Benz A.G. Archive; NA RG 242–HL ML 941, 942; Linge, statement confirms Kempka; Wiedemann, p. 132.

8. BA NS 10/55.

9. Rattenhuber to Frick 25 March 1936, BA R 2/12159; Linge, 'Kronzeuge,' *8. Folge*, p. 24; Dietrich, *12 Jahre*, p. 162; Zoller, p. 175; Hoffmann, *Hitler*, p. 82.

10. Rattenhuber, *Entwurf zum Haushaltsplan für das Rechnungsjahr 1937 des Reichs-sicherheitsdienstes* 28 Feb. 1937, BA R 2/12159.

11. Rattenhuber to Frick 25 March 1936, BA R 2/12159; Rattenhuber to Himmler 13 Apr. 1943, BA R 43 11/1104; *Hitler's Secret Conversations*, pp. 367–8; Schulze-Kossens, letter 16 Jan. 1974; Zoller, p. 32; correspondence between Berlin Presidium of Police and *Reich* Chancellery 1934, BA R 43/II 1093a.

12. *Regierungsrat* Luchmann, travel bureau in *Reich* Ministry of Transport, to Brückner 6 May 1939, BA NS 10/38; descriptions of cars, composition lists for *Führer* Specials, and *Aufnahmezettel* 10 Dec. 1937 for Hitler's Pullman 10206 from files of *Reichsbahnzentralamt* und *Bundesbahnzentralamt*, Minden, in archive of J. Deppmeyer, Uelzen; cf. Paul Dost, *Der rote Teppich: Geschichte der Staatszüge und Salonwagen* (Franckh Verlag: Stuttgart, 1965), pp. 50–3, 174–9 (almost no information on Hitler's trains in this book); correspondence on RSD Berchtesgaden bureau, *Staatsarchiv München* LRA 31931; cf. Zoller, p. 22.

13. Schmundt (successor to Hossbach as Hitler's Chief *Wehrmacht* Aide) to Brückner 22 Feb. 1939, and Wünsche to Schmundt 7 March 1939, BA NS 10/126; KTB FHQ, *passim*, NA T–77 Rolls 858, 859 and T–78 Roll 351; NA RG 242–HL ML 941, 942; Speer, p. 259; Puttkamer, letter 13 Jan. 1976.

14. *Hitler's Secret Conversations*, p. 366; Dietrich, *Mit Hitler*, p. 17; *Reich* Minister of Transport Dorpmüller to Brückner 10 Sept. 1940, BA NS 10/38; *Reich* Transport Ministry to Brückner 4 Oct. 1940, BA NS 10/38.

15. For this and the following: Brückner to Dorpmüller undated, BA NS 10/

38; *Hitler's Secret Conversations*, p. 366; Baur, p. 106; Dorpmüller to *Bahnbevoll-mächtigte der Reichsbahndirektionen Berlin, Halle/S., Erfurt, Augsburg, Nürnberg und München* 26 Sept. 1940, BA NS 10/38.

16.   *Deutsche Reichsbahn, Vorschriften bei Reisen bestimmter Personen (Reisen nach Son-dervorschriften)* No. 470, *Reichsbahndirektion München*, 1937, 1941.

17.   Hoffmann, *History*, pp. 339, 637–8, 387; [Heinrich Himmler], *Telephonge-spräche des Reichsführer-SS am 11.7.1942*, NA T–84 Roll R 25; David Irving, *Die Tragödie der Deutschen Luftwaffe* (Verlag Ullstein: Frankfurt/M., Berlin, Vienna, 1970), p. 336; Heiber, *Lagebesprechungen*, p. 662; correspondence of RSHA con-cerning Specials 1940–4 in BA Slg. Schumacher O. 474, 1492; KTB FHQ, *passim*; Dr. Werner Koeppen, *Bericht Nr. 55 über ein Tischgespräch (Hitlers) vom 6.11.41*, NA T–84 Roll 387; *Kriegstagebuch des Oberkommandos der Wehrmacht (Wehrmachtfüh-rungsstab) 1940–1945* (hereafter *KTB OKW*) IV (Bernard & Graefe: Frankfurt/M., 1961), p. 1869; *Reichsführer SS, Decknamenliste der Sonderzüge* 13 Jan. 1943, EAP 161-b-12/218, NA T–175 Roll 129/2655558; *Eisenbahnabteilungen des Reichs-verkehrsministeriums an Bahnbevollmächtigte* [etc.] 21 Jan. 1943, copy, papers of *Mini-sterialrat* (Ret.) Eugen Kreidler; *SS-Standartenführer* Josef Tiefenbacher (*Komman-dant der Feldkommandostellen* RFSS) to *Reichsverkehrsministerium* 28 July 1944, NA T–175 Roll 122/2647994.

18.   Speer, p. 259; Zoller, pp. 32–3, 134–5; Gerhard Boldt, *Die letzten Tage der Reichskanzlei* (Rowohlt: Hamburg, Stuttgart, 1947), p. 33; Gesche, statement; Günsche, statement 12 Nov. 1974 and letter 7 Sept. 1977.

19.   Puttkamer, letter 24 Jan. 1977; Deppmeyer, letter 16 Feb. 1977; cf. note 12 above.

20.   Baur, pp. 81–6.

21.   Baur, pp. 93–4, 124; cf. Rattenhuber to Lammers 4 March 1942, BA R 2/12160.

22.   Baur, pp. 85, 87, 99–100, 106–7, 124 (Baur incorrectly gives 1935 as the year of the first Condor flight) and photograph of a Rohrbach Roland C 1 before p. 97; Himmler to Schwerin von Krosigk 8 March 1937, BA R 2/12159.

23.   Baur, pp. 127–8; NA RG 242–HL ML 941, 942; William Green, *The War-planes of the Third Reich* (Doubleday: Garden City, New York, 1970), p. 223.

24.   Baur, p. 193; [Karl R. Pawlas], 'Hitlers Reisemaschinen,' *Luftfahrt international* 8, March 1975, pp. 1228–48; [Fabian von Schlabrendorff], *Offiziere gegen Hitler* (Europa Verlag: Zürich, [1946]), pp. 78–9; Otto John, *Zweimal kam ich heim* (Econ Verlag: Düsseldorf, Wien, 1969), p. 117.

25.   Baur, pp. 193, 239, 260–1; Green, pp. 224, 504–10.

26.   Linge, 'Kronzeuge,' *1. Folge*, p. 32; Baur, pp. 124, 211–12.

27.   For this and the following: Baur, pp. 124–5, 200–1, 240, 250; Best, *Anwei-sung für die Überwachung der Regierungsflüge und Bewachung der Regierungsflugzeuge, 1. Juni 1935, SS Absperr-Anleitung*, pp. 53–5, NA T–611 Roll 47; *Der Politische Poli-*

zeikommandeur der Länder [*und*] *Preussische Geheime Staatspolizei an Politische Poli-*
zeien der Länder [*und*] *alle Staatspolizeistellen, Anweisung für die Überwachung der*
Regierungsflüge und Bewachung der Regierungsflugzeuge, BA Slg. Schumacher O. 462;
SS-Fliegerstaffel-Ost to *SS-Gruppe Ost* 16 March 1933, *ibid.*; *SS-Truppführer* Gärtner
(in charge of security service) to *Staatskommissar* Daluege 15 March 1933; *Vorschlag*
zur Sicherung der Regierungsflugzeuge, ibid.

28. Baur, pp. 134, 164, 201.

29. Baur, pp. 104–6, 124; Best, *Anweisung*, p. 53; *VB*, 15 Sept. 1933.

30. Baur, p. 125, misdates the incident '1934;' *VB*, 21–23 March 1935.

31. Baur, pp. 240–2.

32. Baur, pp. 109–11, 240–2; Hanfstaengl, p. 265; cf. Domarus, pp. 1888–90.

33. Baur, pp. 168–9; NA RG 242–HL ML 941, 942; Domarus, pp. 375, 1127–
8; [Martin Bormann], *Daten aus alten Notizbüchern*, Hoover Institution, NSDAP
Hauptarchiv, Roll 1.

34. Baur, p. 212.

Chapter 8

1. [Bormann], *Daten;* Baur, pp. 128–9; Hanfstaengl, pp. 334–5; Speer, p. 57;
Linge, statement.

2. Diels, pp. 59–60; Zoller, pp. 31–2; Linge, 'Kronzeuge,' *10. Folge*, p. 26, dates
the incident for about 1935 so that it might also have occurred in June 1934
when the expedition against Röhm started out from this hotel.

2a. *Schleswig-Holsteinisches Landesarchiv* Kiel (SHLA) 1 II Fasc. 132; Hess,
Anordnung 23 Sept. 1934, SHLA 1 II Fasc. 132; cf. *Verordnungsblatt der Reichsleitung*
der NSDAP. Folge 82, 4. Jahrgang, Mitte Oktober 1934, No. 47/34; Dietrich, *Mit*
Hitler, p. 17; Frick to ministers of the interior in the provinces 12 Oct. 1934,
SHLA 1 II Fasc. 132; cf. Diels, p. 51; Frick, *Anordnung* 1 Dec. 1934, SHLA 1
II Fasc. 132; Heydrich to Political Police in *Länder* Anhalt, Baden, Bayern,
Braunschweig, Bremen, Hamburg, Hessen, Lübeck, Mecklenburg, Oldenburg,
Preussen, Sachsen, Thüringen, Württemberg 12 Dec. 1934, SHLA 1 II Fasc, 132;
Puttkamer, letter 13 Jan. 1976.

2b. *Hitler's Secret Conversations*, pp. 366–7; Rattenhuber to Brückner 26 May
and 29 May 1939, BA NS 10/136; Karl Baedeker, *Berlin und Umgebung* (Karl
Baedeker: Leipzig, 1921), pp. 4, 26; Hans Severus Ziegler, *Adolf Hitler aus dem*
Erleben dargestellt (Verlag K. W. Schütz: Göttingen, [1964]), pp. 53, 56, 70.

3. Hess, *Anordnung* 9 March 1936, SHLA 1 II Fasc. 132; cf. *Verordnungsblatt*
der Reichsleitung der NSDAP. Folge 116, Mitte März 1936, Nr. 13/36; Volz, p. 70.

4. *SS Absperr-Anleitung*, NA T–611 Roll 47; Rattenhuber to Brückner 29 May

1939, BA NS 10/136. *Reichsstatthalter* Röver to *Staatsministerium* Oldenburg 26 Feb. 1935 concerning instances of people breaking through cordons, StA Oldenburg 136 Nr. 2835.

5. Günther Weisenborn, *Der lautlose Aufstand* (Rowohlt Verlag: Hamburg, 1962), p. 30.

6. Rattenhuber to LSSAH and to *Kriminalinspektor* Forster (Berlin) 29 Jan. 1936, Rattenhuber to Police Captain Staudinger (chief of Bav. Pol. Police in Garmisch-Partenkirchen) 29 Jan. 1936, and Rattenhuber's *Minutenprogramm* for 6 Feb. dated 1 Feb. 1936, all in NA T–354 Roll 211; *VB*, 7–17 Feb. and 2–17 Aug. 1936; [Bormann], *Daten*, 1936; Wiedemann, pp. 85–6.

7. *Wachvorschrift für die SS-Leibstandarte 'Adolf Hitler' und Pz. Abw. Abt. 26 bei der Grossen Herbstübung des Gruppenkommandos 2, Schlüchtern*, 17 Sept. 1936, NA T–354 Roll 206; on Hitler's view that the *Reichswehr* was the only bearer of arms of the nation, see O'Neill, p. 41, and Gerhard Engel, *Heeresadjutant bei Hitler 1938–1943* (Deutsche Verlags-Anstalt: Stuttgart, 1974), 19 Apr. and 26 Aug. 1938; *SS-Hauptsturmführer* Collani, *Befehl für die Teilnahme der LSSAH an der Grossen Herbstübung 1936 29. Aug. 1936*, NA T–354 Roll 206; *SS-Hauptsturmführer* Collani (Adjutant LSSAH), *Betr.: Absperrdienst bei der Schlussbesprechung am 25.9.1936*, 22 Sept. 1936, NA T–354 Roll 206.

8. *Generalkommando II. Armeekorps (Wehrkreiskommando II) Abtlg. IIa, Minutenprogramm*, and seating charts, 15 Aug. 1938, BA–MA WK XIII/240.

9. For this and the following: Rattenhuber to Deckert 28 Jan. 1937 and Rattenhuber, *Betrifft: Feierlichkeiten anlässlich des 30. Januar 1937*, dated 27 Jan. 1937, BA R 43 II/1104; *Hitler's Secret Conversations*, p. 367; Domarus, opposite p. 417; Heinrich Hoffmann, *Hitler in seiner Heimat* (Zeitgeschichte-Verlag: Berlin, [1938]); *VB*, 15/16 July 1934, cf. 31 Jan. and 1 Feb. 1937; NA RG 242–HL ML 941, 942.

10. Diels, p. 52; *Hitler's Secret Conversations*, p. 367; Wilhelm Treue (ed.), 'Rede Hitlers vor der deutschen Presse (10. November 1938),' *VfZ* 6 (1958), pp. 175–91; NA RG 242–HL ML 941, 942; circular ordinance of *Reich* and Prussian Minister of the Interior 18 June 1935 and Himmler to *Regierungspräsidenten, Oberbürgermeister, Kommandeure der Schutzpolizei*, etc., 9 Sept. 1936, SHLA 1 II Fasc. 132; *RdErl.d.RuPrMdI.18.6.1935*; Hess, *Anordnung Nr. 112/38*, 3 Aug. 1938; Daluege to *Reichsstatthalter* [etc.] 30 Nov. 1938; StA Oldenburg 136 Nr. 2835; Schulze-Kossens, letter 20 Nov. 1973.

11. NA RG 242–HL ML 941, 942.

12. For this and the following: *VB*, 19–21 Apr. 1939; arrangements, timing and security directives for 20 Apr. 1939 dated 12 Apr. 1939 in BA R 43 II/902 and NA T–354 Roll 200; Domarus, pp. 1144–7; NA RG 242–HL ML 941, 942; cf. Sir Noel Mason-MacFarlane, autobiographical writings (Imperial War Museum: London).

13. Wiedemann, pp. 126–8.

14. Directives, BA R 43 II/902; *Hitler's Secret Conversations*, p. 367; Dr. Werner Koeppen, *Bericht Nr. 28, Führerhauptquartier*, 7 Sept. 1941, NA T–84 Roll 387.

15. NA RG 242–HL ML 941, 942.

16. For this and the following: [Sir Noel Mason-MacFarlane], drafts of interview for A. G. S. Wilson of the *Daily Express* 3 Jan. 1951 and 4 Jan. 1952, and autobiographical writings (Imperial War Museum: London); *Auswärtiges Amt*, letter 27 March 1973; Imperial War Museum, letter 29 March 1973; cf. Ewan Butler, ' "I talked of plan to kill Hitler," ' *The Times*, 6 Aug. 1969, p. 1; Helmut Heiber, 'Der Fall Grünspan,' *VfZ* 5 (1957) pp. 134–72; NA T-175 r. 154/2 684 165–7.

17. For this and the following: [*Gauleitung München*], *9. November 1936: Verlauf der Veranstaltungen in München und Bemerkungen zum Programm 8./9. November 1936*, 20 Oct. 1936, BA NS 10/124; [Bormann], *Daten*, 1935–8; cf. Gordon, p. 184; Schulze-Kossens, letter 2 Apr. 1974; NA RG 242–HL ML 941, 942.

18. *Hitler's Secret Conversations*, p. 367; Peter Hoffmann, 'Maurice Bavaud's Attempt to Assassinate Hitler in 1938,' in *Police Forces in History* (ed. George L. Mosse) (Sage Publications: London, 1975), pp. 173–204; Hitler apparently accepted Bavaud's explanation of his failure to shoot during the November march: see Koeppen, *Bericht Nr. 28* (incorrectly dating the incident 1937); M. Bormann (as Hess's *Stabsleiter*), *Anordnung Nr. 93/38* of 15 July 1938, copy, StA Oldenburg 136 Nr. 2835.

19. *Regie-Programm für den 8./9. November 1939 in München, Gesamtleitung: Gaupropagandaleiter Pg. Karl Wenzl*, BA NS 10/126; *VB*, to Nov. 1939; Domarus, pp. 1414, 1603.

20. For this and the following: Elser, pp. 71, 77, 79–80; Hoch, pp. 393–413; see also the sources cited in Hoffmann, *History*, p. 612 note 11; literal quotations are from *Regie-Programm* and Hoch, pp. 408–10.

21. Hoch, pp. 383–93, 404–13; Linge, 'Kronzeuge,' *11. Folge*, p. 38; Hoffmann, *History*, pp. 120–1; Picker, p. 211; Helmuth Groscurth, *Tagebücher eines Abwehroffiziers 1938–1940* (Deutsche Verlags-Anstalt: Stuttgart, 1970), pp. 222–3.

22. For this and the following: Gruchmann in Elser, pp. 8–9; *Regie-Programm*; Hoch, pp. 410–11; *VB*, 7–10 Nov. 1939; NA RG 242–HL ML 941, 942; *Time*, 20 Nov. 1939, p. 21; Rosenberg, p. 88 (with incorrect times of day); Hoffmann, *History*, pp. 255–8.

23. Hitler confirmed this in two table conversations: Koeppen, *Bericht Nr. 28* for 7 Sept. 1941; *Hitler's Secret Conversations*, p. 366 for 3 May 1942.

24. *Regie-Programm*; Hoffmann, *History*, pp. 257–8.

25. Hoch, p. 405; Hoffmann, *History*, p. 258.

26. Heydrich to *Staatspolizeistellen in Preussen* 12 Dec. 1934, copy, and *Krim. Kom. Anw.* Scholz (*Gestapa*), *Der politische-polizeiliche Schutzdienst*, no date [after 1 June 1935], BA Slg. Schumacher O. 462; Heydrich, *Betrifft: Sicherungsmassnahmen zum Schutze führender Persönlichkeiten des Staates und der Partei* 9 March 1940 and *Reichssicherheitshauptamt—Amt IV, Richtlinien für die Handhabung des Sicherungsdienstes*, dated Feb. 1940, NA T-175 Roll 383; cf. Peter Hoffmann, 'Hitler's Personal Security,' pp. 32–6; [Himmler], *Polizei*.

27.   Gramophone record of the speech in BA; the speech is printed in Picker, pp. 493–504, based on Picker's notes; KTB FHQ, Nr. 6, NA T–78 Roll 351; security plans for 30 May 1942, BA RG 1010/714; cf. Hoffmann, 'Hitler's Personal Security,' pp. 36–8; Jan G. Wiener, *The Assassination of Heydrich* (Grossman: New York, 1969), p. 87; *Befehl Nr. 1* is printed in Hans-Adolf Jacobsen, *1939–1945: Der 2. Weltkrieg in Chronik und Dokumenten*, (Wehr und Wissen: Darmstadt, 5th ed. 1961), p. 643.

28.   For this and the following: Hoffmann, *History*, pp. 283–9; Peter Hoffmann, 'The Attempt to Assassinate Hitler on March 21, 1943,' *Canadian Journal of History/Annales Canadiennes d'Histoire* II (1967), pp. 67–83; Semmler, p. 80; Himmler, *Terminkalender*, NA T–84 Roll R25; [Bormann], *Daten*; Daily Digest of World Broadcasts (From Germany and German-occupied territory), Part I, No. 1343, 22 March 1943 (BBC Monitoring Service: London, 1943); *Field Engineering and Mine Warfare Pamphlet No. 7: Booby Traps* (The War Office: London, 1952), pp. 26–8.

Chapter 9

1.   Dietrich, *12 Jahre*, p. 162; Hoffmann, *Hitler*, p. 82; Friedrich Hossbach, *Zwischen Wehrmacht und Hitler 1934–1938* (Vandenhoeck & Ruprecht: Göttingen, 2nd ed. 1965), pp. 17–18; [Bormann], *Daten, passim*; Speer, p. 132. Compare Hitler's unrestrained consumption of cake, his habitual taking of laxative to control his weight and of opiates to suppress the appetite: Speer, 53, 56, 105; Linge, 'Kronzeuge,' *4. Folge*, p. 46.

2.   [Bormann], *Daten, passim*; Ziegler, *passim*; Kempka, p. 27; Kempka, statement 24 Aug. 1974. For the following also an order from district authority Schluckenau to all police stations 31 Oct. 1929 (translation from Czech), BA R 43 II/963a.

3.   Domarus, pp. 387–9, 2276; Baur, pp. 99–100, 115–17; Hanfstaengl, pp. 335–7 and Wiedemann, pp. 63–4, 128, refer to this visit as the *first* encounter between Hitler and Mussolini; Wiedemann calls it Hitler's first visit to a foreign country; according to Dietrich, *12 Jahre*, pp. 197–8, Hitler visited Austria in 1931 to attend the funeral of Geli Raubal in Vienna; Gebhardt, p. 224.

4.   For this and the following: Volz, p. 75; Wiedemann, pp. 121–4; [Bormann], *Daten*; Baur, pp. 165–6; Mason-MacFarlane, 'Three Curtain Raisers Seen from the Wings' (Imperial War Museum); Dieter Wagner and Gerhardt Tomkowitz, *'Ein Volk, ein Reich, ein Führer!' Der Anschluss Österreichs 1938* (R. Piper: Munich, [1968]), pp. 158–9, 213–15; Rattenhuber, *Befehl für Einteilung der Begleitkommandos, Berlin 11. März 1938*, NA T–175 Roll 241; Hoffmann, *Hitler in seiner Heimat*.

5.   For this and the following: Baur, pp. 165–6; [Bormann], *Daten*; Wagner, and Tomkowitz, pp. 259–60, 270, 279–85, 287–90, 294–6, 307–12, 333–46; Domarus, pp. 817–25; Hoffmann, *Hitler in seiner Heimat;* NA RG 242–HL ML 941, 942; Hoffmann, *Hitler*, p. 95; Kempka, statement 24 Aug. 1974; *Hitler's Secret Conversations*, pp. 366–7.

6. For this and the following: Domarus, pp. 856–62; *VB*, 3–11 May 1938; Baur, pp. 161–3; Wiedemann, pp. 133–44; cf. Zoller, p. 160, giving the wrong year, 1937; NA RG 242–HL ML 941, 942; Daluege (for Himmler) to *Land* governments, district presidents, etc., 4 March 1938, StA Oldenburg 136 Nr. 2835.

7. *Major d. Schutzpolizei Titel (RMfVuP), Arbeitsplan zum Staatsbesuch des japanischen Aussenministers Matsuoka in Berlin*, 22 March 1941, BA NA 10/124.

8. Fritz Dreesen (son of the proprietor of 'Rheinhotel Dreesen' in Bad Godesberg, where Hitler preferred to stay), in Linge, 'Kronzeuge,' *10. Folge*, pp. 24–7, and *11. Folge*, pp. 16–17, 38; cf. Speer, p. 59.

9. Zoller, p. 160; Baur, pp. 161–3; Wiedemann, pp. 136, 140–2.

10. Wiedemann, pp. 137–8; cf. Ziegler, p. 56 (giving the wrong date).

11. *Trial*, vol. XXV, pp. 433–9, 445–7; Domarus, pp. 868–9; Hoffmann, *History*, pp. 90–3.

12. For this and the following: *VB*, 4–9 Oct. 1938; [Bormann], *Daten*; Domarus, pp. 949–61; NA RG 242–HL ML 941, 942; Wiedemann, pp. 185–8; cf. Speer, pp. 77–9.

13. Wiedemann, p. 187; Schacht in *Trial*, vol. XII, p. 531; Domarus, p. 772, cites Schacht's testimony incorrectly and incompletely; *Trial*, vol. XII, p. 531.

14. [Bormann], *Daten*; Linge, 'Kronzeuge,' *2. Folge*, p. 40; Kempka, pp. 59–61; Baur, p. 168; Hoffmann, *Hitler*, pp. 99–100; NA RG 242–HL ML 941, 942; Domarus, pp. 1097–1102; BA NS 10/124.

15. Rattenhuber to Brückner 29 May 1939, BA NS 10/136; Zoller, pp. 31–2.

16. *ADAP*, Serie D, vol. VII, p. 253, Nos. 192, 193.

17. Paul Schmidt, *Hitler's Interpreter* (William Heinemann: London, 1951), p. 158; KTB FHQ Nr. 1–6 (23 Aug. 1939 to 15 July 1942), NA T–77 Rolls 857 and 858, and T–78 Roll 351; *Eisenbahnabteilungen des Reichsverkehrsministeriums* to *Bahnbevollmächtigte* [etc.] 21 Jan. 1943 (copy), in possession of *Ministerialrat* Eugen Kreidler.

18. For this and the following: Schmundt, *Folgende Wageneinteilung . . .*, 3 Sept. 1939, BA NS 10/126; NA RG 242–HL ML 941, 942; KTB FHQ Nr. 1–6; Andreas Hillgruber, *Hitlers Strategie: Politik und Kriegführung 1940–1941* (Bernard & Graefe Verlag: Frankfurt/M., 1965), pp. 659–98 (in cases of conflict, KTB FHQ, which was not consulted by Hillgruber, has been followed); Rommel, *Befehl für Einteilung des F.Q.* 31 Aug. 1939, NA T–77 Roll 858; Baur, pp. 180–1; Irving, *Hitler's War*, pp. 9–10.

19. Brückner, *Fahrt des Führers nach Danzig, Korridorgebiet und Ostpreussen*, 17 Sept. 1939, BA NS 10/126; Schmundt, *Zeiteinteilung für den 19.9.1939*, 18 Sept. 1939, BA NS 10/126; KTB FHQ Nr. 1–6; NA RG 242–HL ML 941, 942; Domarus, pp. 1353–66.

20.   For this and the following: Rommel, *Betr.: Einsatz der Einheiten des Führer-hauptquartiers vom 21–26/12/39*, 20 Dec. 1939, KTB FHQ *Nr. 2*; Zoller, pp. 34–5 (10 May instead of 9 May for departure); Finkenkrug: on line Berlin-Lehrter Bahnhof-Nauen, see *Amtliches Bahnhofverzeichnis 1938 der Deutschen Reichsbahn und der deutschen Privatbahnen mit Güterverkehr (Bfv)* (Reichsbahn-Zentralamt: Berlin, [1938]; [Bormann], *Daten*, confirming the train story; Hoffmann, *Hitler*, pp. 113–15; cf. Hillgruber, pp. 669–71; Hoffmann, *History*, pp. 169–72; Thomas, order for forming front groups 21 May 1940, KTB FHQ *Nr. 3*; 'Grey Column': all the cars together, 15 plus 19 plus 14; Rattenhuber, *Merkblatt*, 14 Dec. 1939, BANs 10/136; Irving, *Hitler's War*, pp. 107–8; Puttkamer, letter 17 Feb. 1977.

21.   [Bormann], *Daten*; KTB FHQ *Nr. 3*; Hillgruber, p. 672, mentions visits to Charleville, 24 May, and to Bad Godesberg, 31 May not found in KTB FHQ.

22.   KTB FHQ *Nr. 3*.

23.   William L. Shirer, *Berlin Diary* (Alfred A. Knopf: New York, 1941), pp. 414–15, 419; Heinz Huber and Artur Müller, (eds.), *Das Dritte Reich*, vol. 2 (Verlag Kurt Desch: Munich, Vienna, Basel, [1964]), p. 476; *Guide Michelin France 1964* (Pneu Michelin Services de Tourisme: [Paris], 1964), see *Clairière de l'Armistice*; Alistair Horne, *To Lose a Battle* (Macmillan: London, 1969), pp. 507–9.

24.   [Franz] Halder, *Kriegstagebuch* (KTB) (Kohlhammer: Stuttgart, 1962–4), vol. II, pp. 22, 24, 28; KTB FHQ *Nr. 3* gives 23 June; Speer, pp. 186–7, gives 28 June, incorrectly, as does Domarus, p. 1534; Baur, p. 192; KTB OKW IV, p. 1869; [Bormann], *Daten*, gives June 23; Schmundt, *Fahrt ins Operationsgebiet am 28.6.1940*, 27 June 1940, BA Slg. Schumacher 1492; NA RG 242–HL ML 941, 942; Arno Breker, *Im Strahlungsfeld der Ereignisse* (Verlag K. W. Schütz: Preussisch Oldendorf, [1972]), pp. 151–66; Hoffmann, *History*, p. 259; D. F. Stevenson, Director of Home Operations, to Deputy Chief of Air Staff 13 July 1940, Public Record Office/Air Ministry 20/2081 (I am indebted to Professor John P. Campbell, McMaster University, for this item).

25.   Halder, KTB II, pp. 30–2.

26.   NA RG 242–HL ML 941, 942.

27.   KTB FHQ *Nr. 6*, NA T–78 Roll 351; [Bormann], *Daten*; Schmelcher, statement 21 July 1971; Hillgruber, pp. 691–8 (in cases of conflict, KTB FHQ was followed, which Hillgruber did not consult); Baur, pp. 206–10. See below for details on 'Wolfschanze' and related installations.

28.   Domarus, pp. 1758–67, 1771–81; KTB FHQ *Nr. 6*.

29.   KTB FHQ *Nr. 6*; Baur, pp. 224–5; Linge, 'Kronzeuge,' *4. Folge*, p. 44.

30.   For this and the following: KTB OKW III, pp. 136–7; Halder, KTB II, III, *passim*; Engel, 18 Feb. 1943; Hoffmann, *History*, pp. 279–80; Baur, p. 231; Kempka, pp. 61–2; Schulze-Kossens, letter 16 Jan. 1974.

31.   For this and the following: Hoffmann, *History*, pp. 280–3; Luther to Schellenberg 16 Feb. 1943, AA PA D II 427g; Bormann to *Reichsleiter, Gauleiter, Verbändeführer* 7 March 1943; *Reichsführer-SS Pers. Stab* to *SS-Sturmbannführer* Paul Bau-

mert 8 March 1943; Himmler to Rattenhuber (teleprint) 10 March 1943; Berger
to *Hauptämter der SS und HSSPF* 11 March 1943, BA Slg. Schumacher O. 487;
Telefongespräche des Reichsführer-SS [*sic*] *am 6. März 1943*, NA T–84 Roll R25; Rat-
tenhuber, *Betrifft: Sprengstoffattentate durch Versendung von Einschreibepäckchen mit
Öffnungs- und Zeitzündung* 11 March 1943, BA Slg. Schumacher O. 487 and also
in *Verfügungen/Anordnungen/Bekanntgaben, 1. Teil aus 1943, IV. Band hrsg. von der
Partei-Kanzlei* (Zentralverlag der NSDAP, Frz. Eher Nachf.: Munich, [1943]),
pp. 587-8; *Telefongespräche des Reichsführer-SS am 24. März 1943*, NA T–84 Roll
R25; Goebbels, *Tagebücher*, p. 469; *Hausinspektion* [*NSDAP-Verwaltungsbau,
München*] *an Reichsschatzmeister der NSDAP* 30 March 1944, BDC.

32.   For this and the following: Hermann Teske, *Die silbernen Spiegel* (Kurt
Vowinckel: Heidelberg, 1952), pp. 172-5; *Rittmeister a. D.* Gustav Friedrich
(then in *Kav. Rgt. Mitte*), letters 19 May and 24 June 1971; [Rudolf-Christoph]
Fr[ei]h[er]r v[on] Gersdorff, *Beitrag zur Geschichte des 20. Juli 1944*, typescript,
Oberursel [prisoner-of-war camp], 1 Jan. 1946, IfZ Munich; Gersdorff, statement 25 May 1964; Fabian von Schlabrendorff, *Offiziere gegen Hitler* (Fischer
Bücherei: Frankfurt/M., 1959), pp. 75–81, 131–2; Walther Schmidt-Salzmann,
letter 14 Feb. 1966; Boeselager, statement 19 Nov. 1964; Schlabrendorff, letter
22 Oct. 1966; Eberhard von Breitenbuch, statement 8 Sept. 1966; the liquor
contained in the package is sometimes described as Cognac, sometimes as Coin-
treau: cf. Hoffmann, *History*, p. 619 note 22; Schulze-Kossens, letter 16 Jan.
1974; photograph collection in Boeselager Archive; John, *Twice through the Lines*
(Macmillan: London, 1972), p. 106; for the story about Hitler's hat: Fabian
von Schlabrendorff, *Revolt against Hitler* (Eyre and Spottiswoode: London, 1948),
p. 82 (this is the English version of *Offiziere gegen Hitler*; the relevant passage
does not appear in the original); Gersdorff, based on what Tresckow had told
him, and on his own examination of Hitler's hat, in statement 25 May 1964.

33.   Baur, letter 10 Jan. 1969.

34.   See Erich v[on] Manstein, *Verlorene Siege* (Athenäum: Bonn, 1955), p. 522.

35.   Speer, pp. 300, 311–12; Semmler, pp. 153, 170, 177; Goebbels, *Tagebücher*,
pp. 469–74; Domarus, pp. 2160, 2035–50; Linge statement.

36.   For this and the following: *Konteradmiral* Gerhard Wagner, letter 17 Nov.
1964; Gerhard Wagner (ed.), *Lagevorträge des Oberbefehlshabers der Kriegsmarine
vor Hitler 1939–1945* (J. F. Lehmanns Verlag: Munich, [1972]), p. 578; Heinz
Linge [*Tagebuch* 14 Oct. 1944 to 28 Feb. 1945], NA T–84 Roll 22; Alfred Jodl,
pocket diary 1944, NA T–84 Roll R 149; KTB OKW IV, pp. 1869–70; Hans
Speidel, *Invasion 1944* (Rainer Wunderlich: Tübingen, 3rd ed. 1950), pp. 112–
19; Speer, p. 336; cf. Baur, pp. 247–8; Irving, *Tragödie*, p. 363; Puttkamer, statement 17 Aug. 1974; Irving, *Hitler's War*, pp. 641–2.

37.   Linge, *Tagebuch*; Domarus, p. 2211; Kempka, pp. 76–7; Irving, *Hitler's
War*, p. 776.

Chapter 10

1. For this and the following: BA R 43 II/1104, *passim*; Lammers, *Vermerk* 16 March 1936, Lammers to Sepp Dietrich of LSSAH and Police Captain Koplien of 16th Police Precinct Berlin 18 March 1936, BA R 43 II/1105; Horst Scheibert, *Panzer-Grenadier-Division Grossdeutschland und ihre Schwesterverbände* (Podzun-Verlag: Dorheim, [1970]), pp. 10, 12–13 (posts of the Watch Regiment Greater Germany at the *Reich* Chancellery, 1936, 1937, 1938 respectively); Lammers, *Dienstanordnung für den Sicherheitsdienst (SD) in der Reichskanzlei* 28 March 1936, Lammers to Meissner, Luther, Sepp Dietrich, Brückner 7 Apr. 1936, *Kommando der Schutzpolizei, Berlin, Dienstvorschrift für den Schutz der Reichskanzlei Wilhelmstr. 77/78* 23 March 1936, [*Polizeipräsidium Berlin*], *Wachvorschrift für die Bezirkswache der Schutzpolizei Berlin im Brandenburger Tor* 20 Oct. 1936, Lammers to Meissner, Lutze, Sepp Dietrich, Koplien, Brückner, *SS-Obersturmbannführer* Ebhardt (in the *Reich* Chancellery) 28 March 1936, Deckert, *Anordnung für den Sicherheitsdienst der Reichskanzlei* 19 Apr. 1936: all in BA R 43 II/1105; LSSAH *Standartenbefehle* 10, 17, 18 Aug. and 15 Sept. 1938, NA T–354 Roll 214; Lammers to Schwerin von Krosigk 3 Nov. 1934, BA R 2/4508, and 14 Feb. 1944 and 19 Sept. 1935, BA R 2/4515.

2. For this and the following: *Tagesbefehle* [etc.], LSSAH files, 26 Aug. 1938 to 31 July 1939, NA T–354 Roll 214; LSSAH *Wachbuch, Wache Reichskanzlei* 15 Dec. 1938 to 4 May 1939, NA T–354 Roll 233; O[stertag] to Sepp Dietrich 21 June 1935, Lammers to Brückner 3 Oct. 1935 and draft 22 June 1935, BA R 43 II/1100; *SS-Untersturmführer* Hammersen to I *Bataillon* LSSAH 5 June 1936, *SS-Untersturmführer* Nothdurft to I *Bataillon* LSSAH 9 June 1936, NA T–354 Roll 208.

3. Albert Blaesing (ret. police sergeant), *Bericht* 12 Jan. 1937, Deckert to Rattenhuber and Wernicke 13 Jan. 1937, BA R 43 II/1104.

4. Captain Deckert to RSD 15 Feb. 1937, Zeitler to State Secretary Meissner 17 March 1937 and Meissner to Deckert 20 March 1937, BA R 43 II/1104; RSD, *Vormerkung* 25 Nov. 1937, O[stertag] to Lammers 24 Jan. 1938, Sidow (of SD *Reichskanzlei*), *Bericht* 23 Jan. 1938, all in BA R 43 II/1104; Kulowski, Hühner [*Sicherheits-Kontrolldienst*], *Bericht* 9 Dec. 1937, BA R 43 II/11016.

5. Thus the balcony was not added in 1933, as Speer claims in a photo caption between pp. 112 and 113; *Akten betr. Dienstgebäude Wilhelmstr. 78/Balkonanbau* 16 May 1935 to 25 July 1935, BA R 43 II/1046.

6. [Bormann], *Daten*; Speer, pp. 116, 117, 127, 128, 131–4.

7. Rattenhuber, *Betrifft: Sicherung der Reichskanzlei* 22 Sept. 1939, BA NS 10/136; Speer, pp. 131–2; Speer, letter 11 May 1972.

8. Erich Kordt, *Nicht aus den Akten: Die Wilhelmstrasse in Frieden und Krieg* (Union-Verlag: Stuttgart, 1950), pp. 370–6; Erwin Lahousen, *Zur Vorgeschichte des Anschlages vom 20. Juli 1944, Institut für Zeitgeschichte* ZS 658; Dr. Hasso von Etzdorf, statement 2 Sept. 1972; Consul I Class Susanne Simonis, letter to the author 8 March 1971; Hans-Adolf Jacobsen, *Fall Gelb: Der Kampf um den deutschen Operationsplan zur Westoffensive 1940* (Franz Steiner Verlag: Wiesbaden, 1957), p. 141.

9.   Rattenhuber, RSD budget explanation Feb. 1935, BA R 43 II/1103; Rattenhuber to President of Police Graf von Helldorf 26 May 1939, BA NS 10/136; *SS-Obersturmführer* Wünsche (SS Adjutant to Hitler) to LSSAH 18 Jan. 1939, BA NS 10/83; General Ernst Seifert (*Wehrmacht-Standort-Kommandant Berlin*) *Betr.: Standartenparade* 16 Feb. 1939, NA T–354 Roll 205.

10.   *Wachregiment Berlin* to *Hausverwaltung der Reichskanzlei* 18 Jan. 1939 and 25 May 1939, BA R 43 II/1104; NA RG 242–HL ML 941, 942; according to Spaeter I, p. 44, the *Wehrmacht* sentries were already present on 12 January; Schmundt, *Betr.: Wachgestellung für das Führerquartier* [*sic*] 25 March 1939, BA NS 10/126; Wünsche to LSSAH 18 Jan. 1939, BA NS 10/83: Wünsche suggested in this letter that new guard regulations had to be written and that it was time for someone from LSSAH to get in touch with the *Führer's* adjutants and arrange to see the new building.

11.   Wünsche to LSSAH 10 and 18 Jan. 1939, BA NS 10/83; Albert Speer, *Die Neue Reichskanzlei* (Zentralverlag der NSDAP, Frz. Eher Nachf.: Munich, [1939]); NA RG 242–HL ML 941, 942; Friedrich Schmidt, letters; *Kriminalsekretär* (RSD) Gregor Karl, letters 18 May 1966 and 17 Feb. 1968; Baur, pp. 98–9, 132; Ziegler, p. 115.

12.   LSSAH *Wachbuch, Wache Reichskanzlei* 15 Dec. 1938 to 4 May 1939, NA T–354 Roll 233.

13.   For this and the following: Rattenhuber to *SS-Sturmbannführer* Wernicke (*Adjutantur des Führers*) 13 Jan. 1939, BA NS 10/136; LSSAH *Wachbuch, Wache Reichskanzlei* 4 and 6 Apr. 1939, NA T–354 Roll 233; LSSAH IIa to Wernicke 3 Aug. 1939, *SS-Oberscharführer* Ommen (12th Company of LSSAH), *Meldung* 14 July 1939, Albrecht to LSSAH 8 Aug. 1939, BA NS 10/83.

14.   Rattenhuber to Deckert 30 Aug. 1939; Rattenhuber, *Betrifft: Ausweise zum Betreten der Wohnung des Führers und der Reichskanzlei* 30 Aug. 1939, BA R 43 II/1104.

15.   Rattenhuber to *Hausinspektion der Reichskanzlei* 19 Feb. 1937, *Ministerialbürodirektor* Ostertag (*Reichskanzlei*) to *Baufirma* Erich Schwanz 26 Oct. and 6 Nov. 1937, Erich Schwanz to *Hausinspektion der Reichskanzlei* 27 Nov. 1937, Deckert, *Verfügung* 3 Dec. 1937, in BA R 43 II/1104.

16.   Rattenhuber 9 Nov. 1939, Brückner 15 Nov. 1939, Rattenhuber to Brückner 10 Nov. 1939, BA NS 10/136.

17.   For this and the following: Correspondence concerning passes for 1940 in files of *Adjutantur des Führers*, BA NS 10/138; Rattenhuber, circular 22 Feb. 1940, List '*Verschiedene*' [March 1940], RSD to Wernicke 7 Feb. 1940, BA NS 10/137.

18.   Order (from *SS-Adjutantur?*) 21 Sept. 1939, BA NS 10/124; [Rattenhuber], *Betrifft: Sicherung der Reichskanzlei*, draft, 22 Sept. 1939, BA NS 10/136; Speer, *Reichskanzlei*, p. 6.

19.   Meissner, *Dienstanweisung für den Sicherheitsdienst in der Präsidialkanzlei des Führers und Reichskanzlers* 16 Nov. 1939, BA R 43 II/1101b.

20. Wünsche to commanding officer replacement battalion LSSAH 18 Nov. 1939, BA NS 10/83.

21. *Wachbataillon Berlin, Anordnungen über das Verhalten der Wache 'Führer' bei 'Luftgefahr' bezw. 'Fliegeralarm'* 15 June 1940, Rattenhuber, *Verhalten bei Fliegeralarm oder Abwehrschiessen der Flakbatterie der Reichskanzlei* 17 July 1941, BA R 43 II/1104.

22. Rattenhuber, *Betrifft: Sicherheit der Reichskanzlei und der Führerwohnung* 5 March 1942, BA R 43 II/1104.

23. Rattenhuber, *Betrifft: Sicherheitsdienst in der Wohnung des Führers in Berlin, Wilhelmstrasse 77 und auf dem Obersalzberg* 31 Dec. 1940, BA NS 10/138; Albrecht (Personal Adjutant to Hitler), *Sicherheitsbestimmung [sic] betreffend Sendungen für die Führerwohnung* 7 May 1941, Hoover Institution Ts Germany R 352 kb.

24. Bormann to Himmler 30 July 1944, BDC; Linge, 'Kronzeuge,' *4. Folge*, p. 46.

25. Rattenhuber, *Betrifft: Sicherheit der Reichskanzlei*, 17 March 1942, BA R 43 II/1104; cf. Wiedemann, p. 128; [Lammers], *Vermerk* Jan. 1939, BA R 43 II/967a.

26. Maser, *Hitler*, pp. 117, 123, 149–165, 293; Maser, *Frühgeschichte*, p. 132; *Fragebogen für Wohnungsuchende [sic] 113683* 13 Sept. 1929, *Stadtarchiv* Munich Zim. 117.

27. Lease contract between Hugo Schühle and Adolf Hitler 10 Sept. 1929, *Stadtarchiv* Munich Zim. 117; Domarus, p. 200; cf. *Stuttgarter Zeitung*, 8 Feb. 1967.

28. *Adressbuch für München und Umgebung* 1930, p. 715; 1931, p. 736; 1932, p. 748; *Münchner Stadtadressbuch* 1933, p. 417; 1934, p. 448; 1935, p. 460; 1936, p. 469; 1937, p. 466; 1938, p. 477; 1939, p. 483; 1940, p. 498; 1941, p. 310; 1942, p. 512; 1943, p. 515; BDC Dietrich and Zaske files.

29. Hossbach, p. 17; Speer, *Erinnerungen*, p. 52; Picker, p. 244; Karl (RSD); Friedrich Schmidt, letters, and statement 7 June 1973; Rattenhuber to *Leiter der Dienststellen 1, 8 und 9 des Reichssicherheitsdienstes* 22 July 1940, BA NS 10/137; Hans Knör (former resident at 16 Prinzregentenplatz), statement 6 Sept. 1966.

30. For this and the following: *Grieben Reiseführer Band 19: München und Umgebung* (Grieben-Verlag: Berlin, 1936), pp. 61–62; cf. pp. 51 ff. above; *Auszug, Dienstanweisung für den Führerbau in München* 3 Nov. 1941, and *Auszug aus der Ergänzung zur Dienstanweisung vom 16.1.43 für die Beamten des Reichssicherheitsdienstes im Führerbau zu München* 24 June 1944, BA NS 1/532.

31. *Hitler's Secret Conversations*, pp. 172–80.

32. *Hitler's Secret Conversations*, pp. 172–80; according to Josef Geiss, *Obersalzberg: Die Geschichte eines Berges* (Verlag Josef Geiss: Berchtesgaden, 1972), p. 65, Hitler leased the place in 1927; Maria Rhomberg-Schuster, *Historische Blitzlichter vom Obersalzberg* (Selbstverlag der Verfasserin: 1957), p. 5, gives 1925 for the initial rental—this small work contains many errors.

33. *Finanzamt München-Ost, Verteilungsplan für die Festsetzung der Rechnungsanteile an dem Einkommensteuersoll des Adolf Hitler, Schriftsteller* 22 Dec. 1930, and further correspondence, *Stadt München* to *Finanzamt München-Ost* 21. Feb. 1931, *Gemeindeverwaltung Salzberg an Finanzamt München-Ost* 12 Mar. 1931, *Finanzamt München-Ost* to *Stadtrat München/Stadtsteueramt* 12 May 1931, all in *Stadtarchiv* Munich Zim. 115; according to Kempka, p. 26, Hitler bought 'Haus Wachenfeld' in 1933.

34. Friedrich Schmidt, statement.

35. Speer, *Erinnerungen*, pp. 52, 59–61, 98–9; Heinrich Hoffmann, *Hitler in seinen Bergen* (Zeitgeschichte-Verlag: Berlin, [1938]); Zoller, pp. 78–9; Wiedemann, pp. 69, 82; Dietrich, *12 Jahre*, p. 213.

36. *SS-Hauptsturmführer* Keilhaus to *Stab* LSSAH 4 Feb. 1937, NA T-354 Roll 208.

37. For this and the following: Speer, *Erinnerungen*, pp. 61, 99; Linge, 'Kronzeuge,' *16. Folge*, p. 14, and *8. Folge*, p. 24; Wiedemann, p. 80; Dietrich, *12 Jahre*, pp. 212–13; Hoffmann, *Hitler in seinen Bergen*.

38. Rattenhuber to Brückner 15 Nov. 1937 and to Brückner and Bormann 13 Dec. 1937, BA NS 10/55; Georg Herrgott (*Kriminalassistent, RSD Dienststelle 1 Obersalzberg*), *Betrifft: Vorfall auf dem Obersalzberg* 12 June 1942, and further eyewitness accounts, NA T–175 Roll 241.

39. Picker, p. 306; Koeppen, *Bericht Nr. 28;* on Bavaud, see note 18, p. 289, above; Himmler to Schwerin von Krosigk 8 March 1937, BA R 2/12159; correspondence concerning RSD bureau 9, 1936, *Staatsarchiv* Munich LRA 31931.

40. Speer, *Erinnerungen*, pp. 98–9: [Bormann], *Daten*; Bormann, *Aktenvermerk für Pg. Friedrichs, Pg. Klopfer und Pg. Zeller* 28 Oct. 1944, BA NS 6/422; *Baedeker's Autoführer, Band I: Deutsches Reich* (Karl Baedeker: Leipzig, 1938), p. 460; Rhomberg-Schuster, pp. 6–7; Geiss, pp. 69–102; Henry Picker and Heinrich Hoffmann, *Hitlers Tischgespräche im Bild* (Gerhard Stalling Verlag: Oldenburg, Hamburg, 1969), pp. 48–59; Linge, 'Kronzeuge,' *1. Folge*, p. 34; Koeppen, *Bericht Nr. 47 über Tischgespräch* 19 Oct. 1941; Kempka, pp. 40–1; *Bergheimat: Beilage zum Berchtesgadener Anzeiger* 3 Aug. 1963, p. 22.

41. Linge, 'Kronzeuge,' *1. Teil*, pp. 34–5, and *5. Folge*, pp. 32–3; Linge, statement; Gesche, statement; Hoffmann, *Hitler*, p. 119.

41a. Karl Zenger (formerly of RSD Obersalzberg), written statement March 1977; confirmed by Schulze-Kossens, statement 11 May 1977.

42. *Präsident des Landesarbeitsamtes Alpenvorland* to *Reichsarbeitsministerium* 27 Nov. 1941, BA R 41/168; Dietrich, *12 Jahre*, pp. 212–15, 223; Picker, pp. 58–9; Speer, *Erinnerungen*, pp. 98–9; Geiss, pp. 68–99, 205; 1642 labourers on Obersalzberg were recorded as employed on 1 Apr. 1942: report by construction management, Berchtesgaden *Gemeinde-Archiv*.

43. Halder, KTB III, pp. 354–5; Walther v. Guendell, *Headquarters Commandant, Army High Command (1941–1945)* (n.p. 1952) NA MS No. P-O41da, pp. 10, 17; Speer, *Erinnerungen*, pp. 230–1, 547 notes 4, 7; Willi A. Boelcke (ed.),

Deutschlands Rüstung im Zweiten Weltkrieg: Hitlers Konferenzen mit Albert Speer 1942–1945 (Akademische Verlagsgesellschaft Athenaion: Frankfurt/M., 1969), p. 72; [Martin Bormann and Gerda Bormann], *The Bormann Letters: The Private Correspondence between Martin Bormann and His Wife from January 1943 to April 1945* (Weidenfeld & Nicolson: London, 1954), p. 103; Geiss, pp. 164–73 (Geiss's information can be verified by a visit to Obersalzberg).

44.   Geiss, pp. 164–5; *Präsident des Landesarbeitsamtes Alpenvorland* to *Reichsarbeitsministerium* 27 Nov. and 11 Dec. 1941, BA R 41/168; Karl Theodor Jacob (*Landrat* in Berchtesgaden during the war), letter 3 June 1976.

45.   [Bormann], *Daten*; Rattenhuber, *Ergänzung zur Dienstvorschrift für die Dienststelle 1 des Reichssicherheitsdienstes für die Dauer der Verlegung des Führerhauptquartiers auf den Obersalzberg* 26 March 1943, Hoover Institution Ts Germany R 352 kb.

46.   Rattenhuber, *Ergänzung*; the list named as shorthand writers and typists: Dr. Kurt Peschel, chief, Dr. Kurt Haagen, deputy chief, Dr. Hans Jonuschat, Ludwig Krieger, Heinrich Berger, Dr. Ewald Reynitz, Karl Thöt, Heinz Buchholz, Hans Helling (in charge of safe), Adolf Lutz, Erna Braun, Hertha Dittrich, Hedwig Keller, Cresc. Winterheller, Frieda Kress, Gertrud Wernich.

47.   Rattenhuber, *Dienstvorschrift für die Sonderdienststelle Obersalzberg des Reichssicherheitsdienstes für die Dauer der Verlegung des Führerhauptquartiers auf den Obersalzberg* 26 March 1943, Hoover Institution Ts Germany R 352 kb.

48.   *Ibid.*

49.   Cf. Baur, p. 295.

50.   For this and the following: Hoffmann, *History*, pp. 322–32; Eduard Ackermann (formerly in FHQ, on Gen. Buhle's staff), statement 20 Nov. 1964; Roger Manvell and Heinrich Fraenkel, 'The Bomb Plot,' *History of the Second World War* (Purnell: London, 1966–9), vol. 5, No. 7, pp. 1961–75.

51.   Hoffmann, *History*, pp. 329, 348–81.

52.   Wiedemann, p. 171; Dr. Paul Collmer, statement 26 Apr. 1977; Dr. Wilhelm Hoffmann, statement 27 Apr. 1977.

53.   For this and the following: Linge, 'Kronzeuge,' *8. Folge*, p. 24, and statement; Kempka, p. 17; Hoffmann, *Hitler*, pp. 155–6, 159; Office of Military Government for Germany (U.S.), Field Information Agency, *Technical DI 350.09–78 (FIAT) EP Report No. 19, Part IV, Intelligence Report No. EF/Min/4*, 25 Feb. 1946, '*Women around Hitler*,' based on an examination of Dr. Karl Brandt conducted by Colonel Pratt of U.S. Forces, European Theater, at 'Dustbin' on 6th August, 1945; Rattenhuber to *Dienststelle 1a, 4, 8, 9* of RSD 23 June 1937, BA Slg. Schumacher O. 462.

54.   See note 22 in Chapter 11.

55.   *SS-Kommando Obersalzberg, Flak-Abteilung 'B,' Erfahrungsbericht an SS-Führungshauptamt Berlin-Wilmersdorf und an Kommandostab RF-SS, Hochwald*, 30 June 1944, NA T–405 Roll 21; Wesley Frank Craven and James Lea Cate [eds.],

The Army Air Forces in World War II, vol. III (University of Chicago Press: Chicago, 1951), pp. 638–9, 743.

56. For this and the following: Kit C. Carter and Robert Mueller (comps.), *The Army Air Forces in World War II: Combat Chronology 1941–1945* (Albert F. Simpson Historical Research Center Air University and Office of Air Force History: Headquarters USAF, 1973), pp. 199, 312; *The United States Strategic Bombing Survey*, vol. II (Garland Publishing, Inc.: New York & London, 1976), p. 61 and figure II–2.

57. Allen Dulles (ed.), *Great True Spy Stories* (Harper & Row: New York and Evanston, 1968), p. 28.

58. Lt.-Gen. (Retd.) Ira C. Eaker, letter 25 July 1977; cf. p. 145 above.

59. Craven and Cate, pp. 638–9.

60. Craven and Cate, p. 743; Headquarters Eighth Air Force AAF Station 101, *INTOPS Summary No. 319*, 15 March 1945, Department of the Army, Albert F. Simpson Historical Research Center, Maxwell Air Force Base, Alabama (henceforth: HRC).

61. Directive by Lt.-Gen. Eaker 24 Feb. 1945, *Fifteenth Air Force Plan for Operation Doldrums* 15 March 1945, *Comments of HQ Mediterranean Allied Air Force* 16 March 1945, comments dated 20, 24 and 27 March 1945, respectively, from Deputy Commander, Operations, HQ U.S. Strategic Air Forces in Europe, Major-General F. L. Anderson, Colonel Alfred R. Maxwell (A.C.), and Colonel Thetus C. Odom (Assistant Deputy Commander), in HRC.

62. Mediterranean Allied Tactical Air Force, *INT/OPSUM No. 572* 4 Nov. 1944, in HRC; Carter and Mueller, p. 488.

63. [Bormann], *Daten*; KTB FHQ Nr. 3; *SS-Sturmbannführer* Dr. Frank (*Kommandeur der Waffen-SS Obersalzberg*), *Betrifft: Alarmierung der Stosstrupps zur Fallschirmjägerbekämpfung* 2 June 1944, NA T–405 Roll 11.

64. Boelcke, p. 308; *SS-Sturmbannführer* Dr. Frank to 26 Flak-Division in Munich-Grünwald 20 June 1944, NA T–405 Roll 11; Lammers to Schwerin von Krosigk 4 June 1944, BA R 2/4494; Oron James Hale, 'Adolf Hitler: Taxpayer,' *American Historical Review* LX (1954/1955), pp. 830–42; Alfons Pausch, 'Hitlers Steuerfreiheit,' *Deutsche Steuer-Zeitung* 58 (1970), pp. 182–5.

65. Geiss, pp. 187–203, also for the following; Picker/Hoffmann, p. 48; Group Captain E. B. Haslam, R.A.F. (Retd.), letter 5 Dec. 1975; Hilary St George Saunders, *The Fight is Won, Royal Air Force 1939–1945*, vol. III (H.M.S.O.: London, 1975 [1st ed. 1954]), p. 277.

Chapter 11

1. For this and the following: KTB FHQ Nr. 1, with situation sketch Bad Polzin; Spaeter I, pp. 60–3. For this entire Chapter, cf. R. Raiber, 'The Führerhauptquartiere', *After the Battle* [London] No. 19 (Feb. 1978).

2. [Rommel], *Befehl für die Sicherung des Führer-Hauptquartiers* [August 1939], NA T–77 Roll 858 says '*Gestapo*' instead of RSD, but obviously refers to the RSD.

3. Rommel, *Befehl für die Verladung des F.Q.*, Karlshorst 14 Sept. 1939, NA T–77 Roll 858.

4. KTB FHQ Nr. 1, Nr. 4; Spaeter I, pp. 60–3, 213, 237; Scheibert, p. 21.

5. KTB FHQ Nr. 1, Nr. 4; cf. above, pp. 161–3; Hillgruber, pp. 659–61; [Bormann], *Daten*.

6. KTB FHQ Nr. 2, NA T–77 Roll 857; Jacobsen, *Fall Gelb*, pp. 44–9; cf. Linge, 'Kronzeuge,' 2. *Folge*, p. 41, for Hitler's impatience when the Polish campaign had not ended after two weeks; Friedrich Classen (one of the architects of the various FHQ), statement 16 May 1973; Siegfried Schmelcher (also an architect involved), statement 27 July 1971; Speer, *Erinnerungen*, p. 184; Zoller, pp. 139–40; Baur, pp. 187–8; Picker/Hoffmann, p. 20.

7. Jacobsen, *Fall Gelb*, pp. 49–51, 141; Captain Spengemann (FBB staff), *Bericht über Aufgabe und Tätigkeit in R* 31 March 1940, KTB FHQ Nr. 2, *Anlagen*; Zoller, pp. 139–40; NA RG 242–HL ML 941, 942.

8. Rattenhuber, *Betrifft: Sicherung des Führer-Hauptquartiers* 19 Dec. 1939, BA NS 10/136, also for the information following below except when otherwise noted.

9. Rattenhuber to Brückner 18 Nov. 1939, BA NS 10/136.

10. KTB FHQ Nr. 2, 3; [Bormann], *Daten*.

11. Thomas, *Befehl für die Bekämpfung feindlicher Fallschirmjäger an der Anlage 'F'* 23 May 1940, KTB FHQ Nr. 3, *Anlagen*.

12. Rommel to Major Stach/FHQ 18 Oct. 1939, KTB FHQ Nr. 2, *Anlagen*; *Flakgruppe Münstereifel*, *Gefechtsbericht* 25 and 26 May 1940, KTB FHQ Nr. 3, *Anlagen*.

13. KTB FHQ Nr. 4.

14. KTB FHQ Nr. 3.

15. *Ibid.*; Speer, *Erinnerungen*, p. 185; Zoller, pp. 140–2; Baur, p. 190; *Hitler's Secret Conversations*, pp. 174–5.

16. Zoller, pp. 140–1; Puttkamer, statement 17 Aug. 1974; cf. Breker, pp. 151–66; Hans-Adolf Jacobsen and Hans Dollinger (eds.), *Der Zweite Weltkrieg in Bildern und Dokumenten*, vol. I (Kurt Desch: Munich, Vienna, Basle, [1963]), p. 197.

17. Classen, statement; Speidel, pp. 112–19; Speer, *Erinnerungen*, p. 366; Walter Warlimont, *OKW Activities—Der Westen (1 Apr. to 31 Dec. 1944)*, Part I–III Supplement, Landsberg 3 Sept. 1952, NA MS C–099a; Raiber, pp. 49–50.

18. KTB FHQ Nr. 3, *Anlagen*: Puttkamer, *Betr.: Verlegung des Führerhauptquartiers* 26 June 1940, *ibid.*; Zoller, p. 142; NA RG 242–HL ML 941, 942; *Oberbaudirektor* (Retd.) Fritz Autenrieth (builder of Installation 'T'), letter 7 Dec. 1974.

19.   KTB FHQ Nr. 3, 4, 5.

20.   Baur, pp. 195–7; Spaeter I, p. 238; KTB FHQ Nr. 5; Hillgruber, pp. 688–9.

21.   Emil Seidenspinner and Fritz Hölter, statements 25 June 1972; Baur, p. 206; Kurt Dieckert and Horst Grossmann, *Der Kampf um Ostpreussen* (Gräfe und Unzer Verlag: Munich, 1960), pp. 36–40 (with errors: underground bunker apparently confused with installation 'Zeppelin' near Berlin; sketch p. 38, taken from Spaeter II, p. 562, largely inaccurate); aerial photographs from *Reich* Photo Reporter's files (now in possession of his son, H. Hoffmann); on burials: dates on gravestones that are still there.

22.   Schmelcher, statement; KTB FHQ Nr. 6; [Bormann], *Daten*; NA microfilm R 60.15 Box 6015, p. 4; cf. reports of Hans Hausamann intelligence service in possession of Peter Dietz, Schaffhausen, and Kurt Emmenegger, *Qn wusste Bescheid* (Schweizer Spiegel Verlag: Zürich, 1965), pp. 44–51; F. W. Winterbotham, *The Ultra Secret* (Harper & Row: New York, 1974), *passim*; Research and Analysis Branch summaries of intelligence reports, prepared by OSS for White House Map Room, Joint Chiefs, Dept. of State, in NA RG 226; Dulles, *Stories*, p. 28.

22a.   KTB FHQ Nr. 6; [Bormann], *Daten*; Schmelcher, statement; Baur, pp. 206–10. The HQ's name is usually spelled 'Wolfsschanze' in the literature, and often in contemporary documents as well. But the many documents consulted for this study indicate 'Wolfschanze' was used and intended as the official spelling at least by those who had the authority to determine the spelling, namely Hitler and his immediate staff. Therefore this spelling, without the genitive -s, has been followed except in literal quotations from other sources. 'Wolfschanze' should not be translated 'Wolf's Lair.' The word 'Wolf' does not refer to a beast but to the cover name Hitler frequently used in the 1920s, and a '*Schanze*' is a redoubt.

22b.   See Peter Hoffmann, *Widerstand, Staatsstreich, Attentat* (R. Piper Verlag: Munich, 2nd ed. 1970), p. 655 and note 73 on p. 876; F. Schmidt, letter 16 Sept. 1974; papers of J. Wolf (maps). Spelling: 'Werwolf' would seem correct, as Hitler's aides agreed, but Hitler insisted on 'Wehrwolf;' Puttkamer, letter 13 Jan. 1976; see also NA T–175 Roll 94 where Himmler uses the spelling 'Wehrwolf.'

23.   For this and the following: Guendell, pp. 5–7; Spaeter II, p. 562, according to whom the outermost wire-barrier was 3 metres wide; Peter Hoffmann, 'Zu dem Attentat im Führerhauptquartier "Wolfsschanze" am 20. Juli 1944,' *VfZ* 12 (1964), pp. 254–65; KTB FHQ Nr. 6; Walter Warlimont, *Inside Hitler's Headquarters 1939–45* (Weidenfeld and Nicolson: London, [1964]), pp. 172–4: Capt. (Ret.) Hermann Kiefer (one-time Security Officer in FBB), statement 23 Apr. 1975; cf. Wilfred von Oven, *Finale Furioso: Mit Goebbels bis zum Ende* (Grabert-Verlag: Tübingen, 1974), pp. 131–2.

24.   These descriptions are based on the author's and Dr. Raiber's investigations at the site in 1972 and 1974; [Karl-Jesko von Puttkamer], *Lageplan Wolfsschanze nach einer im Winter 1945/46 gezeichneten Skizze*, and statement 5 March 1964; sketch of 'Wolfschanze' from papers of Capt. Kiefer, 1943–4; cf. Hans Walter Hagen, *Zwischen Eid und Befehl* (Türmer Verlag: Munich, 1959); KTB OKW IV, pp. 1752–3; Zoller, pp. 145–8; Guendell, *passim*; Hoffmann, 'Zu dem Attentat,' *passim*.

25. Zoller, pp. 138–9, 144–5; Speer, *Erinnerungen*, pp. 245, 400; Boelcke, pp. 5, 238, 381.

26. Baur, pp. 206, 254; Zoller, pp. 147–8; Boelcke, p. 308.

27. Speer, *Erinnerungen*, pp. 391, 547.

28. For this and the following: Note 24 above; report of *SS-Sturmbannführer* Tiefenbacher (Commandant of train 'Heinrich') to *SS-Obergruppenführer* Wolff Jan./ Feb. 1942, NA T–175 Roll 129; Boelcke, pp. 414–15. KTB FHQ Nr. 5, Nr. 6 and *Anlagen*; Heinz Pieper, statement 24 July 1965; Josef Wolf, statement 27 Feb. 1965.

29. Rattenhuber, *Betrifft: Sicherung der Anlage 'Wolfschanze'—Sonderdienstvorschrift (SDV) für die Dienststelle 1 d. RSD.*—24 Dec. 1942, Hoover Institution Ts Germany R 352 kb; KTB OKW IV, p. 1753.

30. Werner Vogel, statement 26 June 1970; Kiefer; cf. map 'Wolfschanze.'

31. Puttkamer, statement; Jacobsen, *1939–1945*, p. 643.

32. For this and the following: Picker, pp. 46, 505–17; [Bormann], *Daten*: *Führer* eats alone from 5 Sept., 7 Sept.; shorthand writer must record military situations conferences, 12 and 14 Sept.; two groups of shorthand writers sworn in; *Trial*, vol. XV, p. 300–1; cf. Linge, 'Kronzeuge,' *4. Folge*, p. 44; Baur, p. 228; Zoller, pp. 25, 145; Walter Warlimont, *Im Hauptquartier der deutschen Wehrmacht 1939–1945: Grundlagen, Formen, Gestalten* (Bernard & Graefe: Frankfurt/M., 1962) pp. 267–9; Günsche, statement 6 Nov. 1972; KTB OKW IV, p. 1753; Rattenhuber, *Sicherung*; cf. W. F. Flicke, *Spionagegruppe Rote Kapelle* (Verlag Welsermühl: Wels, 1957), *passim*.

33. For this and the following: Engel, 16 Nov. 1942; Linge, statement; Hoffmann, *Hitler*, pp. 198–200.

34. Rattenhuber, *Sicherung der Anlage 'Wolfschanze.'*

35. *Ibid.*

36. *SS-Untersturmführer* Giggenbach to Darges (*Pers. Adjutantur des Führers*) 6 Aug. 1943, Hoover Institution Ts Germany R 352 kb; Schmundt, directive 31 July 1943; Darges to *SA-Hauptsturmführer* Vater 3 Aug. 1943, Hoover Institution Ts Germany R 352 kb; cf. Flicke, *passim*, and Hoffmann, *Widerstand*, pp. 678–9, note 95.

37. Sander to concerned agencies, *Betrifft: Abänderung der Hauptanschlüsse Rastenburg-Wolfsschanze* 27 Jan. 1944, Hoover Institution Ts Germany R 352 kb.

38. For this and the following: Schmundt and A. Bormann *an Verteiler* 20 Sept. 1943, NA T–84 Roll 21; KTB OKW IV, p. 1753. Puttkamer, letter 24 Jan. 1977.

39. Streve, *Merkblatt über das Verhalten bei Alarm für die Belegschaft der Sperrkreise und Sonderzüge*, 14 Oct. 1943, NA T–84 Roll 21.

40. Streve, *Merkblatt über das Verhalten bei Alarm für die Belegschaft der Sperrkreise und Sonderzüge während des Einsatzes in allen FHQu.*-*Anlagen* 5 May 1944, and *Alarm-Merkblatt für 'Wolfschanze,'* Hoover Institution Ts Germany R 352 kb and NA T-84 Roll 21; Pieper; Josef Möller, statement 10 Dec. 1964; Guendell, p. 14.

41. Herbert Büchs (then General Staff officer in WFSt), statement 1 July 1964; Baur, p. 253; Heiber, *Lagebesprechungen*, pp. 661–2, also for the following; Himmler, notes for conferences with Hitler 15 July 1944, NA T–175 Roll 94.

42. Streve, *Zusatz zum Alarmbefehl für FHQu. Truppen* and *Merkblatt über Verhalten bei Alarm für Spkr.- und Sdr.-Zug-Belegschaft, gültig während Belegung 'Wolfschanze'* 23 July 1944, NA T–84 Roll 21.

43. On Stauffenberg, see Joachim Kramarz, *Claus Graf Stauffenberg 15. November 1907 – 20. Juli 1944* (Bernard & Graefe Verlag für Wehrwesen: Frankfurt/M., 1965); Kurt Finker, *Stauffenberg und der 20. Juli 1944* (Union Verlag: Berlin, 1973); Christian Müller, *Oberst i.G. Stauffenberg* (Droste Verlag: Düsseldorf, [1970]); Hoffmann, *History*, pp. 315–508.

44. Werner Vogel, *Betr.: 20.7.1944 – eigene Erlebnisse* 26 June 1970 (printed in translation in Hoffmann, *History*, pp. 762–3).

45. *Spiegelbild einer Verschwörung* (Seewald Verlag: Stuttgart, 1961), pp. 83–6, 112–13.

45a. Werner Bross, *Gespräche mit Hermann Göring während des Nürnberger Prozesses* (Verlagshaus Christian Wolff: Flensburg/Hamburg, [1950]), p. 221.

46. Speer, *Erinnerungen*, p. 391; [Alfred Jodl], *Der 20. Juli im Führerhauptquartier*, (n.p., [1946]), in the possession of Frau Jodl; Eugen Dollmann, *Dolmetscher der Diktatoren* (Hestia Verlag: Bayreuth, [1963]) pp. 40–5; Schulze-Kossens, letters 20 Nov. 1973, 16 Jan. 1974.

47. *Spiegelbild*, p. 113.

48. Baur, p. 253; Büchs; Spaeter II, pp. 588–9; *SS-Führungshauptamt/Amt II Org. Abt. Ia/II Tgb, Nr. 4213/44 g.Kdos.* 13 Nov. 1944, made available by Herr Schulze-Kossens.

48a. Günsche, statement 2 May 1975.

49. *Protokoll von Hitlers Hals-, Nasen- und Ohrenarzt Dr. Erwin Giesing vom 12.6.1945 über den 22.7.1944*, made available by Dr. W. Maser; cf. Kempka, pp. 34–5; the tent is visible in NA RG 242–HL–7241–3.

50. Domarus, p. 2137; Dr. Giesing, statement to Dr. W. Maser Nov. 1971; NA RG 242–HL–7241–3.

51. Giesing in *Hitler as Seen by His Doctors*, Annexes II, IV, Headquarters United States Forces European Theater Military Intelligence Service Center 01 Consolidated Interrogation Report (CIR) No. 4, 29 Nov. 1945, and Giesing to Maser; cf. Zoller, pp. 25, 122, and Kempka, pp. 34–8, with a story that Hitler had come to suspect that Dr. Brandt wanted to poison him, after Brandt had accused Dr. Morell of being a charlatan.

52. Widmann to Rattenhuber 14 Oct. 1944, NA T–175 Roll 453.

53. Streve to all *Sperrkreisdienststellen* 22 Aug. 1944; Keitel, '*Der Führer hat befohlen . . .*' 1 Sept. 1944, Hoover Institution Ts Germany R 352 kb; Streve to M. Bormann 7 Sept. 1944, NA T–84 Roll 21.

54. For this and the following: Dr. Widmann's correspondence Oct.–Nov. 1944, Widmann to Rattenhuber 14 Oct. 1944, Hermann Münkner to Rattenhuber 8 Oct. 1944, *SS-Untersturmführer* Sachs, report 22 Oct. 1944, Widmann to Rattenhuber 3 Nov. 1944, Widmann to Rattenhuber 10 Nov. 1944, Heinrich and Bernhard Dräger to *O T-Oberbauleitung* Rastenburg/Herrn Welker 28 Nov. 1944, Widmann, minute 9 Jan. 1945, NA T–175 Roll 453.

55. Col. Schlossmann to Chief, *Führungsgruppe/GenStdH* Major-General Wenck 22 Nov. 1944, Col. von Bonin (*OKH/GenStdII/OpAbtIa*) to Commandant of Fortress Lötzen 26 Nov. 1944, Wenck to G. Z. 4 Dec. 1944, NA T–78 Roll 338.

56. Boelcke, pp. 189, 381; Guderian, orders 12 and 26 Feb. 1945 in files of *GenStdH/OpAbt*, NA T–78 Roll 338/6294129.

57. Linge, [*Tagebuch*]; Speer, *Erinnerungen*, pp. 426, 446, confirmed in similaar terms from another source in KTB OKW IV, pp. 1704–5; Puttkamer, letter 24 Jan. 1977; Günsche, letters 31 March and 7 Sept. 1977; Linge, statement 14 Feb. 1977 (thinks, but is not sure, cars were used from Giessen). A locator list of *Führer* HQ installations drawn up about August 1944 refers to the Giessen–Bad Nauheim area as '*Amt 600*', NA T–84 Roll 255/EAP 47a/1.

58. Cf. Picker/Hoffmann, pp. 68–9; Fest, pp. 991, 1001; Zoller, pp. 29, 148–50; Baur, pp. 257–8, 264–5, 274–6; Speer, *Erinnerungen*, pp. 427–8, 437, 467; Boldt, pp. 11–15, 23; Kempka, pp. 56–7, 65–104. For the construction of air-raid shelters: Lammers to Schwerin von Krosigk 6 May 1936, BA R 2/4508; Lammers to Schwerin von Krosigk 23 Oct. 1940, BA R 2/4510; Office of *Reichsminister und Chef der Reichskanzlei* to Schwerin von Krosigk 10 May 1944, BA R 2/4511.

59. Domarus, p. 2211, based on Morell; Morell, as quoted in *Hitler as Seen by His Doctors*; Boldt, p. 15; BA R 43 II/1060c.

60. For this and the following: Baur, pp. 264–5, 276; Schmelcher; affidavit of Major Edmund Tilley dated 14 May 1946, StA Nürnberg PS–3980; interrogations of Dietrich Stahl dated Kransberg 8 October and 1 November 1945, StA Nürnberg PS–3980; Speer, *Erinnerungen*, pp. 437–9; Baur, pp. 275–6; Boldt, p.67; [Karl R. Pawlas], 'Vierläufige Leuchtpistole,' *Waffen-Revue*, No. 12, March 1974, pp. 1821, 1830–3.

61. Speer, *Erinnerungen*, pp. 466–7; KTB OKW IV, p. 1704; Pieper; Otto Lechler, statement 5 June 1964; Erich Kretz, statement 31 Aug. 1966; Zoller, pp. 66, 164–5; *The Testament of Adolf Hitler: The Hitler–Bormann Documents February–April 1945* (ed. by François Genoud) (Cassell: London, 1961), pp. 50 ff.

62. Guendell, pp. 17–18; Zoller, pp. 151–2; Linge, [*Tagebuch*]; Craven and Cate, vol. III, p. 473.

63. For this and the following: Boldt, pp. 11–15, 38–9; KTB OKW IV, pp. 1700–5; [Xaver Dorsch], interrogation of Dorsch, chief of *Amt-Bau-OT*, at Dustbin, 29 July 1945. Interrogated by Mr. Samuel J. Dennis and Lt. Robert Stern, USSBS Interrogations, NA RG 243; Kempka, pp. 65–104; Günsche, statement 2 May 1975.

64. Günsche, statement 2 May 1975; minute by *SS-Obersturmbannführer* Alfred Franke-Gricksch, Chief of *Amt I* in *SS Personalhauptamt*, 5 Feb. 1945, on conference with *SS-Obersturmbannführer* Grothmann, Chief Adjutant to Himmler, EAP 161-i-12/12, NA T–175 Roll 191/2729608–10.

65. Boldt, pp. 52, 56–7; Günsche, statements 12 Nov. 1974 and 2 May 1975; cf. Hoffmann, *Hitler*, p. 81; Irving, *Hitler's War*, pp. 804–8; Franke-Gricksch, 5 Feb. 1945.

66. H. R. Trevor-Roper, *The Last Days of Hitler*, 3rd ed. (Collier Books: New York, 1965) p. 260.

Chapter 12

1. Frank R. J. Nicosia, *Germany and the Palestine Question, 1933–1939*, McGill University Diss. 1977, *passim*; Lucy S. Dawidowicz, *The War against the Jews* (Holt, Rinehart: New York, 1975), *passim*.

2. Speer, *Erinnerungen*, pp. 430, 446.

3. Reginald H. Phelps, 'Hitlers "grundlegende" Redeüberden Antisemitismus,' *VfZ* 16 (1968), pp. 412, 416; *Trial*, vol. XXVI, p. 330 (Dec. 789–Ps); *ADAP*, Series D, vol. VIII, No. 384.

4. *ADAP*, Series D, vol. VII, No. 192; *Hitler's Secret Conversations*, pp. 367–8, 415.

5. *Hitler's Secret Conversations*, pp. 316, 519.

6. Speer, *Erinnerungen*, pp. 173, 229.

7. Speer, *Erinnerungen*, pp. 54, 466–7, KTB OKW IV, p. 1704; Czarina Elizabeth died on 5 Jan. 1762, and her successor Peter III left the coalition against Prussia and made peace with Frederick the Great.

8. Speer, *Erinnerungen*, pp. 430, 446.

9. Baur, p. 275.

10. Weisenborn, p. 240; *Stiftung 'Hilfswerk 20. Juli 1944*,' name files; Peter Paret, 'An Aftermath of the Plot Against Hitler: the Lehrterstrasse Prison in Berlin, 1944–5,' *Bulletin of the Institute of Historical Research*, 32, (1959), p. 99, note 6.

Source-notes on Illustrations

1. Section of Munich City map 1:50000 (Städtisches Vermessungsamt: Munich, 1936).

2. BA Slg. Schumacher O. 434.

3. NA RG 242–HL.

4. NA RG 242–HL.

5. Erich Kempka.

6. Daimler-Benz A.G. Archive.

7. NA RG 242–HL.

8. NA RG 242–HL; Karl R. Pawlas, archive.

9. *SS-Absperr-Anleitung*, NA T–611 Roll 47.

10. NA RG 242–HL.

11. NA RG 242–HL.

12. NA RG 242–HL.

13a. NA RG 242–HL.

   b. Library of Congress, lot 4320.

14. *Field Engineering and Mine Warfare Pamphlet No. 7: Booby Traps* (War Office: London, 1952), p. 26.

15–22. NA RG 242–HL.

23a. Town Plan of Berlin, Geographical Section, General Staff, No. 4480 (War Office: [London], 1944). The original includes all of Berlin with an address list of Government, Party, Police and SS agencies.

   b. See Notes 1–25 for Chapter 10.

24a. Library of Congress, lot 55420/1.

24b–c. *Topographische Karte 1:25 000 8344 Berchtesgaden Ost* (Bayer. Landesvermessungsamt: Munich, 1971); *Übersichtskarte Obersalzberg-Kehlstein M. 1:50000, Dipl.-Ing.* R. Gerhart, *Baustelle Obersalzberg*, 19 Jan. 1939 to 30 Dec. 1941; *Übersichtskarte Obersalzberg-Kehlstein, Strassen und Wege, M. 1:10000, Dipl.-Ing.* R.

Gerhart, Oberau 17 Oct. 1941; *Übersichtskarte Obersalzberg-Kehlstein M. 1 : 50 000, Ing.* Max Hartmann, Berchtesgaden 10 Oct. 1945; *Obersalzberg*, Berchtesgaden Recreation Area Engineer Section 1964; *Karte des Berghofbunkers* (Verlag Therese Partner: Obersalzberg, n.d.); *Karte des Berghofgeländes* (Verlag Therese Partner: Obersalzberg, n.d.); notes 32–42 for Chapter 10.

25. *Topographische Karte 1 : 25 000 2262 Bad Polzin* (Reichsamt für Landesaufnahme: [Berlin], 1937); note 1 for Chapter 11.

26. *Topographische Karte 1 : 25 000* (*Messtischblatt*) *5617 Usingen* (Hessisches Landesvermessungsamt: Wiesbaden, 1973); sketches and statements from Rear-Admiral (Ret.) K. J. von Puttkamer and *Oberregierungsrat* (Ret.) *Dipl.-Ing.* K. Prädel: notes 1–5 for Chapter 11; examination of the sites by the author, 1974.

27. *Topographische Karte 1 : 25 000 5406 Bad Münstereifel* (Landesvermessungsamt Nordrhein-Westfalen: [Düsseldorf], 1969); sketch and statements from Puttkamer; examination of site by author, 1974; notes 6–12 for Chapter 11.

28a. *Belgique 1 : 25 000 Rièzes—Cul-des-Sarts Édition 1–IGMB 1969 M834 Planche 62/3–4* (Institut Géographique Militaire: Bruxelles, [1969]); sketch and statement from Puttkamer.

b–d. NA RG 242–HL.

29. *Carte de France 1/25 000 Soissons Nos. 1–2, 3–4* (Institut Géographique National: Paris, [1962]); sketch and statements from Puttkamer; Raiber, pp. 49–50.

30a. *Topographische Karte 1 : 25 000 Oppenau* (Landesvermessungsamt Baden-Württemberg: [Stuttgart], 1972); note 18 for Chapter 11.

b–c. NA RG 242–HL.

31. *Österreichische Karte 1 : 50 000 106 Aspang, 105 Neunkirchen* (Bundesamt für Eich- und Vermessungswesen (Landesaufnahme): Vienna, 1960); note 20 for Chapter 11.

32a. *Karte des Deutschen Reiches 1 : 100 000* (*1-cm-Karte*) *Grossblatt 30a Rastenburg-Lötzen-Arys* (Reichsamt für Landesaufnahme: Berlin, 1941); notes 24, 28 for Chapter 11.

b. *Messtischblatt 1994 Rastenburg* (*Stand v. 1.10.38*) ([Berlin], n.d.); *Messtischblatt 640 Gross Stürlack Neue Nr. 1995* (*Stand v. 1.10.38*) ([Berlin], n.d.); sketch by Max Müller (stationed at Rastenburg airfield to 1942); Hoffmann, *History*, p. 663 note 3.

c–f. Note 32b above; notes 21–24 for chapter 11; NA RG 242–HL.

33a, b. *Deutsche Heereskarte Russland 1 : 50 000 Winniza M–35–105–B*, and dto *Mal. Kruschlinzy M–35–106–A*, (OKH GenStdH Chef des Kriegskarten- und Vermessungswesens 1943); papers of Major (Ret.) J. Wolf (formerly Commander, *Führer-Nachrichten-Abteilung*); sketch and statements from Puttkamer and F. Schmidt.

34a.   NA RG 242–HL; notes 23–24 for Chapter 11; author's investigations, 1972, 1974; author's photographs, 1974.

35.   *Plan Lager Fritz u. Quelle M 1 : 2500*, ([OKH] 1943), from papers of *Ministerialrat* (Ret.) E. Kreidler; *Messtischblatt 640 Gross Stürlack Neue Nr. 1995 (Stand v. 1.10.38)* ([Berlin], n.d.).

36.   NA RG 242–HL.

37a–c.   NA EAP 105/16.

38.   Note 23b above; Erich Kempka, *Ich habe Adolf Hitler verbrannt* (Kyburg Verlag: Munich [1950]), pp. 65–104; Picker/Hoffmann, pp. 68–9; Trevor-Roper, p. 171; statements from Erich Kempka and Otto Günsche.

Index